ID0375052

Nobody's Girl Friday

NOBODY'S GIRL FRIDAY

The Women Who Ran Hollywood

J. E. Smyth

OXFORD
UNIVERSITY PRESS

Oxford University Press is a department of the University of Oxford. It furthers
the University's objective of excellence in research, scholarship, and education
by publishing worldwide. Oxford is a registered trade mark of Oxford University
Press in the UK and certain other countries.

Published in the United States of America by Oxford University Press
198 Madison Avenue, New York, NY 10016, United States of America.

© Oxford University Press 2018

Library of Congress Cataloging-in-Publication Data
Names: Smyth, J. E., 1977– author.
Title: Nobody's girl Friday : the women who ran Hollywood / J. E. Smyth.
Description: New York, NY : Oxford University Press, [2018] |
Includes bibliographical references and index.
Identifiers: LCCN 2017026978 | ISBN 9780190840822 (cloth : alk. paper) |
ISBN 9780190840853 (Oxford Scholarship Online) | ISBN 9780190840839 (updf) |
ISBN 9780190840846 (epub)
Subjects: LCSH: Women in the motion picture industry—California—
Los Angeles—History—20th century. | Hollywood (Los Angeles, Calif.)—
History—20th century.
Classification: LCC PN1995.9.W6 S639 2018 |
DDC 384/.80820979494—dc23
LC record available at https://lccn.loc.gov/2017026978

9 8 7 6 5 4 3 2 1

Printed by Sheridan Books, Inc., United States of America

In memory of Mary Caldwell McCall Jr. (1904–1986),
Ruth Elizabeth Davis (1908–1989),
and Barbara Pollut McLean (1903–1996)

Nothing and nobody would take her place away from her. She was fighting every minute of the time, and you gloried in her battle. She was a supreme success; she knew it, we knew it. And the theaters reaped a golden harvest.

Hedda Hopper, 1949

CONTENTS

FIGURES

PREFACE

This book was planned many years ago when I was a rebellious and unrepentant defender of the Hollywood studio system. Growing up, I spent more time after school with Barbara Stanwyck and Ginger Rogers than with my peers. I never took classes in film or media studies in college. Film was an essential part of my life—I felt that it would have been as ridiculous to take lessons in breathing. Behind the scenes, I wrote scripts, read old Hollywood memos, and collected production material the way others did comic books. Looking back, I can almost smile at that anxious, driven, double life. I still felt some need to impress people back then.

I've grown out of it.

As a graduate student, I tried the odd film class and cringed when I read Andrew Sarris and Laura Mulvey. Hollywood, for me, was always more than male directors—and who said that you couldn't identify with Errol Flynn or Cary Grant as a girl or that studio-era Hollywood films always objectified and punished strong women? Look at who's writing, editing, and starring in some of them occasionally, I grumbled under my breath, and you'd been teaching us a different story—and maybe one that could be an inspiration to girls and women today.

And so the idea for this book was born. I started off writing to Janet Leigh, and, miraculously, she wrote back. She was fed up with people wanting to interview her, only to ask about Orson Welles (*Touch of Evil*, 1958) and Alfred Hitchcock (*Psycho*, 1960). We met, and talked about her "discovery" by colleague Norma Shearer, early career struggles, and commitment to her work. Over the next decade, I would spend more time in the archives, trying to reconstruct a picture of a film industry where women remembered their points of view being taken seriously, fought for and achieved a measure of success, and produced films with women protagonists. Acquaintances often asked why I didn't look at contemporary films. "Why bother?" I said. "Have you seen the kind of image Hollywood is pushing of women these days? Things were better for women in the studio era." They raised their eyebrows, skeptical. "I'll prove it," I promised.

Although I admired histories of the silent era by Cari Beauchamp that recalled a period when women were a force in the industry, I didn't like the prevailing scholarly picture that was emerging: that as Hollywood matured in the late 1920s and 1930s, women were forced out and disempowered, visible only as actresses and, invisibly, as secretaries and seamstresses—good little "girl Fridays" at their boss's beck and call. When people did talk about Bette Davis, they always skipped her off-screen life as president of the Academy of Motion Picture Arts and Sciences and of the Hollywood Canteen. I read about the blacklist, but no one ever mentioned Mary McCall, except in footnotes when she was backing up the careers of male screenwriters. Even the Writers Guild seemed to have forgotten about their first female president.

Bob Sklar was a great source of encouragement in the early stages of this project. He liked encouraging rebellions, and he was also one of the kindest people I've ever met. I was struggling with a foreign university system and a marriage I didn't like. On one of my rare visits, the remains of lunch in front of us, he just said, "Stop letting life get in the way."

So, Bob, it took me a while, but I came back to the original plan.

Part of that original plan was to spend most of my life in film archives, but I had two problems: I can't eat scripts, and my job was thousands of miles from Los Angeles.

Archivists and colleagues came to my rescue. I owe a lot to Ned Comstock, Hilary Swett, Valerie Yaros, Joanne Lammers, Sharon Smith Holley, Lisa Dosch, Pauline Wolstencroft, André Bernard, Heika Burnison, Sarah Weinblatt, Amanda Stow, and Kristine Krueger for sending me material. I remain grateful to Eric Hansen and Candace Bothwell for access to Katharine Hepburn's papers prior to her estate bequests. Hilary, J. C. Johnson, Adriana Flores, Tal Nadan, John Leroy Calhoun, Laura La Placa, Mary K. Huelsbeck, and Jenny Romero sustained me on my marathon trips to the archives.

But I have to say a special thank you to Ned Comstock. I've known him for nearly twenty years, and in that time I've benefited from his knowledge, enthusiasm, generosity, and open-mindedness. When I've had to cancel trips because I can't get a babysitter for the kids, he sends me what material he can. Ned gives the best presents—script memos for Christmas, New Year's clippings, and a Hollywood phonebook that absorbed me for weeks. The person who says anyone is replaceable has obviously not met Ned. He is one of a kind, and I will always associate him with library basements, boxes of script memos, air conditioning, and the best-spent days of summer.

I'm deeply grateful to Mary-David Sheiner and Sheila Benson for their memories of their mother and access to the private papers of Screen Writers Guild president Mary C. McCall Jr. It's true they each have contrasting assessments of her (so different, their mother could be two different women). Sheila's childhood coincided with a period when "Mamie" was one of the most visible and vocal women in Hollywood; Mary-David grew up with her in the blacklist era, when she had more time on her hands to read bedtime stories and cook.

But if my research on studio-era Hollywood women has proved anything to me, it's that these women were never easily described female "types," with all the traits fitting together like pieces of a jigsaw. How else could one explain Hedda Hopper's consistent support and defense of working women in Hollywood—even Democrats like Davis, Ida Lupino, and McCall? That really resonated with me. Whatever their political affiliations, women during this era tended to support each other off-screen. Sometimes it was a positive comment or celebration of a career move in a column; other times it was recommending another woman for a job; sometimes they supported each other on a committee, on a radio show, or in working together on an enterprise such as the Hollywood Canteen. Certainly women competed for jobs. Davis and Joan Crawford disliked each other; sisters Joan Fontaine and Olivia de Havilland did feud. But too often, the media has reduced women's presence in Hollywood's past to a series of catfights. And, to paraphrase Davis, while the studio system was no place for sissies, many women gave the industry credit as a space where they could thrive as professional women.

I wasn't taught this history, and I didn't read it because it didn't really exist except in the archives and in dusty newspapers. I never heard about Mary McCall until a few years ago. She was a workaholic, tough, articulate, charismatic, but also domineering and stubborn. She was a working woman, a mother of four, and the creator of Maisie Ravier, the role Ann Sothern made her own in 1939. When I first began to grasp McCall's public and private lives, I was astounded, but also felt that I had found an ally who would have understood the challenges women of my generation still face. I wish I could have told her that nothing in life has any business being perfect. When you try being the perfect parent, very often you are agonized to be away from what you feel most fulfilled doing—in McCall's case, writing and guild leadership. Motherhood is sometimes boring, and marriage—well, show me a successful and fulfilled woman and I'll show you a woman who's divorced or single! But colleagues can be even worse than in-laws . . . It's finding the balance. Whatever the contrasting perspectives of her children, McCall struggled and she did her best. Both

Mary-David and Sheila went on to make their own careers in the world of film and television. They are a phenomenal family, and I hope that I've done some justice to their faith in this book.

As far as I have been able, I've tried to give a full picture of women's lives during the studio era. Not just their studio careers, but also their work in the guilds and unions, their interviews for fans, their political lives, and their roles as wives, partners, and mothers. Like McCall, Bette Davis worked hard in all her roles. Her son Mike Merrill gave me permission to reprint images from his mother's papers and was very encouraging with my project. I am also indebted to Olivia de Havilland, Marsha Hunt, Samantha Eggar, Peter Jeakins Dane, and the late Janet Leigh, Ann Rutherford, and Noel Taylor for reflections on their careers and for being sources of inspiration.

Gary Crowdus, Vera Dika, David Eldridge, Desirée Garcia, Mark Glancy, Hannah Graves, Helen Hanson, Kristin Hole, Dijana Jelača, Julia Kostova, Paula Massood, Nahid Massoud, Sarah Onions, Robert Rosenstone, Alvin Sargent, Tom Schatz, Art Simon, and Tom Stempel have been great colleagues and friends. I am especially grateful to Tom Stempel for a copy of his oral history with Bobbie McLean, certainly the best example of the genre I've ever read. Thank you, Tom, for giving us such a lively portrait of Hollywood's "Editor-in-Chief." But it's so typical of the American Film Institute that the only reason we have McLean's oral history is because it was to be a part of the Darryl F. Zanuck oral history project. Not that I don't like Zanuck; he hired McLean, after all! And Dorothy Spencer. And Mary Steward.

Even when we've been thousands of miles apart, Cynthia and Ray Lucia, Roy Grundmann and Mark Hennessy, Robin Vaccarino, and Donna Vaccarino have been there with invaluable friendship, conversation, and irreverent laughter. I look forward to the next time we can sit down and have a drink and not look at clocks.

At first, my kids Zachary and Zoe did not want to talk about the book at all. The trade-off was they loved Claudette Colbert and the Ale and Quail Club, were thrilled when Bette Davis got rid of another dull lover (the quick but often illegal way), and shared Kate Hepburn's addiction to Mondel's chocolates and eyebrow-raising disdain for the idiots we can't completely get rid of in our lives.

The British Academy supported this project with—by their standards— a small grant. The Writers Guild of America West, the Writers Guild Foundation, and the guild's women's committee sponsored the articles, exhibition, and screenings honoring Mary C. McCall Jr. in 2017. They also let Sheila, Mary-David, and me sit down on a Beverly Hills stage and talk about McCall, careers, and motherhood. Hopefully now Madam President's name is a bit more familiar to the members, although I don't see any McCall biopic on the horizon at this point. If it happens, I hope to hell they have enough sense to hire a woman to write it.

It's been a true pleasure working with my editor, Norm Hirschy, and the staff at Oxford University Press. And I want to thank my anonymous reader whose encouragement and astute criticism helped shape the final draft of the manuscript.

This book is meant to challenge and to inspire people who love Hollywood and believe in gender equality. It targets the beliefs, reinforced in too many histories and public comments, that feminism died between 1930 and 1950, that women were not important within the Hollywood studio system and had little creative control, that directors called all the shots, that the most important Hollywood writer you should know about is Dalton Trumbo, and that Katharine Hepburn is the best example of studio-era feminism. On that last point—yes, sad to say, she admitted she was not a feminist.

Today, actresses such as Reese Witherspoon and Geena Davis are taking Hollywood to task for its lack of substantial roles for women. Yet the focus is still on actresses' salaries and the number of women who direct pictures. There was a time when Hollywood recognized and supported a collaborative, creative environment and women achieved positions of power and influence in the American film industry. Sadly, this disappeared with the decay of the studio system. Even the memory of these women's achievements has faded. The only historical period currently of any box-office interest, the blacklist, has become a minifranchise enabling white males a space to reenact heroic victimhood. The poor little dears.

Hollywood may be a bastion of male privilege these days. It may have been for the past sixty-odd years. But there was a time when things were a bit different.

Let me take you back to 1942 . . .

Nobody's Girl Friday

The Equal Right to Be the Best

This industry is a generation ahead of the rest of the world in its attitude toward women workers.

Julie Hunt, 1939[1]

Film Daily was never a complete directory of creative and management departments in the Hollywood studios. In any given year, a studio could choose to report a different or abbreviated portion of its employees. At other times, jobs could be omitted or incorrectly reported. But in the absence of complete studio employment records, it gives a fairly comprehensive map of the various professions, guilds, unions, and clubs operating in one of the United States' largest and most powerful corporate enterprises in the first half of the twentieth century.

Anyone expecting list of uniformly male names is in for a few surprises.

A quick scan of Cecil B. DeMille Productions, Inc., for 1942–43 reveals that half of his board of directors were women. Cecilia DeMille Harper and Constance A. DeMille were vice presidents of the company. Cecilia was head of the reading department, Anne Bauchens head of editing, Beatrice Warner was the company's librarian, and Marion Crist was head of research.[2] For many years, DeMille's chief screenwriter had been Jeanie Macpherson, a woman DeMille referred to as not only his right hand, but also his "left brain."[3] But DeMille's employment of women in senior creative and management positions was not unique. Of the smaller production companies, Charles Chaplin's studios on La Brea Avenue listed Lois Watt as treasurer and on the board of directors, Catherine Hunter as the studio press representative, Lois Runser as bookkeeper, and Corresponding Secretary Kathleen Pryor.[4] At Samuel Goldwyn's studio, Irene Lee was story editor, and Goldwyn's wife, Frances, was the company's treasurer and also served on the board of directors.[5] That "most remarkable girl" Leila Alexander ran his research department and also made key decisions on hiring set and production designers for Goldwyn's major features. Alexander had been in the papers recently given her role in coordinating the research on Goldwyn's latest production "about the young people of the Soviet Union" (*The North Star*, 1943).[6] The other person heavily involved in the production at that stage was another woman: Lillian Hellman. In the 1930s, Goldwyn was famous for employing female writers, among them Hellman, Jane Murfin, Rachel Crothers, and Dorothy Parker.[7] Writer Phillip Dunne remembered the producer gloating beside Hellman and Parker at one working lunch: "You know, I'm delighted with the work that's being done. From now on I'm going to hire nothing but women writers. . . . But [after noticing Alan Campbell, aka Mr. Parker, at the table] if one wants to bring her husband along, that's okay too."[8] David O. Selznick's new production company, Vanguard Films, listed Barbara Keon in charge of scenario, Joyce Allen as chief purchasing agent, Margaret McDonnell as head of the story department, Harriet Flagg as head of the New York office, and Nellie Dunham as head of the stenographic department.[9] By this time, Katharine "Kay" Brown, who began as eastern story editor at Radio-Keith-Orpheum (RKO) and went on to work as Selznick's right hand on *Gone with the Wind* (1939) and head of the New York office, had moved on in 1942 to work as a top agent at the Music Corporation of America (MCA) and as Goldwyn's eastern story editor in 1943.

Larger studios also reported women in executive positions, and women did particularly well working for Harry Cohn at Columbia. Eve Ettinger was chief East Coast scenario editor; Hortense Schorr was head of publicity; Hannah Kass was head of the Title Department; Karen DeWolf, Gina Kaus, Adele Comandini, Connie Lee, and Sonya Levien made up nearly half of Cohn's contracted writers; and Roberta Thomas ran the research department.[10] At RKO, Renie Conley was head of design and Claire Cramer was head of wardrobe. Bessie McGaffey, said to be "the first woman to originate a research department in a studio," was RKO's head of research, and Helena Sorrell was head of talent.[11] At Republic Studios, Harriet Parsons was an associate producer (having formerly worked at directing and producing shorts at Columbia from 1934), Frances Manson was chief West Coast story editor (and would become a producer when she moved to Columbia Studios in 1943), Adele Palmer directed women's wardrobe, Mary Mariani was head of the Stenographic Department, Hinda Means directed the film library, and Hortense Stahl was head of contracts.[12] Universal's Vera West was the studio's chief designer, Gwen O'Brien was story editor, and Nanette Grant was head of research.[13] Movietone News, a subsidiary of Fox, had two female department heads.[14] The head of the print department at the Producers Releasing Corporation of America was Janet Rosenthal.[15]

There were a robust number of female agents with successful independent offices, including Mary Bran, Kathryn Burns, Sue Carol, Ruth Collier, Malvina Fox Dunn, Clara Elison, Betty Fairfax, Jessie May Hirsch, Lola Moore, Dorothy Preble, Rosalie Stewart, Jessie Wadsworth, Minna Wallis, Pauline Cooke, Sara Enright, Sylvia Hahlo, Frances Robinson, and Leah Salisbury. Many other women worked for the William Morris Agency, MCA, and the Jaffe Agency (co-run by Sam Jaffe and the formidable Mary Baker).[16] Agent Marcella Knapp had started as a "telephone girl" at Metro-Goldwyn-Mayer (MGM) in the late 1920s, and within ten years had become "one of the most efficient casting directors in the business,"[17] working as head of MGM's radio activities under Louis K. Sidney before turning agent. By 1942, she had an impressive clientele, including rising star Robert Walker.

Former silent actress Helen Ferguson also changed careers, becoming one of Hollywood's most influential publicists. She acted as "suppress agent" for Barbara Stanwyck, Henry Fonda, and Loretta Young. Publicist Margaret Ettinger, frequently mentioned in the columns for her influence in brokering film deals (it helped that she was columnist Louella Parsons's cousin), was vice president of the Independent Screen Publicists.[18]

Women were instrumental in the founding and development of two major Hollywood guilds and unions, the Screen Actors Guild (SAG; officially recognized in 1937) and the Screen Writers Guild (formed in 1933, recognized in 1939, but the last major guild to secure a contract with the producers in 1942). Although SAG was quickly dominated by star names such as Adolph Menjou, Fredric March, Robert Montgomery, and Spencer Tracy (who resigned from the Academy over producers' attempts at wage controls), SAG was established by less well-known supporting players, including Lucile Webster Gleason, who was not only a founding board member, but the organization's first treasurer as well (she remained involved in SAG through the 1940s). Ann Harding, who served a term as third vice president in 1933, as second vice president in 1934, and three years on the executive board, was the most active female star to be involved in the guild's early negotiations for a contract with the producers.[19] She chaired part of the guild's first formal meeting on October 4, 1933.[20] Harding would also speak at the famed October 8 meeting at El Capitan Theatre and was the only woman to be quoted in ensuing press coverage, stating in the *Hollywood*

Reporter, "There are rumors that we wish a strike. This is not true, but we do want to be ready for anything that might happen."[21] Actresses Isabel Jewell, Jeanette MacDonald, Miriam Hopkins, Marion Davies, Jean Muir, Mary Astor, Marsha Hunt, Olivia de Havilland, and Joan Crawford were all active organizers in the actors' union. By 1942, Gleason was still serving as treasurer, while Heather Angel, Beulah Bondi, Elizabeth Risden, Nydia Westman, Emma Dunn, Carole Landis, and Jane Wyman were all on the board of directors.[22]

By the late 1930s, when SAG began a more cordial relationship with the Academy, many actresses were involved in Academy governance, and later in coordinating war activities. The Academy, of course, was dominated by the producers and their conservative Republican interests, and there was a fair share of women among their ranks, including founders Mary Pickford, Bess Meredyth, and Jeanie Macpherson, and active member Frances Marion. By and large, extras, bit players, supporting players, and younger stars were committed to SAG, and following union recognition, more actresses involved themselves in a variety of committee work. In 1942, Bette Davis, Rosalind Russell (who served on the Academy's board of governors with Jane Murfin), and Marlene Dietrich were on the executive board of the Hollywood Victory Committee, and Davis was the founder and longtime president of the Hollywood Canteen.[23] These wartime activities were comparatively safe ways for women to develop their public profiles and to demonstrate patriotism in a studio political climate that, during the 1930s, was dominated by anti-Roosevelt, corporate interests. Yet, given the Republican Party's early sympathy with the Equal Rights Amendment, many of Hollywood's wealthier working women were comfortable with publicizing their political affiliations. Both Republican and Democratic women in Hollywood pursued a more prominent political role when their parties committed to the Equal Rights Amendment in the party platforms (1940 for Republicans, 1944 for Democrats).

Although 1942 was the first full year of US involvement in World War II, with many of Hollywood's men being called up for active service, the overall number of women in executive positions or as heads of department was in line with other years. In addition to Ann Harding's work as a leading officer of the Screen Actors Guild, Bette Davis was head of the Academy of Motion Picture Arts and Sciences in 1941, and a number of women had served on the executive committees of the Academy and the Screen Writers Guild from the early 1930s. Women's membership in the writers' guild from the early 1930s through 1950 fluctuated between 23% and 26%, although a casual look at *Film Daily* in 1942 reveals that women were only listed for 15% to 20% of the produced films. It's easy to speculate that women members simply weren't being assigned to projects in proportion to the men. However, evidence of script development in several studio archives makes it apparent that they were not receiving screen credit for all their contributions (something that unfortunately happened to screenwriting men and women, since packs of writers were routinely hired by the studios and credit arbitration was notoriously bad prior to the 1942 contract).

Writers most active in the 1930s and 1940s included Edna Anhalt, Sally Benson, Leigh Brackett, Adele Buffington, Lenore Coffee, Adele Comandini, Betty Comden, Viña Delmar, Helen Deutsch, Phoebe Ephron, Frances Goodrich, Ruth Gordon, Eleanore Griffin, Joan Harrison, Lillian Hellman, Dorothy Hughes, Fay Kanin, Virginia Kellogg, Dorothy Kingsley, Erna Lazarus, Gladys Lehman, Isobel Lennart, Sonya Levien, Anita Loos, Jane Loring, Josephine Lovett, Clare Booth Luce, Frederica Maas, Jeanie Macpherson, Doris Malloy, Frances Marion, Sarah Y. Mason, Bess Meredyth, Jane Murfin, Dorothy Parker, Laura Perelman, Gertrude Purcell, Betty Reinhardt, Marguerite Roberts, Louise Rousseau, Jean Rouverol, Madeleine Ruthven, Florence Ryerson, Tess Slesinger, Adela Rogers St. Johns, Jane Storm, Wanda Tuchock, Catherine Turney, Virginia Van Upp, Salka Viertel, Irma von Cube, Claudine West, Mae West, and Elizabeth Wilson. Many of these women would be nominated for or win Academy Awards and even, in Murfin's, Van Upp's, Deutsch's, and Harrison's cases, move into producing.

In 1948, even after the return of men serving overseas in World War II, women still made up nearly 25% of writers in Hollywood, comparable to female numbers prior to the war.[24] In 2016, the Writers Guild of America West conducted its own survey of gender representation in screenwriting. Over eighty years after the founding of the guild, women make up 24.9% of the overall film writers with guild membership, up from 24% in 2009 (numbers are now slightly better for television).[25] These figures are more positive than 1974 and 1984 reports revealing that women accounted for only 14% of feature film writers and guild members.[26] The statistics give sobering evidence that the real gains for women's equality in screenwriting were made in the 1930s and during the war.

But, as a glance at *Film Daily* reveals, 1942 was a particularly good year for the women of the guild. Not only did they have the benefits of their first contract (co-negotiated by Mary C. McCall Jr.), but also the union had elected McCall its first female president (an office she would hold three times). Jane Murfin and Gladys Lehman were part of her executive board.[27] McCall appears in several other places in *Film Daily*'s records for that year. She was the vice president of the Motion Picture Relief Committee, with emeritus president Mary Pickford, art director Julia Heron, and her close friend SAG leader Lucile Webster Gleason all trustees.[28] McCall was also on the national committee of the War Activities Committee in her capacity as president of the Screen Writers Guild and also as president of the Hollywood branch of the War Activities Committee.[29] She worked alongside Pauline Lauber (secretary to the recently formed Hollywood Writers Mobilization), Dorothy Jones (chief of the Movie Analysis Department of the Office of War Information [OWI]),[30] and Evelyn Edwards (the vice president of the Screen Readers Guild). McCall also served on the Academy's board of governors that year (as did Rosalind Russell, the board's third vice president), and women had served or would continue to serve in other years.[31]

Women were more active in the administration of the Screen Writers Guild than in the Society of Motion Picture Film Editors, where they sometimes worked sixty-hour and seven-day weeks before the contract. They obtained wage increases and a framework for overtime and bonuses in 1938, and were offered their own local by the International Alliance of Theatrical Stage Employees (IATSE) in 1943, before becoming the Motion Picture Editors Guild (MPEG) in 1944. Though *Film Daily* doesn't list any women on the editors guild board of directors for 1942, Barbara McLean, Sylvia Reid, Monica Collingwood, Hazel Marshall, Dorothy Spencer, Florence Leona Lindsay, and Mary Steward were founding members, joining the union in the spring and summer of 1937.[32] In the guild's early years, women's jobs were protected. Fox assistant cutter Mary Steward remembered a meeting she had with a male union executive soon after joining up: "With his feet up on his desk, he told me, 'My dear, we don't get jobs for girls.' He didn't last long."[33] Steward was one of several key women who worked in Fox's editorial department, including supervising feature editor Barbara McLean (who held the record for Academy Award nominations until 2002), Dorothy Spencer (who coedited *Stagecoach*, 1939, before joining Fox), and Irene Morra (*Captain January*, 1936). Steward edited *Drums along the Mohawk* (1939) and *The Grapes of Wrath* (1940), both directed by John Ford, as well as the classic young woman's coming-of-age drama, *A Tree Grows in Brooklyn* (1945, co-edited with Spencer). Women were well respected as editors across the industry, and during the studio era, press coverage of women's film jobs often began with the achievements of editing women such as MGM's legendary Margaret Booth, McLean, Spencer, Blanche Sewell, Anne Bauchens, Irene and Eleanor Morra, Viola Lawrence, Frances Marsh, Alma Macrorie, Eda Warren, Monica Collingwood, Helene Turner, Adrienne Fazan, and many others.[34] Journalists mentioned their technical skill and endurance as often as their creative control and intuition, disproving stereotypes of the mechanically challenged female.

However, there was one branch of the film industry which maintained a rigid gender membership: the American Society of Cinematographers. Founded in 1919, the organization only admitted its first female member, Brianne Murphy, in 1980, and to date, only 4% of its members are female. In 1938, the *Los Angeles Times* reported that Mexico's budding cinematographer, Maria Alicia Abitia, was visiting director of photography Lucien Andriot on the Twentieth Century-Fox lot, but there was no rush to train Hollywood equivalents. However, that same year, Dorothy Arzner was elected the first female member of the Screen Directors Guild. Writer-director-producer Ida Lupino followed in 1950, heralded in the press as the new Orson Welles.[35]

Women fared far better as producers during the studio era. Though a handful of women had served as associate producers and production executives during the 1930s, in the 1940s, *Film Daily* listed some new names. In addition to Harriet Parsons, there was Anna Bell Ward, and within twelve months Harry Cohn would promote Virginia Van Upp at Columbia, and Universal would hire Joan Harrison, whose production *Phantom Lady* was released in 1944. In the summer of 1943, Una Smith Stanley would become vice president and director of the Producers Corporation of America, an independent company releasing through Mary Pickford's United Artists.[36]

Women held offices in major and minor guilds and unions (such as Margie Ring, secretary to the Motion Picture Costumers Union, and Margaret Bennett, president of the Screen Office Employees Guild), OWI and wartime committees, and benevolence funds, and won Academy Awards in editing, writing, acting, and later, from 1948 to 1949, the year the award was created, costume design.

In the press, Rose Pelswick was the chairwoman of the New York Film Critics, with members Kate Cameron, Wanda Hale, Dorothy Masters (who also served as secretary), Irene Thirer, Jane Corby, and Louise Levitas constituting seven of the eighteen members. The gender balance isn't nearly so favorable to women currently (only five of the thirty-one members were women in 2017). Louella Parsons, Hedda Hopper, Elsa Maxwell, and Dorothy Kilgallen covered industry scuttlebutt, reaching tens of millions of readers and radio listeners. Many of these women drew special attention to Hollywood women's employment gains in their columns and programs. The Hollywood Women's Press Club, founded in 1928 by Parsons, was a formidable force in and outside of the industry. Its frequent lectures and luncheons brought Hollywood's women together to discuss art, industry, and politics. Columnist Elsa Maxwell expounded on French resistance leader Charles de Gaulle, and actress Ann Dvorak gave a lecture on why American women should be drafted.[37] From 1940, the fifty presswomen held annual Golden or Sour Apple Awards for the most and least cooperative Hollywood stars.[38] By the mid-1950s their numbers had risen to well over one hundred,[39] but they were still chastising the prima donnas and grumpy egomaniacs and praising the team players—such as Bette Davis and Janet Leigh—who helped other women do their jobs.

Hollywood's women were, by and large, loyal to the system that sustained their careers. In 1943, when women were enjoying a period of strength at all levels of the film industry, head of the Hollywood branch of the War Activities Committee, Screen Writers Guild president, and member of the Academy's board of governors Mary C. McCall Jr. stepped in to defend Hollywood from a damaging press campaign from the *Chicago Tribune*. Ironically, the scourge was another woman, reporter Marcia Winn. Her front-page exposés, with lurid headlines like "City of Magic, Fantasy and Filth: It's Hollywood," "Hollywood Vice Swallows 300 Girls a Month," and "Blackmail King in Hollywood—Anything Goes," guaranteed an avid readership.[40] Winn targeted agents and sleazy publicists who arbitrarily broke stars' careers, egomaniacal producers (Colonel Darryl F. Zanuck), lecherous stars (Errol Flynn and Charlie Chaplin were recently involved in sex scandals), and movie-struck young girls abused by the system (countless but unnamed). McCall, responding in *Motion Picture–Hollywood*, was in her element, refuting each accusation with the rapid-fire prose synonymous with her cinematic alter ego at MGM, Maisie Ravier (played by Ann Sothern, 1939–47). Hers was a tough, no-nonsense defense of the industry that had rebuilt its wild reputation through war service, improved negotiations with the various guilds and unions, and successful star-oriented press campaigns. While she occasionally drew upon metaphors of the studio "family" (particularly when praising the charitable work of the Motion Picture Relief Fund and its country house in the San Fernando Valley for elderly or unemployed members),[41] McCall argued that Hollywood was not a benign or predatory patriarchy, but rather a place where women and men had an equal chance of success.

Like many journalists before her, Winn claimed that the road to fame in Hollywood was paved with corruption. McCall responded with the classic American immigrant success story, focusing on the experience of her close friend from her New York City days, James Cagney, who had just won an Oscar for Best Actor. Cagney, who, McCall noted, paid the second or third largest personal income tax in 1942, "once stood on Broadway with his dancing shoes worn down to the pavement, wondering where he could promote a dime for coffee and a doughnut because he hadn't eaten in two days. I don't resent the money James Cagney makes today. I think he's worth every penny of it." For some, she admitted, "Right now the going may be tough. But I believe that genuine talent has a greater chance of being recognized in the motion picture business than in most large industries."

For it wasn't only Cagney who could rise from the streets of New York to become one of Hollywood's wealthiest but still politically committed citizens. In her article, McCall created a subtle portrait of Hollywood as a community of working women who succeeded on both sides of the camera.[42] Responding to Winn's slander of "soiled-faced" agents, the writer pointed out that her own agent, "a young woman named Mary Baker," always had a clean face, "except when she's spading up the back yard to enlarge her Victory Garden." Women could be intelligent, honest, successful agents, McCall argued, but she also disarmed potential misogynists or critics of working women by mentioning not only Baker's patriotism but also her marriage to an army lieutenant serving overseas.

In her attack on Hollywood's legions of stage mothers, Winn again trotted out all the classic stereotypes (many of them familiar in Hollywood scripts, as well as Philip Wylie's recent vituperations on "Momism" in *Generation of Vipers*, 1942), but McCall blandly turned Winn's veiled references to cinematic pimping into praise for the strong mother-child relationships that nurtured so many careers, including Mary Pickford, Shirley Temple, Mickey Rooney, and their mothers. Without the matriarchy, the Hollywood star system would not be as powerful. McCall named no names, but it was her MGM colleague Ida Koverman who had been instrumental in developing a studio school and child welfare initiatives, models copied at RKO by the likes of Lela Rogers, another friend. McCall's discussion of the studios' careful education and labor protection of child stars might appear like press damage control from a highly placed insider, but it also adds another dimension to Hollywood as a family-oriented organization managed by women.

When Winn complained about the industry's exploitation of unknown starlets, McCall responded with reminders about Ginger Rogers and Joan Crawford, working-class actresses who had used the Hollywood system to escape punishing careers in dance halls. And, McCall added, "It wasn't an acting role I was avid for as a young girl. It was a writing job. Hollywood gave it to me, and freed me from the eviction notices and the shame of borrowing money from friends." Although popular histories of studio-era Hollywood have given the impression that women were on one side of the camera and men on the other, McCall told a different story of an industry that supported women in many branches of filmmaking. This perspective had appeared in coverage from the 1930s about Hollywood as "a generation ahead of the rest of the world" in terms of its commitment to women's careers, and would be echoed by syndicated journalist Bob Thomas and others through the 1940s and early 1950s. But it is worth pointing out that McCall's perspective also goes against the grain of the majority of post-1970 academic and popular histories that have painted the industry as monolithically male and hell-bent on disempowering women.[43]

All this may sound surprising to fans, students, and historians schooled to believe in a strict division of gender in screen work during the studio era (1925–1960). Men were supposed to run the studios and call all the shots in film production. Women were supposed to be sexualized objects, standing obediently in their chalk-marks on the soundstage, speaking lines written for them by men. But these are some of the most inaccurate, pervasive, and damaging myths about Hollywood.

Inside Hollywood, each studio had a monthly newsletter, which attempted to create a shared home/corporate environment for its range of employees. Hollywood studio newsletters reported the activities and work and family achievements of male and female employees and were often run and published by a mixture of men and women. Script, research, scenario, reading, cutting, sound, stenographic, and transport departments all met for suppers, picnics, softball competitions, golf matches, and bowling nights-out, and photographs of the events show a near fifty-fifty split of smiling male and female employees. In some cases, women dominated the departments. Journalist Hubbard Keavy claimed in 1934 that at the larger studios, 40% of all employees were women and that women's overall employment in the industry was increasing.[44] (At the time, women's employment in the United States was climbing from 22% to 25%. It was only in 1970 that women made up 40% of the national workforce.)[45] Outside the studios, Louella Parsons's and Hedda Hopper's syndicated columns frequently focused on women working in Hollywood—and not just the romantic sagas of the top stars. During the 1930s, a number of columnists were covering the range of work open to women in the film industry, going beyond the typical role of the screen-struck girl who wanted to be the next Carole Lombard. Keavy was fascinated with the power wielded by Hollywood's top female editors, but in 1939, he published a more ambitious, wide-ranging piece, and sought the expertise of Paramount's head of publicity, Julie Hunt. Women had been writing to her for years about getting jobs in Hollywood, and she stated: "Serious-minded girls, with ingenuity, need have no fear of knocking at the forbidding gates."[46] She asserted: "Hollywood would as soon hire a woman for an important job as a man, and very often does."

Hunt was hired by Paramount back in 1924, and although the reporters were "amazed" at finding a woman in a traditionally male job, "her name always appeared in stories about women in the movies." She had a list of women's jobs in Hollywood ready for Keavy to consult: they were editors, animal trainers, casting agents, writers, architects, talent agents, makeup artists, designers, nurses, purchasing agents, stunt women, and fliers.[47] She drew special attention to Mary Eicks, longtime head of transportation at Paramount.

But Hunt, who was divorced because she had been putting in fifteen-hour days at the studio, stated flatly: "Careers and marriage don't mix here." It wasn't that the studios fired married women, or even discouraged the institution. Marriage sometimes worked. Hunt named Barbara McLean, top editor at Fox, and Marcella Bannett Rabwin, David O. Selznick's executive secretary from 1937 until 1941, who seemed to be able to handle a partnership with a husband. But when it worked, it was usually because their spouses also had jobs at the studios and understood the time demands. But even McLean's marriage would dissolve over career issues after a few years. Women working in Hollywood tended to be single (either unmarried or divorced) or to live with other female colleagues. This way, they didn't have the added complication of spending more time soothing male egos when they earned less than their wives. However, when Hollywood press agents found those rare happy couples (Edith Head and Wiard "Bill" Ihnen, Frances Goodrich and Albert Hackett, Tess Slesinger and Frank Davis, Barbara Stanwyck and Robert Taylor, and, for a while, Virginia Van Upp and Ralph Nelson and Mary C. McCall and Dwight Franklin), they endorsed the benefits of married women working.

Legendary film historian Bob Thomas began his studio writing career after the war Richard Isomaki pointing out the many important job opportunities open to women aside from acting, and there is evidence that his coverage was part of a wider publicity campaign spotlighting the surge in female producers and executives, among them Ida Koverman, the "power at MGM," Anita Colby, Harriet Parsons, Joan Harrison, Virginia Van Upp, past guild president Mary C. McCall Jr., press agents Margaret Ettinger and Helen Ferguson, and star managers and ex-wives Edna Skelton Borzage and Sylvia Fine, who continued to manage Red Skelton's and Danny Kaye's careers after their marriages fell apart.[48]

Unfortunately, the gains in gender equality in Hollywood did not last. With the end of the 1950s and the decline of the studio system, women no longer played dominant roles in the administration of the Screen Writers Guild and Screen Actors Guild. They were no longer heading major departments in individual studios. Women were no longer promoted to jobs as first cutters, and senior women were not replaced upon retirement or after their deaths. Scenario, costume, and research departments downsized as studios attempted to cut costs in a shrinking market following a series of economic crises forced by expensive new star contracts (Olivia de Havilland's decisive victory against Warner Bros. became law from 1944), the rise of percentage deals, government-spearheaded trust-busting initiatives (in *United States v. Paramount Pictures*, 1948), competition from television, independent production companies, and shifting competition in overseas markets. Even in departments where women predominated, their positions were no longer mentioned in *Film Daily*. Some women, sensing the diminishing opportunities in a dying industry, moved to theater or television work. Lucille Ball, Joan Harrison, Ida Lupino, Dorothy Hechtlinger, and Gail Patrick did rather well. Others maintained a career foothold, but at reduced salaries.

And of course, beginning in 1947, many female writers and actors were blacklisted, graylisted, or under intense investigation by the FBI, including Jean Muir, Marsha Hunt, Gale Songergaard, Lillian Hellman, Isobel Lennart, Marguerite Roberts, and Mary McCall. Only a few years after McCall defended Hollywood on behalf of her guild, director Sam Wood would claim screenwriters were "the most dangerous group in the movie industry," and Jack Warner would concur, stating that those with "un-American leanings" in Hollywood were "in the writing division."[49] The Hollywood Ten—longtime heroes of Hollywood leftist lore and film history—were ten men. Though Hollywood's black- or graylisted women didn't go to jail, they were named and shamed in the papers, called to testify, lost their jobs, and faced years of poverty and anonymity. The male victims snagged most of the headlines.

Writers, whose final push toward unionization had coincided with the introduction of the infamous *Paramount* case in the courts, were, more often than not, the scapegoats for power struggles that were as much about payback from America's strong labor and feminist eras as about anticommunism. Women working in various administrative or clerical capacities in the film industry also lost their jobs, and others moved from film to television or theater. But Hollywood actresses Bette Davis and Katharine Hepburn were also branded communists by various right-wing organizations and had to curb their political voices in order to remain a viable force on screen. Liberals Paulette Goddard, Ava Gardner, and Olivia de Havilland moved to Europe. Younger stars such as Elizabeth Taylor, Janet Leigh, and Lana Turner, who mixed on the fringes of the Left but matured in an environment in which the media and industry executives destroyed women's careers, chose to remain silent. It was easier for Republicans June Allyson and Esther Williams, both decorative supporters of the young Richard Nixon. Producers such as Y. Frank Freeman, Jack Warner, and L. B. Mayer participated in a climate of fear that encouraged the witch-hunt.

Certainly no actress in the 1950s dared to take the career path of former stage and screen star Helen Gahagan, who, after marrying her costar, Melvyn Douglas, turned politician, won three terms of office as a California congresswoman for the Fourteenth District, and served as one of the nation's most prominent Democrats. A good friend of Eleanor Roosevelt, Douglas was responsible for introducing many of Hollywood's top women to the First Lady while on her visits to the West Coast. One of her last acts before running for Senate was to introduce a bill that would treat working women's childcare "as a business expense deductible for income tax purposes."[50] But in 1950, she was defeated by Republican Richard Nixon in a race "infamous" for its red-baiting. Douglas, the "darling of the Hollywood liberal establishment," had participated with Lillian Hellman in the November 1945 Conference on American-Soviet Cultural Cooperation, which many in the media regarded as communist-fueled propaganda.[51] Her defeat by Nixon, engineered by Republicans such as outgoing senator Sheridan Downey, who smeared her as a communist, ended her political career and paved the way for Nixon's election two years later as Dwight D. Eisenhower's running mate.[52] Douglas's experience not only set back Hollywood women's political ambitions for a generation (Nixon would later be accused of trying to "personally blacklist Jane Fonda" over her opinions on Vietnam and Watergate),[53] but also served to break the cross-party coalition of working women in Hollywood who supported each other professionally for twenty years.

Another even more insidious factor contributed to the erasure of women from Hollywood. However much Hollywood acted as an advocate for working women during the heyday of the studio system, male historians tended to edit out women's roles, leaving them on the cutting room floor of conventional film histories. These classic "professional" studies of Hollywood would later be taught in universities as film history emerged as an academic discipline, perpetuating the belief that women had no creative role in Hollywood save acting. Terry Ramsaye (1926), Benjamin Hampton (1931), Lewis Jacobs (1939), Leo Rosten (1941), and Arthur Knight (1957) all focused on a progressive historical model founded on technological, artistic, and commercial innovation dominated by a male cast of producers and directors.[54] Though there are occasional references to Mary Pickford, Jean Harlow, and Mae West in their books, Pickford's work as a producer and West's skills as a screenwriter are glossed over. While Leo Rosten acknowledged the film industry as unique in its ability to empower professional women, he was concerned only with actresses such as MGM's Norma Shearer and Greta Garbo.[55]

New York Times film critic Bosley Crowther's classic history of MGM, *The Lion's Share*, portrays the studio as an almost exclusively male domain where directors "handle the girls [actresses]."[56] Though his studio story is populated with vignettes from the careers of Jeanette MacDonald, Garbo, and Lana Turner, the woman many said "ran" MGM and Mayer from 1928 to 1954, Ida Koverman, gets three one-line references, while executive Eddie Mannix gets twenty-four. The pattern is repeated elsewhere: top-paid screenwriter Frances Marion gets four references, while Charles MacArthur gets eleven pages, and fellow critics Parsons and Hopper get a meager one and three references respectively. Crowther's story is one about moguls Irving Thalberg and L. B. Mayer and the male directors controlling a legion of pretty girls. Long before popular auteurism had taken hold in mainstream newspapers and magazines, Crowther embraced the idea of filmmaking as a man's—and principally a director's—game.[57]

But something as simple as a 1934 telephone directory for the studio suggests a different story.[58] Scroll down the list of names. In MGM's cutting department, rooms 1 and 2 were occupied by Blanche Sewell and Margaret Booth. Adrienne Fazan, who worked in the music department, had a separate office. Muriel Lambert and Peggy O'Day worked in sound. These women weren't secretaries fetching coffee, transcribing Dictaphones, and fending off their boss's wandering hands. Look in another column: Marjorie Haddock headed censorship, Frances Edwards ran the commissary, Peggy Coleman was chief nurse, Mrs. J. Terrell was the matron, Pearl Porter was head of the Planning Department, Florence Hannemann and Marcella Knapp worked in casting, Mary Hill, Mary Mayer, and Kate Mulvey handled publicity, Lillian Rosine was head of women's makeup, Beatrice Langley was in charge of transportation, and Dorothy Pratt headed the Reading Department. But that wasn't all. The formidable Nathalie Bucknall (who Hubbard Keavy said was educated in Russia with the czar's daughters and was "a member of the second woman's battalion of death" during the Russian Revolution) was in charge of the Research Department, Edith Farrell was in charge of Script, Kate Corbaley ran the Story Department, "Mother" Coulter ran Women's Wardrobe, Dolly Tree was chief designer, Mary MacDonald ran the school for child stars, and Lola Shea ran the studio's telephone operators and exchanges. All MGM's key secretaries (including Silvia Schulman, future author of the best-selling Hollywood exposé *I Lost My Girlish Laughter*, 1938) were women; Ida Koverman was chief executive. Running over the list of individual names, it becomes obvious that women dominated the studio's screenwriting department: Vicki Baum, Zoe Akins, Maureen Watkins, Claudine West, Anita Loos, Sarah Y. Mason, Frances Marion, Zelda Sears, Ruth and Mitzi Cummings, Katherine Lane, Frances Goodrich, Eve Greene, Lenore Coffee, Salka Viertel, and Mercedes de Acosta were all on the payroll and were important enough to merit their own offices and private phones. Garbo was only one of dozens of women who had positions of power in the studio hierarchy.

A phone book is a useful metaphor for the way films were made in the studio era. In the phone book, everyone looks equal in the MGM family. Mayer was listed alphabetically alongside the women who ran his payroll, phones, publicity, transport, hospital, research library, sound and editing departments, makeup, wardrobe, story, script and reading, the writers who penned the films, and the stars who raked in the money at the box office. Hubbard Keavy's 40% industrial statistics may have been conservative. Each of these female-run departments was integral to the running of the studio. But the idea of studio collaboration, more popular with industry people and critics writing in the studio era, was eliminated and was replaced in the 1960s and 1970s with a model of production overdetermined by male-dominated, director-based auteurism. Auteurism academically legitimized sexism in film history and criticism in more than one way. Academics from the 1970s reproduced the assumption that women did not have any creative or administrative control in the studio system, and even feminist film critics, while grasping at the impressive careers of Dorothy Arzner and Ida Lupino for some respite, by and large lambasted Hollywood for its assumed denigration of women on screen via scopophilic "gaze" theories pioneered by Laura Mulvey.[59]

Although today, with a renewed attention to archival research, film historians are gradually coming to terms with the substantial number of women working in Hollywood during the twentieth century, most of the research has focused on so-called pioneers of the silent era, such as director-producer Lois Weber (who died penniless in 1939), star and United Artists' cofounder Mary Pickford, serial star Pearl White, and, via the work of Cari Beauchamp, screenwriter Frances Marion.[60] It is certainly true that there were many women involved in screenwriting, editing, directing, producing, and journalism in cinema's early years, and that the strong presence of women in these branches of the filmmaking profession undoubtedly made it easier for the next generation of women to gain employment in the late 1920s and 1930s.

But Karen Ward Mahar and Mark Garrett Cooper have argued that masculine managerial business practices all but closed the directing profession to women by the mid-1920s, and this has led many to assume that women lost professional prominence in the industry.[61] This belief has added weight to Erin Hill's research on the high number of low-paid, powerless female drones working in the studio system. If women did hang onto their jobs after the closure of the "pioneering" days of the silent era, it was in repetitive, menial "women's work"—sewing hundreds of beads on gowns, typing someone else's letters, cutting negatives. The end of the Hollywood frontier was tied to Lois Weber's depressing career trajectory and Mary Pickford's shorn curls.

It certainly is tempting to use western metaphors to characterize the narrative of women's presence in Hollywood during the first few decades of the twentieth century—reading these women as female "pioneers" in a wide-open cinematic frontier town—but this discourse, as well as the argument that women were utterly disempowered and lost creative control during the 1930s and throughout the studio era, is specious. Keavy, writing in 1934 about the impressive 40% employment figures for women, actually claimed that "fifteen years ago the picture plants were almost wholly masculine," but that "gradually the number of women has increased until today women are to be found in nearly all the 100 trades, professions, vocations, and avocations needed to make a photoplay."

Certainly Louella Parsons's advertisement of Hollywood as a new "West" for women and David O. Selznick's eulogy to Hollywood as screen-struck Esther Blodgett's "El Dorado" in *A Star Is Born* (1937) have encouraged film historians to apply the discourse of the American frontier to their work, singling out great female filmmakers as "pioneers" to promote early Hollywood as a "free" space for modern women.[62] Usually these pioneers are directors. But how appropriate is it to reconstruct a women's filmmaking "canon" using the same exclusionary language that erased women from active participation in earlier eras of US history? So often we have been inculcated with the belief that the American West was a *man's* space; are we also to believe the same for Hollywood or blithely apply these misogynistic and racist metaphors to other contexts without consequences? Similarly, while classic historians of the American West have argued that a few great women carved "pioneering" paths out of the wilderness, they tended to privilege the rare Annie Oakleys and ignore the scores of anonymous women who conceived of their experience through familial and community networks, kinships, and collaboration.[63] In the same way, film historians schooled in conventional auteurism are committed to a hierarchy of work emphasizing directors as the definitive creative force in filmmaking,[64] a position that masks women's wider presence in the industry during the studio era.

Yet it's hard to get around the fact that silent film historians' assumption of women's decline in the Hollywood workforce from the 1920s parallels the arguments made by many women's historians writing about the years between First and Second Wave feminism.[65] As historian Susan Ware commented, "Historians traditionally have thought that the women's movement fell apart after the vote was won."[66] Nancy Cott, William Chafe, and Stephanie Coontz have drawn attention to the opposition to women working during the Depression, particularly married women, and the limited educational and job opportunities. With the exception of the war years, they have argued that American women were not an important or respected group of workers, and that any efforts to push forward women's economic and social equality were derailed by the Depression.[67] However, as Ware points out, "Many now believe that feminist activity continued in the 1920s. Instead of being united behind the single goal of suffrage, the movement splintered into a variety of causes: pacifism, professional politics, business and the professions."[68] Feminism had arguably entered the mainstream, becoming part of the *Oxford English Dictionary* supplement in 1933. But others continued to insist on its unpopularity among working women, requoting a hostile 1936 Gallup poll and a contemporaneous article asking, "Is Feminism Dead?"[69]

It would be wrong, however, to assume that press coverage was uniformly negative or that women's employment declined in the 1930s. As Ware points out, "In the midst of the greatest economic crisis this country has ever seen," women still increased their overall participation in the workforce from 24.3% to 25.4%, which was an increase of over two million jobs.[70] Women were particularly well represented in the media (Anne O'Hare McCormick, Margaret Bourke-White, Dorothy Thompson, Martha Gellhorn) and in the Roosevelt administration, where women held more positions of power than ever before. Molly Dewson, Mary Bethune, Hallie Flanagan, and Frances Perkins were in many ways the face of the New Deal, and many of Hollywood's most powerful and outspoken women were Roosevelt supporters. Still, many other Hollywood women took sustenance from the Republican Party, which committed earlier to the passage of the Equal Rights Amendment.

Ware's acknowledgment of the diversity of approaches to women's empowerment, and a renewed if dispersed commitment to furthering women's careers and feminism, is useful to bear in mind when profiling studio-era Hollywood women's attitudes toward being working women. Many of Hollywood's top women were Republicans, and others were Democrats. Some supported the recognition of guilds and unions; others did not. Some, like secretary and best-selling writer Silvia Schulman, acknowledged that they were cautious about publicly admitting their feminist commitments since they worked with men who might be ambivalent or fearful of the term.[71] No one wanted to lose her job, so often there was a "Don't ask, don't tell" policy. Others, such as Bette Davis, Louella Parsons, and Hedda Hopper, were proud advocates for other women and publicly criticized sexism in their industry.

For many working in the United States during the 1930s and 1940s, gender equality could only be achieved when women were able to do their work well without the public constantly drawing attention to their identities as women. Frontiers were not broached, but ignored. The transition that cultural historian Kathy Peiss saw from exclusively women's social groups in the late nineteenth century to a more mixed workplace and leisure space advocated by Hollywood after 1920 didn't mean a rejection of feminism, commitment to other women, and women's equality, but a belief in "the single standard." Take, for example, writer and soon-to-be producer Virginia Van Upp's response to actor Gene Kelly's "compliment" to her on the script of *Cover Girl* (1944). Happy that a man actually had a strong part in a musical, he told her, "You write just like a man." The journalist reported, "Miss Van Upp sniffs at that. To her notion, writers of either sex are writers. They have to know people—both men and women."[72]

Over the years, writers and historians have attempted to make a classic feminist out of Lillian Hellman. It was tough work. In her heyday as one of Samuel Goldwyn's top writers, Hellman relished being "the only woman in an all-male group," and was said to have been responsible for getting writer Virginia Kellogg fired by complaining to the producer about her clacking typewriter.[73] Female solidarity was not really a priority for Hellman. Even after the blacklist had ended her lucrative career as a screenwriter, Hellman annoyed many contemporary feminists who wanted to see her as an advocate for women. At a lecture on writing in New York in 1951, Hellman responded to questions from the audience: "Should women playwrights organize to promote the work of women in today's theatre?" she read out. "Why certainly not," she responded in a slow, deliberately paced put-down. "Why would anybody want *women* playwrights? This great desire to have women do things is . . . I don't understand it. They do them or they don't do them. Why would women be of any more benefit than men would be of benefit? Why should one think of it that way?"[74] There were audible gasps from the women in the audience. But Hellman's response was in line with many prominent Hollywood women speaking about gender and work during the twentieth century. They believed that qualifying it, even by pointing out their exceptional status, was offensive and derisory to women's complete equality with men.

This was, for example, why her colleague McCall brushed aside proposals to establish a women's committee at the Writers Guild of America in the 1970s. Several decades later, critic Lizzie Francke dismissed McCall's position as symptomatic of "the small band of career women" who "could not or did not want to . . . bring about larger changes."[75] Similarly, Nancy Cott has also argued that equal rights feminism was problematic since "it urged women to disregard sex" and "the paradoxical realities of women's situation."[76] But, as far as McCall was concerned, the Hollywood "system" had been pretty good to women; what needed changing were wider social assumptions about gender-specific roles and expectations.

One of the most revealing stories about McCall comes from a guild press biography from around the same time she was elected to her third term as president (and when Hellman made light of encouraging women writers). Most people want to know where the "Jr." came from in McCall's name, the release noted. "Her mother's name was Mary McCall, and when mama, on Mary's seventh birthday, opened a savings account for daughter at the same bank where mama banked, the pass book said Mary C. McCall, Jr. . . . When subsequently she was challenged by the boys at school with 'Aw, gee, a girl can't be a Junior,' she was grimly determined to hang onto it." She did, through college and Hollywood and two marriages, rejecting stereotypes of what was masculine and feminine, just as she refused to be typecast as a writer of women's romantic stories (she adapted Sinclair Lewis's *Babbitt* [1934] and Shakespeare's *A Midsummer Night's Dream* [1935] while pregnant with twins, and wrote war pictures and westerns). McCall wasn't alone in her "Jr." female status, either: actress Cobina Wright Jr. (who interrupted her honeymoon to go back to work at Fox) and screenwriter Harriet Frank Jr. (whose mother was also in the film business and who started her career at MGM in the early 1940s as an MGM reader) adopted the suffix after McCall and kept their "maiden" names throughout their careers. Whether you were a writer (Goodrich, Slesinger, Murfin, Lennart, Ryerson), a producer (Van Upp, Harrison, Parsons, Bennett, Deutsch), or an actress (Stanwyck, Davis, Colbert, Gardner, Dunne, MacDonald, and even Hepburn), you kept the name you were born with, even after marriage, for reasons of finance and fame.

Years later, the debate would rage among historians and critics shaped by the different contexts of the 1960s women's movement over whether the women working between 1925 and 1960 were "true feminists" or believed in women's equality at all. But if independent working women's struggle for equality from the mid-1920s through the early 1950s wasn't synonymous with the more confrontational discourse of the Second Wave, does this really mean that feminism disappeared between 1925 and 1960— ironically the period we have come to know as the Hollywood studio era?

While Ware points out the range of responses to the women's movement, there was nevertheless a growing, shared commitment to the Equal Rights Amendment that influenced many of Hollywood's women during the studio era and united them regardless of their political affiliations. In the 1930s, feminism did not disappear as a term in political and cultural life. It was defined by the tenets of the ERA, "the out and out feminist policy" that was the next important step in achieving gender equality, as one 1937 article alleged.[77] After years of struggle between National Women's Party members and opponents of the ERA, there was growing cross-party support for the amendment, first introduced in 1923, thanks to the protective labor legislation made possible by Secretary of Labor Frances Perkins, the Wagner Act (1935), and the Fair Labor Standards Act (1938). As Ware points out, "When the government protected both men and women alike with minimum wage standards, unemployment insurance, and a forty-hour week, women no longer needed to be singled out for special treatment."[78] Additionally, given the range of discriminatory state laws that still prohibited women from entering into contracts or running for public office, allowed husbands to collect wives' wages, and sanctioned unfair divorce laws, ERA advocates believed it was time to have a national law to end the legal discrimination. Business and professional women supported the bill in 1937, with the American Alliance of Civil Service Women, the American Medical Women's Association, and the National Association of Women Lawyers following suit in 1938. In 1940, the Republican National Convention supported the ERA, and Roosevelt's party added it to the Democratic platform in 1944.

While feminist historians of the silent era have turned to the archives and the industry trade papers to reconstruct women's widespread presence in the US film industry in the first two decades of the twentieth century, this book is also built on research in existing studio archival collections, guild reports, trade papers, local reportage, and nationally syndicated journalism. And the startling truth emerges: women working in studio-era Hollywood were experiencing a golden age of employment. Although overall numbers of female directors declined from the silent era, women remained active in the industry as producers, writers, script readers, researchers, actors, costume and makeup designers, set dressers, secretaries, publicists, agents, and editors. Yet, given the dominance of auteurist ideologies in the writing of Hollywood history, these other branches of filmmaking, more heavily represented by women, have been marginalized or ignored. There is certainly no shortage of fine studies of directors Dorothy Arzner and Ida Lupino, as film scholars celebrate their rare, stand-alone success and push them into the boys' club of Hollywood auteurs. But these women were tied to networks of other Hollywood women that promoted and sustained a range of women's careers in film.

Mary C. McCall Jr. served as three-term president of the Screen Writers Guild (1942–1943, 1943–1944, 1951–1952), was a driving force in securing the first contract with the producers, and chaired more committees than most other writers had film credits, but again, historians of the guild, the blacklist, and women in Hollywood have all but ignored her.[79] Supervising feature editors Margaret Booth and Barbara McLean had as much creative control over their studios' final cuts as Irving Thalberg and Darryl Zanuck, but again, they are mere footnotes in the historiography. Those in the know in Hollywood were aware that "executive secretary" Ida Koverman wielded as much power as Thalberg or Mayer; Eve Ettinger was Harry Cohn's right hand in Columbia's script department, Gwen Wakeling and Vera West directed the costume departments at Fox and Universal, and Frances Richardson was director of research supervising all of Zanuck's famed costume pictures at "Nineteenth Century-Fox" during its golden age, but they are not remembered.

Given her shrewd grasp of publicity and the work of costume historian David Chierichetti, Edith Head is remembered as Paramount's longtime head of costume design. Recent publications have discussed Hedda Hopper and Louella Parsons as some of the most influential and political critics in Hollywood. However, these women are usually recognized for their unpleasant professional sides—in Head's case, as an administrator rather than a creative force (who claimed credit from "real" designers like Hubert de Givenchy in *Sabrina*, 1954) or as red-baiting gossip gorgons (in Hopper's case, very right-wing) responsible for destroying careers.[80]

Thanks to Molly Haskell's *From Reverence to Rape* and Marjorie Rosen's *Popcorn Venus* (both 1973), critics and fans have drawn sustenance from the surprisingly feminist elements of some actresses' performances in the 1930s and 1940s. The grim reality of post-studio-era Hollywood in the 1970s forced the question: when did Hollywood forget the women? What happened to feminism, equal representation, and respect? We are asking the same questions today. Academics have continued to find feminist respite, not from contemporary Hollywood's image of women, but from the studio era. Thomas Schatz's work on Bette Davis's conflicts with Warner Bros. acknowledged an important off-screen dimension to her image of independent femininity, and Emily Carman's recent study of freelance actresses in the 1930s and 1940s adds another facet to Carole Lombard's, Irene Dunne's, Barbara Stanwyck's, and Constance Bennett's career images as independent women.

However, comparatively little is known about Bette Davis's founding and direction of the Hollywood Canteen and tenure as president of the Academy, Joan Crawford's front-line union work for SAG in the 1930s, Myrna Loy's support for the United Nations, and Katharine Hepburn's political involvements in the 1940s. We know their films, their attitudes, and what they did for their own pocketbooks and star status, but what did they do, if anything, for other women, for the film industry, and for their country? Were any of them really feminists?

This book offers an overview of the diverse careers open to women in Hollywood between 1925 and 1960, and looks at the rise and fall of prominent women in the industry, from secretaries to stars. There are individual chapters on studio administrators and producers, actors, writers, editors, and designers. Attention is paid not only to career trajectories, work on individual productions, and involvement with studio policy, but also to union activities, political commitments, war work, and home life. Not all of Hollywood's working women were single, pretty girls waiting for husbands to come along, and even fewer resembled the rich and lazy "five-letter females" of Clare Booth Luce's and Anita Loos's *The Women* (1939). They worked, and "women's work" in Hollywood was not always low paid and anonymous. Many were graduates of women's colleges; many came from families with ties to the silent picture business. Some siblings worked for the same studio; sometimes wives and husbands did. Some women were single; others were married. More were divorced. Some were at one time members of the Communist Party; some were fiercely anti-communist. Some were Democrats, some were Republicans, and many, usually the overworked editors, were too busy to care about which party was in office. Even more were prounion and proud of being working-class women. Most, apart from actresses such as Hattie McDaniel, Lena Horne, Anna May Wong, Dolores del Rio, Lupe Velez, and Rita Hayworth, were white. There are some stars in this book, but they aren't all actresses. Mary C. McCall Jr., Barbara McLean, and Bette Davis are the most prominently featured, given their range of work and commitment to the industry, but this book aims to name as many names as possible, patched from fragments of studio archives, payrolls, union lists, items in the *Hollywood Reporter* and obscure national papers, House Committee on Un-American Activities testimonies, memoirs, and yes—even studio phone books.

Hollywood has a unique history of supporting a diverse range of careers for women, and women's achievements in Hollywood were celebrated by the industry for at least twenty-five years, from the Depression through World War II and the postwar era. Although the decline of the system, economic downsizing, and the political pressures of the blacklist certainly contributed to a decline in women's employment in Hollywood, the studio era—long dismissed as a corporate patriarchy by historians and critics— remains the most important and empowering chapter in women's employment in the film industry. In 1977, at the height of popular Second Wave feminism's praise for "golden age" Hollywood stars, Bette Davis acknowledged that contemporary Hollywood was not a place where women had much of a voice. However, she reminisced, "Women owned Hollywood for twenty years, and we must not be bitter." Few historians seem to have listened to her.

This book is the largely untold story of the women who once ran Hollywood during its true golden age.

CHAPTER 1
The Fourth Warner Brother

There's a French saying, an actor is less than a man and an actress is more than a woman. Men weather better. But women owned Hollywood for 20 years, and we must not be bitter.

Bette Davis to Mel Gussow, March 1977[1]

On December 13, 1930, a shy, mousy young woman from Massachusetts waited on the station platform in Los Angeles. She had recently signed a contract with Universal, and a representative was supposed to have met her train. No one was there. She later found out that the studio man had arrived, looked over the passengers—herself included—and departed alone, feeling that no one on the train looked like a prospective star. The young woman was Bette Davis, and she would remember this event for the rest of her life, retelling it in autobiographies, articles, and television appearances with her trademark brand of wry humor and tart satisfaction at having had the last word.[2] Nobody remembers the name of the studio representative.

Davis had come to Los Angeles as one of the new generation of sound-era contract players. She was well educated, a successful Broadway actress, and with an impressive list of references, including actress Blanche Yurka, director Marion Gering, director of the Provincetown Players James Light, and Richard Bennett (father to actresses Constance and Joan Bennett).[3] But she, like so many of Hollywood's female stars, from Mary Pickford to Ginger Rogers, was also raised by an independent single mother who put the career of her daughter above everything else. Ruth Elizabeth Davis's mother would divorce her husband when Bette and her younger sister

Barbara ("Bobby") were aged seven and six (figure 1.1). Although he would occasionally appear to take the girls out at the weekends on excursions, Ruthie was a single mother and supplemented the meager alimony checks by working as a photographer's assistant. She was proud of her independence, but wanted something much better for both her daughters. Years later, when Bette Davis was well established in Hollywood, an article in her hometown paper noted that "her ambition to become an actress caused dissention between her parents."[4] As Davis remembered, "My father thought I ought to be something nice and respectable like a stenographer. Mother told him she would support me in any career I chose. I wanted to be an actress and mother said that was all right with her."[5] In another early interview, she recalled, "When I first started clamoring to be an actress, my mother said, 'Go ahead and try it. It's a job like any other. Think of it that way, not in terms of glamour and glory and your name in lights. All that's a bi-product, pleasant enough if it comes. Only it has nothing to do with acting.' "[6]

Ruthie's New England work ethic, self-reliance, and the hard times she and the girls endured before her elder daughter succeeded on Broadway transformed Bette Davis into the ideal star for Depression-era American women. She was beautiful, but didn't seem to care about it and even dismissed her looks. She was famous, but never behaved like a star. As Ruth Rankin noted in *Photoplay*, "She isn't given to romantic attitudes or postures. . . . Nobody has tried to kidnap her or steal her jewels. . . . People suspect her of having brains."[7] Bette Davis was proud of being a working woman—or, as her family members only half-jokingly nicknamed her, "The Golden Goose." Rather than dwelling on her own success and enhancing her star status with publicists and members of the press, she formed links with others inside and outside the studios to help women's careers. While historians and critics have claimed that the opportunities for women in the film industry declined from the late 1920s, slowed by the failing momentum of the women's movement and "First Wave" feminism, the aims of late nineteenth- and early twentieth-century social feminism lived on in Bette Davis, who subtly adapted them to her New Deal politics and Depression-era practicality.

In the 1930s, she crafted her career in opposition to conventional images of femininity, battling for equal treatment and pay, and by the end of the decade, the media, her legions of fans, and the Hollywood industry itself paid tribute to "Queen Bette," the "Fourth Warner Brother." And while Harry, Albert, and Jack Warner concealed their often repressive studio practices behind the mask of a paternal family brand, as the fourth Warner Brother, Davis shrewdly promoted filmmaking's capacity for transparency,

*Homes Girls at Aunt Mildred's wedding.
in Winchester, Mass at our house.*

Figure 1.1 Bette Davis with mother Ruthie and sister Bobby, 1919

realism, and equality, from her public contract dispute in 1936 to her unconventional roles and off-screen persona. But perhaps most striking was her strategy of acquiring top star power by working within the studio system. While a number of her actress colleagues kept their distance from long-term studio contracts, brokering successful careers as "freelancers" that financially outdistanced their more compliant contract sisters, from 1937, Davis put her "team player" capital to good use. As president of the Academy of Motion Picture Arts and Sciences, president of the Hollywood Canteen, and public Democrat, she built networks of working women inside Hollywood and inspired her female fans to develop their independent political voice and faith in equal rights. If, as she later put it, "Women owned Hollywood for twenty years," then she is the Warner brother to remember.

Bette Davis's backstory, whether told to local or syndicated Hollywood journalists, reflected the star's frankness and dislike of artifice, traits that, perhaps surprisingly, Hollywood publicists and journalists appreciated and respected. As Ida Zeitlin wrote, "She has no tricks. She keeps her acting for the screen."[8] During the height of her stardom in the 1930s and 1940s, she was repeatedly praised for her ease and cooperativeness with journalists, many of whom were young women struggling to make ends meet on a journalist's paycheck. In 1941, even the notoriously hard-to-please Hedda Hopper was her fan, naming Davis the "wisest" and the "best" actress in the business.[9] Hollywood's influential columnist was tougher on Davis's male colleagues, however, listing Donald Duck and Mickey Mouse as Hollywood's top men that year! In 1942, the Women's Press Club named Davis "hands down" the "most cooperative" female star in Hollywood. As *The Movie Radio Guide* commented, "This is an honor which should be treasured by its recipients because it reflects so clearly how gracious 'big people' can, if they choose, help 'littler people' do their jobs."[10]

Davis could be gracious, but she wouldn't tolerate sexism in the industry—period. While at Universal making a film called *The Menace* (1931), her sense of moral outrage and filmmaking inexperience made a hilarious combination. As she recalled, one day "an electrician on the set suddenly shouted, 'Get that broad out of the way!' I flared up. 'He can't talk to me that way!' I screamed. Then I was informed that a broad is the Hollywood term for a certain kind of light."[11] Playwright Wilson Mizner, a close friend and mentor of writer Anita Loos, admired Davis's attitude but sensed her frustration with a career that at this point seemed to be going nowhere. The Hollywood insider advised the young star to dye her hair blonde, and Davis took his advice. The change coincided with veteran actor George Arliss's decision to cast her opposite him in *The Man Who Played God* (1932). Arliss had become Warner Bros.' top prestige star due to his reputation as one of the stage's most distinguished actors, and he had won the Academy Award the previous year playing the title role in *Disraeli* (1929). He too flouted the glamour of Hollywood stardom, and Davis, to a certain extent, was influenced by the older actor's professionalism. But she also developed her own, powerful, and startlingly feminist voice, on screen and off, to describe her attitude toward work and her commitment to her career.

Playing Arliss's young love interest in *The Man Who Played God* coincided with a move to his studio, Warner Bros., where she appeared as a succession of sweet young things, perky working girls, and the occasional siren—but Davis preferred playing the hardboiled bitches. As she complained, "The trouble is, I look like an ingénue is supposed to look. . . . That came close to being my Waterloo in pictures. . . . [G]ood creatures are usually saps. Dreadfully dull." She was quickly bored at Warner Bros., a studio notorious for squandering its female talent on poor scripts, and leaped at the chance of playing Mildred in RKO's adaptation of Somerset Maugham's *Of Human Bondage* (1934). Mizner sent her the script, and director John Cromwell wanted her to test for the role. Studio head Jack Warner was initially skeptical, but Davis and Cromwell persisted. Playing Mildred would cure every Hollywood casting agent of recommending her for any virginal ingénue role. In many ways, Mildred was the ultimate femme fatale in contemporary literature, a cool, Cockney, promiscuous bitch who drives protagonist Philip Carey (Leslie Howard) to the brink of self-destruction. But, as she later revealed, she also had her own misgivings about playing the part: "I knew I was taking chances with my career when I played Mildred."[12] Eventually Davis talked it over with playwright and friend Lynn Riggs, who said, "Things couldn't be much worse than they are now, so you might as well try it."[13]

Mildred redefined Davis's career. It was the first of many shocking physical transformations she made to achieve the cinematic realism she craved. While RKO's top contract star, Ann Harding, praised by still photographer Ernest Bachrach as having "the most nearly perfect face" in the industry, was famous for refusing to cut, dye, straighten, or curl her naturally white-blonde hair and only wore powder in front of the camera, her stubbornness was seen as the right of a beautiful and intelligent woman "to refuse to be standardized."[14] Harding also refused "to be used as a manikin for RKO's dress designers": "Harding clothes have to express the simplicity and straightforwardness of the Harding personality." RKO shrewdly marketed Harding as unique in Hollywood and a role model for other young women who resented being typecast by a male-dominated beauty industry. But unlike Davis, Harding's roles were carefully tailored to her educated demeanor and regal appearance (*The Girl of the Golden West*, 1930; *Holiday*, 1930; *The Animal Kingdom*, 1932; *The Silver Cord*, 1933; *The Age of Innocence*, 1934; *Gallant Lady*, 1934).

Davis took Hollywood realism in a direction that only Lon Chaney equaled in his 1920s horror films. In order to appear more like the dying East London prostitute, she overbleached her hair so that chunks of it fell out of her scalp, stopped eating to approximate the protagonist's wasted appearance, and chain-smoked to get the right rasp in her voice. Later in the decade as Mary in the Lucky Luciano–inspired *Marked Woman* (1937), Charlotte in Edith Wharton's *The Old Maid* (1939), Elizabeth I in *The Private Lives of Elizabeth and Essex* (1939), mentally ill Charlotte Vale in *Now, Voyager* (1942), and typhoid victim Fanny Skeffington in *Mr. Skeffington* (1944), Davis went out of her way to transform and deglamorize herself. Warner Bros. designer Orry-Kelly was at his wit's end from trying to make her wear underwire bras to lift her heavy bust, but she refused, believing the wiring caused breast cancer.[15] When he bought her one of the new strapless bras, she allegedly threw it at him. At the height of her fame in 1939, she balked at being photographed by the legendary George Hurrell, protesting: "I will not be turned into a piece of shiny wax fruit!"[16]

She behaved this way away from the studio as well, refusing to wear any bras or foundation garments, doing her own nails at home, and while journalists warmed to her frank discussion of work and personal issues, she could take her informal behavior too far. When she attended the Academy Awards in early 1936 to accept her award for *Dangerous*[17] (a role based on the life of actress Jeanne Eagels, who'd broken even more taboos than Davis during her short lifetime), she shocked the company for another reason. As she recalled, "My first Oscar also involved one of my major clashes with Hollywood precedent and custom. Then, as now, it was the habit of film actresses to appear at the Awards affairs wearing glamorous gowns of lace and tulle. Instead I had bought an expensive but simple navy-blue and white dinner dress. Particularly shocked was a well-known Hollywood newspaperwoman who followed me into the ladies room and said, 'How dare you appear like that?'"[18] But snubbing contrived images of feminine beauty worked for Davis's audiences. Exhibitors routinely voted her the top box-office draw among adult female stars in the 1930s and 1940s.[19]

Davis may not have bothered to dress up for another reason: she and many in Hollywood viewed her win for *Dangerous* a cop-out consolation prize for not even being nominated for *Of Human Bondage* the year before.[20] While the role of Mildred had been too brash and startling for the Academy's conservative and predominantly male members, Hollywood's actresses broke with tradition—for the only time in Academy history—and responded in solidarity with Davis. Norma Shearer had initiated a write-in campaign for her performance in *Of Human Bondage* (allowed under Academy bylaws), and Davis nearly beat rival Claudette Colbert (for Columbia's *It Happened*

One Night). Until Shearer's subversive act, producers routinely ordered their employees to vote their way on the ballot—before the guilds began to challenge this practice in the late 1930s—and staff complied.

Although much of the trade press coverage in the mid-1930s had emphasized Jack Warner's reluctance to loan out Davis to RKO for *Of Human Bondage*, the actress, perhaps angling for better roles after her Academy Award for *Dangerous* and hoping to win a higher salary from the cheapskate studio, attempted a more diplomatic PR solution. In the spring of 1936, she wrote a column for *Screen Guilds' Magazine*, stating, "The most encouraging thing to me today in regard to our mutual industry is the trend toward realism."[21] According to Davis, films such as *Ah, Wilderness!* (1935), *Alice Adams* (1935), and *Of Human Bondage* were part of a wider shift toward giving screen audiences real life rather than mindless escapism. Much of this resulted, she believed, from actresses being more assertive with the glamour industry, and rejecting ultrafeminine and unrealistic standards.

In another article, she wrote that the casting issues with *Of Human Bondage* were a question of her having to reject the arbitrary rules dictating female glamour and "raise her game" as an actress: after all, she claimed: "A story like that only comes once in a lifetime."[22] The role required a personal and professional courage, and she argued in many press interviews and articles during the 1930s and 1940s that all American women should stretch themselves this way. In her interviews, Davis consistently reached out to other women through shared experiences rather than focusing on her exceptional individuality and talent. After her success with Mildred and the consolation Academy Award, she advised young women to make a name for themselves on Broadway before attempting to break into Hollywood.[23] She formed lifetime friendships with fellow Warner Bros. actress Joan Blondell and writer Mary C. McCall Jr., and also sought out other prominent actresses, forming a mutual admiration society with Helen Hayes after the two met in New York in 1937 (figure 1.2). She acknowledged that it was Hayes's work on Broadway in *Coquette* (1927) that influenced her performance as prostitute Mary Blake in *Marked Woman*,[24] and Hayes would later write to her to express her pleasure on finding out "that my sincere enthusiasm should have reached your ear, and that it had such a happy effect on you! You must *know* how fine you are in your work, but I'm grateful that you like hearing it from me. *Please* let's meet whenever we find ourselves in the same town again."[25] They did a few months later, when Hayes paid a well-publicized visit to Davis on the set of *The Sisters* (1938).

What is striking about Davis's development from starlet to rebel to mature artist is that, while at first, a cluster of older, established men mentored and encouraged her to break the mold (mirroring the dynamics of the

Figure 1.2 Davis with new friend Helen Hayes on the set of *The Sisters*, 1938

Hollywood genre film about female stardom from *What Price Hollywood?*, 1932, to *A Star Is Born*), she quickly formed a network of like-minded (though not always politically synched, as in Hayes's case) working women to support and encourage their careers and those of other women. This was Hollywood feminism in action.

Yet, unlike fellow actresses Joan Crawford and Miriam Hopkins, with whom Davis was said to have had more than a friendly rivalry, Davis was not actively involved in the development and administration of the Screen Actors Guild. After Ann Harding retired from office and Hollywood in 1936 to concentrate on winning a protracted custody suit for her daughter, it was Crawford who served as second vice president from 1937 to 1939 amid calls for a strike, and again was "one of the motivating forces in the fight" for the contract with producers that they accepted in May 1937.[26] In 1937, as SAG secured its contract, Bette Davis was uncharacteristically dutiful to Jack Warner and the executives at Warner Bros. Several months before, she had taken matters into her own hands, and without securing the assistance of the guild, had attempted to break her studio contract. It nearly cost Davis her career.

Despite a Broadway résumé, an Academy Award, and the respect of her coworkers, even Davis could not escape the punishing enslavement of a studio contract. In many ways, Hollywood was decades ahead of its time in awarding comparable pay to men and women; as actress Rochelle Hudson stated in 1935, "Hollywood is the only place in the world where a girl can earn as much money as a man."[27] Davis, though making Warner Bros. huge amounts with her growing stardom, still earned substantially less than other stars of her caliber at other studios. As Davis remembered in 1955, "I suffered numerous suspensions during my twenty-five years in Hollywood—mostly because I refused to do things that I felt were patently phony. At Warner Bros. I had a friendly competition with Jimmy Cagney in this respect. We kept a box score, and when we both left the studio in the 1940s we were tied at sixteen suspensions apiece."[28] However, as Emily Carman has pointed out, other actresses had negotiated more favorable contracts with the studios through wily agents such as Leland Hayward and Charles Feldman, and there were a number of independent contract free-lancers, including Carole Lombard and Irene Dunne, who could pick and choose their roles.[29] Locked into a traditional seven-year studio contract, Davis was forced to take demeaning women's roles or face unpaid suspension that would simply extend the term of the original agreement. *God's Country and the Woman* was the last straw. In 1936, she went on strike.[30] It was a carefully considered decision. As Davis wrote to Jack Warner, explaining her commitment to her career: "I also am ambitious to become known as a great actress . . . I would be willing to take less money, if in consideration of this, you would give me my 'rights.'"[31] When he didn't, Davis left for England, attracted by the offer of a film with Maurice Chevalier for Toeplitz Productions in London.[32]

Warner Bros. brought a suit against her in Britain, and while the prosecuting council tried to paint her as a frivolous and avaricious woman, her lawyer William Jowett revealed that even if Davis wanted to quit Hollywood and become a waitress or a hairdresser, under the contract system, she "cannot engage in any other occupation, whether for love or money."[33] And, he continued, "If she becomes a mother, the employers have the option of terminating the contract for the period in which she is unable to act."[34] Jowett's argument appealed to the court by emphasizing Davis's rights as a married working woman, but even more unusually, acknowledged the injustice of terminating a woman's career because she had children. While the judge remained unimpressed, journalists widely reprinted the text of Jowett's defense, which was designed to garner sympathy from her female fans.

Davis lost over $100,000 defending her case—and, allegedly, the much-coveted role of Scarlett in Margaret Mitchell's *Gone with the Wind*, for which Warner Bros. would now neither purchase nor loan her out.[35] Back in Hollywood, she was walking on a knife's edge. On the one hand, though the studio had taken her back, she could have been forced to play in additional demeaning roles, like colleague Kay Francis, whose career was sabotaged by the studio after she complained too much about the lousy scripts she was given. Remaining aloof from the producers' bête noire, the Screen Actors Guild, and working within the studio contract system, may have been the price for her career. Warner's offer of *Marked Woman* may also have represented a conciliatory gesture on the studio's part, even if some columnists thought it had an "ominous ring" for Hollywood's rebel.[36] Davis, however, though smart enough to make some concessions, was not willing to be a dutiful daughter in the studio hierarchy. Shortly after returning to Warner Bros., she was asked to represent Hollywood actresses in an edited collection of professional essays on working in the Hollywood motion picture industry, documentary filmmaker Nancy Naumburg's *We Make the Movies* (1937).[37] Anne Bauchens, longtime editor for Cecil B. DeMille at Paramount, was also involved and contributed an essay on film editing. Although as many stars later admitted, studio publicity departments falsely attributed press articles to stars in order to garner fan readers, Davis, still outraged over the outcome of her court case, wanted a forum to defend herself from allegations the suit had been frivolous in the midst of a worldwide economic depression.

In the essay her much-discussed Yankee practicality is apparent in her half-joking introduction, "If the studio weather department will hold off the artificial fog of glamour for a while," where she asserted first and foremost that "we are just plain workers here" who serve the audience.[38] Davis, still burning from her dispute with the studio, explained the pre-eminent importance of story quality and the counterproductive structure of the star system, which forced stars to play poor parts or "refuse." She outlined the twelve- to fourteen-hour days involved in shooting where she got "dog-tired," but also revealed that "endless hours must be spent in reading" about historical characters she played, "until I know them so well I couldn't possibly do anything inconsistent with their characterization." Davis stated flatly that far from seeing herself as some special artist, she was "extremely workman-like," and paid tribute not only to the paying audience for supporting her work, but to the anonymous "women in the workroom" who receive "no credit for the final product" but are unflaggingly loyal to their stars and their work standards.[39] To journalists, she may have been Hollywood's "one-woman revolution,"[40] but it is to Davis's credit that she understood and acknowledged the work of women above and below the screen credit line in making Hollywood films. Davis's well-organized, clear outline of the collaborative filmmaking process and her own attitude toward her work are in stark contrast to Warner Bros. star Paul Muni's more elaborate, "arty" approach, which highlights the actor's social importance in shaping hearts and minds. As Muni concluded his article, "Perhaps the actor can reach people and influence them so that they will go forth with a new strength and a new vision in combatting the evils of our own society."[41] One can almost hear Davis spitting "Bunk!" in the background (one of her favorite words to describe highfalutin nonsense).

In early 1939, *Life* speculated that had she won her contract dispute, Davis "would have become the Joan of Arc of a cinema revolution."[42] But her action spurred the studio to agree to her choice of three pictures a year and a raise. Close friend George Arliss knew that the studio not only would take Davis back after the court case, but also would go to great lengths to appease her. Though she had lost, the publicity from Jowett's speech gained her sympathy among non-Hollywood women and made public the hitherto unknown details of the Hollywood studio contract. She remembered his reasoning: "The last thing the movie moguls wanted was to have the harsh terms of their contracts revealed to the public." Davis was proud that her case had done just that.

Yet, despite the tantalizing financial rewards of freelancing, negotiating with and remaining part of Warner Bros. gave Davis more control over her career and earned her roles and longevity that escaped other actresses. The films Davis selected following the 1936 dispute built upon the independence she experienced at RKO with Mildred. Though initially she had hoped to continue working with Leslie Howard, playing Beatrice to his Benedict in an adaptation of Shakespeare's *Much Ado About Nothing*, she would choose roles that traditionally were regarded as unsympathetic or even a case for censorship—prostitutes (*Marked Woman*), adulteresses (*Jezebel*, 1938; *The Old Maid*), murderesses (*The Letter*, 1940), and dying heiresses (*Dark Victory*, 1939).[43] *Jezebel* was the distillation of the Davis persona, and the industry recognized her contractual stamina and industry fellowship— as well as her performance—with a second Academy Award. As Thomas

Schatz has pointed out, the star had more creative control over this project, something she would hang onto throughout the 1940s.

Journalist Sonia Lee gloated, "She is the protagonist of the bad, the heartless, the selfish, self-preserving woman who grabs everything by instinct. The kind of woman who always makes demands but never gives."[44] But rather than putting audiences off with these roles, Davis regularly topped exhibitors' lists in the late 1930s and became the top box-office actress of 1940.[45] "Bette has been in effect a one-woman revolution in Hollywood, who has upset all the long-held, cherished notions of producers that the heroine must be wronged, salvaged, and live happily ever after," Lee continued. "Bette's women stand alone, take the consequences, and usually finish in the gutter—if not physically, at least spiritually." Male producers' penchants for blondes with nice legs, big breasts, and no brains were no match for Davis's popularity with female fans who loved her for simply being the best at her job. The struggles she handled on and off screen added zest to her fans' devotion. Davis articulated women's rage and anger as an empowering force. Lee concluded, "Without compromise she believes every ambitious woman must burn her bridges behind her. Bette's contention is that it puts steel in the spine to know that you must go ahead—that there's no going back."[46]

Certainly Davis inspired her friend Olivia de Havilland, who, by 1939, was tired of playing a succession of good girls in Errol Flynn swashbucklers (Arabella in *Captain Blood*, 1936, and Maid Marian in *The Adventures of Robin Hood*, 1938). She was increasingly on suspension at Warner Bros., and during her 1943–44 contract dispute, was shrewd enough to put out publicity that Warner Bros.' enforcement of her contract was unpatriotic. Journalists explained that she wanted "to go overseas to entertain the boys and has put in a request with the USO."[47] Warner Bros.' miserly insistence on contractual obligations was hurting the war effort. De Havilland also became more involved in the running of the Screen Actors Guild and campaigned for Roosevelt in 1944 alongside Davis.[48] When the court ruled in her favor in 1944, Warner Bros. retaliated, holding back the release of *Devotion* until 1946. Other studios shunned her. Although Paramount signed her to two productions, they also had delayed releases.[49]

De Havilland's return to screens in 1946 revealed almost as violent a screen transformation as Davis's a decade before. Audiences now saw the winsome, wide-eyed Warner Bros. ingénue as unglamorous, brusque, and over forty (*To Each His Own*, 1946), mentally unstable (*The Dark Mirror* 1946; *The Snake Pit*, 1948), and a shrinking wallflower dominated by a stern parent (*The Heiress*, 1949). All of these screen choices were variations on roles Davis herself had played (*The Old Maid; The Letter; The*

Great Lie, 1941; *Now, Voyager*), and would win de Havilland the career recognition she craved. As de Havilland later admitted, the traditional female roles of her youth and typecast Hollywood stardom bewildered her: "I didn't really become adjusted to the life of a movie star until the period when I made *The Snake Pit* and *The Heiress*."[50] Yet, unlike Davis, de Havilland was not a true organization woman who would negotiate within the system. De Havilland wore her "uncompliant" attitude like a badge, and this would adversely affect her career within a few years.

The younger star was also far less comfortable with the press and maintained a chilly distance from female journalists hoping for in-depth interviews. Even when she was still a charming Warner Bros. heroine on screen, off screen she was blunt: "When I am ready to marry, I shall announce my intention. Until that time my affairs are my own."[51] Davis, in contrast, appealed to average women through her personal struggles and solidarity with other women. From the beginning, she didn't try to hide her problems with marriage to bandleader Harmon "Ham" Nelson. During the production of *Bordertown* (1935), press coverage emphasized the problems associated with couples working in the entertainment industries. Davis's nine-to-six workdays conflicted with Nelson's 6:00 p.m. to 4:00 a.m. orchestra stints, so "they left notes for each other and carried on a more or less extensive correspondence six days out of every week that Bette worked."[52] When the couple did meet on Sundays, it was "on the golf links." They were active and equal partners, and the article emphasized difficulties that many couples might be facing with incompatible shifts at work. Her higher salary was pooled every month with his smaller earnings and divided equally between them, while ironically her clothes and jewels were listed as "business expenses." Davis presented her marriage as a practical partnership, and one based on a simple acceptance of equal rights. Following their fifty-fifty divorce split, she moved into a much smaller house in the unfashionable Los Feliz district, but didn't complain to the press about her husband's generous cut of her earnings.

Things weren't so pleasant for Ann Harding. She was one of the few stars to give birth to a child and maintain her identity as a mother and a film star in the late 1920s and early 1930s. Like Davis, she had also joined the Provincetown Players as a novice, leaving her own unsatisfactory job as an insurance clerk. She married film star Harry Bannister, thirteen years her senior, and accompanied him to Hollywood, planning only to look after their young daughter Jane while he worked. But she "rose swiftly to a stardom that threatened to overshadow her husband's," and in May 1932, Bannister divorced her, saying he was "gradually losing his identity" and was "becoming known as 'Ann Harding's husband.'"[53] His career over, he spent the next three years financially draining Harding in the courts in a series of lengthy custody battles over their daughter Jane. He even threatened blackmail, as Harding revealed, demanding "one-half the value of my property, which amounted to robbing the baby of whatever I am able to save for her."[54] But it kept Bannister's name in print, even though his film career was over. Harding retained sole custody October 24, 1935, despite countless legal battles in which her ex-husband accused Hollywood's well-known "lady" to be an unfit working mother. She married again, but still had to obtain court permission to take Jane on any trips involving her new spouse's work. In 1936, she took her daughter to Europe while she finished a film, and after her ex-husband's failed attempt at charging her with abduction, temporarily retired from the screen. She realized that any attempts she made to return to her Hollywood career would be thwarted by a deranged and embittered ex-husband, and so she remarried and tried to live quietly. Though Harding continued to work into the 1960s on stage and screen and in television, she never recovered her former status as a major star. Instead, in the 1930s, she reminded her female colleagues that it was often safer to sign a traditional studio contract than a marriage license.

Davis watched the Harding-Bannister court cases unfold and knew that her first instinct to delay having children was the right one. Her divorce from Nelson had to be managed more carefully; she needed the public on her side. A few years and several public affairs later, journalists interviewed Davis about the struggle for personal happiness, her relationship with frequent costar George Brent, and her eventual decision not to marry him following her divorce from Nelson. While Davis had won concessions from Warner Bros. in terms of salary (though she was still paid less than Greta Garbo and Claudette Colbert, who did not earn as much for their studios), her separation and divorce made real headlines.[55] She was frank as ever with the mostly female reporters, and rather than dwelling on the past, she set an example of a woman who needed to exercise her mind, social responsibility, and political voice. Instead of playing the Hollywood romance game, she took her cousin Johnny Favor to the 1940 Oscars as her "date" (she was nominated again for *Dark Victory*, but lost to Vivien Leigh in *Gone with the Wind*).[56] It was a smart move and deflected any potential backlash from her less-than-perfect private life (Greer Garson, also trying to build a wholesome image at her new studio, MGM, played this game, taking her mother along with her to the Oscars).

But in the early 1940s, Davis took other risks and developed into one of Hollywood's most high-profile Democrats. She was also an unapologetic advocate for the Equal Rights Amendment, a conviction not shared by all

Democrats or Mrs. Roosevelt, who from 1933 had been against the amendment given its removal of "all the special protective legislation" in the workplace for wealthy women's "less vocal sisters."[57] However, the measure had been gaining national momentum because of the New Deal's protection of working-class women's labor and women's gains in the media and other professions. Davis was also a committeewoman who created organizations as diverse as the International Tailwaggers Association (where she supported the first animal hospitals and shelters in California) and the Hollywood Canteen.

While a few years earlier, Carole Lombard revealed her personal value system to *Photoplay* ("Work—and Like It!") and an unqualified admiration for "the outstanding success" of businesswoman Mary Pickford, she presented her qualities of firm fairness, honesty, and hardworking toughness as essentially masculine: "How I Live by a Man's Code."[58] Davis, in contrast, saw no reason why these same traits weren't naturally feminine. As Marian Young reported, "She doesn't think it unfeminine to be well informed. In fact, Miss Davis has little patience with the woman who reads news headlines but never the stories under them, or thinks that editorial pages are written for men only." As Davis commented in that interview, "'I think it's sad for any woman to let herself slip mentally as she walks down the years. . . . If she's in business, she simply can't let herself get into the habit of fuzzy thinking—not if she expects to stay in the business—any kind of business. And the home woman who, at 50, has no interest in anything outside of her home, is apt to lead a pretty dreary existence.'"[59]

In an era where stars were increasingly penalized for expressing views on current world affairs, Davis remained a defiant critic of nativists such as Charles Lindbergh, speaking out about his "really shocking" criticism of Canada's declaration of war on Germany in 1939 and making a barely veiled reference to his fascism: "I wonder who is really behind him."[60] She routinely dined at the White House,[61] the president selected her film *Watch on the Rhine* (1943) for the annual "command performance,"[62] and articles of the late 1930s and 1940s comment on her daily engagements, the range of her social and political commitments, and her work at the studio as "Queen Bette," Hollywood's most popular actress (figure 1.3).

In early 1940, Durward Howes, editor of the *Biographical Dictionary of American Women*, published his fourth annual selection of the nation's ten outstanding women whose "talents, their technological achievements or their civic and social activities" had benefited society. Davis was named because "her colleagues love her and she is the best," and she was part of a diverse group: Lilia Bell Acheson, editor of the *Reader's Digest*; Katherine Burr Blodgett, developer of a glare-proof glass; Mrs. Elias Compton, mother

Figure 1.3 Davis with Ed Sullivan receiving her "Queen of Hollywood" crown, 1940

of a Nobel Prize winner, a college president, and a lawyer, and who recently received an honorary LLD in motherhood; Anne Hummert, the largest producer of radio material, former journalist, and vice president of a media company; hostess and columnist Elsa Maxwell; Anne O'Hare McCormick, foreign correspondent; Anna Eleanor Roosevelt; novelist Nora Waln; and Margaret Webster, actor, director, and producer. Regardless of the fact that a man was selecting the top ten women in his editorial capacity, the choices were nonetheless diverse and reflected a range of professional roles. Interestingly, even motherhood was seen as a profession, with Mrs. Compton being honored with a university "degree" for her services. The press continued to present a portrait of Davis as a woman with both a public and a private life, with career and personal needs, who belonged to a diverse community of powerful women. Hedda Hopper would spotlight Hollywood's civic-minded women, from Frances Marion to Joan Crawford and Rosalind Russell, in a column a year later. The columnist noted that Davis continued to help her friend Mary McCall on the Motion Picture Relief Fund, stating that "if anybody suddenly drops out on the Screen Guild Show," they can "always get her to go on at the last minute."[63]

Within that national community, more and more women were becoming heads of households: 15% by 1940.[64] The following year, Bette Davis became head of hers: she was appointed the first woman president of the Academy of Motion Picture Arts and Sciences. An industry ad shows Davis putting flowers in a vase looking pleasantly surprised as the headlines read, "Three cheers for Miss Davis, first woman president of the Academy of Motion Picture Arts & Sciences."[65] Her election in early November 1941, supported by a board including Rosalind Russell and writer Jane Murfin, made the front page of the conservative *Hollywood Citizen-News* and was mentioned in industry tradepapers.[66] Darryl F. Zanuck had also been one of her strongest supporters, and in one of her first actions as president, she appointed him to a third term as chairman of the Research Council. Zanuck had built a good working relationship with the War Department, and the move was noted with approval by the rest of the board, who recognized that a declaration of war against the Axis would be announced any day.[67] However, one journalist seemed to know that Davis's job would be no bed of roses: "The morning after Bette Davis was elected president of the Academy of Motion Picture Arts and Sciences she had to come down to earth and take an awful slapping around from Dennis Morgan. It was a scene from *In This Our Life*. Bette told him to let her have it and not pull his punches. They had to make three takes to get the scene, too."[68]

Her tenure as president quickly became one of the most controversial periods in Academy history—and not just because it overlapped with Pearl Harbor and America's entry into World War II (figure 1.4). The woman who had worn plain business dresses to the Academy Awards ceremony had big plans to transform the banquet and the organization's membership. In order to support the war effort, she argued that the ordinary glitzy ceremony should be suspended for the duration and that places at the dinner be raffled off at $25 a ticket, with the proceeds going to war relief. As Louella Parsons reported, "This would give the public a chance to see the annual presentation and would not be a foolish expenditure of money."[69] Mindful of restrictions on war materials, she even proposed wooden Oscars, with winners having the option of redeeming metal versions after the war was over. It would be a "morale" booster for the industry to pitch in at such a symbolic level. Furthermore, Davis argued, Academy membership needed reformation. Currently even extras could vote, and Davis wanted them removed since she argued they only ever voted for the studio currently employing them. But in publicizing this nepotistic practice, Davis was also hinting at another unpleasant truth: the fact that studio heads routinely pressured *all* of their employees to vote a certain way and resented any checks on their power. After Norma Shearer's notorious write-in campaign for Davis was allowed by then-president Howard Estabrook back in 1935–36, the Academy board changed the guidelines so that such embarrassing female-led revolts could not happen again.

As one of Hollywood's most outspoken advocates for realism, Davis was instrumental in creating two separate Academy Awards for documentary film (short and feature-length).[70] Although the Society of Motion Picture Film Editors had a number of women as founding members in 1937, few had been involved in the union's governance. In one of her last acts as president, Davis appointed Anne Bauchens to the committee branch considering Academy rules on editing awards.[71] Davis's refusal to be a mere

Figure 1.4 John Huston, stunned to read his orders to report for army duty, with Olivia de Havilland and Davis, 1942

figurehead and her decision to reform Academy policy were too disturbing for Hollywood's wealthy conservatives. They demanded her resignation, outraged over her revelations about the corruption in Academy voting and her puritanical suggestions about curbing Hollywood luxury in the midst of war.

Well, if they wanted a scene, they got one. Citing "pressure of her film work and reasons of health" as the cause, Davis resigned on December 24.[72] The conservative *Motion Picture Herald* complained about the timing of the resignation, as a slap in the face to Hollywood's elites, and as "at variance with Academy practice," whereby more formal statements were supposed to be issued to the press.[73] Her "plain" explanation also slammed the Academy's behind-the-scenes corruption and addiction to empty ceremony. But the Monday after her resignation, her opponents planted rumors in the columns that the feeling to reinstate the banquet had "gained some momentum." Others were gossiping that the only reason she had resigned was to avoid potential conflicts of interest should she win the best-actress award a third time for her role in Lillian Hellman's *The Little Foxes*. On January 7, the Academy elected her predecessor, producer Walter Wanger, whose "discharge of the presidential duties," *Motion Picture Herald* noted smugly, was "widely approved." But Hollywood's two top presswomen stood by her. Louella Parsons had the guts to tell fans the truth: the Queen of Hollywood was forced out. Hedda Hopper would praise Davis in 1942 for being able to "fight her weight in wildcats" as "our only woman president of the Motion Picture Academy."[74] The star was bitter. But she soon took up a more important administrative role on August 28, 1942: the presidency of the Hollywood Canteen.

The Hollywood Canteen was Davis's idea and was inspired by the New York Stage Door Canteen, where servicemen could get free drinks and food and could dance with stars for an evening before going overseas. With Davis and her colleague and fellow Roosevelt supporter John Garfield pitching and pushing that spring and summer, Hollywood's organization was eventually supported by forty-two craft unions and prominent people in the industry.[75] The Canteen building, which would open for business in November 1942, was a converted club on Cahuenga Boulevard once known as El Rancho, refitted by volunteers and regularly staffed by the likes of Marlene Dietrich, Hedy Lamarr (who met future husband John Loder at the Canteen on Christmas Day, 1942), and Olivia de Havilland (although as Jean Gabin was put to work as a dishwasher and not a dancer, one female correspondent noted, "It's easy to see the Canteen does *not* cater to WAACs and WAVES").[76]

Davis combined her work overseeing the Canteen and working there each night with a happy second marriage to non-Hollywood industrialist Arthur Farnsworth, creating some of her best-loved film roles (Charlotte Vale in *Now, Voyager*; Sara Muller in Lillian Hellman's *Watch on the Rhine*; and spoiled flirt Fanny in *Mr. Skeffington*), giving frequent interviews and editing a *Photoplay* advice column, and leading an extensive war bond campaign for which she wrote her own speeches.[77] Although one might have expected Hollywood journalists to criticize the election of a woman as president of the Hollywood Canteen, the reality was quite different. As writer James Hilton acknowledged, she was the "moving spirit" and John Garfield "her first lieutenant."[78]

Though Davis was a lifelong Democrat, she worked well with a group of powerful Republican women on the Canteen's administration, including Hopper, Ida Koverman, and Lela Rogers.[79] In April 1943, Hopper again named Davis the "best all-around woman in Hollywood," praising her for starting the Canteen "against many odds." Remembering the trouble she'd had with the Academy, Hopper observed sharply, "Because it wasn't producer-inspired, she's had to fight for all the co-operation she's gotten. Yet singlehanded, the Canteen is selling Hollywood to our soldiers as no other Hollywood endeavor."[80] But the Hollywood insider also took note of the women Davis got to work with her, including Ann Sothern, Barbara Stanwyck, Irene Dunne, Claudette Colbert, and Mary Martin. In her coverage of "Stars at War," Louella Parsons acknowledged the men fighting overseas, but gave equal space to Davis for "starting" the Canteen and recruiting a group of committed women, singling out Lamarr, Bonita Granville, Rita Hayworth, Lana Turner, Betty Grable, Ann Rutherford, and Linda Darnell.[81] Parsons was modest—her coverage did much to make the Canteen a success. Hedy Lamarr and Davis became close friends thanks to the Canteen, with Lamarr saying Davis "is the one actress who has lived up to her expectations, both on and off the screen."[82] Though gossip columns were usually full of real or imagined conflicts between Hollywood actresses, Davis formed a coalition of women that transcended political, professional, and romantic rivalries.

In fact, given Davis's impact, members of the press even drew attention to the changing times and gender equality in the American family. As Sgt. John Whitehead noted in *Los Angeles Radio Life* in the early days of the organization, "Typical of a wartime spouse is Bette Davis's husband, Arthur Farnsworth. During a recent period of two weeks, Bette spent so much of her time at the Canteen that he had to get a special pass to work as a bus boy in order to get a few words or a smile from his wife."[83] Again, it is Davis who is characterized as the primary war worker—and while her husband and actors such as Jean Gabin and pal Humphrey Bogart were in aprons washing dishes, she was running the show, supported by a cast of powerful Hollywood women.[84] Noting Davis's "fine executive and directorial mind" in the running of the Canteen, Adela Rogers St. Johns said that "Hollywood has changed!"[85]

The Canteen also made Davis's relationship with Jack Warner as warm as it would ever get. Given Davis's success, Warner Bros. wanted to make a film, *The Hollywood Canteen* (1943), starring Davis and an all-star cast, to promote Hollywood's war effort. The profits would go to the Hollywood Canteen and to canteens throughout the country. But when SAG and producer Y. Frank Freeman made trouble about hiring stars from different studios for bit parts, Davis was firmly on her studio's side, arguing "the picture was more important to all groups than anything that had ever been produced in Hollywood."[86] Shortly after the success of the film, Davis formed her own production company with the studio's blessing, taking her "fine executive and directorial mind" to a new level.

But there was occasional dissention within that strong coalition of women. Davis had her work cut out for her on more than one front. Although opening press coverage in Hollywood included shots of men and women working and African American hosts including Eddie "Rochester" Anderson, most press coverage of the Canteen showed white actresses and white servicemen dancing. Both black male and female stars worked in the Canteen, and black and white actresses danced with both black and white servicemen. The venue, orchestra, and the dances were also mixed—unlike the segregated armed forces and most of middle-class Los Angeles society and movie theaters. Some members of the board did not hold with Davis's attitudes toward racial equality and tried to break up the mixed dances. As *Liberty* magazine reported in 1943: "An investigation conducted by *Down Beat* uncovered evidence that there is a faction within the Canteen administration, which, if not actually anti-Negro, is fearful of progressive attempts to overcome prejudice." It went on: "This faction, led by a non-professional Beverly Hills woman who is very active in the affairs of the Canteen, attempted at the recent meeting to pass a rule forbidding 'mixed dancing.'" But there was a big fight at the meeting, and "strong remarks involving various races were passed as the representatives of Local 767 and their supporters fought to prevent adoption of the discriminatory regulation. It is understood that one reason the rule was not passed is because Bette Davis and John Garfield threatened to resign from the board and withdraw the support of the Screen Actors Guild if any such action were taken."[87]

Davis believed in the Double V campaign to win rights for African Americans, and her stance on racial equality never wavered: "Let them dance if they want to," she was quoted as saying.[88] In addition to helping guide the careers of Pamela Caveness (radio), Jane Bryan (*Marked Woman*), and Richard Travis (*The Bride Came C.O.D.*, 1941; *The Man Who Came to Dinner*, 1942), she got African American Ernest Anderson, a former "service boy" at Warner Bros., a part as a young law student in *In This Our Life*.[89] By the spring of 1944, she had been elected president three times, and the Canteen had served 1.58 million black, Latino, and white servicemen.[90]

Though the novelty of working for the Canteen had vanished for most performers by 1943, Davis was still in attendance every Saturday night she was in town in 1945.[91] Working at the Canteen helped tie her even closer to her female fans. After suffering a fall, Farnsworth died suddenly at the age of thirty-five at the end of August 1943. Davis hid her grief like any other war widow and pushed herself into making the Canteen a success. *Screenland*'s editor Delight Evans noted in an open letter to the star, "As the leading lady of the Canteen, as its guardian angel and hardest worker, you could not be spared—and so you came through."[92] Hollywood owed Davis an enormous debt in directing its most important wartime public relations gig. When the Canteen closed, holding its last Thanksgiving dinner on November 22, 1945, it had served three million servicemen, with Davis known coast-to-coast as the organization's "guiding light."[93]

But though directing the Canteen was an important component of her war work, it was not her only job. In her war bond speeches for radio and on tour in the Midwest, Davis emphasized the importance of the working class and women's and men's equality. In one speech to war workers in Oklahoma, she stated, "I'm an actress, and I do my job, and I also try to do what little I can for the war, to buy bonds, to ask other people to buy them. You as the people who know most about the war, have the greatest responsibility. You know what fascism means to the working class, what life is like for workers in Germany and Japan, and in the occupied countries. The weapons you make are liberating these workers and all others."[94] Later, in the seventh war bond drive, she would ask people to continue the fight at home because "Our soldiers and all the fighting men and women of the free nations . . . never let down."[95]

Her feminist political philosophy was most clearly articulated in a speech she wrote in favor of Roosevelt's re-election in September 1944, delivered at Madison Square Garden on September 21, 1944, as part of a rally organized by the Independent Voters Committee on the Arts and Sciences for Roosevelt.[96] Unlike other stars, Davis wrote her own speeches off screen, and drafts of her war and Democratic speeches exist in her archive in longhand and typescript, with her comments and revisions. The war was drawing to a close, and in seven weeks, women, as 60% of the electorate, were faced with a great political challenge. "For such a stake, there is not one woman of us but should pledge that she will bring five others to the election headquarters to register; pledge that she will make sure every one will vote." Women were playing the "major role" in this election because "for the first time in history, there are more women eligible to vote than men" because so many servicemen were facing complications with the ballot while overseas. Women were to be "the conscience of those silent soldiers and sailors." But, with so many men overseas, women were also the closest they would ever get securing cross-party support for the Equal Rights Amendment.

Davis was well aware that women's participation in national politics had not lived up to the expectations of the Nineteenth Amendment, and she cited statistics indicating that thirty-nine out of one hundred eligible women would not vote. She appealed to those thirty-nine to remember the Great Depression, Nazi atrocities, and the war that was claiming the lives of their men overseas. But, she concluded,

> In the victorious war which we are waging—the war against those bloody, wicked villains who would relegate women to the bawdy slavery of the brothel or the humdrum inferiority of the kitchens—in this war women have learned much. They have learned the dignity of work, in factory and mill. Unpleasant necessity has forced on them the maturing lesson of independence. They have watched their children growing up with no man in the house. These citizens are no longer the citizens who were reluctant to vote for fear they would have to swear to their true age. These are not the timid Mrs. Milquetoasts who were fearful of the complexity of the voting machine. These are the first-class citizens who have learned their responsibilities, the hard way, who know that their security, and that of their returning husbands, and that of their unborn sons, is bound up in the single, simple gesture that will pull the voting lever down over the name of Franklin Delano Roosevelt![97]

She made the speech of a lifetime, connecting her lifelong Democratic affiliation with Roosevelt and the New Deal, the rights of the working class, and gender equality. She knew those thirty-nine out of one hundred women could be persuaded to vote for FDR, not necessarily for his liberal politics or even to endorse gender equality, but to see their men come home victorious.

By 1944, Davis didn't see anything incompatible with her own assertive brand of feminism and supporting the presidential patriarch. For many of her Hollywood colleagues, including Myrna Loy, Olivia de Havilland, Katharine Hepburn, Mary McCall, Paulette Goddard, and Joan Crawford,

Roosevelt was always the choice for women, not only because of his high-profile appointments of women to cabinet and administrative positions, including Frances Perkins, Mary Bethune, and Hallie Flanagan, and his support of his very political First Lady, but also because of his commitment to organized labor and the rights of the working class. But Davis's fervent campaigning for FDR coincided with Democrats' decision to adopt the ERA. Never before had the Equal Rights Amendment come so close to being passed by Congress. Female business leaders and politicians left and right were rallying to the cause.

But the political tide had turned by the mid-1940s. Although Roosevelt's fourth term began on the wings of victory in Europe, the days of labor and outspoken women were numbered. Even as far back as the 1940 election, Roosevelt's margin of electoral support had shrunk despite increased commitment to organized labor and visible support from stars such as de Havilland, Dorothy Lamour, and Mickey Rooney.[98] Davis's liberalism had first attracted the attention of the House Committee on Un-American Activities (also known as the Dies Committee) back in 1938, but her good PR with colleagues and fans and her work with the Canteen gave her some political insulation from conservative critics. But, with the failure of the ERA in 1945 and 1946 and New Dealers increasingly rebranded as communists, Davis realized she had gambled on political visibility and lost. In July 1946, William R. Wilkerson, publisher of the *Hollywood Reporter*, named prominent screenwriters as communists. In March 1947, Davis's political profile had attracted the attention of California senator Jack B. Tenney, whose committee investigating un-American activities reported to the state legislature that Davis, along with colleagues John Garfield, screenwriters John Howard Lawson and Albert Maltz, producer Walter Wanger, and director John Cromwell, was at the center of communist agitation in Hollywood. The committee alleged that "the Communist Party infiltrates every conceivable mass organization in the country—in trade unions, farm organizations, ladies clubs, in Harlem, the deep South, and among intellectuals."[99] Film critic Jack Moffitt, a former screenwriter and a member of the Motion Picture Alliance for the Preservation of American Ideals (MPA), wrote to Congressman Norris Poulson in April 1947, naming Davis, Hepburn, de Havilland, and Gale Sondergaard as pro-communist actors.[100] It also didn't help that *Daily Variety* had an item noting that an "unnamed commie correspondent" had recently alleged that the Soviet Union had many friends in the US film industry, "notably Bette Davis and Charlie Chaplin."[101]

By the time a re-energized HUAC began calling prominent industry professionals to testify in Washington, Davis realized the seriousness of the situation and refused to lend money or public support to the Hollywood Ten and Hollywood Nineteen. In October 1947, FBI reports noted that since "the big names" Davis and de Havilland had refused to lend their support to fundraisers for the newly formed Committee for the First Amendment, "the entire movement will fall flat locally" because Hollywood would only follow "the big toppers."[102] Evidently CFA members Fredric March, Bogart, and Gene Kelly weren't in the same star and political league as Davis and de Havilland! Because of her war record and more careful stance in the fall of 1947, Davis managed, by the skin of her teeth, not to be named publicly or accused in *Red Channels*, the tract that named 151 actors, writers, and others as communist sympathizers. Colleague and rival Joan Crawford also distanced herself from her support of organized labor and active leadership in the Screen Actors Guild; friend Louella Parsons planted items showing Crawford denouncing communism and expressing her interest in appearing in a film Parsons identifies as *The Patriot* (more likely the 1943 Founding Fathers play *The Patriots*, purchased by Warner Bros. in 1947, than the adaptation of Pearl Buck's 1939 novel about the wartime battle for China!).[103]

Though CFA members Lauren Bacall and Marsha Hunt only played "supporting roles" as the wives of liberal husbands Bogart and writer Robert Presnell Jr. when they flew to Washington to protest the October 1947 hearings, actress Myrna Loy was one of the CFA's founders.[104] Loy had recently survived an attack by Matthew Woll, a vice president of the American Federation of Labor, who in 1946 alleged that she was a communist. Louella Parsons defended her, calling the accusations "laughable," and Loy sued, demanding a retraction from Wilkerson's *Hollywood Reporter*.[105] Wilkerson, not wanting to pay $1 million for libel, published his retraction, and Loy felt politically vindicated enough to risk working for the CFA a year later. But it would cost her. She was conspicuously not nominated for an Oscar for her role in *The Best Years of Our Lives* (1946). Film roles were diminishing. After spending two decades performing the ideal wife at MGM (*The Thin Man* franchise, 1934–47), she left MGM to star as the famed American feminist and businesswoman Lillian Gilbreth (*Cheaper by the Dozen*, 1950; *Belles on Their Toes*, 1952, both Twentieth Century-Fox), but these were her last major roles.

In 1948, Loy was asked by Marshall Stimson, acting president for the Los Angeles chapter of the American Association for the United Nations, to make a speech about freedom of information and the press's impact in Hollywood.[106] This began her second career as a UN spokeswoman. She would later address women's and national clubs on these and other topics, including the UN's appeal for children (1948–49) and the need for social problem features and documentaries in Hollywood. Writing a profile on its ambassador in 1950, UNESCO argued that Loy had outgrown Hollywood: "What impresses you most about Miss Loy is how the Montana lass has progressed from glamorizing, slant-eyed, at Grauman's Chinese, to the role of good citizen of the world."[107] Loy commented on her industry, "Our entertainment pictures . . . are, of course, the finest possible mass communication method." She acknowledged that "people go to the movies, as we think of them, for entertainment," but now, "the success of such pictures as *The Snake Pit, Home of the Brave, Pinky* and the like" had "surprised the producers because they're outside of the usual mold."[108]

According to Loy, Hollywood's old genre films, the musicals and westerns, represented an old style of filmmaking that did not address the wider world or its complex social and political challenges. Hollywood producers (particularly message-filmmaker Darryl F. Zanuck), along with everyone else, had "matured so greatly in the past decade," but for this to truly make an impact, the film industry and the UN had to work together. This kind of policy work was responsible for her being named in anti-communist literature into the 1960s and for ending her Hollywood career.[109] In contrast, star Douglas Fairbanks Jr.'s postscreen career as a cultural go-between for Great Britain was viewed with universal political approval. Although the Kennedy administration would later recognize Loy's work with the United Nations, it was not compatible with a Hollywood career during the blacklist.

Davis wanted to continue to work as an actress, not as a UN ambassador and diplomat. But given her years as a fearless political woman and New Deal Democrat, it is surprising that Davis did not take a more prominent role in defending the liberal establishment in Hollywood during the late 1940s. It's easy to speculate that things simply got too hot for her, and as with many other Hollywood liberals of her generation, she ran for cover (or, as in Hepburn's and de Havilland's cases, to Broadway)—to preserve her career. But the star, like her friend Mary C. McCall Jr., former president of the Screen Writers Guild, had also remarried, had a baby, and tried domestic life for a few years. After a lifetime of hard work performing on and off camera, Davis realized that if she wanted to have it all—home and children included—her approaching fortieth birthday was a serious deadline. She had always acknowledged to fans the difficulties facing any woman who wanted to combine work, romance, and family life, and after four years administering the Canteen (during which she was widowed), and increasing involvement in producing her own films, culminating in *A Stolen Life* (1946), she felt entitled to a career break. When trying to explain her chaotic romantic life to her fans several years later, Davis mused,

Another pitfall for the high-powered woman is a tendency to choose weak men. The successful Hollywood actress is often attracted to rather neutral characters from outside her profession. Then there's no basic understanding by him of what her job involves—and she ends up like a hardworking businessman with a wife who is only interested in going out every night. I also think the Hollywood actress often shies away from marrying a man in her profession because she's afraid that he would run her career.[110]

Davis, delighted at becoming a mother at thirty-nine, nevertheless had her hands full with a physically abusive third husband and finished the decade ridding herself of a bad marriage and her contract with Warner Bros.

But even in the midst of her transitioning career, chaotic home-life, and the political minefield of HUAC, she remained close to Hollywood and continued to be a role model for American women. In 1948, an article appeared discussing her dissatisfaction with her Warner Bros. contract, since the star wanted more leeway in making one outside picture per year. The journalist commented that for many years, she has had "almost complete authority over her own pictures. She has had the final word on the choice of stories and a big voice in determining the detailed development of her shooting scripts. She has had—and reportedly has used—the right to 'okay' supporting casts, directors, and cameramen. In short, Bette Davis, rather than the men who normally have 'produced' her pictures, has been the boss."[111] Davis's role as a producer on all of her films was acknowledged outright by Hedda Hopper and other journalists,[112] but she was not the only actress to expand her creative role in film (Hepburn, *Woman of the Year,* 1942) or to consider producing films in an attempt to revive, or add another dimension to, a flagging career (Constance Bennett, Kay Francis, Claudette Colbert, Shirley Temple, Mary C. McCall).[113] Yet in 1949, the year Warner Bros. terminated Davis's contract, Hopper would look back on Davis's career at its fighting peak—to *Jezebel,* a period when she claimed "no propaganda found its way into movies," but when women were strong role models who defied the odds. "Nothing and nobody would take her place away from her. She was fighting every minute of the time, and you gloried in her battle. She was a supreme success; she knew it, we knew it. And the theaters reaped a golden harvest."[114]

Davis began the 1950s working with Darryl F. Zanuck at Fox, appearing in arguably her most famous role, Margo Channing, in *All About Eve* (1950), and coverage around the role and her new freelance status commented that she had entered "a new era of freedom" when she no longer had to ask any studio head's permission to do a role. While film critics have often seen Channing's decision to take a career break from the theater to marry a younger man and potentially start a family as part of a wider, postwar anti-feminist media plot to domesticate independent women, Channing is not so easily dismissed. While the biological clock is undoubtedly ticking for the forty-year-old theater star, she sneers that wealthy Radcliffe-educated friend Karen (Celeste Holm) is merely a "happy housewife" who essentially wasted her education and talents on becoming nothing more than a domestic decoration for her second-rate playwright husband (Hugh Marlowe). By the time she's decided to marry Bill Sampson (Gary Merrill), she's one of the most famous women in the world and wants to work at another side of "being a woman." It was also Davis's choice, too, when she married her younger costar Merrill and moved back to Cape Elizabeth, Maine, shortly after filming.

Ironically, colleague Barbara McLean, editor of *All About Eve* and Zanuck's longtime top editor, made a similar decision around the same time to finally marry partner Robert Webb, move into producing, and devote less around-the-clock time to the editing room. But McLean had done her best to train other young women in her profession, such as Mary Steward and Marjorie Fowler, and did not give up her career after marriage. Though the limited time-frame of *All About Eve*'s narrative doesn't show Margo returning for other stage productions, Davis certainly did not give up her career after embarking on the longest of her four marriages. She involved her daughter B. D. in the production of *The Story of a Divorce* (1951), believing "her daughter should know something about her mother's work,"[115] and mentored the maturing Natalie Wood on the set of *The Star* (1952). Wood idolized Davis, even going to far as to copy her gardenia perfume and hairstyle. And, to give credit to her legions of female fans, Davis remained the only entertainment professional to top polls on the most influential women after the war, remaining popular with both housewives and working women.[116] In 1947, the Treasury listed her as the top female earner in the United States, at $328,000 to Bogart's $467,361 and in 1948, she out-earned top male-earner Dennis Morgan, $364,000 to $315,476.[117] It was quite an achievement for an industry obsessed with youth.

In 1955, Davis was asked to present the Academy Award for Best Actor. Even though she would eventually call out Marlon Brando's name for *On the Waterfront*, Davis, at age forty-seven, still managed to upstage Hollywood's newest version of the rebel. The woman once known as "The Queen of Hollywood" had been shooting her second film as Elizabeth I, *The Virgin Queen* (1955), and rather than using a skull cap and makeup to simulate the aging monarch's appearance, Davis had shaved her head. But instead of hiding away from the photographers and crowds, Davis courted the attention, the jeweled "Juliet" cap covering her pate only emphasized Davis's commitment to her work and the symbiotic relationship she had with England's legendary diplomat, stateswoman, and patron of the arts. It was an unprecedented public move by a major Hollywood star. Although Laurence Olivier created a minor sensation when he arrived at Buckingham Palace in 1947 to accept his knighthood sporting his bleached-blond hair for *Hamlet* (1948), he quickly redyed it after shooting wrapped. Davis's more substantial disfigurement was part of a career pattern resisting traditional images of femininity that was twenty years in the making, starting from her work on *Of Human Bondage*. Her appearance challenged the conceits of postwar Method acting, which set itself in intellectual opposition to old-fashioned Hollywood methods. Method had a gender bias as well; most of the coverage circulated around Brando and James Dean and teachers Elia Kazan and Lee Strasberg. In contrast, the embodiment of great Hollywood acting was female: Bette Davis.

But in an extensive article with *Colliers* released not long after the 1955 awards, she avoided the temptation to set old and new Hollywood and actresses and actors at odds, reflecting: "I felt a strange kinship with Marlon as I stood up there with him. Both of us were nonconformists, battlers for realism and individuality. We had refused to allow ourselves to be cast in the artificial mold set by Hollywood. We were loyal but not craven subjects of the absolute monarchs who ruled the town—and yet they had come to honor us on our own terms." She remembered that the next day, costar and friend Paul Henreid told her, "'It was fitting for you and Marlon to share that moment together. He is what you are and were 20 years ago. People like you have helped make the American motion picture far better than it would have been.'" She continued, "I would like to believe that Henreid is right—that I have made some contribution to the improvement of the medium—because my life in Hollywood has been tempestuous, to say the least. It would have been far easier to knuckle under." While she loved Hollywood, Davis saw herself in active, long-term opposition to the patriarchal forces in Warner Bros.:

> If I had always been the obedient little daughter that the Great Fathers of Hollywood wanted me to be, perhaps I would have escaped the personal tragedy and unhappiness that stalked me for 20 years. . . . But on the other hand I would not have become the first and only woman to be elected president of the Academy of Motion Picture Arts and Sciences. I would never have attained the box-office position that led people to call me "the Fourth Warner Brother" in the 1940s.

Davis's self-confessed search for realism in her work had a political edge in the 1950s. So did her demands that the studio system live up to its highest standards for both men and women. Ten years after Roosevelt's death, she was still well known as a committed Democrat and defender of civil liberties. She spoke for Maine's first Democratic and Roman Catholic governor, Edwin Muskie, at a rally in Brewer in 1955. The following year, she would star in Daniel Taradash's better-late-than-never critique of anti-communism, *Storm Center* (1956), in which she played a librarian who refused to remove a communist book from the community's shelves. Publicity photographs and lobby cards emphasized her role as a mature, independent woman who had a role in educating the next generation about civil liberties. Both the political appearance and her latest film represented her continuing commitment to the principles of the New Deal and Franklin Roosevelt in the face of widespread retrenchment and attacks on free speech. As she stated to the crowds in Brewer, "Why am I a Democrat? I feel we care more about people—every kind of people."[118] Although, she remarked, "I am the daughter of an Augusta Maine Republican, my political father was Franklin Delano Roosevelt. He brought me up to be aware of the differences in ways of thinking—I chose his way—and I've been trying to be worthy of him ever since." Of *Storm Center*, she said proudly, "As I played librarian Alicia Hull I felt the old Bette Davis coming back—and I don't think I'll ever lose her again."[119] Davis's words on a woman's ability to change and to choose her own political and spiritual family (Roosevelt and film work in Hollywood) represented a careful postwar negotiation of new roles for women within a redefined sense of public networks.

But Davis did have a difficult time reclaiming her career in the late 1950s before remaking herself as a horror star in *Whatever Happened to Baby Jane?* (1962) and *Hush Hush, Sweet Charlotte* (1964). It's difficult to ignore the fall of the studio system and the decline of Davis's career as a prominent star during the late 1950s. In the absence of the female-centered roles orchestrated by the old studio system, she, and costars Crawford and de Havilland—some of the most vocal and politically astute women of their generation—were marketed as aging monsters. Ironically it was only in the 1970s, and with a twin resurgence of women's history and women's film in Hollywood, that Davis returned to the public eye as a feminist legend. Television appearances on talk shows, a one-woman traveling review covering the comic highlights from her career, an American Film Institute Lifetime Achievement Award (1977), the Distinguished Service Medal for her work for the Hollywood Canteen (1980), and a Women in Film Crystal Award (1983) all followed, as Davis's views of feminism and a woman's view of Hollywood returned with a sharpened focus.

On November 19, 1971, Bette Davis was a guest on Dick Cavett's popular talk show, which competed successfully against Johnny Carson's *Tonight Show* for a number of years. Unlike Carson, the younger, courtly, and openly star-struck Cavett would let his guests take center stage. Davis, clad in a sexy black dress and unafraid of showing her legs at sixty-three, walked on stage to wild applause from the audience. After initially flirting with her younger host, Davis got her first cigarette out and prepared to light up. Cavett offered to light it for her and then hesitated. "Go ahead, I'm not women's lib," she growled, and the audience exploded in laughter. Yet, despite Davis's joke, they spent the majority of the interview talking about her historic fight to be "liberated" from her repressive Warner Bros. talent contract in the 1930s, a controversial move that could have destroyed her career but ended up serving as a precedent for de Havilland's successful case against the studio in 1944.

After forty years as a Hollywood star, on and off camera, Davis still put her career, public image, and responsibility to her audience ahead of everything else. She made no apologies. "Bette Davis and her career are one and the same thing," she wrote.[120] Her career in film and television was still flourishing despite her advancing age, and she had no plans to retire when she reached sixty-five. Despite her jibe at the women's movement, it was easy to see why she was so sought after as a feminist icon in the 1970s and 1980s. Yet her early crusade to reform studio employment contracts was intended to better the system for both women and men. Rather than arguing for special protection for women in the workplace, Davis was a fierce, lifelong advocate for equal opportunities and for increasing women's participation in all areas of public life. Her image in 1971 as a tough, practical, but very feminine woman was meant to reach out and build bridges with working men, rather than to alienate them.

Like many of her successful actor colleagues from Humphrey Bogart to Joan Crawford, Davis had married four times, had children, and adopted more. She believed "being married was the ideal way for a woman to live," but was quick to point out that at nineteen she had rejected a Yale man's proposal of marriage because he had wanted her to give up her career. There was never any reason why women couldn't have it all, she reasoned, arguing that "working women make better wives" because they understand the value of money and the need to take it easy and have a quiet drink in the evening rather than going out on the town on a spree.[121] On the other hand, she understood why more and more women preferred the single life and was fond of quoting the lyrics to one of her hit recordings, "Single" (1965): "It's so good to be single. It's so good not to listen to some idiot who's convinced he's Heaven's gift to womankind, who criticizes whatever you do and spouts about a man's superior mind."[122]

Davis embraced the conflicted struggle for equal rights, the privilege to befriend, negotiate with, and fight with other women, and the right to remain feminine. Gender equality at home had always been a struggle: "Adam didn't cook and he never spent enough time with Cain and Abel,"[123] she said flatly. But, writing and speaking in the 1970s and 1980s, she still spoke to women of all ages as she had at the height of her Hollywood stardom: put yourself and your career first and spare yourself the greatest regret of all: not fulfilling your full potential. She was studio-era Hollywood's greatest advocate for working women who "did it the hard way" so other women would have a role model.

On March 1, 1977, Davis became the first woman to receive a lifetime achievement award: director John Ford, close friend James Cagney, and actor-writer-director Orson Welles preceded her. In an interview given later that spring, Davis was asked specifically about her "feminist beliefs" and feelings about the Equal Rights Amendment. Davis replied, "It's only the most important bloody thing in the whole wide world! And they're still fooling around with it, as you know. I believe violently with Germaine Greer's book *The Female Eunuch*, men will change when we demand it; it's up to women. Men won't automatically change. And it doesn't mean, to achieve equality, that we women have to be unfeminine."[124] At her tribute in 1977, Hollywood's self-proclaimed "Year of the Woman," her devoted fan and surrogate daughter, Natalie Wood, sat by her side, while Jane Fonda, the little girl born to her *Jezebel* costar and fellow Democrat, gave her oration. Nearly forty years back, Davis had very graciously let Henry Fonda leave the set early to see his new child in the hospital. Davis relished the all-too-rare treat of seeing a man put his family before work! The grown-up child pleased her even more; Jane had matured into Hollywood's political conscience, and it was a lonely role.

Davis was well aware of how her female fans and the production trends in studio-era Hollywood created a world where women could succeed. In the 1970s and 1980s, she offered a female-oriented picture of the film business that was at odds with new Hollywood and growing bibliographies on old Hollywood. She said of her career, "I didn't work with any big male stars. Female stars didn't in those days. We were meant to carry the picture by ourselves." She continued: "It was the woman's era in pictures mainly because the industry made mostly romances. Which is what people wanted to see then and what they still want to see, only Hollywood can't seem to understand that now." Her frequent male costar George Brent said that "all a leading man had to do was worry about whether the back of his hair was combed right. Women ran the show, during the war years at least, because there were very few male stars around to play leads. They were all in the military." But, as she mused, things changed, and not for the better: "After the war, of course, movies became consumed with the problems of men. And they're still writing men's problems." "Of course," she added with more than a touch of devilish humor, "men do have enormous problems today I must admit."[125]

Of all women in studio-era Hollywood, Bette Davis came closest to having it all: feminist, actress, star, producer, rebel, politician, war worker, administrator, defender of civil liberties, role model, wife, mother, and legend. Through it all, she maintained her commitment to engaging a community of women in and outside Hollywood, and to making New Deal equal-rights feminism a way of life.

CHAPTER 2
Organization Women

Organization is within yourself. . . . You simply cannot grow old unless you are bored, and I think professional women look younger than housewives for this reason.

Virginia Van Upp, 1947[1]

Though Bette Davis and many other of her female colleagues' career stories were profiled over and over by *Modern Screen, Photoplay*, and *Life*, critically acclaimed Hollywood novels were usually by and about men: Nathaniel West's *Day of the Locust* (1939), F. Scott Fitzgerald's *The Last Tycoon* (1940), and Budd Schulberg's *What Makes Sammy Run* (1941).[2] The anonymous working girl's story, when told on screen, made a lot of money for the studios—but tales of making it in Hollywood usually focused on a young actress's experience (*What Price Hollywood?*; *Bombshell*, 1933; *A Star Is Born*). Although these films showed women working in Hollywood in other capacities (as casting agents, script girls, stenographers, publicists, journalists, makeup artists, and costumers), they rarely had more than a few lines of dialogue and were kept to the margins of the shot.

But one Hollywood novel, comparatively neglected in the "canon" of the Hollywood literary genre, told a radically different story: Jane Allen's *I Lost My Girlish Laughter* (1938). Allen's short novel was about Madge Lawrence, a Hollywood newcomer who gets a job as private secretary to a big-time producer, Sidney Brand. The book created quite a buzz on both coasts in 1938—it was rumored to be autobiographical, and "Sidney Brand" was a sharp and unflattering portrait of one of Hollywood's moguls. "Jane Allen" had insider status that drew critics and readers eager for a real scoop on the picture business, and the press kept her identity a secret at first, knowing this would boost sales. Her "personal comments" may have been "master-pieces in humor and irony" to the critics, but with "a laugh on every page" directed at a real-life top producer, the author had to be careful.[3] Allen was the pen name of Silvia Schulman (better known to history as the ex-wife of future blacklistee Ring Lardner Jr., whom she married in 1937).[4] For a time in the 1930s, Schulman was secretary to producer David O. Selznick at MGM. She was able to get a little of her own back by parodying Madge's "hateful boss," who calls his employees "boys and girls," forces her to work appalling hours without paying her overtime or thinking of letting her have a coffee break or a meal, and, though married, overweight, and crass, sexu-ally harasses her nonstop.[5]

Madge tells her story in a hilarious series of first-person letters to her girlfriend back home. When she arrives in town, she goes—as a proper young woman should—to stay at a woman's hotel similar to the one famil-iar to contemporary audiences in RKO's *Stage Door* (1937), in which the-atrical hopefuls (Ginger Rogers and Katharine Hepburn leading a mostly female cast) struggle for success in a cutthroat entertainment business. As Madge jokes in one letter, "It's not a bad little hostelry although it sim-ply crawls with femmes and wherever a mob of femmes gathers there is something depressing about the atmosphere." She went on: "I wouldn't for the world admit that to a gentleman, because I still have something in me of the old guard feminists who broke out in bloomers and smashed windows."[6] Madge is a self-proclaimed feminist, but it's something she dis-cusses with women friends and keeps from the opposite sex, whether pro-spective employers or future romantic partners. But she is less shy about advertising her college education, since it is already seen as an advantage on the Hollywood job market—even for a lowly secretary. On her first night out, she ends up serendipitously drinking with one of the industry's top directors, and he is delighted when he realizes that she is a job-prospecting college woman. Madge will be perfect for Sidney Brand's new secretary, he says. "I will fit the bill," she tells her friend, "because Mr. Brand believes in higher education for women and won't have anything less than a college girl for his secretary."[7] How sweet of him.

In her descriptions of Hollywood, Madge indicates women's presence in many branches of the filmmaking profession. Although she acknowledges that "the majority are extra girls on the break for the big chance, frighten-ingly young for the most part and devastatingly pretty," there are also "an odd sprinkling of stenographers, script girls, assistant cutters, designers, a librarian or two" and—the pièce de résistance—"one honest-to-goodness writer who has actually had her name on screen credits but is very Scotch in makeup and is saving her money against a rainy day."[8] Given that writers were the last of the major branches of the industry to secure union status and that it was well known that the average Hollywood writer made far less than a secretary during the 1930s, Allen's penny-pinching screenwriter is a particularly apt character!

Far from seeing Sidney Brand as one of the "geniuses of the system," Madge gradually realizes that her boss is nothing more than a neurotic mama's boy desperate to screw everybody over, from his secretaries to the public. He may be powerful, but he is far from intimidating. As she brings his lunch to him each day on a little tray, she feels "like a mother with a chick."[9] Madge, cool, capable, and hardworking, manages the egos running through the office, prompting one publicist to remark: "In your modest way you are an important guy in this studio; you have access to the great man and can do a lot of favors.'"[10] Unfortunately, the "great man" is a jerk, and the "favor" this smooth-talking male publicist wants from Madge is for her to sleep with him. Madge won't at first; she has a fling with an up-and-coming actor instead. However, at the end of the story she succumbs to marriage, which naturally prompts Brand to fire both Madge and her enterprising publicist. But Hollywood producers' logic doesn't sack Madge because she will soon be a married woman and, as historians have claimed over the years, married women were discouraged from working during the Depression. On the contrary: married men are just as much a liability as married women in Hollywood. Marriage represents a betrayal of loyalty to the producer and therefore both future husband and wife have to go. The novel ends with both of them losing their jobs.

However, while she's in the system, Madge frankly relishes the power she attains and is able to exert some creative control over various projects and her actor love-interest. Although Brand is patronizing and under-pays all of his workers—the men and women—he does admit that the female patron keeps him in business: "'It is women whom we are trying to please. It is women who are responsible for paid admissions.'"[11] One could certainly imagine Selznick saying as much. Throughout his career, Selznick made films about strong women aimed for a female market, from *Christopher Strong* (1933) to *A Star Is Born*, and he would later produce *Gone with the Wind* and *Duel in the Sun* (1946), two of the all-time highest box-office grossers in the studio era.

As a best seller written by an anonymous Hollywood insider, *I Lost My Girlish Laughter* kept critics talking about its potential as a screen block-buster. One claimed sassy Joan Blondell had "the inside track" on the role of Madge, and another argued that Jean Arthur, who frequently starred as a plucky news reporter (*Mr. Deeds Goes to Town*, 1936) or savvy secretary (*Mr. Smith Goes to Washington*, 1939), would be equally good in the role.[12]

Like most headlining novels, it was serialized in *Cosmopolitan* prior to publication and was popular with critics.[13] It reached wider audiences as one of Orson Welles's radio shows for CBS in 1939 starring Ilka Chase (in which Welles introduced the show with an interview with his "secret guest," Silvia Schulman).[14] By then, Schulman was raking in royalties and didn't have to worry if she "would never have lunch in that town again." MGM optioned the property, but undoubtedly so that it could prevent other studios from adapting it.[15] Although he had left MGM by then, Selznick allegedly used his leverage to prevent Schulman's and his own former employer from adapting it for the screen. He had leverage to burn: L. B. Mayer was his father-in-law.

Selznick's work producing *What Price Hollywood?*, *Bombshell*, and *A Star Is Born* had given him a reputation for crafting sympathetic stories about working women "making it" in Hollywood. It was well known that he had launched the outspoken Katharine Hepburn's career at RKO. Schulman's semiautobiographical novel showed a less pleasant side of the producer on-the-make. Had the film reached screens, it would have been unique as a women's social "history from below," but Selznick could have sued Mayer for libel. Instead, allegedly, he soured prospects for Schulman's writer-husband, Ring Lardner Jr., working for the studios. Because Katharine Hepburn kept Lardner's coauthorship of *Woman of the Year* a secret, the studio purchased the property and built it up into a major vehicle for Hepburn and Spencer Tracy. In March 1943, the film won the Academy Award for Best Original Screenplay. However, Lardner may not have forgiven Schulman for her success; they were divorced in 1945, and he remarried soon after.

One of the many interesting aspects of Allen's novel is its indication that Hollywood's production system worked very much like a dysfunctional family, with Madge's maternal interest in Brand and even her up-and-coming actor boyfriend dominating day-to-day work. At one point, Madge is even running the studio's latest production, averting disaster with a terrible foreign leading lady by keeping Brand out of the loop on the set. Was this simply another Hollywood fantasy, where instead of becoming the wife, the secretary briefly functions as Hollywood insider and de facto studio head? Certainly, Hollywood had its share of important executive secretaries and "girl Fridays," including Schulman, who didn't always have to marry and divorce the boss à la Rosalind Russell in *His Girl Friday* (1940) to maintain their career profiles. Sometimes, as in the case of Dorothy Arzner, who began as a stenographer in 1920 and ended up Hollywood's most famous woman director, they *were* the boss.[16] Others, including Kay Brown, Dorothy Hechtlinger, Molly Mandaville, Eve Ettinger, Marguerite

Roberts, Ida Koverman, Kate Corbaley, and Anita Colby, would redefine the concept of women's work in the Hollywood office, carving out impressive careers, and proving they were nobody's girl Fridays but their own.

Most of the women in this chapter do not follow Madge Lawrence's exciting but brief Hollywood storyline. They aren't Bette Davis, but they aren't the lowly, comparatively anonymous, and often powerless women in Erin Hill's portrait of Hollywood, *Never Done*, either. Instead, they changed jobs, hauled themselves up the career ladder year after year, married, continued working, rose higher, divorced, and continued working—sometimes for more than one studio and often turning to television when opportunities for advancement in Hollywood disappeared. No one wrote their memoirs or had them serialized for publication. Usually their names are unrecorded in film credits. Hollywood's white-collar organization women worked as executive secretaries, assistant to the vice president in charge of production, heads of scenario, heads of research, independent publicists, technical advisors, readers, screenwriters, and agents. The range of work, managerial and creative, knew few boundaries for women with the drive to succeed, but these women had an easier time working with producers and studio heads Harry Cohn, Irving Thalberg, Darryl F. Zanuck, and even—surprise, surprise—David O. Selznick. Hollywood had legions of organization women from stenographers to producers; none of them simply took dictation. But there was no time for comedy or much girlish laughter at the top. Only one of them would be unscathed by the blacklist.

In many ways, Derek Granger Katharine "Kay" Brown was a perfect example of Hollywood's organization woman. Born in 1902 on Hastings-on-Hudson, Brown came from a wealthy New York social register family. Her parents were important patrons of the arts and helped to found the Museum of the City of New York. She went to Wellesley College (then more socially acceptable than academically rigorous among the eastern Seven Sisters women's colleges) and majored in English. After graduation in 1924, she got a job working in the Mary Arden Theater School in New Hampshire, and in 1926, Joseph Kennedy, one of the owners, was impressed enough to hire her as a talent scout and reader for his new FBO Studios, which would shortly become RKO. "When I first started at FBO," she remembered, "You just read a story in some magazine, *Argosy* or *Red Book* or something of the kind, and called up the agent to say you'd pay $300 for the rights. They were always delighted."[17] Kay loved a good novel and was instrumental in fixing the deal to buy Edna Ferber's number-one best seller of 1929, *Cimarron*, for the studio.[18] The western novel about an Oklahoma pioneer woman went on to win the fledgling studio Oscars for Best Picture and Screenplay and launched Irene Dunne's screen career. Brown paid Ferber's record-breaking price, $110,000, in addition to agent's fees of $15,000. In 1939, she mused on the long-term impact of the Depression: "Those are prices seldom met in Hollywood these days."

When David O. Selznick joined RKO in 1932 after leaving Paramount, Brown had acquired a reputation as a headlining dealmaker who was ahead of the curve in nabbing popular women's and historical material for her young and ambitious studio. She attended all the top executive sales conventions, usually the only woman photographed alongside vice president of distribution Ned Depinet and eastern production head Lee Marcus.[19] When forming his own independent studio, Selznick International Pictures, in 1935, he hired Brown as eastern story editor and later appointed her eastern representative at $300 a week.[20] After opening her office on 654 Madison Avenue, she crisscrossed the country with assistants Dorothy Modisette and later Elsa Neuberger, identifying and optioning the best books on the market.[21] Another find, also written by a woman, Margaret Mitchell, became Selznick and Hollywood's all-time greatest domestic box-office success: *Gone with the Wind*. Selznick, astoundingly, didn't want to buy it at first. Brown had the good sense to read it and push for the acquisition before the reviews had appeared. "I kept badgering and badgering him," she recalled. "I didn't get very far with him. In those days, quick purchases weren't made." Growing exasperated with her "nagging," Selznick wired her, "If you can, buy it for $50,000. Buy it and don't bother me." She did, and negotiated a raise to $400 a week in 1937.[22]

Without Brown, there would be no *Gone with the Wind* as we know it today. Whatever modern audiences may think of its sympathetic picture of the slave-owning, Civil War South and the heroine's convoluted love life, *Gone with the Wind* starred the most independent, ambitious, practical working woman in American literature and film and became an inspiration to generations of women worldwide.[23] Brown also was involved in the purchase of Daphne du Maurier's *Rebecca*, later adapted by Joan Harrison for Selznick and Alfred Hitchcock in 1940. These two purchases would make Selznick the first producer to win consecutive Academy Awards for Best Picture.

Brown was invaluable during preproduction on *Gone with the Wind*, and some of Selznick's correspondence with her is preserved in Rudy Behlmer's classic compilation, *Memo from David O. Selznick* (1972).[24] Unfortunately, none of her memos to him are included, and readers only get Selznick's retrospective gloss on his film productions, which tends to downplay Brown's role.[25] But to give Selznick his due, during her tenure at SIP, he allowed numerous press interviews with Brown revealing her key role in developing his productions and stars. In the midst of the excitement over *Gone with the Wind*'s Atlanta premiere, Brown laughed she was "the highest paid office girl in the world." But she was no secretary: at SIP, Brown "buys stories, looks out for plays, arranges screen tests, signs up actors, and even, in the case of the Atlanta opening of *Gone with the Wind*, helps with hoopla premieres."[26]

Life with Selznick was always unexpected, and in early 1938, the producer, considering the possibilities of making a film about the *Titanic* disaster, told Brown to go down to the Hoboken docks and buy the remains of the *Leviathan*.[27] Brown, "a true soldier of her then king," went down to price it, and the officials regarded her with "alarm," speaking in "those tones reserved for very young children or adults who, plainly, need psychiatric care."[28] When they asked why she wanted to buy it, she, "a woman used to direct action," replied, "To sink it." Luckily, the crazy British government had already bought the liner—for scrap. One can understand where some of Sidney Brand's antics came from in *I Lost My Girlish Laughter*!

She was a great talent scout as well, with an eye for faces and names. Brown discovered Ingrid Bergman after viewing one of her Swedish films "and persuaded David Selznick to sign her." Brown would remain Bergman's agent and, as the star wrote fondly, one of "the three main pillars of my life."[29] While Selznick, rather ungraciously, called his biggest box-office star "the Palmolive Garbo," to Brown, Ingrid Bergman would always be "my darling." A few years later, she found Viveca Lindfors, a Swedish mother of two, and groomed her for Hollywood stardom at Warner Bros.[30] She also was responsible for changing "Phyllis Walker" to Jennifer Jones. None of these women were mere single, sexually available sirens on whom male producers and audience members could project their real or imagined fantasies. Instead, these stars were, like Brown, young mothers who did not conceal from their fans the challenges in balancing work and family life.

Brown was entranced with Bergman's lack of pretense, simple enjoyment of being a mother, and willingness, early in her career, to allow her first husband to manage her business transactions so she could concentrate on acting. She was less impressed with Bergman's decision to throw her Hollywood career away on Roberto Rossellini a few years later, remarking, "If she'd decided to live on the Solomon Islands with a cannibal chief, I would still have loved her . . . but that did not necessarily mean I felt that Ingrid was right."[31] Eventually, though, it was Brown who identified *Anastasia* as a potential property for her and persuaded Bergman to do it. Rossellini thought it was "junk."[32] Bergman had, by then, spent enough years with her husband to know whom to trust. She trusted Kay. Her performance earned the actress her second Academy Award in 1956 and regenerated her Hollywood career. Shortly after that, Brown flew to Paris with the script of *Indiscreet* (1958). At the time, Rossellini's affair with the wife of Indian documentary filmmaker Harisadhan Dasgupta was all over the tabloids and Bergman was in the middle of a divorce. Brown, always multitasking, had business to handle with Swedish producer Lars Schmidt. She introduced him to Bergman at dinner, and in December 1958, Bergman married him.

Despite her close friendship with Selznick and their shared interest in making films with strong female protagonists (in addition to advocating *Gone with the Wind* and *Rebecca*, Brown explored a potential remake of *Little Women* in 1942 and showed an early interest in Horace McCoy's Amelia Earhart story), their partnership drew to an end in 1942. That summer, there were rumors that Selznick was cutting costs and jobs. Brown was on the list. She had done her work too well. Selznick had a backlog of potential stories and could no longer afford her when he was not actively producing anything. *Rebecca* had been his last great success.[33] Selznick International was dissolved, and Vanguard Films, Inc. attempted to fill its place. Sam Goldwyn tried to hire her straight away, but Brown took her time accepting his offer, preferring to look after Bergman and her other clients, spending time with her daughters, and vacationing at Lake Placid. She took over Goldwyn's New York office in July 1943, but only remained with him for a year, before turning full-time agent and theatrical producer.[34]

Brown, as well as her colleague Mary Baker, partner of the Sam Jaffe Agency, had two young children, and, as columnist Elsa Maxwell noted approvingly, both women "forget the office the moment the door is locked at night."[35] For years, Brown and Baker crisscrossed the country closing deals for Selznick and Jaffe. But Kay, an authentic, blue-blooded New Yorker, disliked living in Southern California, where the locals' idea of culture was discussing their latest preview, and remained an important force in the studio's East Coast enterprises. As a working mother, she emphatically did *not* want to raise her children in a Hollywood environment. She was cultured, brilliant, and a noted Anglophile, and when she left Hollywood to focus on her career as an agent in 1944,[36] she represented primarily English talent in the United States, including Laurence Olivier, Alec Guinness, Ralph Richardson, John Gielgud, and Rex Harrison. Politically left, she also represented blacklisted actor Fredric March, screenwriter and playwright Lillian Hellman, and playwright Arthur Miller, and, with her and her clients' declining influence in Hollywood, moved from film representation to more New York–based theatrical work in the 1950s.

Kay Brown might appear to be unique among office executives, a woman whose family name bought her the prestige and advantages at work that poorer Madge Lawrences and Silvia Schulmans couldn't afford. But even setting her wealth and family name aside, she was more typical than one would assume of Hollywood's female employees. Women who started as script readers, editors, or secretaries often moved into editorial positions in the scenario department or screenwriting or became agents. Frederica Maas worked as both writer and agent, Eve Ettinger began as a scenario reader before moving up to head of her studio's scenario department, and even Selznick's first wife, Irene Mayer, who could have sat on her brains and family name, worked as a top agent and theatrical producer.

But longtime personal executive secretaries who never formally moved into the writing department routinely worked on scripts (almost always without credit). Take, for example, Dorothy Hechtlinger, who worked as Darryl F. Zanuck's chief secretary at Twentieth Century-Fox until 1943,[37] when Molly Mandaville took over. Hechtlinger, born in 1902, emigrated from Galicia, Austria, before coming to Hollywood. She was one of five children, and all of them worked for the film industry. Her sister Helen was secretary to Gene Markey, and her other sister Sally also worked as a Fox secretary for several years before the Second World War. Brothers Louis and David worked for Zanuck, with Louis working in publicity at the studio from 1933 to 1941. But Dorothy's career easily eclipsed those of her siblings.

Maas was a close friend of Hechtlinger and remembered: "When I was an agent for Edward Small, performing my daily rounds of the studios, Dorothy's offices, adjacent to those of Darryl Zanuck, always held out a big welcome mat to this unhappy agent. Over steaming cups of coffee brewed in her office, we exchanged confidences, impressions, and opinions about the not-so-glamorous film industry we have both been a part of for so many years. Zanuck was the manipulator, Dorothy his good Girl Friday, his right hand, the perfect foil for his diabolical creativity. She had no set working hours, and neither did he. Her time was adjusted to his time, even if it ran late into night hours and sometimes even into dawn."[38]

But Dorothy was never just a factotum. A 1937 article profiling top women in the industry called her "the lady behind Darryl F. Zanuck's scenarios." She served as "story editor" and "story coordinator" at the studio from 1934 to 1945, when she moved over to Universal-International to be the assistant to William Goetz.[39] In the rare photographs of Zanuck's story conferences, Dorothy was often the only woman in the room. Often, when stories were mere ideas of Zanuck's, she and the other writers would work things out orally around the conference table, and Hechtlinger would be the one who wrote "the first draft of the scenario."[40] At later stages of production, she and her successor, Molly Mandaville, would take down Zanuck's notes as best they could in shorthand, edit, and then distribute them as his famous story and production memos. In these documents, widely reproduced now by film historians and excerpted in Behlmer's *Memo from Darryl F. Zanuck* (1995), Zanuck is witty, tough, insightful, brutal, and occasionally profane.[41] So posterity's understanding of Zanuck, his tone, organization, and outrageous sense of humor are all mediated through Hechtlinger's and later Mandaville's editorial skill.

As many of the production files on Zanuck's films at Fox attest, Hechtlinger and Mandaville were also reading potential properties, giving Zanuck their opinions about relative strengths and weaknesses of material for the screen, and commenting on writers' evolving script drafts. They were joined by Frances Richardson, Zanuck's longtime head of the research department, who worked closely with writers on the studio's specialty in the 1930s and 1940s—period costume dramas.[42] Richardson also acted as a conduit of information about studio research practices and library innovation in the 1930s and 1940s, as the studios became more concerned with their public image and educational capacity.[43] In addition to Zanuck's screenwriters, who included Wanda Tuchock and Sonya Levien, Fox's story and script departments included a range of women readers, including Winifred Aydelotte, Joan Maples, Ruth Goddard, Tammy Cotter, Marge Decker, Dorothy Lebedoff, Edith Youngmeyer, and Dorothy Robinson, who all worked with Hechtlinger and Mandaville.[44] Although the work of these women in reading, critiquing, recommending, purchasing, adapting, typing, and collating script and story material may not have made the credits on Fox's finished films, their work did make headlines in monthly studio newsletters, which profiled their work, accomplishments, decisions to change departments, marriages, divorces, children, and promotions.

Mandaville, even in her typed story conference notes, wasn't above voicing the occasional dissenting opinion in Zanuck's memos. In 1955, Zanuck was preparing his personal production of the year, the adaptation of Sloan Wilson's best seller *The Man in the Gray Flannel Suit*. He asked Mandaville to look over Nunnally Johnson's script and give her opinion. Although Johnson was one of Zanuck's closest friends, and a writer he had personally promoted to director, Mandaville was blunt. She disliked the lifeless adaptation and wrote a lengthy critique, which, among other things, lamented the limited construction of Betsy (Jennifer Jones) and Tom Rath's (Gregory Peck) domestic life in the suburbs. She wrote to Zanuck and Johnson: "I wouldn't have gone to quite this much trouble with this report except that I liked the book and I was disappointed in the script, and I hope you will feel impelled to make it better!"[45] Mandaville was never simply Zanuck's personal secretary, but like Hechtlinger, worked as "liaison between writers and as a script coordinator" during Zanuck's tenure and remained at the studio until her retirement in 1968.[46]

In 1948, as Hollywood personnel came under increasing scrutiny by HUAC and the media, Hechtlinger left Hollywood to work for former Columbia Pictures producer and noted liberal Theresa Helburn at the Theatre Guild in New York before moving into television, primarily at CBS, where she was script and later story editor for the Desilu Playhouse. In television, she had more power and more opportunities for screen credits than as a studio secretary. She was story producer for the US Steel Hour in 1954 and 1955 (where she produced the production of *Hedda Gabler*, starring Tallulah Bankhead, airing in January 1954), and she served as story editor of *Keep Me in Mind* for *Climax!* (1957), *The Time Element* for the Westinghouse Desilu Playhouse (1958), and episodes of *The Untouchables* (1959), *Checkmate* (1961), and *Wide Country* (1963). Hechtlinger was also associate producer on episodes of *Checkmate, Will the Real Killer Please Stand Up?*, and *The Bold and the Tough*, in 1962. She was also mentor to a number of young television writers, including Rod Serling. But in the early 1960s, she returned to Universal Studios and worked there as chief story editor until her retirement in 1967. Television offered qualified opportunities for women who had achieved a certain power in Hollywood, but who, as secretaries in a shrinking studio job market, had found it difficult to rise to heads of story or producing departments. Lucille Ball (*I Love Lucy*, 1951–57), Gail Patrick (*Perry Mason*, 1957–66), Joan Harrison (*Alfred Hitchcock Presents*, 1955–62; *The Alfred Hitchcock Hour*, 1962–75), and Ida Lupino (*Have Gun, Will Travel*, 1957–63) achieved a certain creative autonomy and respect in the business, but writers Anita Loos (*The Buick Circus Hour*, 1952–53), Virginia Kellogg (*Ethel Barrymore Theater*, 1956), Brenda Weisberg (Fireside Theatre, 1951–54), Mary C. McCall Jr. (*The Millionaire*, 1955–56), and Helen Deutsch (*Producers' Showcase*, 1956) didn't find it a particularly rewarding career shift.

In the 1930s, amid the struggles for the writers' union, Harry Cohn had been one of the more politically tolerant producers, hiring both Mary C. McCall Jr. and Dalton Trumbo after they were fired by Warner Bros. for union activities. Under Harry Cohn, Columbia Studios also employed a significant number of women at all levels of production—editor Viola Lawrence, director Dorothy Arzner, writer-director-producer Harriet Parsons, and writer and executive producer Virginia Van Upp all worked for Cohn. But Eve Ettinger, less well known than the producer of *Gilda* (Van Upp) or the longtime editor of countless hits including Bogart's classic 1950 noir, *In a Lonely Place* (Lawrence), had a lasting impact on the studio's output.

Ettinger was chief of scenario development and writers at Columbia. She began as a poorly paid screen reader at Paramount before moving to a better job in New York as a reader and assistant in the story department at Columbia. She helped to organize the Screen Readers Guild to get better pay and negotiated to have readers included in the Screen Writers Guild's 1942 contract with the producers. She worked for Columbia's New York office until 1945, reading and commenting on potential screen material, until Cohn asked her to move to Los Angeles and be his chief script reader. She helped Cohn pick her replacement in New York, Janet Wood, who would later move to CBS-TV as a story editor. As Ettinger remembered,

> I was unhappy at the time I came out here, I was sensitive, I was frightened. This was a new world to me and I came into a job in which I had to learn. I had to learn screenplay writing, I had to learn how to choose writers. . . . Cohn called me one day and said, "Do you want to come out? Make up your mind in a day," and the next day I made up my mind.[47]

It was a demanding job. "I hadn't done much script reading in New York and I certainly didn't know Hollywood writers, so I didn't know their capabilities, which meant I just had to kill myself to read every script that came in the studio."

We know some of Ettinger's story only because she was one of many men and women named as a former Communist Party member by top HUAC fink Martin Berkeley. Berkeley accused everyone from writers Madeline Ruthven, Dorothy Parker, and Lillian Hellman to script reader Jessie Burns and secretaries Ann Roth and Helen Slote of being communists.[48] But Ettinger was also accused of being a communist by Columbia executive B. B. Kahane and was called to testify on September 10, 1951, along with a range of female screenwriters. She was ordered to deliver the list of 930 writers employed by the studio, and after an exhaustive search, the committee reported that 38 of them had been Communist Party members.[49]

Kahane had suggested that Ettinger used her position to employ or push communist writers at Columbia. They were particularly interested in the period around 1947. After two years of her work in Los Angeles as head of scenario, in 1947 Ettinger had asked Cohn to let her out of her contract and so she could return to New York. She wanted to form her own company in the manner of agent Charles Feldman, who would nurture writing clients and then sell scripts independently to the studios for massive amounts of money—as much as $150,000 apiece. Milton Pickman, a former Columbia employee, and Nat Goldstone asked her to join them in a new business partnership. As she put it,

He [Pickman] thought I knew writers, he thought that I knew scripts. I had often talked to him about a dream of buying my own stories, hiring writers, writing scripts and selling them to studios at enormous prices. . . . And I thought, I really know how to develop scripts, why shouldn't I do it. I had visions of being very rich.

The backers pulled out and the business collapsed, but Cohn offered Ettinger her old job. After six months, "Mr. Cohn called me up and said, 'You made a mistake.' I realized full well." But though Cohn liked her imagination and honesty, Columbia executive B. B. Kahane did not. He found out that Ettinger, while in New York in the 1930s, had briefly been a member of the Communist Party. Shortly after she returned to Los Angeles, she recalled, "Mr. Kahane said he had gotten information from somebody who claimed that when I left Columbia . . . I was going to get young writers to write scripts and I was going to sell these script to the studio with the writer, and presumably these writers were going to be communists." She concluded, "This is, of course, ridiculous, and I was amused by it at the time because I didn't realize the implications in it."

Ettinger explained the attraction of the Communist Party as a space for intellectual discussion, something stimulating for a young woman who opposed racism and fascism but knew comparatively little of what was going on in the world outside the United States. She admitted, "I had no—what is the word—no goal." The news in Europe was of "people being killed, people dying," and she wanted to know why. Ettinger was a reader; the group's meetings and book discussions thrilled her. "This is what happened, we discussed."

Ettinger's candor and defense of her early political beliefs as a stand against fascism did not save her job at Columbia. It took a year for her testimony to become public, and then in the spring of 1952, she was widely mentioned in her capacity as chief Columbia story editor.[50] Kahane won; Cohn let Ettinger go. One of her last acts for the company was listening to struggling writer Daniel Taradash tell her how to "lick" the script of *From Here to Eternity*. She recommended him to producer Buddy Adler in early 1952, and the rest, as they say, is history.[51] Despite her strong relationship with Harry Cohn and years of experiences as a top story editor, Ettinger could not survive Columbia's changing corporate culture, which, by the early 1950s, seemed equally intolerant of women and former Communist Party members in the organization. Ettinger's friend and colleague, Janet Wood, would resign from her job at CBS-TV in 1953. But Ettinger's career wasn't entirely over. Gary Cooper, who had testified as a friendly witness for HUAC back in 1947, announced in September 1954 that he had hired

Ettinger "as a story consultant" who would "comb the market for suitable film subjects" for his new film company, Baroda Productions.[52] Cooper was anything but predictable politically, but he certainly knew the value of a good story editor, like his longtime friend Harry Cohn.

As Elizabeth Spector points out, the public and historians talk a lot about the blacklist "and focus on Trumbo . . . and those people who were able to survive in Mexico, working under the table, working through fronts." When great party leaders or speakers were mentioned in the press coverage of HUAC, it was an almost exclusively male list. This male collective would calcify in film histories of the blacklist. Trumbo, Lester Cole, Albert Maltz, Alvah Bessie, and John Howard Lawson were the big names, the "brilliant" writers and speakers and forces for the party line in the guild, as writer Karl Tunberg would argue.[53] But, as Spector reminds us, this was only a fraction of those hundreds of people "who lost their jobs in the industry, secretaries and so forth. I knew one who was thrown out of the studio she'd worked in her whole life, and she developed a terrible drinking problem. For many people the blacklist was the end of their lives.'"[54] Most of these blacklisted women are, as with Spector's example, nameless. Some of the names we know through their HUAC testimony, including Actors Laboratory Theatre secretary and John Garfield's secretary Helen Slote. Other women, such as Leona D'Ambrey, Ann Roth, and Alice Goldberg, were accused by the mostly male writers who agreed to name names.

During the war, Pauline Lauber was an important industry figure, coordinating the relationship between the Screen Writers Guild and the Office of War Information. She was executive secretary to the Hollywood Writers Mobilization (another secretary, Ann Roth, was also named as a communist). Lauber was an early critic of Jack Tenney's California House Un-American Activities Committee, and with journalist and civil rights lawyer Carey McWilliams (*Factories in the Field*, 1939), Carlotta Bass, editor and publisher of the liberal *California Eagle*, and Margaret Pennett, executive secretary for the Council of Hollywood Guilds and Unions (of which Mary McCall was president), formed the Mobilization for Democracy. Conceived as a union of "all progressive organizations in Los Angeles" to protest the political scare tactics, the organization targeted Tenney, John Rankin of Mississippi, and Gerald L. K. Smith in a rally in Los Angeles in February 1946.[55] A few years later, Lauber was named a communist by Richard Collins, former *Song of Russia* writer, who also named Elizabeth Leech Glenn, Norma Hallgren Blaché, and writer Madeline Ruthven.[56]

Herta Uerkvitz was called to testify on September 20, 1951, and she was one of the few women whose profession in Hollywood was "architectural research." Originally from Wisconsin, she was educated in Washington, graduated from business school, and did a two-year extension course at UCLA. Although Uerkvitz had worked in Hollywood since 1922 in minor clerical and research capacities, she moved to MGM in 1929 and was appointed head of her department in 1936 shortly before Irving Thalberg's death, one of many high-profile women within MGM's studio structure. Fifteen years later, Uerkvitz was denounced as a communist and, although she took a swipe at the committee for listing "dozens and dozens and dozens of organizations as subversive" based "purely upon hearsay," invoked the Fifth Amendment, refusing to answer questions. But when the counsel reminded her that she had been named by Martin Berkeley, Uerkvitz bristled, saying, "That reminds me of a tale on witch hunts where a five-year-old child was condemned because a man testified that he saw devils running out of her mouth."[57]

Another prominent employee of MGM would testify before the committee that summer. Nebraska-born Marguerite Smith started working during her summer vacations when she was fourteen. She graduated from high school and worked her way through six months of business college before moving to Hollywood and getting a job as a secretary at Fox Studios in late 1926. But secretarial work being as flexible as it was in Hollywood, she began commenting on story material and writing her own stories on the side. After a few years, she was promoted to reader. By 1930, she sold her own story, and when "they gave me an opportunity to do the screenplay," she became a full-time screenwriter, using her pen name, Marguerite Roberts. In 1938, she moved to MGM and wrote some of the studio's biggest hits, including a number of films for Clark Gable, who became her close friend and advocate at the studio. She later wrote Lana Turner's *Ziegfeld Girl*, the early anti-fascist adaptation of *Escape* (1940), *Somewhere I'll Find You* (1942), *The Bribe* (1949), *Ivanhoe* (1952), and the Hepburn films *Dragon Seed* (1944) and *The Sea of Grass* (1947). But, as Roberts noted in 1951, "I have been continuously employed at the studio for 12½ years and naturally I worked on other things that I did not receive screen credit on."[58]

In spite of her impressive list of screen credits, little is known of Marguerite Roberts; the most comprehensive information about her career is in her testimony before HUAC in September 1951. She was another casualty of colleague Martin Berkeley, who referred to her simply as "Marguerite Sanford, wife of writer John Sanford." Roberts never used her married name in Hollywood, and Berkeley and the committee's description of her was intended to diminish her professionally as just the wife of another writer (even though she had been instrumental in getting Berkeley a six-month contract at MGM in 1941). She was one of the few called to testify who criticized the committee for the wanton damage it had done to people's careers in Hollywood. She stated flatly, much to the dismay of her lawyer Sidney Cohn: "I don't think you really have uncovered any subversive acts, and no one has seriously alleged that there has been any communist propaganda in the pictures, and a lot of people really have suffered a lot by this. I honestly think that the bad outweighs the good."[59] Roberts's blunt outspokenness did her no good, and although some committee members wanted her cited for contempt, the industry did enough by blacklisting her.[60] Even Gable, "the King of Hollywood," and the "secret boss of MGM,"[61] Ida Koverman, could not help her. And as everyone in Hollywood had known for twenty years, if there was a problem Ida "Kay" Koverman couldn't fix, it really *was* a problem.

In the early 1960s, critic and commentator Hedda Hopper published her long-awaited and feared memoir, *The Whole Truth and Nothing But*. Women dominated press coverage and film criticism in Hollywood during the 1930s and 1940s, with Kate Cameron, Irene Thirer, Alice Hughes, Sheila Graham, Elsa Maxwell, Cobina Wright Jr., and, of course, rival Louella Parsons the biggest names. Hopper, though known today as the ultimate anti-communist shrew thanks to biopics such as *Trumbo* (2015), was a committed studio-era feminist. Throughout her career, she consistently used her column to promote other Hollywood women's career achievements, often regardless of their political affiliations (she liked Democrats Davis, McCall, and Lupino a lot). Those following her column would remember Ida Koverman as one of Hopper's close friends. Since Koverman's death in 1954, traces of Koverman's once formidable power at MGM had begun to fade. So, in her book and in the accompanying press coverage, Hopper focused on the "wonderful" woman who "carried the title of assistant to Louis B. Mayer but . . . was the real power behind the throne." As Hopper concluded, "To all intents and purposes, she ran MGM."[62] It was a stunning revelation for readers who had been exposed to Bosley Crowther's *The Lion's Share*, which eulogized Mayer as Hollywood's cinema pioneer and mogul. Of all the forgotten people included in Hopper's memoir, Koverman was the one Hopper was utterly committed to redeeming. And L. B. Mayer could spin in his grave for all she cared.

During the studio era, however, all industry people knew of "Kay" Koverman, the "tall, stately, gray-haired queen mother" who stood behind Mayer.[63] It was no secret that she changed Spangler Arlington Brugh to Robert Taylor.[64] According to the columnists, Mayer mishandled Taylor's career in its early stages, trying him "as a 'heavy,' in a gangster picture" before Koverman "suggested" Taylor "was unfit for that type of role."[65] He moved into straight roles and became one of the biggest heartthrobs of the decade, thanks to Koverman. She also discovered Nelson Eddy, Robert Montgomery, and Clark Gable, convinced Mayer to pin back Gable's ears and promote him as a star, and "fought like a tigress" to get the best roles for her pets.[66] Paramount and MGM had tried for years to find the right child star for *National Velvet* in the 1930s, and in 1937, it was Koverman who suggested twelve-year-old Leatrice Joy Gilbert to producer Hunt Stromberg after the youngster appeared in full equestrian garb in her office (Koverman had a soft spot for her father, John Gilbert, and felt Mayer had destroyed his career). Koverman's star-making touch was well known by then, and Louella Parsons reported the story as if casting were a done deal (it wasn't, and MGM waited several years before young Elizabeth Taylor, another one of Koverman's surrogate children, could star in Helen Deutsch's classic adaptation of an English schoolgirl who wins the Grand National steeplechase).[67]

But though Koverman took a motherly interest in MGM's heartthrobs and junior talent, her closest relationships were with the studio's other powerful women, from top writer Frances Marion to actress and Academy representative Rosalind Russell. Columnist Jimmy Fidler commented in 1938:

> The other day in the MGM cafe, I made a mental note of six women who were lunching together at a table near mine. Anyone in the world would have recognized five of them—Jeanette MacDonald, Myrna Loy, Norma Shearer, Maureen O'Sullivan, and Rosalind Russell. Few even in Hollywood would have known the sixth, whose name is Ida Koverman. And yet she happens to be one of the most powerful personages in the entire motion picture industry; when she pulls the strings, world-famous stars dance, like puppets. . . . Mr. Mayer's interests are so many that Ida Koverman, gradually, has assumed almost dictatorial power in the studio. I don't know her salary, but it must be fabulous. I do know her authority, and it is colossal. She will be a great power in Hollywood when nine-tenths of today's stars are only vague memories.[68]

Later that year, the *MGM Studio Club News*, a monthly newsletter, did a biographical profile of her career. The picture of a dapper little girl in a rickrack pinafore and straw hat stared out from the front page. Even at the age of ten, Ida Koverman had the self-possession and confidence of a miniature Winston Churchill. This was a little girl who looked ready to conquer the world. "She is known to us all as a good friend, and is nationally and internationally famous," the caption read. Born Ida Brockway in Cincinnati, unlike most of Hollywood's "Cinderellas," she "chose a surer way to a surer success . . . possessing the joy of achievement for a girl who did want to go places in the world but who early saw the value of rising by one's own efforts."[69]

Koverman's story was pitched to the mostly female readership of the *MGM Studio Club News*, hoping to "inspire" other women in administrative positions to rise in their profession. After completing school, Ida chose a business career over teaching school, working as an executive of a jewelry business. She eventually became an executive in the New York offices of the Consolidated Gold Fields of South Africa, where she first met Herbert Hoover. After helping get Calvin Coolidge and Hoover elected (she was executive secretary of both of their presidential campaigns in 1924 and 1928), she accepted Mayer's offer to head "public relations" at the studio. As a *Los Angeles Herald* staff writer commented, "Although her official title at MGM was executive secretary to Louis B. Mayer and later after he left, director of public relations, she was credited with exercising as much influence in the film world as many top executives, and her standing in Republican political circles was equally high."[70]

According to Hopper, Koverman's biggest public relations job was in teaching Mayer table manners: "Ida transformed the once inarticulate ex-peddler of scrap iron into an after-dinner orator in love with the sound of his own voice."[71] Koverman was instrumental in helping Mayer develop his political contacts. In March 1929, the Mayer family, including his two daughters Irene and Edith, were the first nonfamily visitors invited to dine at the White House. The other guest present at that dinner was Ida Koverman. After his visit, Mayer reported that he and the president had discussed "using the 'talkies' in the schools and colleges for educational purposes" as well as "the effect of the talking pictures on our foreign trade." The article claimed Mayer was "one of the 'original Hoover men' in California" and was a key delegate at the Republican National Convention in Kansas.[72] Koverman had arranged the alliance. In 1930, one paper described Koverman's job in highly unusual terms. Mayer "employs continuously a political expert" whose job was "to keep Mr. Mayer advised politically." The article continued, "Mrs. Koverman knows everyone worthwhile in the civic and political world, and on the walls of her office hang personally autographed portraits of President Hoover and former Presidents Wilson, Harding, and Coolidge."[73]

In the early 1930s, there were rumors that Mayer coveted an ambassadorship to Turkey. Had this panned out, Koverman would have had even more day-to-day power at the studio. But if we are to take society and entertainment columnists Elsa Maxwell and Hedda Hopper seriously, Mayer's real interests were not in the running of the studio, but in politics, horses, and chorus girls. Koverman, through her political contacts, quietly pushed Mayer away from studio details and took over much of the running of MGM in his stead.[74] When Mayer's political and diplomatic career didn't materialize, he blamed her and allegedly retaliated by keeping Koverman at her starting salary of $250 a week for twenty-five years (so much for Fidler's guess about her salary!).[75] Annoyed that Koverman "was running the show instead of him," he even tried to get rid of her completely after Thalberg's death. But, according to Hopper, "she had too many friends" for this to happen. It was another woman, Mayer's attorney Mabel Walker Willebrand, who ensured that Koverman would not be fired. When the Roosevelt administration developed a reform bill to prevent racehorse owners from writing off losses and claiming tax deductions unless horses were their one-and-only business, Mayer believed FDR was out to get him. Willebrand told Mayer he couldn't fire Koverman because she was the only one with enough political influence in Washington to help defeat the bill. The bill died, but when Mayer insisted it was *his* influence alone that had killed it, Willebrand allegedly waived her fees for a year in a deal to protect Koverman's position.

Smiling, motherly Kay Koverman was also a veteran of a hundred business and political deals, and not fazed by Mayer's vindictiveness. Though she wasn't a conventional studio star, top still photographer Clarence Sinclair Bull, another of her devoted admirers, made her one in his 1930 portrait (figure 2.1). Seated, her soft, shingled graying hair catching the light, Koverman looks off to the left, a slight smile on her generous mouth. Wearing a draped collarless variation of the business suit, a long silver and pearl necklace causally knotted at her throat, she appears relaxed, efficient, and approachable. It is easy to see why male and female stars alike preferred to take their career and personal problems to Kay rather than L. B. Mayer. Koverman's photographs weren't for MGM publicity; she gave the prints to her friends, and this one is inscribed to Charlotte and Martin Broones, former head of the MGM Music Department, simply "two real people."[76] With so many roles to play at the studio, the pressure was daunting.

During the 1930s, she maintained her own political contacts and developed a group of like-minded and powerful women in the industry. Recall that Jimmy Fidler saw her seated in the MGM commissary with Russell, Shearer, O'Sullivan, MacDonald, and Loy—a heady gathering of the studio's most powerful women—Democrats and Republicans. All of MGM's players and stars ran to "Kay" for protection, whether it was Jeanette MacDonald, whom she advised to invent an engagement to keep the predatory mogul off her, or the young students of the "talent school" she created, including Elizabeth Taylor, Mickey Rooney, and Donna Reed. She stayed close to her

Figure 2.1 Ida Koverman, MGM studio portrait by Clarence Sinclair Bull, 1930

discoveries, and one of them, Jean Parker, was married at Koverman's Santa Monica beach house in 1941.[77] She also did her best to support stars in trouble, but was thwarted by Mayer's obsession with exploiting Judy Garland. According to Hopper, Garland had always been "as close to [Koverman] as a daughter,"[78] at least early in her career. When Mayer ramped-up Garland's work schedule and the exhausted young woman turned to Koverman for help, he engineered an end to their "old intimacy," pushing the star toward drugs rather than a mother figure.[79] Several years later, when Garland's career at MGM was on the skids, the star reached out to Koverman. During Garland's alleged suicide attempts following her suspension from the studio in 1950, only "close friend" Katharine Hepburn and Koverman were admitted to her house on Sunset Boulevard.[80]

Though she was undoubtedly the most powerful woman within the studio hierarchy, Koverman was not alone. When Koverman arrived at MGM, Kate Corbaley had been chief story editor for three years. Corbaley was one of many female story editors and heads of studio writing departments, including Warner Bros.' Irene Lee, appointed in 1939, Elsa Neuberger,

Universal's chief eastern story editor, Columbia's Eve Ettinger, and RKO's heads of story Nan Cochrane and Lillie Messinger.[81] Corbaley, a graduate of Stanford University, made a career as a writer of fiction for popular women's magazines to support herself and her four daughters after her divorce. Following a short stint in Hollywood as a screenwriter, she was hired by Irving Thalberg to head the Story Department in 1926. During her tenure, "An average of 2,000 stories passed through her hands weekly,"[82] and she and Koverman worked together to decide which properties were appropriate for their stars, and then pair them with the appropriate writer. Clark Gable, deeply devoted to both Kay and Kate, remembered the latter as "a wonderfully kind, white-haired, brilliant woman."[83]

Although Hubbard Keavy noted the discrepancy between her power at the studio and the small number of published news items about her, one of the few noted Corbaley's influence in picking Ann Austin's *A Wicked Woman* for Helen Hayes (to be scripted by Josephine Lovett).[84] Although the project was later abandoned, it is worth pointing out the number of women involved in the production. Keavy's article appeared as discussion of women's broader employment across the industry, but his examples were mainly drawn from MGM staff. It is likely that Koverman and heads of publicity Mary Hill, Mary Mayer, and Kate Mulvey were influential in spinning this piece. But Koverman was also directly involved in cultivating a wider press awareness of MGM's coterie of powerful women. In 1933, a series of syndicated press articles quoted her drawing specific attention to two youthful, lively women chatting in the studio commissary, Margaret Booth and Blanche Sewell, in Koverman's opinion "the two best 'cutters' in the business."[85]

In 1935, Louella Parsons covered Koverman's luncheon for Madame Olga Revillion-Masarykova, daughter of the president of Czechoslovakia. Invited to the luncheon were Parsons's journalist rival Hedda Hopper, actress Constance Collier, writer Frances Marion (Koverman's close friend and political associate), and actress Laura Hope Crewes.[86] In the 1940s, Hopper's column took an increasingly political turn, and in the mid-1940s she was often describing the strong political presence of women in Hollywood—Democrats and Republicans. Koverman was mentioned hosting a luncheon for Mrs. Earl Warren where she and Gracie Allen talked about Hopper's "entertaining" column. Hopper revealed that Allen spent most of the afternoon swapping political views with Alice Longworth, "which, if put into script form, would get the comedy rating of the year."[87] In 1945, Koverman again was "seeing that everybody met everybody else" at a tea and reception given in honor of ex-governor of Minnesota Harold Stassen, one of the few prewar anti-isolationist Republicans and then currently part of the US delegation to the UN security conference in San Francisco. A range of Hollywood people attended, from Edward G. Robinson and the Walter Wangers to Virginia Zanuck and Hedda Hopper, and the affair attests to Koverman's ability to reach across party lines for the good of the industry's profile.[88]

She was also a major cultural figure in Los Angeles and in New York. As a young woman, she organized the Women's Athletic Club of Brooklyn and, following her move to Hollywood, chaired the Women's Swimming Association in Los Angeles, served on the Opera Board of Southern California, the Southern California Symphony Association, the St. John's Hospital Guild, the Business and Professional Women's Club, the Los Angeles Advertising Women, the John Tracy Clinic, and the Hollywood Canteen. All of this committee work linked her to other men and women of the film industry and civic culture of Southern California. Koverman was invested in developing her own and other women's visibility in networks of cultural and political power.

Still deeply involved in the day-to-day running of the studio and support of its stars, Koverman stayed out of the early stages of the HUAC controversies. In contrast to Mayer, Koverman did not approve of the Hollywood witch-hunts and continued to offer her tacit support for liberal "message" films such as *Cross Fire, Gentleman's Agreement*, and *Body and Soul* (all 1947), which were all attracting condemnation from conservative groups. In her capacity as "public relations executive" at MGM, she represented Mayer at the third annual Interracial Unity Awards.[89] MGM star Lena Horne attended with her. But Koverman also continued her work for the Republican Party. In October 1947, she, Robert Montgomery, and George Murphy formed the Hollywood Republican Committee, whose members included Ginger Rogers, Barbara Stanwyck, Harriet Nelson, and Jeanette MacDonald.[90] The organization was pitched as a Republican reconquest of Hollywood and dovetailed with Republican efforts for the 1948 election campaign. The next year, she and Murphy, former president of SAG, organized a massive rally for presidential candidate Thomas Dewey at the Hollywood Bowl. Gary Cooper wrote his speech in longhand and then couldn't read his own writing (making the audience and himself break up with laughter), while Ginger Rogers and Frank Morgan also appeared.[91]

Being the top woman at MGM for decades took its toll on her health. In 1948, her heart gave out, and she was in hospitals recovering for months. MGM, Hopper noted with venom, paid for none of her hospital costs. In fairness, Mayer may have had his hands full with Nick Schenck in a corporate war to control the studio. But once Nick Schenck appointed Dore Schary vice president in charge of production, he was persuaded to reinstate Koverman as head of public relations. No longer was she on the books as "just a secretary." And, once officially promoted and less accountable to Mayer, something changed with Koverman.

Although long widowed and childless, the older woman had been the reason MGM had any pretense of a family environment. It was she who was the guiding spirit behind *The MGM Studio Club News* (established in 1936), which celebrated the achievements of all of its employees and displayed a thriving family culture, with picnics, baseball matches, and golf tournaments. Outside the studio, she had mixed with Democratic and Republican women alike. But in 1950, Koverman alienated many of her Democratic female colleagues when she took part in Richard Nixon's divisive senatorial campaign. As one of California's leading Republican organizers, she could not have abstained from the campaign without raising eyebrows. Still, the 1950 election was significant. Helen Gahagan Douglas not only represented the legacy of the New Deal but also, more importantly, Hollywood women's political achievements over the past two decades. Both were under increasing threat by anti-communist smear campaigns. Koverman persuaded fellow Republican Irene Dunne "to make her first television appearance" with Richard Nixon and also encouraged June Allyson, Frances Marion, Esther Williams, and Hattie McDaniel to campaign for him (with McDaniel also agreeing to appear on television in support of the young candidate).[92] Douglas lost.

Koverman was an equal rights advocate; her actions make sense in this framework. The fact that Gahagan Douglas was a woman who fought for many women's issues made no difference to Koverman. But in choosing political party over other women, and urging other Hollywood women to do the same, Koverman did much to break the strong, cross-party alliance that had linked Hollywood's working women since the 1920s. Two years later, Koverman, Dunne, Leo McCarey, Gary Cooper, Cecil B. DeMille, and Hedda Hopper all traveled to the Republican National Convention in Chicago as state delegates (Koverman was also a delegate in 1944 and 1948), thrilled to see the first Republican president in power since Hoover's doomed term in 1928, and a young Californian by his side as vice president.[93]

Although "she lived to see King Louis [Mayer] deposed from his throne" in 1951, she never lived to see Nixon elected twice—or resign in disgrace. Ida Koverman died in November 1954, her good friend screenwriter Virginia Kellogg at her side.[94] Eddie Mannix, then the studio's manager, appointed Koverman's old friend, Republican George Murphy, to take over "the public relations post," and according to Murphy, it was Koverman's "work in keeping touch with the political scene" that was most important to him.[95] By then, of course, no amount of political fixing could stop the film industry's hemorrhaging profit margin. Mayer's death may have signaled the end of an era to some, but with Koverman's death, there was no one to pick up the pieces of the studio system she maintained or the political regime she helped set in motion.

If Ida Koverman quietly shaped MGM's family culture and forever broke the mold of the corporate secretary, then the career of Anita Colby represents a second-generation variation of Hollywood's organization woman. She was born in Washington, DC, in 1914, the daughter of well-known *New York World* cartoonist Bud Counihan, but had little interest in politics. Although she would be elected the president of the Women's News Service in 1957, Colby was not interested in journalism as a young woman and instead concentrated on modeling. When she concentrated on anything, she became the best. Once "the highest paid photographer's model in New York," she launched campaigns for cigarettes, cosmetics, and fashions—her specialty was hats.[96] Colby appeared on over fifteen hundred magazine covers in the late 1930s and early 1940s and was so well known as a Broadway first-nighter and Stork Club regular that Alfred Hitchcock based Lisa Freemont on his memories of Colby when he made *Rear Window* with Grace Kelly in 1954.[97]

Although she half-heartedly tried a film career at RKO in the late 1930s (where executives made her drop her family name Counihan in favor of Colby and cast her as one of Katharine Hepburn's ladies-in-waiting in *Mary of Scotland*, 1936) and dated Cary Grant and dozens of other bachelors, she left, realizing that even America's most beautiful face needed a different act to conquer Hollywood. Fortunately, while at RKO she met Lela Rogers, screenwriter, actress, executive, and mother to Ginger, who gave her and friend and future television producer Lucille Ball acting and career lessons.[98] It was something she also did from the pages of *Photoplay*, advising women on how to become "tops" in their professions.[99] Acting, like modeling, only offered women limited power and financial rewards. And women, more than men, were on a time clock.

It was only in 1943 that Colby was able to put this into practice. She was the original big-city "bachelor girl" and made friends and played the field. Her rule about mixing with everyone at parties made her a variety of useful business contacts. Harry Cohn liked her enough to hire her to play, not a starlet or ingénue, but herself—the one and only "Face" in his new prestige musical, *Cover Girl*. But when she arrived from New York on the *Santa Fe Chief* in early 1943, it was announced she would also "double as technical advisor and publicist."[100] Colby was thrilled: "It's the first time I've been hired for my brains."[101] Cohn was the most important of a handful of producers who promoted women's talent as filmmakers rather than as mere actresses, and he would make screenwriter Virginia Van Upp a producer shortly after she finished writing *Cover Girl* and handling his top star, Rita Hayworth. Van Upp recognized a kindred spirit in Colby, who worked what could have been an informal stint as technical adviser into something bigger. With Van Upp informally managing Rita Hayworth, Colby served as the film's chief press agent or "advance man," touring twenty-four key cities promoting the film on a fifty-nine-day tour.[102] In 1952, she looked back on her early career, remembering the advantages of using the fact that she wasn't just another pretty face: "In my *Cover Girl* job, generalities just wouldn't do—and I was thankful for the explicit working knowledge I had on camera angles, make-up and beauty care, fashion and promotion. I used every bit of it in getting my bevy of modeling beauties before the camera."[103]

Colby was shrewd enough to realize that competing with Van Upp for executive dominance at Columbia would be more difficult than striking out on her own and marketing her talents to another studio. Through agent Kay Brown, she had become best friends with Jennifer Jones, David O. Selznick's future wife, and so Selznick hired Colby as "feminine director" of his studio (figure 2.2).[104] There she worked with Jones and Shirley Temple, and foreign imports Ingrid Bergman, Ann Todd, and Alida Valli. On January 8, 1945, she was on the cover of *Time*, with her star pupils surrounding her in smaller supporting photographs (figure 2.3). " 'The Face' has a brain to match," the caption read. Colby's work with Selznick focused on his follow-up to *Gone with the Wind*—a controversial western about mixed-race Pearl Chavez, *Duel in the Sun* (1946). It was she who pushed Selznick to make *Duel* with Jones in the lead. When shooting finally wrapped, Colby handled the film's lavish publicity with a trio of other women, former MGM writer Inga Arvad, radio star Florence Pritchett, and Powers model and society editor Laura Wells. Selznick was marketing *Duel* as a women's western on many levels, and having Colby manage the publicity was key to this campaign tactic.[105]

But Colby rose still higher when in 1947 Paramount made her "executive assistant to the vice president and production head of Paramount," Henry Ginsberg. She was making over $150,000 a year supervising the careers of top stars Barbara Stanwyck, Paulette Goddard, and Diana Lynn.[106] Though women often served as producers of individual films, and, for a while, Van Upp worked as an executive producer at Columbia, Colby, like Edith Head at Paramount and Ida Koverman at MGM, was in control of aspects of an entire studio's feature output, a "Jill-of-all-trades on the staff" of the studio.[107] Hollywood's women celebrated this major coup for Hollywood's

Figure 2.2 Glamorous executive Anita Colby with David O. Selznick, 1944

"ambassadress of charm."[108] Who needed to be a screen siren when you could be the assistant to Paramount's vice president in charge of production? As Inez Gerhard wrote: "Add brains to beauty and you have Anita Colby."[109]

But Colby wasn't the only one to have this kind of opportunity. Model, future fashion editor, and "close friend" of John F. Kennedy, Florence Pritchett worked something similar out for William Goetz at Universal, and Dorothy Ford, an actress at MGM and, as Louella Parsons put it, a six-foot-two "glamazon," was sent on a three-month tour of the country to talk to editors about *A Miracle Can Happen* (retitled *On Our Merry Way*, 1948).

THE WEEKLY NEWSMAGAZINE

HOLLYWOOD'S ANITA COLBY
"The Face" has a brain to match.
(Cinema)

Boris Chaliapin

Figure 2.3 Colby on the cover of *Time,* 1945, flanked by her charges Shirley Temple, Jennifer Jones, Ingrid Bergman, Joan Fontaine, and Dorothy McGuire

Parsons noted: "She'll do the same kind of job Anita Colby did when she walked into editorial offices and gave a selling talk about *Duel in the Sun*."[110]

Colby was fortunate in her powerful female friends (Koverman and Hopper were particularly close to her),[111] but she knew the risks of being at the top. She kept out of politics, and when pressed, would turn the conversation back to her favorite topics: her businesses and money. These were things working women of whatever party could understand. She used the same tactics with boyfriends who pressed her to marry her, knowing nothing cooled romantic temperatures more than discussions of finance! In order to offset any criticism of a woman wielding that much power in a largely male corporate environment, she countered in one interview that women's work should be in a separate sphere. According to columnist Betty Clarke, Colby argued that "the trouble with American career women" is that "they try to compete with men. If a woman wants to pursue a career she should choose a field which can't be handled successfully by men. This way, she can retain her femininity and skip the tough talking lingo she feels is a part and parcel of a career job when she is competing with men."[112]

This credo partly explained Colby's ability to get to the top of a male-dominated corporation without making too many enemies and maintaining job security. As "executive assistant to the head of Paramount Pictures," she was "called in to give technical advice as to grooming, makeup, and fashion on any studio picture involving women."[113] Colby believed that all career women had to embrace their independent fashion sense, femininity, and simplicity, and like Paramount fashion director Edith Head, she advocated a simple, interchangeable wardrobe with muted colors for all working women. Colby also had some unusual advice for cultivating male business contacts: get to know and like the wives—because they are the ones who will invite the career women back for further business networking dinners!

Unlike Koverman's quarter-century as top MGM woman, Colby remained at Paramount only eighteen months before moving back to New York and becoming her own boss. She was shrewd enough to see how bad politics was for Hollywood business—and social life. As Anita Colby, Inc., she could advise all of the studios and claim higher fees.[114] She also put her writing skills to good work and served as an editor for *Harper's Bazaar*. But her crowning achievement was the publication of her best-selling, multitranslated *Anita Colby's Beauty Book* (which she promoted with her own syndicated column). For several years, Anita Colby's empire dominated American beauty and fashion. And, recognizing the end of Hollywood's control of the media, she moved into television, taking over as *Playhouse* host from Arlene Dahl in 1954, appearing with Ed Murrow on *Person to Person* in 1958, acting as commentator on *The Dave Garroway Today Show*, and producing and hosting her own morning show in the 1960s and early 1970s. A young Barbara Walters began her television career writing copy for Colby.

While Koverman supported both MGM actors and actresses, Colby, in contrast, worked exclusively with women and was proud of it. Although famous on both coasts and in Europe for juggling dozens of beaux, she never married, stating in 1961, "I love working, you know, I'd have to work if I married the richest man in the world."[115] For thirty years, the gossip columnists were kept busy guessing whom she was currently dating or engaged to, but Colby had the last laugh, writing articles and drafting a second book on the joys of being a single woman in the late 1950s.[116] Her glamorous, smiling, successful face beamed from the pages of the New York newspapers, giving the lie to conventional gender assumptions that unmarried career women were disappointed wallflowers and unattractive spinsters.

In her syndicated beauty and fashion column, Colby gave empowering life and career advice to all women, encouraging them to find their own "hidden dynamo that will release your talents."[117] She did not tell women to stay in the home, marry, and settle down, but instead argued that romantic love was only one part of a woman's life. She continued, "Order your mind, and plan your days—your career—your life. Keep remembering that you can always improve—your mind, your viewpoint, your face, figure, and clothes."[118] Colby advocated independence and a classical Greek sense of balance and perspective in every undertaking. She blamed many of Hollywood's men—makeup and hair artists, who had a "rubber stamp" formula for female beauty that tried making every starlet into another Ginger Rogers. With Colby as beauty "director," women in Hollywood and throughout America were encouraged to achieve things on their own terms by finding "a rounded, full life" where mind and body were made beautiful by embracing difference and individuality. Being single was seen as an independent, exciting lifestyle choice. It was a heady mixture of progressivism, glamour, self-reliance, and feminism, and made Colby one of the most successful executives in postwar America.

Anita Colby never lost her girlish laughter. But she manipulated Hollywood as deftly as her string of lovers, and got out of a dangerous relationship at just the right time.

CHAPTER 3
Jills of All Trades

It does my heart good to see a woman get a job of that magnitude.
Louella Parsons, 1944[1]

Ask someone to describe a typical studio-era Hollywood producer. Short. Thickset. Cigar. Gold cufflinks. Receding hairline. Ulcers. A well-upholstered wife at home, and a line of unnatural blondes queuing up for the casting couch at work. The image of studio power is emphatically and obnoxiously male. Whatever Ida Koverman may have achieved at MGM, she still operated in the large shadow cast by L. B. Mayer's egocentric bulk. Anita Colby created her own executive niche, but even at $150,000 a year, she was no mogul calling all of the shots at Paramount. Those in charge of studio production were mostly (with the exceptions of Fox chief of production Winfield Sheehan and his successor, Darryl F. Zanuck) Jewish men. Harry and Jack Warner. Irving Thalberg. David Selznick. Harry Cohn. But all of these men employed women as producers during the 1930s and 1940s. Thalberg made his favorite editor, Margaret Booth, a producer. Jane Loring would later follow this career path at MGM with Pan Berman. Warner Bros. spent years watching Bette Davis virtually produce her own films before accepting the inevitable with B.D. Productions and *A Stolen Life* (1946). After a brief but successful stint in the 1920s producing films starring her dog Strongheart, Jane Murfin returned to work as a producer and screenwriter at RKO in the 1930s. Selznick nurtured teenager Shirley Temple with an eye to turning her into a producer. Harry Cohn outdid everyone at Columbia, employing Theresa Helburn, Harriet Parsons, Virginia Van Upp, Helen Deutsch, and Frances Manson as producers.

Though women worked as assistant producers in the 1930s without credit, during the war and immediate postwar eras, they became a force in Hollywood production and attracted considerable attention in the press. The role of the producer, and Hollywood itself, was in upheaval. In the 1930s and early 1940s, supervising producers such as Irving Thalberg, David O. Selznick, and Darryl F. Zanuck okayed the development of story material and worked closely with a handpicked writer or group of writers to construct the screenplay. Only after a series of script meetings, when the screenplay was deemed ready with a particular set of stars in mind and a budget, did producers assign a director to a picture. Even as the picture was being shot, film editors assigned by the producers had as much creative control on the emerging and final product. But after the war, directors began to lobby for control of the final cut and, through an increasing number of independent production deals, exerted more influence over material and script. The creative process became more and more under the control of one figure, and though occasionally producers in the late 1940s and 1950s maintained a creative foothold in the industry directors, more and more, absorbed the work formerly managed by producers.

The 1940s did have a handful of producers who did more than finance and put a studio stamp on their products; Zanuck and Selznick still dazzled with individual projects, and Hal Wallis and Mark Hellinger were independent names to be reckoned with. But the most significant shift in the wartime and postwar history of the Hollywood producer was the rise of women. Joan Harrison and Virginia Van Upp are best known to film history, but comparatively little has been written about the producing careers of Harriet Parsons, Helen Rathvon, Ruth Herbert, Frances Manson, Ginger and Lela Rogers, Constance Bennett, Joan Bennett, Helen Deutsch, Jane Murfin, Theresa Helburn, Bette Davis, Katharine Hepburn, Kay Francis, and Rita Hayworth. Together with Mary Pickford, longtime partner of United Artists, and Ida Lupino, actress turned writer-director-producer, they formed a formidable contingent of women who were actively seeking to redefine and re-energize the creative role of the producer. Many of these women combined screenwriting, editing, acting, and producing duties. Much of the publicity surrounding their ventures was supportive and even glowing. During this period, two factors converged to advance women's executive roles in Hollywood: women outnumbered men in the United States (millions of whom had been exported to Europe and the Pacific to fight the Axis), and public and cross-party support for the Equal Rights Amendment was at its peak. For a brief time, women in Hollywood were truly calling the shots.

First introduced by Alice Paul's National Women's Party in 1923, the Equal Rights Amendment demanded an end to any sexual discrimination in public or private life. In many states, women still could not serve on juries, have custody of their children, or retain their earnings if they were married. In some states, women were forbidden to run for public office. For professional women earning a living and wanting to protect their property, the gains of the ERA were obvious, and it is significant that support for the movement came first from business and professional women with ties to the Republican Party. Opponents of the proposed amendment used scare tactics, claiming that the "Amazons" were attempting to "thrust women into ruthless competition with men which would precipitate sex war."[2] Prominent Democratic women such as Secretary of Labor Frances Perkins and First Lady Eleanor Roosevelt opposed the amendment in the 1930s, arguing that equal rights were "unrealistic" and, in Perkins words, "equality is sometimes an empty word." Many financially disadvantaged working women believed that "women's problems are somewhat different from those of men," and women with children needed protective employment legislation that the ERA would potentially invalidate.[3]

But in the summer of 1937, bolstered by the New Deal's protective labor measures covering both sexes, the National Federation of Business and Professional Women's Clubs voted unanimously to endorse the ERA. Los Angeles businesswoman Gertrude Mallory proposed the measure. "Times had changed," and Myra Blakeslee concluded, "We shall lack courage if we do not face the issue."[4] In 1940, the Republican Party included the ERA in its election platform. By 1942, more and more Democratic women were pushing for their own party to adopt the amendment. "Now, more than ever before, the Equal Rights Amendment should be passed," they urged. New Deal policies began a cultural change, but, as Mary Padgett stated, the war made up even more minds: "Women are taking their places side-by-side with men in the industrial and civilian defense to meet the needs of the Nation, as well as wearing the uniforms of the fighting forces."[5]

Eleanor Roosevelt and president of the National Consumer League Elizabeth Magee still opposed the amendment, stating it was "a gold brick that may glitter, but would hurt if it hit," and that women would always be physically inferior to men.[6] But given the passage of the Fair Labor Standards Act in 1938 and overtime provisions that "blurred" old labor's objections and their gains in war work, fewer women believed in the "natural limitations" Mrs. Roosevelt spoke of and found them outdated and chauvinist. In addition, many states had already suspended the old protective legislation for women's work during the war, and wages were higher than ever.[7] There were frequent calls to equalize wages, and in 1942, the government began to pressure war industries to comply.[8]

Women viewed these gains and the ongoing struggle for the ERA with equal measures of exaltation and alarm. If Silvia Schulman's Madge was shy about admitting her feminism publicly in 1938, the "Don't ask, don't tell" policy still constrained many women in the 1940s. During the war, columnist Alice Hughes acknowledged the importance of the Equal Rights Amendment, but felt it was "old stuff"; women had come very far since 1923 without it: "We now compete, often successfully, with men in business and the professions, and I know that many men hate this, and fear it too."[9] It was this hatred and fear of empowered women that Hughes knew would cripple her sex in the postwar years. Some women weren't afraid of nailing their colors to the mast. As *The Hollywood Citizen-News* reminded the public, women now made up a quarter of all employees at General Electric, with college women taking over top engineering jobs. Between 1940 and 1945, women jumped from 25% to 36% of all workers, with polls indicating that they wanted to continue working after the war.[10] Women officially gave notice: "Mama won't go back home after the war."[11]

Would the New Deal's labor laws and the transformation of the wartime industrial job sector be enough to protect women's gains in the workplace? Without the ERA, Hughes's unfinished "old stuff" might well return to haunt the next generation. With American men and some of the native misogyny posted to remote locations in the Pacific and European theaters of war, and with women represented equally on the platform committees of the national conventions, women's votes counted more in the elections. In 1944, the National Women's Party urged the president "to throw the full weight of his vast influence" behind the amendment. "The greatest spiritual resolution in the world today," the organization stated, "is the elevation of women to equality with men." If the world war had demonstrated anything, "Without the mobilized power of women, the world cannot be reconstructed as a fit abode for men and women."[12] Women were riding a political tide, but knew their time was limited. They were successful "only because in this election year—with so many men overseas—women are expected to cast 60% of the total presidential vote and thus dominate the election."[13] Toward the end of the war, there was support in both parties for the passage of the amendment, but though it went up for debate, it was tabled in committees.[14]

But in 1946, the measure attracted only a small majority in the Senate, not the two-thirds majority necessary to pass the amendment. Republican senators kept their party's word more than Democrats: twenty-three (70%) voted in favor and ten against, as opposed to fifteen Democrats in favor

(38%) and twenty-four against. However, "A number of Senators who are champions of the proposal were not present to vote," a flagrant disregard for the parties' promises and popular support for the amendment.[15] Defenders of the amendment reminded the public that in some states women still could not engage in independent businesses or keep their wages without their husband's consent, with Susan B. Anthony's grand-niece acknowledging the unpleasant truth, "Women are still second-class citizens."[16] The amendment continued to be introduced in the Senate, and in 1950, it passed in the Senate sixty-three to nineteen, but was defeated in the House.[17] Thereafter, the ERA continued to be reintroduced in the Senate, but it lost momentum until the early 1970s, when it passed both congressional houses in 1972. But, in spite of widespread support from the likes of Bette Davis, the measure failed to be ratified by the required thirty-eight state legislatures by the March 1979 deadline and the June 1982 extension. Women had to be content as an afterthought in the Civil Rights Act of 1964.

Most of Hollywood's top female producers were Republican business-class supporters of the ERA. This made sense, given the party's longer association with the amendment. In the fall of 1943, there were rumors from RKO that Lela Rogers, who for several years had been an executive in charge of RKO's young stars, would be given a producer's job to manage her daughter Ginger's next film.[18] There was never any doubt about where mother and daughter Rogers stood politically—they were straight-down-the-line Republicans. But more than that, both were unashamed feminists, who came from a family whose "independent" women had always "pitched in" and worked for a living.

One columnist claimed Ginger Rogers would sign her next contract "only if she can be assured that her mama, Lela Rogers, will produce all of her pictures."[19] But shortly after completing *Heartbeat* with Cornel Wilde (released 1946), Rogers announced that she would produce her own pictures, with mother Lela and husband Jack Briggs on the board.[20] Warner Bros. star Bette Davis announced a deal around the same time, though she arguably had always "had something to say about story, about choice of director, and casting."[21] Davis, one of Hollywood's most outspoken Democrats, read the shifting political landscape well and opted for an "easy" women's romantic melodrama (*A Stolen Life*) that had no pretensions to being anything but entertainment, but enabled her to play two very different roles. Lela Rogers stated up front that their production company would produce entertainment, not leftist "propaganda," yet apart from Rogers's own media pontificating in the evolving HUAC investigations over alleged communist content in motion pictures in 1947, nothing substantive came of this partnership. Signing Briggs on as coproducer may have been the problem. Rogers had married him during the war, perhaps—like many women—dazzled by the uniform. When the ex-serviceman returned on leave and then for good, she realized her mistake. He was a heavy and abusive drinker, and in a few years, both the marriage and "family" production company were over.

Constance Bennett outdistanced all her actress-producer colleagues. The daughter of Broadway great Richard Bennett became one of Hollywood's most glamorous stars in the 1930s, and in 1931, she was earning $30,000 a week. Her astronomical salaries attracted a great deal of press attention, and Bennett was respected around town as "a shrewd businesswoman." She also ran a successful cosmetics line. Women liked her. It also helped that the much-married Bennett had Elsa Maxwell's seal of approval as "a wonderful mother." She had two daughters, Lynda and Gyl, with her fourth husband, actor Gilbert Roland, and an adopted son Peter (from her second marriage). Equally at ease in comedy or drama, a glamour queen who upstaged even the likes of Joan Crawford and Marlene Dietrich, during the war, she also had her own radio show, and "in her broadcasts," Maxwell reported, she "is seriously tackling many of the women's problems not only of this war but postwar questions as well."[22]

Although her sister Joan had formed a production company with her husband Walter Wanger and director Fritz Lang during the war, *The Woman in the Window* (1944), *Scarlet Street* (1945), and *The Secret Beyond the Door* (1948) were produced and credited to her husband. Similarly, screenwriter Bess Meredyth would form a production company with her husband, director Michael Curtiz, in late 1946. Though Curtiz "will never be without story material as long as his writer-wife is associated with his new company," the company was strictly "Michael Curtiz Productions, Inc."[23] Connie wanted to do the work and have her name in the credits. Thanks to her acute business sense, she had enough personal fortune to pay for the privilege. Bennett's interest in feminism and equality drew her to Etta Shiber's memoir, *Paris Underground* (1943). Adapted by Gertrude Purcell, Dorothy Parker, and Boris Ingster, the book was based on real-life experiences of women saving British airmen from capture during World War II.[24] Bennett worked closely with her writers and supervised every aspect of the production, releasing her World War II female Scarlet Pimpernel spy story through Mary Pickford's United Artists in 1945. The only "message" Bennett's film had, Maxwell said, was in showing "the courage and quick thinking of two women caught in a crisis." According to Maxwell, the blonde star had "wisdom and experience" and "a mind and determination" that made her a natural producer. Bennett was no egoist interested in getting as many close-ups as possible; in fact, critics noted that there were hardly any in this tight thriller.

Being "one of the first woman producers" was one of many jobs Bennett handled with ease. She timed the release of her new clothing line with the premiere of *Paris Underground*. Her beauty secret, typically, was hard work: "If there's a secret, it's working like a beaver to be happy," she laughed. "What I mean is, I've always been interested in everything I did, or else I wouldn't do it. When you're that interested in anything, you're happy."[25] *Paris Underground*, praised as a "vigorous" production, did well at the box office. Critic Irene Thirer set it a cut above the rest of the wartime espionage films audiences had seen since 1942 and toasted Bennett's multifaceted career: "Here's luck to her future enterprises."[26] Although Bennett was working on her next production with her writers (a comedy), sadly it never materialized. Her last starring role, as a lawyer in *Smart Woman* (1948), was released through her production company, but did not bear her name as producer. But Bennett had so many concerns going, including reviving her Broadway career, she was content to let critics hail her as "the busiest star in Hollywood." "I still find time," she grinned, "to do a little knitting."[27]

Bennett succeeded in producing a critical and box-office hit on her own, but she was nearing the end of her Hollywood career. Similarly, though Rogers and Davis may have been at their popular peaks when they formally embarked on producing ventures, both soon experienced career declines. After aging child star Shirley Temple left Fox in 1940 at age twelve and was picked up and dropped by MGM in 1941, she signed a contract with David O. Selznick in 1944. Columnists announced that she was said to be "learning every angle of the picture business" from Selznick so that when her star days were through, "she'll be prepared to move in as a director-producer."[28] Was producing the kiss of death for the powerful Hollywood actress? This question is particularly worrisome when considering the career of Kay Francis, who produced a trio of films for Monogram, *Divorce* (1945), *Allotment Wives* (1945), and *Wife Wanted* (1946), her last film.

Francis, once one of the biggest box-office draws in women's melodramas, had been badly treated by Warner Bros. when she, like Bette Davis, began to complain openly of the exploitation of her career. Although a top box-office draw and all over the covers of 1930s film magazines, Francis's scripts were poorly written and repeated too many stereotypes of home-wreckers and high-class whores. Warner Bros. responded to her complaints by demoting her to B pictures and let her contact run out. The other studios refused to hire her, but old Paramount friend Carole Lombard stepped in and persuaded her studio to hire Francis for a supporting role in her latest picture with Cary Grant, *In Name Only* (1939). Francis entertained the troops during the war and appeared as part of a uniformed quartet in Carole Landis's autobiographical *Four Jills in a Jeep* (1944), which narrated her story of entertaining the troops overseas. The film, given a prestige treatment by Twentieth Century-Fox, represented something of a comeback for Francis, but the Monogram producing deal was the best she could do on her own after the war.

Though her friend Louella Parsons took note of the deal ("Our women are really going places and doing big things in the movies"),[29] this was, of course, nothing to what Mary Pickford, once "the most famous woman in the world," had been doing since 1916. Pickford not only starred in material she approved, she also wrote scripts and occasionally directed (though without credit). With her retirement from acting in the early 1930s, the star had concentrated on her professional role as one of the heads of United Artists' distribution company and was known as "the wealthiest woman in Hollywood."[30] She was no longer actively producing her own films with screenwriter Frances Marion, and her colleague, director-producer Lois Weber, had been on a downward career spiral since the mid-1920s. By the early 1930s, the female directors of the silent era had dwindled to Dorothy Arzner. Mae West, hired in the early 1930s by Paramount to "write and star in a play of her own,"[31] was in a class by herself.

Pickford admitted that she was reluctant to combine acting with off-camera control of the material. She was getting older and recognized that "one can't ponder over business details and look one's best for the camera."[32] Nevertheless, the Hollywood Women's Press Club lived in hope, and there were repeated rumors of deals in the 1930s and 1940s that kept her name in the columns. In 1933, she had plans to make *War Horse* with Gary Cooper and was "enlisting" her old friend and silent-era collaborator Frances Marion to write the script.[33] Though Marion, as a two-time Academy Award winner and MGM's top writer, was interested in the project, it never materialized. Paramount wouldn't loan Cooper. In 1935, following Nick Schenk's withdrawal from the company, she opted to develop a production unit within United Artists. However, the prospect of carrying the complete burden of productions costs must have seemed daunting in the current economic climate. As journalists pointed out, "Miss Pickford's personal fortune is at stake."[34] Only one woman, journalists claimed, "had ever got away with it on a big scale": Lois Weber, who in 1917, headed her own studio. And Pickford remembered what happened to her.

But Pickford pushed ahead, and later that summer, on a trip to New York, she announced that she "will produce as many as six pictures as soon as she chooses a working partner."[35] For her, it was as difficult as choosing another husband—and she was shopping for both. Pickford said, "I have worked actively with men, so I have a male viewpoint—besides my natural feminine intuition." Jesse Lasky coproduced her romantic comedies *One Rainy Afternoon* and *The Gay Desperado* (1936; both starring future director-producer Ida Lupino),[36] and former costar Buddy Rogers agreed to be Mr. Pickford in 1937. After her marriage, journalists again announced she was considering starring in an adaptation of Faith Baldwin's *Portia on Trial*.[37] Again in 1941, she and David Selznick, a consecutive Academy Award winner for producing films aimed at women (*Gone with the Wind* and *Rebecca*) and new partner of United Artists, were allegedly "mulling a new producing combine."[38] Although no Pickford-Selznick productions emerged, Pickford continued to purchase scripts by and about women for potential productions, including Sally Benson's novel *Junior Miss* (1941). Pickford paid a staggering $350,000 for the novel and adapted play, and it was rumored that "after the first picture she will probably make a series."[39] Unfortunately the additional 35% of the royalties was too exorbitant, and after making a few screen tests, Pickford sold the property to Warner Bros.

Even less successful was her purchase of a stake in the Broadway musical *One Touch of Venus* in 1945. After several years since her last picture, Hedda Hopper remained skeptical of Pickford's return to producing: "Things have changed mightily since Mary produced pictures."[40] Pickford soon fell out with Gregory La Cava, who sued her for breach of contract and kept her in the courts for two years, despite superior, appellate, and appeals court judges all ruling in Pickford's favor. Pickford allegedly "reneged" on their agreement for his "producing and directing."[41] But La Cava was notoriously litigious. In 1938, he made use of the House Committee on Un-American Activities to escape having to pay child support to his ex-wife Beryl. When she pursued him in the courts for nonpayment, he tried to gain sole custody of his son "on the ground the boy's mother is teaching him to be a communist."[42] The press had a field day: "His former wife, La Cava set forth, frequently brings persons of radical tendencies to her home and encourages William to listen to them and accept their ideals and manners." Beryl sniffed, "Anyone who does have liberal ideas is classed as a radical, it seems."[43] The courts, smelling a deadbeat dad and a rat, sided with her.

While *One Touch of Venus* stalled and was eventually picked up by Universal for Ava Gardner, Pickford executive produced a series of comparatively unimpressive properties through United Artists (*Little Iodine*, 1946; *Susie Steps Out*, 1946, *High Fury*, 1947; *The Adventures of Don Coyote*, 1947; *Stork Bites Man*, 1947; *Sleep, My Love*, 1948; *Love Happy*, 1949). But columnists weren't really paying attention to her productions. Instead, they were profiling younger women such as Bennett, Virginia Van Upp, and Harriet Parsons who had access to more substantial scripts and female stars. One exception was Bob Thomas, who, in 1947, devoted a large section of one of his columns to Pickford, writing that she had plans to shoot F. Scott Fitzgerald's *Babylon Revisited* and conduct a nationwide search for an eight- to eleven-year-old girl to fill one of the lead roles. Pickford wanted to "nurture" her prospective star "with the possibility of reviving old Pickford vehicles."[44] She had a similar ambition with *Junior Miss*. But when the Fitzgerald project did not work out, she instead toyed with producing her life story. The project would be "the greatest Cinderella story the world has known," Louella Parsons claimed.[45]

Most of Pickford's efforts to become a viable producer centered on reviving the old formulas that had made her a star decades before. Stories of impish adolescent girls still had a market (with Peggy Ann Garner and Margaret O'Brien taking over Shirley Temple's mantle in the 1940s), but it was far more limited than in Pickford's heyday. Similarly, while historical stories about Hollywood were certainly gaining momentum in the late 1940s, with *Sunset Boulevard* (1950), *Singin' in the Rain* (1952), and Edward Small's *Valentino* (1951) in the future, none of these productions represented silent screen divas in a particularly flattering light. In 1956, Pickford sold her remaining shares in United Artists.

Despite her failure to build upon her producing career in any meaningful way, Pickford served as an inspiration for one of her stars, Ida Lupino. Lupino, long in the shadow of Olivia de Havilland and Bette Davis at Warner Bros., became a force in independent filmmaking from 1949. Going the way of an increasing number of actors, writers, and directors, in 1949, Lupino formed The Filmmakers with Melvin Wald and then-husband Collier Young to release several pictures through Howard Hughes at RKO. While other actresses such as Claudette Colbert had "always wanted" a "chance to direct,"[46] only Lupino succeeded. It had been six years since Dorothy Arzner's retirement tribute at the Screen Directors Guild, and Louella Parsons was in Lupino's corner, noting the "young woman with ideas" and her shrewd judgment on story material.[47] Lupino produced and directed *Not Wanted* and *Never Fear* (both 1949) and made even greater strides with *Outrage* (1950), *Hard, Fast and Beautiful* (1951), *The Hitchhiker* (1953), and *The Bigamist* (1953), often working on the script and acting as an uncredited producer. Tough films focused on male protagonists were "her cup of tea," according to Hedda Hopper, who also looked on Lupino's eclectic career with approval.[48]

Her films were a success for RKO, but the rare press profiles of her played up the fact she was the one woman attending directors guild meetings: "Film star Ida Lupino, in forsaking her acting for a career as a producer-director of motion pictures, has discovered that being the lone woman in a 'man's world' can be slightly uncomfortable, to say the least." Although she thrived on the complexities of the job, the article insisted that being the only woman at the job made her "lonesome for female companionship."[49] Unfortunately, her partners decided to go into distribution in 1955 (her films were still making money, and it seemed purely a financially driven decision). So she, like fellow producer Joan Harrison, moved from film to television in the mid-1950s, directing episodes for Harrison on *Alfred Hitchcock Presents, Have Gun–Will Travel, The Untouchables, The Donna Reed Show,* and *Mr. Adams and Eve* (which she starred in with third husband Howard Duff). She and Duff would form their own production company after The Filmmakers disbanded, and Lupino would continue to direct the odd feature film (her last was in 1965).

Lupino was one of the rare women who, at the height of her career, managed to combine work, marriage, and motherhood. Duff, whom she married in 1951, was also her costar and partner in her film company, and their daughter Bridget would later be the company's president. "Ghouls in Hollywood predicted unpleasant consequences for the Duff-Lupino marriage when Howard and Ida joined forces on motion pictures Ida directed," one columnist noted. "After all," another critic asked, "how can you expect a husband to take orders from his wife . . . well, at least in public?" But Duff and Lupino stuck together until 1984. The only inequity Lupino complained about was that because she was directing, "Howard generally gets to sleep longer in the morning."[50]

Despite Hedda Hopper's admiring comments about her hard-boiled proclivities, Lupino liked doing work about women's issues and stories for children. She gave Sally Forrest her big break, starring her in two features that focused on rape (*Outrage*) and unwed motherhood (*Not Wanted*).[51] When Ida was "awaiting the stork" in early 1952, she was writing a story, *The Magic World of Cathy,* about a GI cartoonist who regains his faith in humanity through a child.[52] Shortly after Bridget's birth, she was producing television cartoons for children with Duff. Her "motherly" role extended into her film-directing career. Lupino's set was a matriarchy, with her known popularly as "Mother"—though she often likened herself to a "bulldozer" in her quest for funding.[53] As her career changed from actress to producer-director-writer, Lupino abandoned rules of feminine glamour learned at Warner Bros., wearing Hepburn-esque trousers and sports shirts on location and pushing her trademark curly hair under baseball caps and golf visors as she studied scripts and called the shots.

While Hedda Hopper covered Lupino's career with interest, other critics seemed invested in seeing her alone and embattled, as the only successful female director-producer in Hollywood following Dorothy Arzner's retirement. Yet by the 1970s, in an interview for Bob Thomas, the fifty-two-year-old stated, "I never meant to be a director. I had no driving ambition; it all happened quite by accident. I was making *Not Wanted* for our own company when the director [Elmer Clifton] got sick and couldn't continue. So I moved in and finished the picture. Then the backers said they wouldn't finance our next one, *Never Fear*, unless I directed. So I stuck."[54] Lupino's drive and ambition, though praised by Hopper, had to be managed when she was dealing with male colleagues. Whether it was getting up an extra hour early to fix her unruly hair, or wording directorial orders as "wild" impromptu suggestions to her cameraman rather than carefully considered orders, Lupino did what she had to succeed. A native of England with an acting pedigree that went back to the Renaissance, and, like Davis and de Havilland, a survivor at Warner Bros., it was hard to find anyone with better credentials for succeeding in the world of film production.

Though Lupino was the only woman to act as a prominent producer-director-writer of Hollywood features in the late 1940s and early 1950s, there were a handful of leading full-time female producers working closely with the industry's top actresses, within a range of studios and genres. Joan Harrison, also born in England, had a privileged background similar to a number of other Hollywood writers, executives, and actresses.[55] She was a graduate of St. Hughes College, Oxford, and studied at the Sorbonne before becoming Alfred Hitchcock's secretary in 1933. She was very blonde and photogenic, and played a bit in Hitchcock's *The Man Who Knew Too Much* (1934) with Peter Lorre. To his credit, Hitchcock promoted her to writer in the late 1930s. Daphne du Maurier's romantic best seller about lawless Cornwall, *Jamaica Inn*, was her first major script. In 1939, David O. Selznick brought her and Hitchcock to Hollywood. That June she began adapting another du Maurier property, *Rebecca*, and wrote *Foreign Correspondent* (1940) with Charles Bennett. In 1941, on her impressive $600-a-week salary, Harrison was one of the few writers to have two Oscar nominations in one year, something that irked the misogynistic Bennett, who would claim she did nothing on the script and was nothing but a glorified secretary.[56] However, it was she, not Bennett, who collaborated with Hitchcock on *Suspicion* (1941) and *Saboteur* (1942) and was hired to write the unrealized *The Sun Is My Undoing* (MGM) and *Attack by Night* (later retitled *First Comes Courage*, Columbia, 1943), Dorothy Arzner's last film.

Although Harrison signed a deal to produce with Universal in early 1943, several months passed before she was given a property she liked. During this period, she remained unfazed, and after chatting with her, Hedda

Hopper commented, "She's got her head screwed on in the right way, and I believe she'll open the door for many other women."[57] Harrison revealed that it was her own reluctance to doctor "poor" scripts at Universal that led to her being asked to write and to associate produce in the spring of 1943.[58] Hitchcock sent her three dozen roses for her first day of shooting on *Phantom Lady*, but Harrison, with a touch of humor, took out a big cigar in full view of cast and crew and prepared to light up: "Just to prove I'm the producer," she laughed.[59]

The horror-noir film, starring Ella Raines, was often presented as a contrast to the pretty blonde producer's demeanor. The material was actually a perfect match. Harrison's father was a newspaperman and ran the tri-weekly *Advertiser*; her Uncle Harold was once Keeper of the Old Bailey. She grew up hearing about Britain's most lurid crimes. By the early 1940s, she had made women a significant part of the genre that would one day be known as "film noir." Harrison's landmark script for *Rebecca* is one of the earliest examples of a woman's voice-over (Joan Fontaine, playing Maxim de Winter's unnamed second wife) introducing the story. A poor, frightened ingénue in the past, the older Mrs. de Winter reclaims power over memory and the construction of the story as author and voice (just as du Maurier, who based the story partially on her own troubled marriage to General "Boy" Browning, controlled her depression through writing the novel). Although Ella Raines's "Kansas" had been a minor part in William Irish's original material, under Harrison's supervision, she took on the traditionally male role of private investigator.

As columnist Alice Hughes pointed out, with women patrons dominating film audiences, "It is odd that so few women are boss-filmmakers."[60] Harrison was definitely the boss on her set (as Bob Thomas wrote in 1946, "a no woman" in a yes-man world),[61] but she knew how to balance herself in a workplace often beset by sexism. She commented, "I have to convince the men I'm not a woman, just a producer," and revealed that her strategy was based on dress and manipulating her male coworkers. At first, she would wear "business-like" suits to keep the set orderly, but if there was "any difficulty in cooperation," she switched to more feminine clothes. This was a strategy she used when marketing herself as Universal's only female producer in 1943 and something Lupino occasionally admitted to doing a few years later on the set. When the photographer was shooting straight publicity portraits for her new job, Harrison was reported to have asked "sadly," "Don't you want any leg art?"[62] She did have a nice set. Harrison knew the value of exploiting her looks and disarming men who feared or distrusted women with power and bigger salaries (figure 3.1). But, far from complaining about being a woman in a so-called man's world, Harrison later claimed: "Being a girl helps in business. I think my crew works harder for me because I am woman. They also know I know my job."[63]

Harrison worked at Universal, United Artists, and RKO and, like her colleagues, oversaw moderate hits and melodramatic disasters. Although *Uncle Harry* (1945) was hampered by Production Code Administration (PCA) censorship, she had more control over her director, *Phantom Lady* veteran Robert Siodmak, and the film was well received.[64] Eileen Creelman was full of praise for Harrison's cowritten and coproduced "spine-chilling melodrama" *Dark Waters* (1944), but the critic ripped into her "sloppy" work producing the popular detective drama *Nocturne* (1946).[65] The murder plot had comic sides that undoubtedly tickled Harrison: a dead composer has at least ten girlfriends—all with murder motives. George Raft, one of the town's most notorious womanizers, was cast, not as the victim, but the grim-faced detective.

Perhaps more than Van Upp, Harrison suffered from comments that she was Hitchcock's former secretary and "protégé": press of the time indicates that Harrison was "given" tailor-made suspense stories by the

Figure 3.1 RKO Producer Joan Harrison, unimpressed by her *Nocturne* writer, John Latimer, 1946

studio bosses, rather acting as a free agent making her own decisions about properties to develop.[66] This was an unfair charge, given her often uncredited work on the scripts of her films, including *Ride the Pink Horse* (1947), directed by and starring Robert Montgomery. But by the late 1940s, Harrison's career in Hollywood was largely over. She produced one more major film, Montgomery's *Your Witness* (1950), for Warner Bros. in the United Kingdom, which also reunited her with Leslie Banks, the star of her first collaboration with Hitchcock back in 1934.

Television had cut Hollywood's profit margin, and Harrison knew when to leave the party. The real opportunities were now on small screens. In 1954, she produced *Janet Dean, Registered Nurse* (starring her *Phantom Lady* star Ella Raines), before returning to work with Alfred Hitchcock as associate producer (1955–57) and then producer (1957–62) of *Alfred Hitchcock Presents* and the *Alfred Hitchcock Hour* (1962–65). As Hitchcock's television producer, "She selects the story material, supervises the script writing, casts the actors, and keeps a watchful eye on the final editing."[67] Harrison commented that her job was essentially "bringing together in harmony all the elements that go into a series."[68] But, even in an era increasingly dominated by director-driven auteur theories (and worse, directors who believed them!), she told Bob Thomas it was crucial for a producer "to make certain that his conception of the story is carried out."[69] When she had differences with directors, she met with them privately rather than having it out on the set. "After all," she reasoned, the producer "is the one who has selected the story, had it written, arranged the casting and sets."[70] The original values—the producer's values—were paramount.

Though Harrison, with her Oxbridge diction, used the singular "his" in her interview with Thomas, *she* was the producer on *Alfred Hitchcock*. It was her way on her set. In another interview, she insisted that women could still become producers with enough drive and determination, but that most women "won't spend the time required. . . . It's a full time career that doesn't leave much time for early romance and a family."[71] But these weren't things she wanted: "A healthy salary, professional recognition and the sense of a job well done are enough." Truth be told, she didn't have time for anything else. Whereas in Hollywood she would be working on, at most, one to two film scripts a year, in television she was "up to my neck" in "more murders than I ever thought existed in print."[72] It was the life she loved.

By that time, Harrison, who had put early marriage aside to pursue her Hollywood career (and date Clark Gable), wed screenwriter and novelist Eric Ambler in 1958. The pair continued their separate careers and quiet home life amicably, with Harrison pointing out that sometimes the happiest marriages weren't the most traditional. Although people "might find our home life a little dull," the couple had "no pool, no poodle, and no psychiatrist."[73]

Harrison's colleague Gail Patrick, a former actress, had also made a high-profile transition to television producer following her decision to quit screen acting in 1948, remarry, and adopt children (her twin boys from an earlier marriage died soon after birth). She had been one of the screen's most accomplished unsympathetic bitches, known for *My Man Godfrey* (1936), *Stage Door*, and *My Favorite Wife* (1940). But by the early 1950s, Patrick was tired of "being a mass of frustrated femininity"—a pampered housewife—and, with the help of literary agent and husband Cornwell Jackson, developed one of his client's properties for television.[74] The client was Erle Stanley Gardner, and the property was the *Perry Mason* mystery series. Gardner allegedly suggested that Patrick be the executive producer and stated, "With her experience in films, Gail was a natural." Star Raymond Burr was full of praise: "'She is the most fabulous woman I know,' he gushed. 'She's not only a great success as a wife, actress, producer and woman, but she's extremely well-liked by every member of this company. She never orders, only suggests. She never raises her voice, never pulls rank. I tell you this. . . . She is the closest thing to a dream I've met in this business.'"[75] But Patrick was also a superwoman, it seemed. She dropped the kids off at school, did all the cooking, and fixed their lunches—all this while looking chic and managing one of the most popular shows on the networks (1957–1966). But in spite of the way journalists dwelt on her equally stunning work ethic and feminine charm, they indicated that she was not alone: "Married career women are of two types: those who work because they have to, and those who work because they want to."

But there were more than two categories of working women in Hollywood.

Virginia Van Upp began her career another way. She was born into the business. Her mother, Helen Van Upp, was an editor and screenwriter, and at the age of five, Virginia was a child star. When she grew up, she became secretary to director Fred Niblo, and later worked as an assistant film editor before moving into the script department at Paramount. As one critic pointed out, it took longer for her to reach screenwriter status, but she learned things about filmmaking few writers had any knowledge of: "Maybe it isn't exactly typical, because there were eight years between her decision to become a writer and the accomplishment in 1934. She typed scenario writers' manuscripts, gratis, to learn the mechanics of fashioning stories. She learned more in other jobs, which included tedious script copying, stenography, and secretarial work. She also was a reader, synopsizing novels and plays."[76] She quickly became one of the studio's most successful writers, specializing in fashionable modern comedies starring Carole Lombard and Madeleine Carroll and aimed at women. In 1937, she had plans to adapt *Are Husbands Necessary?* for the studio's top star, Claudette Colbert,[77] and her vehicle for Madeleine Carroll and Fred MacMurray, *Café Society* (1939), won critical and popular success in a year dominated with major films. In the late 1930s, she was profiled to explain how to create a working set to mainstream film fans. In the feature article, Van Upp was introduced "striding through" her latest script, dictating to a secretary, and the inside scoop on Hollywood production showed a uniformly male group of set designers having to "project" her ideas.[78] As other critics had noted, Van Upp was at that time "one of the country's highest paid scenarists."[79]

One critic called Van Upp a "typical" successful Hollywood woman in 1939. At that time, she was in the $1,500-a-week class of writer.[80] Although a number of women could be counted among Hollywood's most highly paid and successful writers, fewer of these were happily married unless their collaborators were also their spouses (Sarah Y. Mason, Frances Goodrich, Tess Slesinger, and Florence Ryerson are among the few). But Van Upp was one of a minority of married Hollywood women (husband Ralph Nelson also worked for Paramount).[81] For a while, she was able to balance work and family life and wield surprising cultural influence in the columns. In 1941, "one of Hollywood's foremost scenarists"[82] could be found on the train back from Nassau talking with former New York governor and presidential candidate Al Smith about "writing his biography for a movie."[83]

But it was her move to Columbia and Harry Cohn that redefined her career. Van Upp met Rita Hayworth when both were near the peaks in their careers. They became close friends making *Cover Girl*, which Van Upp wrote. Van Upp's writing was carefully tied to Hayworth's persona and appearance. She gave interviews about the use of Technicolor for the film and how it influenced the creation of Hayworth's character, "Rusty."[84] It was the first of several pairings with director Charles Vidor, and because the film became the studio's biggest success of the year, Cohn promoted Van Upp to associate produce as well as writer. Although Bob Thomas credits Rita Hayworth with persuading Cohn to appoint Van Upp the producer of her next film, *Gilda,* it was not a particularly radical move for Cohn to hire Van Upp in this capacity, and in fact she would produce other films prior to *Gilda.*[85]

Van Upp was not the only woman at Columbia to call the shots. In the early 1930s, in addition to having Harriet Parsons produce and direct shorts, he hired Theresa Helburn of the Theatre Guild as a top production executive. For four months of the year, Helburn, "one of the outstanding women of the theater," would oversee the Theatre Guild, and for eight months, she would remain in Hollywood.[86] Before signing the contract, Helburn had spent "a three-months' period of observation" at Columbia. As columnist Lloyd Pantages commented, "Columbians will have first call on all Theatre Guild Productions which Miss Helburn heads. This bit of information will irk the other studios a-plenty."[87] Helburn found the strain of handling both jobs too much. After the first year of her contract elapsed, she returned to New York, overseeing the production of *Porgy and Bess* and *The Taming of the Shrew*.[88] But while at Columbia, Helburn had purchased screenwriter Oliver Garrett's *Gentleman in High Boots* with an eye to producing it independently on Broadway. The producer and writer promptly abandoned Hollywood "to produce something worthwhile."[89]

In the 1930s and early 1940s, Cohn was one of the few producers to support Dorothy Arzner's career. *Craig's Wife* (1936) had been a huge critical success for the studio in the 1930s, and in 1943, Columbia proudly advertised her as "back in business" with the wartime *Attack by Night* (later renamed *First Comes Courage*, 1943, starring Merle Oberon as a Norwegian resistance worker and edited by Arzner's old friend on *Craig's Wife*, Viola Lawrence). Though illness kept her from finishing the film, and Charles Vidor was brought in to finish the work, Cohn gave Arzner sole credit. The columnists called for the studios to develop the careers of "two or three other women directors if they can be found," arguing, in line with the Equal Rights Amendment language of the time, "If women taxi drivers, and women scenarists, and women film cutters, and women barbers, why not women directors?"[90]

At Arzner's retirement dinner at the Screen Directors Guild in 1943, friend, colleague, and Screen Writers Guild president Mary C. McCall Jr., Rosalind Russell, and Joan Crawford paid tribute to their friend's career, which had long focused on powerful narratives about women (*The Wild Party*, 1929; *Christopher Strong*, 1933; *Craig's Wife*, 1936; *The Bride Wore Red*, 1937; *Dance, Girl, Dance*, 1940). But at the back of their minds, they wondered how to continue to push for women's representation at higher levels of film production. The studios responded with appointments of women to top production roles: Harrison (Universal), Parsons (RKO), and Van Upp (Columbia).

But Harry Cohn would again lead his colleagues in appointment of women producers. In 1943, in addition to hiring Van Upp, he made Frances Manson a producer. She was originally in Columbia's script department and then transitioned to screenwriter. In the summer of 1946, Cohn also hired Helen Deutsch, who had been instrumental in developing successful women's pictures at MGM, to be a producer.[91] She worked on two Columbia films, coproducing *The Guilt of Janet Ames* (1947) with Van Upp and Sam Fuller's *Shockproof* (1949), but received no credit on either picture. Deutsch preferred working as a writer, and often guild affiliations prevented writers from receiving screen credit as both writers and producers. She returned to MGM and her roots on Broadway, where she had first worked as a secretary to Theresa Helburn at the Theatre Guild after graduating from Barnard. But for a few years in the 1940s, Harry Cohn made history for not only having the only female studio executive producer in the industry, but also "the greatest number" of women producers at one studio "in the history of the industry"—three.[92] As Dorothy Manners admitted, "Harry has done all right with women producers."

Van Upp's first film as producer was *The Impatient Years* (1944, coproduced with director Irving Cummings), about quickie wartime marriages, starring Jean Arthur and Lee Bowman (who had been part of *Cover Girl*). Later in 1944, Van Upp was reportedly working on a romantic comedy re-pairing of Boyer and Dunne (who had made a success in Leo McCarey's *Love Affair*, 1939) "for her first solo as producer."[93] In *Together Again* (1944), Dunne would play a widow who had succeeded her husband as mayor of their Vermont town. Boyer arrives with his continental charm and unthaws the frigid New England town and its mayor. Later in September, Van Upp was set to produce a property for Rosalind Russell, *Some Call It Love* (retitled *She Wouldn't Say Yes*, 1945), about "a busy woman psychiatrist."[94] Louella Parsons noted the trend toward films about professional women, citing the film's obvious connection to Ingrid Bergman's world-renowned psychiatrist in Alfred Hitchcock's *Spellbound* (1945). But more and more, columnists drew attention to her as one of three key Hollywood producers who were women, and emphasized that since she had at one time held every job in Hollywood from cutter to secretary to actor's agent: "You can learn about films from her."[95]

Cohn kept Van Upp busy in 1944, and in December he promoted her to "the biggest executive job yet given to any woman in the movies": chief executive producer.[96] It made her "next of importance to Monsieur Cohn." But as far as Louella Parsons was concerned, Van Upp had "what it takes" and concluded, "It does my heart good to see a woman get a job of that magnitude."[97] As another staff writer commented, "In Hollywood, Virginia Van Upp is known as the 'Jill-of-all-trades-of-the-movies.' And she is acknowledged to be past-master of all."[98] While the old studio moguls had started as glove salesmen before venturing into exhibition and production, Van Upp was profiled as a Hollywood insider who knew every job in the film business inside out. One critic explained her executive producer's job to the public: "She bosses eight other producers at Columbia."[99] Cohn seemed to delight in shaking up the studio's male egos. According to Bob Thomas, when the nine male candidates refused to congratulate her, he sacked them.[100]

As an executive producer, she could also pick and choose "to personally produce such stories as attract her individual interest."[101] The zenith was her second Hayworth film, *Gilda* (Van Upp's cowriter on *Cover Girl* and future television producer Marion Parsonnet also worked on the script). Publicity around the film emphasized it as a Van Upp production.[102] After the success of *Gilda*, Cohn planned to reunite Van Upp with Hayworth and Vidor, but things stalled. Van Upp was rumored to be ill in early 1947, either strain from overwork or difficulty with Columbia egos, but she returned to the studio in March.[103] Allegedly, Van Upp was slated to write the original story, *Woman Order*, with Charles Vidor to direct. Vidor had a recent spat with Cohn after the director "had decided against continuing there as an independent producer" but was said to have returned just for this one production.[104] Van Upp's name, strangely, was mentioned only as writer. Although she had stepped down from her role as executive producer by then, she still operated as one of Columbia's producers. Possibly Vidor's ego was bruised by Van Upp's former executive role at the studio (and the fact that Hayworth was also getting a percentage of the gross). In any case, the film wasn't made, nor the subsequent *Loves of Carmen* with the same Hayworth-Ford-Vidor-Van Upp team.[105] Instead, her Columbia producer colleague Helen Deutsch wrote the script, and Hayworth, who learned a thing or two from Van Upp, coproduced with Vidor.

Van Upp's plans to write and produce a film for Lucille Ball in 1948 (inaptly titled *Pink Lady* in view of the HUAC hearings and Ball's liberal reputation) and her planned biography of silent-era heartthrob Rudolph Valentino were also abandoned.[106] Although she worked on Florence Ryan's original 1939 script, Edward Small did not hire her to coproduce and gave George Bruce sole credit (the film was eventually released in 1951 with Anthony Dexter and Eleanor Parker). Only *The Guilt of Janet Ames*, made prior to her leave of absence, has her name on it.

But journalists marveled at her energy and drive, and Van Upp took a shot at her domesticated sisters in an interview with Josephine Lowman: "You simply cannot grow old if you are bored and I think professional women look younger than housewives for this reason."[107] Although she was one of a handful of professional women in Hollywood to combine career, marriage, and motherhood (her daughter Gay Nelson was also a child actress), her marriage to associate producer (and at one time, her assistant) Ralph Nelson fell apart soon afterward, and they divorced in 1949. Van Upp admitted that the same "enthusiasm" and "optimism" that kept her career moving "frightened her husband."[108]

In the early 1950s, both she and Rita Hayworth were in need of career facelifts (both Van Upp—again behind the scenes—and Viola Lawrence had done their best to prevent Orson Welles's *Lady from Shanghai* [1948] from destroying Hayworth's career, but the damage was done). Hayworth's marriage to Orson Welles was over, and she had left Hollywood for an extended tour of Europe, where she met her next husband, Aly Khan. When this marriage also fell apart, Hayworth was left with no savings and needed to go back on salary. In the summer of 1951, she and her two little girls took up the required residence in Nevada for her divorce from Khan, but she made a quick trip with them to Hollywood, her first in three years. The purpose? "To confer with writer Virginia Van Upp on her next picture at Columbia."[109] Shortly before beginning work on *The Rita Hayworth Story* (later renamed *Affair in Trinidad*, 1952), Van Upp was quoted as saying, "My heart goes into any story I write for Rita. She is not only a star but as you know she has my personal love as well as my professional admiration."[110] But within a few months, Van Upp left Columbia over a basic story disagreement with Cohn. According to Cohn, "She could not stay away from the *Gilda* story," and James Gunn was brought in quickly for "some new ideas."[111] Unfortunately, Gunn had no new ideas, and *Affair in Trinidad* made less at the box office than Hayworth's other pictures.

After leaving Columbia in the middle of writing *Affair in Trinidad*, Van Upp went to Germany for eighteen months, "making propaganda films for the U.S. government."[112] She negotiated a new deal with Republic to produce, direct, and write a film based on her original fiction story about "the Allied underground" called *The Big Whisper*, getting 50% of the cut for herself.[113] Evidently, Chancellor Adenauer, the newly elected anti-communist leader, gave her "full cooperation" on the project, which was to have "many escapees from the Russian zone" working as actors.[114] Unfortunately, the film was never made. Her reputation as a producer had slipped so much that in 1953, when the papers revived interest in Hollywood as a career place for women, Van Upp was mentioned only as "one of the highest paid" of the industry's screenwriters (a quarter of whom were identified in the article as women).[115] Even Van Upp's rumored film for newcomer actor Robert Stack at Twentieth Century-Fox, *Mock the Midnight Bell*, came to nothing.[116]

It was at this point, in late 1955 in a career low, that she and Ralph Nelson remarried.[117] The couple had divorced during the peak of her career as producer-writer. It did not help that, as Hedda Hopper put it in 1946, "Maj. Ralph Nelson, out of uniform, becomes assistant to wife, Virginia Van

Upp."[118] Divorces were frequent among Hollywood's professional women. Joan Harrison married Eric Ambler only after her Hollywood career was over and she was comfortable with a new career in television, and Harriet Parsons's brief marriage to "King" Kennedy fell apart as her career began to take off in the early 1940s.

The mid-1940s and the immediate postwar era were an all-too-brief golden period for female producers. In 1945, Harriet Parsons's mother, Louella, described the high-powered female world of the media: "Mary Anita Loos's and Richard Sale's farewell cocktail party for Dorothy Kilgallen went on way past dinner time. About twenty people stayed on for dinner. Harriet Parsons and Joan Harrison with their heads together talking over—what? A woman producer's troubles, I reckon. Joan was there with Billy Wilder and Harriet with DeWitt Bodeen."[119] They were hardly there with their dates—even though both were single (Parsons had divorced her husband of five years in 1944, due to jealousy over her career). Wilder was, like Harrison, one of the few successful writers to transition to directing or, in Harrison's case, to producing. Bodeen was Parsons's handpicked writer for *The Enchanted Cottage*, her recent RKO production. But Kilgallen was a big Hollywood player in her own right. Known from 1936 as the "New Nellie Bly" for her round-the-world correspondent's stint (she raced two other male reporters around the world and won),[120] by 1946 she was one of Hollywood's top columnists for *Modern Screen*, competing with Hopper and Parsons for eight million readers a month and forty newspapers.[121]

While in recent years, film historians have looked predominantly at Hitchcock collaborator Joan Harrison and Virginia Van Upp's careers as exceptional female producers in the studio era, less is known of Harriet Parsons (figure 3.2). Like Harrison, she was well educated. An alumna of Wellesley College, class of 1928, Parsons began as a journalist covering Hollywood shortly after graduation. She had her own syndicated column and often focused on women's issues and film projects. In 1934, she was put under contract at Columbia to write, edit, direct, and produce shorts, and by the early 1940s, fed up with not receiving screen credit, she made a move to produce, first at Republic and then at RKO from 1943. She became one of the industry's leading producers in the 1940s, responsible for Dorothy McGuire's *The Enchanted Cottage* (1945) and Irene Dunne's critically acclaimed *I Remember Mama* (1948), directed by George Stevens. As with Anita Colby and Virginia Van Upp, Parsons's greatest achievements involved female-centered films for major stars. Her work kept RKO a viable artistic and financial presence in the late 1940s, capitalizing on the long-established trend in women's historical films and melodramas.

Figure 3.2 Harriet Parsons on the set of *Night Song* with mother Louella and director John Cromwell, 1947

Parsons took longer to emerge from her mother's oppressive shadow in journalism. In 1931, Harriet Parsons took over her mother's syndicated press column while the elder Parsons devoted more time to radio programming. Harriet Parsons was then in her midtwenties, and the majority of her articles focused on women in Hollywood, as well as the more bite-sized gossip entries in "Hollywood Snapshots."[122] She continued writing the column throughout the 1930s, and when Warner Bros. decided to develop a film based on her mother's radio show *Hollywood Hotel*, reported that Bette Davis had been given the leading role.[123] It was wishful thinking. Davis might have been happy to star in a biopic about Louella Parsons's career in journalism, but by 1937 she was tired of Hollywood ingénue roles, and the film became a Busby Berkeley musical starring the milder song-and-dance talents of Rosemary Lane and Dick Powell.

Parsons began her career as a producer of short films at Columbia, working on the *Screen Snapshots* documentaries (the series lasted from 1924 to 1958). Although originally Jack Cohn, Harry's brother, had developed the idea for one-reel short documentaries about contemporary Hollywood to run before all of the studio's feature output, by 1934, when Harriet began to work on the thirteenth series as an executive producer, Harry was in charge of hires on the project, and originally asked her mother to produce the newsreel "which takes audiences behind the scenes with picture people." "Mother couldn't do it," she reminisced to Irene Thirer, "so it was handed over to me. And I was thrilled to accept."[124] Her work writing, directing, and producing fifty-six shorts released between 1934 and 1940 was uncredited and attributed instead to Ralph Staub. However, she demanded and received screen credit on a new series for Republic, *Meet the Stars* (1940–41). In her last short film before turning feature producer, Parsons focused on Mabel Normand, the famed comedian and silent star. Old and new stars gathered at Republic Studios to witness the dedication of their new soundstage in her memory. In 1942, she acted as associate producer on Republic's Nazi spy-ring drama *Joan of the Ozarks*, starring comedian Joe E. Brown.[125] But Parsons was ambitious and wanted control of bigger productions more suited to her talents. She moved to RKO, where, until 1935, Jane Murfin had been an associate producer.[126]

But turning feature producer in a field entirely dominated by men was difficult. Parsons thought she had solved this dilemma by purchasing Arthur Wing Pinero's World War I veteran love story, *The Enchanted Cottage*. It had been a successful film for May McAvoy and Richard Barthemess back in 1924, and Parsons believed that an updated version for World War II audiences would be a box-office success. Sam Goldwyn agreed to lend her Teresa Wright to star.[127] RKO executives then took the property away from her and handed it over to Dudley Nichols. The same thing happened again when she dug up Kathryn Forbes's 1934 book, *Mama's Bank Account* (eventually produced and retitled as *I Remember Mama*). When Hedda Hopper heard about this, she was outraged, and wrote a column published February 21, 1944, in the *Chicago Tribune* blasting the studio for its gender bias. As she wrote,

> What goes on at RKO with Harriet Parsons? The studio signed her as a producer. She digs through its files and finds *Enchanted Cottage* and arranges a deal with Sam Goldwyn to borrow Teresa Wright for it. Then it's snatched away and given to a big writer-producer. Then she digs up *Mama's Bank Account* and gets Katina Paxinou all set for it. Now that, too, has been snatched away from her. What goes on? Harriet's clever, and I think this is pretty shabby treatment, even for Hollywood.[128]

The day after the item appeared in her column, RKO executives gave *The Enchanted Cottage* back to her. Hopper was triumphant: it was a credit to her influence in Hollywood and her commitment to opening up filmmaking opportunities to other women. Her liking for Louella's daughter led to a temporary truce in their press feud; Harriet persuaded her mother to call and thank Hopper for her help in the column, and the three sat down to lunch together at Romanoff's. But, as Hopper ruefully recalled, the "Versailles Peace Treaty" extended only as far as Harriet's career.[129]

Parsons wrote the outline and script with collaborator DeWitt Bodeen and selected John Cromwell, who had worked so well on women's pictures for Selznick (Cromwell's *Since You Went Away*, 1944, had outdistanced even *Gone with the Wind* in its first week at the box office), to direct. Selznick also helped Parsons by loaning out youthful Broadway star Dorothy McGuire (*Claudia*, 1943) to play the homely girl who marries a wounded soldier and who gradually transforms into a beauty as their romance grows. MGM, through Hopper's connections, lent Robert Young, who had recently starred with McGuire in the successful *Claudia*. The ugly duckling, wartime romantic story was popular, making a nearly $900,000 profit for the studio. A great deal of publicity focused on Parsons. She and McGuire worked well together, with McGuire noting that Parsons gave in to her star's instincts about subtle rather than exaggerated makeup for the film: "She is so intelligent and so understanding," McGuire enthused.[130] *New York Evening Post* journalist Irene Thirer devoted her column to the growing ranks of female producers (Mary Pickford, Constance Bennett, Joan Harrison, Virginia Van Upp) and focused on Parsons. Thirer rather daringly emphasized Parsons's drive and enjoyment of being a power broker in Hollywood. While in her interview, Parsons also avoided discussing the behind-the-scenes struggle to keep *The Enchanted Cottage* as her project, the producer was quoted: "There's no resentment, no opposition to women producers in Hollywood. It's the women themselves who, for the most part, prefer other jobs in the industry. They're scared of the headaches involved: budget trouble, cast difficulties, wardrobe, sets, properties, a thousand and one other responsibilities."[131]

Other interviews focused on the contrast between her feminine persona and powerful new job—a tactic used in many of Harrison's early media appearances. In a major interview with Parsons shortly after *The Enchanted Cottage*'s New York opening, Margaret Mara opened with Parsons's advice "to the girls in increasing numbers who will hold jobs after the war": "Be feminine!"[132] Mara was focused on making Parsons appear the antithesis of the typical male producer, and dwelt on her diminutive 5'1" height and rose-topped hat—things that *New York Sun* columnist Eileen Creelman and Thirer mentioned.[133] Parsons was no "Amazon" and was even quoted saying she did especially not want to become a producer: "I don't approve of mannish, masterful women and I think men resent them in business. It has been my experience that men prefer dealing with women who allow them to open doors for them and perform all the gallant services due to a woman. Men like being gallant. It satisfies their ego."

Both Mara and Creelman stayed far off the topic of RKO executives' misogyny and near derailment of her career as a producer. Instead, in Mara's interview Parsons emphasized her women friends in Hollywood, from her tennis chum Claudette Colbert to silent star Billie Dove and Ethel Barrymore. The articles, more than anything, attempted to package Parsons's success to other women, neither man-eater nor man trap, who worked hard for her success as a producer but would be just as happy cooking at home. Creelman was more invested in Parsons's experience as a producer of shorts for Columbia and at Republic, and in her desire to "keep on doing something different" rather than being typecast for particular genre films.

With some exceptions, journalists' approach to women in positions of power in the postwar period tended to follow this pattern. While coverage from the Depression era focused on their hard work and commitment to their careers, and columnists continued to note the growing number of female producers in postwar Hollywood, Colby, Parsons, and even Dorothy Kilgallen advised women to be careful about showing men just how smart they were. Rather than the brash, tough spirit that dominated so much coverage from a decade before, professional women were advocating a careful kind of diplomacy. In a write-up in the *Woman's Home Companion*, Dorothy Kilgallen, newspaper columnist and radio broadcaster, "who hardly hides her brain under a bushel," admitted, "I'd rather be mistaken for a cutie than a quiz kid any day. Ladies should be subtle about showing their brains and they usually get along better if they let their gray matter operate on the QT."[134]

This strategy worked for a while at RKO. Parsons went on to produce *Night Song* (1947) with Merle Oberon and Ethel Barrymore; *Never a Dull Moment* (1950), originally planned for Ann Sothern before Irene Dunne was assigned to costar with Fred MacMurray;[135] Barbara Stanwyck and Robert Ryan's steamy noir *Clash by Night* (1952); and the Debbie Reynolds comedy *Susan Slept Here* (1954), all for RKO. But her most famous production was *I Remember Mama*, her first of two films with Irene Dunne, and one of the two early properties RKO had tried to steal from her and give to male producers. Hedda Hopper was still a great fan of Parsons, and reprinted the text of her original February 21, 1944, column to shame executives one more time, something that delighted another one of Parsons's fans, Ginger Rogers.[136]

In looking at high-powered female screenwriters, Lizzie Francke would argue that these women were out for themselves and lacked the feminist commitment to creating a women's working culture to nurture or at least sustain other prospective women in the industry—hence the scarcity of powerful women in Hollywood. While women's presence in the screen-writing profession was too significant to give credence to Francke's speculations, there were fewer female producers during this period (though certainly more than historians have realized). But certainly, a culture of support existed among female journalists, writers, producers, and actresses to negotiate and celebrate achievements. As Hedda Hopper exclaimed over Van Upp's big break as a producer: "Hurray! Another Hollywood woman gets her chance."[137] When Van Upp signed another seven-year contract with Columbia in 1947,[138] the buzz about women producing only increased: at twenty-two, actress Joan Leslie was rumored to be setting up her own production company (her first comedy to be titled *Shut Up, My Love*), and Ruth Herbert, former story editor at *Cosmopolitan*, was said to be producing *Career in Manhattan* for Eagle-Lion. But columnist Jack Lait reported equably, "The men-folk don't resent the female invasion. The ladies are pleasant to work with and they pretty up the place."[139]

Parsons's success at RKO also inspired Helen Rathvon, the wife of a former boss at the studio, to produce. But the noir drama directed by Paul Sloane, *The Sun Sets at Dawn*, was an independent production released through Eagle-Lion and not RKO in 1950.[140] Interestingly, Eagle-Lion was the studio slated to release Ruth Herbert's unrealized *Career in Manhattan* in 1947.[141] Parsons remained the only woman member of the Screen Producers Guild after Virginia Van Upp resigned and Joan Harrison moved into television (there were 140 members in total in 1954). But still, critic Jane Corby quoted Parsons's advice: "A woman has to want to be a producer more than anything in else in the world."[142] Even in the 1950s, it was still possible, but Hollywood's last great period of creativity and box-office security was over. With profits down, opportunities for women producing films disappeared. Alone, Parsons could do little to open the profession to other women, and by 1954, her days in Hollywood were numbered. Even Mary Pickford was quoted in a 1954 interview: "I dislike business heartily. A lot of career women may not agree with me, but I don't think business is a woman's world."[143] True, Pickford's career as a producer had been crippled by alcoholism more than missed chances and misogyny, but her words were not well timed for other women hoping to enter the profession. In contrast to early coverage of her career, Hal Boyle, the interviewer, completely ignored her work as head of United Artists and as a producer. Instead, she was "America's Sweetheart."

In 1955, Parsons made a move to form an independent production company after twelve years at RKO.[144] Her plan was to produce a biopic of sports figure Mickey Walker, with Gordon MacRae in the title role (Lupino's successful penchant for masculine-themed projects may have inspired her). It never happened. Instead, a year later she signed a contract with Irving Asher at Twentieth Century-Fox Television Studios to "prepare a pilot" on "How to Marry a Millionaire," a decidedly more conventionally feminine narrative for her talents.[145] This, too, did not work out. In 1959, Louella Parsons reported her daughter was going to produce Dwight Taylor's novel *Joy Ride* as *Billie* on Broadway, with an eye to repackaging it for Hollywood.[146] When this fell apart, Louella reported that the comedy *I Married a Psychiatrist* was her daughter's next film venture.[147] By the mid-1960s, Harriet Parsons was back where she started, cowriting the "In Hollywood" column with her mother.[148]

In one column from 1965, she profiled Ida Lupino and used some of the same journalistic contrasts that columnists had attached to her during her successes twenty years ago. On the one hand she played up Lupino's star good looks and set them in opposition to the hard work ethic that directing and producing required: "Oddly, the very feminine Miss Lupino has established herself in TV as an excellent director of male stars in the action field,"[149] noted Parsons. And, even more remarkably for Parsons, who knew both Pickford and Lois Weber in her youth, covered Arzner and Mae West, and competed with Bennett, Van Upp, and Harrison, she claimed: "In the entire history of Hollywood there has never been anyone like Ida Lupino." In spite of the sometimes-admiring coverage accorded them by Irene Thirer, Bob Thomas, and others, only Louella Parsons and Hopper, whose professional memories extended back to the silent era, avoided these charges of individual singularity and dared to say the truth: there were several women in Hollywood who got to call the shots in their own pictures—as producers, writers, directors, and performers.

Parsons's career tapped into the studios' long-term reliance on film material authored by and focused on women, a reliance dating from the silent era and helped along by her mother's column. Her prestige films of the 1940s starred established actresses who shared her own Republican political convictions, Irene Dunne and Barbara Stanwyck. Indeed, it's very likely her strong Republican ties and friendship with Hedda Hopper, Dunne, and Ginger and Lela Rogers enabled her to succeed in Hollywood during the blacklist, and to last longer in the film industry than her less-active Republican supporters Joan Harrison and Virginia Van Upp.[150] RKO producer Dore Schary's Scandinavian immigrant project, *The Farmer's Daughter* (1947), about an assertive, progressive housemaid (Loretta Young in an Academy Award–winning performance) who becomes a successful politician and congresswoman, is miles away ideologically from Parsons's more nostalgic family tale, where the sweet, stay-at-home, and submissive Dunne takes center stage. Loretta Young's Katie is, by contrast, looking firmly at the future for the working class and for women. Although Young's performance won a great deal of popular acclaim, Schary's progressive film about working women would earn him widespread political disapproval and charges of communism by the likes of *Esquire* critic Jack Moffitt. Parsons, by contrast, was praised to the skies by Hopper, and Ginger Rogers wrote to Hopper thanking her for her glowing review of Parsons's production.

Over a decade later, Hopper would remark sadly that women producers were "as scarce as hens' teeth,"[151] but for several years, she and colleague and sometime enemy Louella Parsons were staunch supporters of the handful of women who held their own ground for a decade. One of the great ironies of Harriet Parsons's career was in that one of her last

Figure 3.3 Parsons joins Teresa Wright and her mother on the set of *The Louella Parsons Story*, 1956

television-related press items, she appeared as part of the publicity for *The Louella Parsons Story* (figure 3.3), a 1956 feature for CBS's popular *Climax* (one of Dorothy Hechtlinger's productions).[152] Teresa Wright, initially cast in Parsons's ill-fated first attempt to produce *The Enchanted Cottage*, played Louella. She's shown grinning in her prim turn-of-the century dress and incongruous 1950s pixie cut, while her long Parsons wig hangs from her hand. Louella, one hand on a typewriter, and still glamorous in a taffeta tea gown, sits between Wright and her standing daughter Harriet. Harriet, the only one of the three with poise enough to look at the camera, was not involved in the production and was just a visitor. Although she was trying to remake her career on television, the "Harriet Parsons story" had less longevity and has been virtually ignored by Hollywood historians and fans since the 1950s.

CHAPTER 4

Madam President

It's a wonderful field for women in that I have never found it "sex-conditioned." You can earn equally with men. It is one of the few careers that combines pretty well with marriage and a family. There must be adjustments made, certainly, but to be a writer . . . it is easier than having to go to a factory or a department store. And it's also more satisfying.

Mary C. McCall Jr., 1970

On the evening of November 12, 1942, the Screen Writers Guild held its annual election of officers. Forty-two men and women stood as candidates for the executive board; of these, eleven were elected. Two candidates each ran for treasurer, secretary, and vice president. Sometimes a candidate ran unopposed if he was especially popular. It happened this year, with the one candidate for president, who received 177 votes and a handful of abstentions. But there was one unusual thing about this election: the new president was a woman, Mary C. McCall Jr.[1]

McCall had been an active member of the guild since its formation. As a short-story writer in New York City, she had been a member of the guild-affiliated Authors League since the late 1920s, and therefore, as she later explained, "as soon as I came to Hollywood, I went and joined the SWG."[2] McCall continued, "I believe very strongly in the necessity of a strong writers' union, not only for the financial benefits which can be obtained by collective bargaining, but also for the professional advantages." While some members like Joseph Mankiewicz had to be chased for their dues, McCall wanted to make the guild a viable writers' union in the most notorious open-shop city in America. That meant work. She received associate membership in 1934 and served her first term on the executive board in

1935.[3] Following the birth of her twin boys, she stood again for the executive board and was elected in 1938, 1939, 1941, 1945, and 1950.[4] She would serve a total of three terms as SWG president, and twice as acting vice-president under Sheridan Gibney in 1940 and again under Emmet Lavery in 1946–47, when she was also vice president of the Board of Governors of the Academy of Motion Picture Arts and Sciences.

McCall was one of many women to belong to the Screen Writers Guild during the studio era. Membership lists in the guild archives confirm that between 20 to 25% of SWG members in the 1930s were women, and in the 1940s, membership remained stable at over 25%, with more women employed at Columbia and MGM (McCall's former and current employers) and far fewer at Warner Bros. (where she was famously fired for union activities in 1936).[5] Jane Murfin and Gladys Lehman would support McCall on the executive board in her first term as president and were later joined by McCall's young collaborator on her lucrative *Maisie* franchise, Elizabeth "Betty" Reinhardt. In any given year between 1933 and 1954, Dorothy Parker, Doris Malloy, Frances Goodrich, Lillian Hellman, Marguerite Roberts, Olive Cooper, Brenda Weisberg, Laura Perelman, Gertrude Purcell, Frances Marion, Anita Loos, Erna Lazarus, Wanda Tuchock, Virginia Kellogg, and Dorothy Hughes were running and getting elected as guild officers. Guild representatives empowered to arbitrate disputes with the studios included Gladys Lehman (Fox), Doris Malloy (Universal), and Mary McCarthy (independents).[6] Statistically speaking, when McCall was serving as president in the 1940s and 1950s, there were always two female members on the executive board to support her, but women were also well represented in Charles Brackett's and Dudley Nichols's presidencies (both men, though politically dissimilar, were lifelong friends of McCall).

In her first public speech as president, McCall did not draw attention to herself as the first female head of the guild.[7] Instead, with characteristic diplomacy, she began with a list of male colleagues who were now "in service" overseas or in intelligence work. While some 172 men were in branches of the armed forces, "To all of us," she said, "the war has brought a heightened sense of responsibility." In this war, she argued, writers were more important than ever before, because "the ideas are ours." Through the Hollywood Writers Mobilization, McCall noted that SWG members had already accrued a "fine record" of accomplishments "as *writing* men and women [dedicated] to the cause of freedom." Although some guild members, remembering the heavy-handed propaganda of World War I, were worried about the potential for government censorship and manipulation, McCall argued that "the pictures we write will be better pictures, more entertaining, more exciting, and quite possibly more profitable, because the war has demanded from us that the screen shall not be used to tell vapid stories, meretricious stories." Bad writing was false writing, whether it was heavy-handed propaganda or escapist fare. "Screen writers have in their hands a weapon not only mightier than the sword—mightier than the Garand rifle. It's our job to see that it is trained always on the enemy, that its fire never wounds one of our own."[8]

Over the past decade, the guild's enemy had been the heads of the studios and the producers. She, Murfin, Goodrich, Lehman, Hellman, and Parker had served on numerous committees and meetings with producers who saw the writers' efforts to improve pay and normalize working conditions as the end to executives' control of the studio system. But now, after years of struggle, McCall could say confidently that the union contract guaranteed by the New Deal's National Labor Relations Board was in place and changing the status of writers across the film industry. They had a guild shop percentage of 85% in 1942. "It's become almost natural for writers to use the front stairs," she joked.[9] Wages and flat-price deals had gone up, while the agreement had given "protection from having our brains picked by predatory producers" and longer notice periods between jobs. McCall had been on the front lines of securing the contract and recognized that even now, the fight was not over. Her speech was focused on the future of the guild. "You must not let yourself be cajoled, wheedled, browbeaten, coaxed, kidded, or stalled into speculative writing. . . . Every member can help the guild live up to the contract, every member can help the guild see to it that the producers live up to the contract." With income going up for everyone, the first order of business was to establish a clear basic agreement with agents, so that writers weren't impoverished by the system. She imagined a day when agents' fees would be treated as work-related tax deductions, but the first step was drafting a basic agreement between writers and agents (this was finally achieved in 1948).

But ever since her first days in Hollywood, McCall had recognized that writers needed to be trained across the industry in the interests of good screenwriting. It wasn't enough to be a smart dialogue writer from New York. Writers needed to know their colleagues' jobs and the whole mechanics of the film industry. In 1935, she wrote an only half-joking article for the Screen Guilds' Magazine, entitled "Let's Have a Motion Picture Kindergarten."[10] In it, she noted that new writers needed a "training period" if they had never written a shooting script before, and that "cutters, cinematographers, and directors, sound men, process experts, might well be glad to talk and answer questions." Directors would only have to shoot what was on the page, she reasoned cannily. McCall was tired of directors who changed the script to suit their own egos, and with this system, more knowledgeable writers would be more powerful writers. Producers might have worried about all these other screen professions talking with writers (as their own get-togethers often revolved around questions of unionization). But McCall argued that even holding the school on company time would eliminate production waste, since "In a business where two highly paid writers often spend twelve weeks pumping the arms and depressing the ribs of a story which has been dead so long even the nose knows it, there must be stringent economies somewhere."[11] Though her dream of studio-run technical schools never happened, she believed in the guild's educational capacities. The key to the guild's future lay in its next generation of screenwriters. In her presidential address, she hoped that "I live long enough to see the guild establish its own school of screen writing. The training and developing of new writing talent should certainly be the job of the Screen Writers Guild."[12]

She ended the historic speech: "By nominating me unopposed for the Presidency of the guild you have given me the greatest honor which I've ever received. I'll work hard for you."[13] Always succinct, always good for her word, politic and a master negotiator with producers, a woman whose petite physique masked a take-no-prisoners commitment to collective bargaining and the needs of the many, McCall was the guild's most valuable asset from its earliest days through the blacklist. Eventually, she would publicly sacrifice her career in Hollywood defending the basic right of screen credit against a new breed of politically repressive producers. But, like her most famous creation, Maisie Ravier, Mary C. "Mamie" McCall Jr. did not give up on herself or her show business industry. Sadly, over the years, the guild and historians of Hollywood have denied her the screen credit she deserves. She was one of the most politically active and powerful of all Hollywood writers, and yet is one of the least discussed in scholarly accounts of the film industry: nonexistent in Clayton Koppes and Gregory Black's classic *Hollywood Goes to War* and Richard Corliss's *Talking Pictures*, a minor character in Lizzie Francke's glib account of Hollywood "script girls," Nancy Lynn Schwartz's *Hollywood Writers' Wars*, and Miranda Banks's chronicle of the Screen Writers Guild, and a footnote in Larry Ceplair and Steven Englund's testosterone-driven history of the blacklist.[14] Much of the scholarship on studio-era Hollywood screenwriters has focused on the men who led the Hollywood Left. But during the studio era, McCall wielded more power than any Hollywood woman before or since. This is her story.

Mary C. McCall Jr. was one of a number of young women who arrived in Hollywood in the early 1930s with a college degree. She came from a wealthy New York Irish American family. Her father, Leo McCall, was the son of John McCall, the former president of the New York Life Insurance Company, and her mother, Mary Burke, was a well-to-do debutante pretty enough to have had her portrait painted. McCall's mother was not a suffragette. Young Mary grew up in comfortable Englewood, New Jersey (an only child until her teens), and she was not going to follow in her mother's footsteps. As she recalled, "From the time a composition of mine written in first grade was well received by the teacher and even most of the kids, I had had only one ambition—to be a professional writer."[15] Though hard times had pinched the family finances, her father had budgeted enough money to educate her until she was twenty-two. McCall wanted to attend a women's college and went to Vassar in Poughkeepsie, New York, edited the college newspaper, studied English and political science, and graduated at twenty-one, a self-styled "big wheel" on campus. But she wanted to see a foreign country, as she put it, "before I settled down to earning my living by writing," and asked college president Dr. Henry Noble MacCracken where she should go in her last year of family-financed higher education. "You are the most Irish looking girl in the College, and it seems appropriate that you should go to Trinity College," he told her, so she accepted an offer at Trinity College Dublin over University College London. An up-and-coming foreign service officer from Massachusetts she met on her year abroad tried to marry her, but, as she recalled with a sigh of relief, "fortunately for me this romance broke up in '27."[16]

McCall had a career on her mind, and when she returned to New York, worked in an advertising agency concocting snappy copy, writing short stories, and eventually producing two novels on the side. Her first book, *The Goldfish Bowl* (1932), was serialized before publication, and, as it was loosely based on her old friend from Englewood, Elizabeth Morrow, her sister Anne, and Charles Lindbergh, the book attracted the attention of Hollywood.[17] Douglas Fairbanks Jr. was quickly assigned to the film version, *It's Tough to Be Famous* (1932), perhaps due to the connection her new husband, designer Dwight Franklin, had with Douglas Fairbanks Sr. The two men had met over their shared love of pirates (both the men *and* the women). Dwight was an authority and had done several exhibitions at New York's Natural History Museum, and when Fairbanks planned *The Black Pirate*, he brought Franklin out to work and even act in the film. Shortly after her marriage to Franklin, Mary McCall met Fairbanks and his wife, Mary Pickford, and ten years later, the two Marys would work together in their capacity as leaders of the Motion Picture Relief Fund.

Though McCall would always be miffed that Darryl F. Zanuck didn't hire her to adapt *It's Tough to Be Famous* (Robert Lord got the assignment), she landed a ten-week job at Warner Bros. writing *Street of Women* (1932), "a dog" of a picture the studio undoubtedly thought was more suitable material for a new female writer (figure 4.1). With baby daughter Sheila vacationing in Arizona with her grandparents and Franklin back east for most of the time, she stayed in town long enough to have an affair with Fairbanks Jr. and see the adaptation of her novel have a good preview. Then, as she recalled, "At breakfast . . . I saw a newspaper with banner headlines: 'Lindbergh Baby Kidnapped.' My first thought was of Anne, but my second thought, I admit, was: 'There goes the book!' And how right I was!" The large bookstores stocked the book, but refused to feature or promote it, "since, as a satirical comedy, it was in such execrable taste, with the Lindberg family undergoing such suffering."[18] McCall sold another book to the studio for Fairbanks, a tragic Russian Revolution love story called *Revolt* (later retitled *Scarlet Dawn*, 1932), but though the film was action-packed and displayed the star's aristocratic good looks, it didn't lead to any immediate studio offers for McCall.

McCall and Franklin went back to New York briefly, and she continued to add to her writing profile, publishing stories with *Colliers* and other

Figure 4.1 Mary C. McCall Jr., 1932

"slick-paper magazines," but the Depression convinced the couple that "more and better paid employment for both of us lay in Hollywood rather than New York". In early 1934, they relocated permanently to the West Coast, taking four-year-old Sheila and her governess, Justine Prickell, along. Franklin went on to become research and technical adviser on MGM's *Treasure Island* (1934), working closely with Cedric Gibbons, and he later designed the men's costumes in *Naughty Marietta* (1935), before joining Cecil B. DeMille's company at Paramount, where he specialized in period films across the 1930s and 1940s. He was a gifted designer who would go on to work (without credit thanks to the rapacious Edith Head) through the production of George Stevens's *Shane* in 1953. Franklin had a flair for fabric and detail and loved wearing his own designs to parties. Early in their marriage, he had dressed his wife as an eighteenth-century aristocrat and even—at her request—as William Shakespeare (complete with skullcap and false whiskers!) (figure 4.2). They would astonish everyone at the Astor Ball in 1930 when they appeared as a Renaissance couple—even down to the makeup and hair! McCall put the parties aside when she returned to Warner Bros., this time for a long-term writing contract, and became active in the Screen Writers Guild.

Through it all, she remained Mary C. McCall Jr. She and Dwight Franklin had a sound, equal partnership that was based as much on mutual respect for each other's intellect and talent as on physical attraction. She never stopped working after marriage, and it was Franklin who encouraged her to go back to writing short stories to escape the boredom of her advertising job. When they married in 1928, she presented him with a "Sonnet for a Partnership," and this, more than anything, expressed her view that even in love, women and men had to preserve their equality and individuality:

> Let us keep something secret and unknown
> Always. Possessed, you would be dead, clay-cold
> And pitiful. It is the free, alone
> And living you I love. Dear, let us hold
> Inviolate the spirit's solitude.
> Adventuring together, we shall be
> Gay fellow-players in the salty, rude
> Boisterous comedy of life, yet we
> Will never lose our joy in quiet things.
> Sharers in laughter and in ecstasy,
> Loving each other while the young blood sings
> Thru all our veins, such friends shall we two be

Figure 4.2 McCall as Shakespeare, 1930

> There will enfold us when our youth is spent
> The lovely mantle of a deep content.[19]

Because there was a sixteen-year age gap between them, Mary McCall benefited from Franklin's knowledge of Hollywood as much as from his amused detachment from the crassness and glitz of Southern California. Franklin needed perspective, particularly when his wife had affairs with Fairbanks and later Leslie Howard, but he loved her and tolerated what was—even by Hollywood standards—a very modern, open marriage. Years later in the supposedly straight-laced 1950s, McCall would discuss the advantages of premarital sex, reasoning with Sheila, "Before you buy the shoe, you have to try it on first."[20]

In spite of the fact that a number of prominent female screenwriters in the 1930s had well-publicized relationships with other writers (Lillian Hellman and Dashiell Hammett, Dorothy Parker and Alan Campbell, Frances Goodrich and Albert Hackett, Tess Slesinger and Frank Davis, Florence Ryerson and Colin Clements), these partnerships were focused on their shared careers as writers. Mary McCall was unique in being married with three (and, from 1944, four) children for the most productive period in her career, something that very few working women in Hollywood dared—or were allowed—to do. Her friend Louella Parsons, a big fan of McCall's *Maisie* series, reported McCall's career successes, remarriages, and new children with equal measures of praise and admiration.[21] Things were not so easy for other women in Hollywood. McCall's close friend Bette Davis only became a mother after terminating her long-term contract with the studio in 1949 and would add to her family as a freelancer in the 1950s.

But in the 1930s, McCall came closest to having it all as a woman in terms of public career and private life. She wrote or worked on half a dozen scripts for Warner Bros., including a sweet May-December romance for newcomer Jean Muir (the future television blacklistee also starred in McCall's *Midsummer Night's Dream*), two hot code-bending stories for freelancer Barbara Stanwyck (*The Secret Bride*, 1934, and *The Woman in Red*, 1935), and a prestige adaptation of Sinclair Lewis's *Babbitt*. She was at the studio all day, and little Sheila was with her governess. At night, instead of reading bedtime stories, she was attending guild meetings and hosting many of them in the McCall-Franklin home. Though she shared a love of designer hats with her friend Hedda Hopper, McCall had little time to shop or fuss with her appearance. The mass of curly dark Irish hair stayed wild. She'd dab a finger in a pot of lip rouge and apply it without looking at a mirror, already halfway out the door in the morning. When she was hard at work writing the script for *A Midsummer Night's Dream* (starring her old New York Irish pal, James Cagney, as Nick Bottom), she was very pregnant with twins. Years later, she described the situation simply in a collection of reminiscences intended for her children: "Gerald McCall Franklin and Alan McCall Franklin were born on November 16, 1934, just 24 hours after my last conference—at home—on *A Midsummer Night's Dream*."[22] She was back at work in two weeks, adapting the gangster drama *Dr. Socrates* (1935), before being loaned out to Columbia Pictures in 1936.

Being loaned out to Columbia was the best thing that could have happened to her. For there she met two people who would change her attitude toward screenwriting and women's career independence: Dorothy Arzner and Harry Cohn. Arzner was Hollywood's last remaining prominent female director. She had her start in the silent era and would remain a viable director of strong women's pictures through the 1940s. McCall would become her good friend and would speak at both Arzner's Hollywood retirement tribute a decade later and at the 1975 event organized by the Committee of Women Members of the Directors Guild of America.

George Kelly's Pulitzer Prize-winning play about an acquisitive housewife was first adapted by Clara Beranger in 1928 as a silent film (William C. de Mille directed, and Anne Bauchens edited the film). Columbia's prestigious, sound-era production capitalized on the trend for lavish literary adaptations and was intended to outshine Samuel Goldwyn's adaptation of Sinclair Lewis's *Dodsworth* (1936). Arzner wanted the best writing possible, and McCall's former colleague at Warner Bros., Edward Chodorov, now a producer at Columbia, recommended McCall. As she remembered, "Miss Arzner's belief that a writer should be a part of the making of a picture from start to finish, and that I had the makings of a good writer for the screen, encouraged me to stay [at Columbia]."[23] McCall had been contemplating returning to New York given how "discouraged" she was at Warner Bros. merely cranking out smart dialogue. She wrote the first draft, and then writer and director worked through each line. "She questioned every move I made," McCall remembered. "In the script, I would write, 'She walks to the window.' Dorothy would say, 'Why?' And I would answer, 'Well, she's getting the worst of the argument, so she is running away. She turns her back and looks out.' 'All right, all right, but I have to know why she moves. Otherwise I cannot direct it.' "[24] McCall had a unique opportunity to shape the production and performances, because, unlike other directors McCall had worked with, Arzner "wanted the writer to be on the set."[25] (figure 4.3).

Actress Rosalind Russell was taking a big career risk playing as unsympathetic a character as Mrs. Harriet Craig. But like Bette Davis's decision to play Mildred in *Of Human Bondage* in 1934, Russell's recreation of Kelly's selfish, remote, and unlikable middle-class matron brought the actress the career rewards and praise for realism she craved. As film critic Mildred Martin wrote, "*Craig's Wife* may give many women the thrill of recognizing themselves, not retouched. . . . Miss Russell has stopped being a carbon copy—however charming—of Myrna Loy and has played Harriet Craig uncompromisingly and sincerely."[26] But Archer Winsten was anxious about the recent cinematic "open season" on women and the range of films that depicted nasty housewives, remarking that although the film was "a serious study," like other less intellectual misogynist fare, it "will keep our fair womanhood in the doghouse."[27]

Figure 4.3 McCall taking a break with Dorothy Arzner and John Boles on the set of *Craig's Wife*, 1936

While Winsten was uncomfortable with what he perceived to be the film's misogyny, he seemed unaware that it was directed only at non-working housewife, Harriet Craig. He was vaguely perplexed that women filmmakers were responsible for the production. However, other critics, looking at who was on the other side of the camera, praised the film as a "revolution." "Women scenarists, women film editors and cutters, as well as women stars, have been for too long taken for granted in the film world," one wrote.[28] Mildred Martin found it liberating that women dominated the film's production. In addition to McCall and Arzner, Viola Lawrence edited the film (figure 4.4). Martin took note of the fact that although a man had written the stage play, the film was better because "Only women could so deeply get beneath the skin of another woman and so devastatingly expose her."[29] Though Kelly's narrative was sound, as Martin noted, McCall had provided additional scenes and "a number of her own" biting lines. In his review, Winsten also took particular note of Harriet Craig's backstory, in which "a childhood experience of seeing her mother trust her father, while he, the sly fellow, mortgaged the roof off their heads for his girl friend, made too deep an impression." However, he appeared unaware that this material was McCall's, for in addition to adding scenes and bitter

Figure 4.4 The women who made *Craig's Wife*: Viola Lawrence, Rosalind Russell, McCall, and Arzner, 1936

new dialogue, McCall's fundamental humanizing of Harriet Craig gave her personal history a depth that it had lacked in the original play. Critic Marsha McCreadie, the only post-studio-era film critic to take McCall's career as a writer seriously, has drawn attention to McCall's reworking of the script to focus on the motivation behind Craig's materialism and personal coldness.[30]

McCall frankly relished working with Arzner, and the two became great friends. As she remembered, "At the end of each rehearsal she would turn to me and say, 'How is that for you?' For the first couple of days I couldn't believe it. I had never been assigned to a set before."[31] Theirs was a true collaboration, and toward the end of production, they had a serious talk about McCall's career. Arzner was worried that the younger woman would give up and return to New York rather than remain at Warner Bros. McCall remembered, "When Dorothy asked me how this assignment had been, I said, 'It's been the finest weeks of my professional life. I have stopped the work reluctantly every night and have gone to it eagerly the next day.'" Arzner told her, "'Well, it can be like that, you know, and you can make it increasingly like that if you stick with it. But if you turn your back on it and run away, then you will never have anything to say about how a motion picture is made.'"[32] McCall took her advice, but knew she couldn't remain at Warner Bros. as, in her words, a mere "corpse-rouger."

At Warner Bros., McCall was on a rigid schedule. Salaries were low, and it was the worst studio to work for if you were a member of the fledgling Screen Writers Guild—or a woman. Though her name was on several moneymakers, she was usually one of several contract writers on a project and preferred to work alone. As McCall remembered, of the thirty full-time writers at Warner Bros., only two were women—herself and Lillie Heyward.[33] In a speech at the guild delivered in 1978, she stated flatly, "The average pay of screen writers equaled that of the body makeup men. Employees were bullied by the High Brass—told, not urged, to donate campaign funds—given a list of films, players, directors to vote for in the Academy's balloting." McCall was fed up and started a petition protesting the studio's methods. As she recalled, "All the men who had signed it were summoned to Jack Warner's office. He demanded to know what individual had written this. They all said, 'We wrote it.' But J. L., through native shrewdness and information from a fink, knew I was the culprit."[34] She was fired in the middle of *Craig's Wife*, but Harry Cohn arranged to buy out the remainder of her contract so she could resume working for him straightaway.

Cohn didn't give a damn whether his writers belonged to the guild or not; he didn't care if they were male or female. What Cohn cared about was good writing. Though today, the mogul is often dismissed as one of many crass, womanizing boors running the Hollywood studios, Harry Cohn had the best record in Hollywood for promoting women's careers at all levels of production. Blunt, challenging, and aggressive, he was also fair. He had a sense of humor too, if you knew how to push his buttons right. McCall did. One day, as she walked across the Columbia lot on her way out, Cohn yelled out the window at her, "Where are you going?" When she replied, "I'm going to lunch," he bellowed, "No one goes off the lot to lunch here." "Well, I do, and I'm going," she yelled back and continued off the lot. Cohn and McCall liked each other. Any woman who yelled right back at him had his respect, and as McCall said of Cohn, "Whereas he might break your jaw, he would never stick a knife in your back."[35]

But though Cohn may have been more easygoing with guild writers, for several years things had been difficult. McCall reasoned later in life, "We were the first of the talent groups to form a guild. The actors borrowed the use of our offices to form *their* guild, and were recognized and got a contract. The directors weren't even a gleam in Frank Capra's eye until several years later, but the studios would never sit down and bargain with *us*." McCall's guild work consisted of talking to young writers, persuading them to join the guild, and involving herself in cross-professional initiatives, whether it was writing articles in the *Screen Guilds' Magazine*, which at first represented both writers and actors, or serving on the board of directors of the benevolence fund, the Motion Picture Relief Committee, with friends Jean Hersholt and Eddie Mannix. It was hard to remain cordial with the likes of Jack Warner and Darryl Zanuck when, in 1936, there was a "blacklist" against employing SWG writers, and right-wing producers and writers had created the company-affiliated Screen Playwrights as a way of breaking the writers' union. Guild members were laid off or not given assignments. Sonya Levien was a supporter of the guild, but given Zanuck's violent antiguild feelings, masked her political affiliations so well that even her colleague William Ludwig said of her "She was the least political person I ever met."[36]

For several months in 1936, the guild dissolved before reforming in 1937. Although many historians have speculated that the resurgent Communist Party was responsible for the formation of the new guild, as writer John Howard Lawson acknowledged, "The majority of the people who sustained the organization were not communists. They were just individuals who saw the need for an organization, who realized that the struggle for the guild was both economic and creative."[37] McCall, Jane Murfin, and Frances Goodrich were some of the more prominent women in this category and were instrumental in developing the membership base and a sense of collective identity that went beyond getting members to pay their dues. The Communist Party–affiliated members, McCall felt, often let their wider political interests obscure their commitment to the guild and the interests of screenwriters' unionization. In the *Screen Guilds' Magazine*, she deplored the recent absence of her colleagues at a SWG meeting—they had all gone to hear a British war correspondent speak about the Spanish Civil War. McCall joked: "Nobody goes to anybody's house any more to sit and talk and have fun. There's a master of ceremonies and a collection basket, because there are no gatherings now except for a good cause. We have almost no time to be actors and writers these days."[38] She believed that for the good of the fledgling guild, radical politics should not take over the primary job of the writer, which is to write, not pass collection plates for the Spanish Civil War or the Communist Party.

In the next issue, communist writer Donald Ogden Stewart, displaying a remarkable lack of humor, accused McCall of defending the Hollywood system of half measures and compromise: "Miss McCall's indignation at the efforts of the organizers of the good causes sounds not so much like the desire of the true artist for the high lonely peak as the reminiscent whine of the well-fed [screen playwright] to be let alone in his feather bed." He continued, "It is a painful surprise to find so courageous a fighter as Miss McCall . . . counseling . . . adherence to the banners of those defenders of the goose that lays the golden eggs."[39] But McCall was neither a conservative stooge nor a fellow traveler; she was merely doing her best to secure the contract and protect her fledging union from too many debilitating political links and "a tenuous existence in a hostile industry." There was a well-justified fear that too many political encumbrances would "further weaken the union." Ten years later, all her predictions would come true.

When the remains of McCall's three-year contract with Columbia expired, she moved on to the more prestigious MGM, beginning her seven-year contract at $1,250 a week with *Dramatic School* (1938), a picture for two-time Academy Award winner Luise Rainier (*The Great Ziegfeld*, 1936; *The Good Earth*, 1937). When McCall moved to MGM, she moved to the studio with the largest number of full-time employed writers—nearly fifty. In the 1930s and 1940s, the studio's writing roster was composed of 23% to 26% women and was a who's who of screenwriting. Frances Marion, Anita Loos, Lenore Coffee, Salka Viertel, Ruth Gordon, Isobel Lennart, Frances Goodrich— name the best, and they worked at MGM, a studio that Dorothy Parker, half-satirically, half-enviously, called "The Mothership."[40] And, as Dorothy Kingsley recalled, the women writers of MGM stuck together.[41] McCall's rising status as an adapter of prestige literature (*Babbitt, Midsummer Night's Dream, Craig's Wife*); her knack of creating contemporary women's stories about work, sex, and love; and her friendship with MGM writer and fellow Vassar alumna Frances Goodrich (*The Thin Man* franchise) all helped to land her the job.

Many of MGM's top female screenwriters had been in the business for decades. Frances Marion was easily the most famous. She had been Mary Pickford's favorite scenarist, and at one time was the highest paid writer in Hollywood. By the late 1930s, most of MGM's scripts passed through her hands for approval. Together with Loos, Lenore Coffee, and Bess Meredyth, she represented a strong, powerful block of screenwriters who began their careers in the silent era and flourished in the early years of the studio system. Marion, in particular, created and nurtured a strong network of Hollywood women during the 1910s and 1920s, and, as Cari Beauchamp has argued, was able to use her influence with Thalberg to help the careers of a number of women, including writer Lorna Moon and star Marie Dressler.

These networks had become more tenuous by the 1930s. Marion, though fond of Ida Koverman, was wary of L. B. Mayer. She sensed a growing hostility to women's power as writers and was careful not to use her own work as an example of a perfect screenplay when she published her popular book, *How to Write and Sell Screenplays* (1937). [42] She even made light of her abilities in the press. The diminutive Loos, though one of MGM's star writers with hits such as *San Francisco* (1936) and *The Women* (1939), had perfected the role of the lighthearted child-writer who took nothing seriously—especially not her career. But this act made her "a producer's darling" in the 1930s. It also helped that Marion, like her friends Mary Pickford and Koverman, was active in the Republican Party, the MGM executives' party of choice. Though Marion briefly agreed to serve as vice president of the fledgling writers' guild in 1933, she functioned more as a prestigious figurehead than as an advocate for unionization, and quickly withdrew her membership when an irate Thalberg demanded it. Meredyth was downright hostile to the founding of the Screen Writers Guild, something that earned her brownie points with Mayer. [43]

While acting humble, scatterbrained, and politically conservative may have earned these older women some measure of protection, it potentially isolated them from the younger generation of women writers who were building their careers and forming their own networks in the Screen Writers Guild. More than one writer of the time saw the founding of the guild as "an assault on a paternalistic kingdom," but Hollywood's first generation of powerful women writers was, at the very least, ambivalent about women's participation in this rebellion. Though a Democrat, like her friend Bette Davis, McCall appealed to many, from Hopper to Pickford, as a moderate and a feminist. As McCall rose to power, she attempted to maintain the informal "old girl" networks Marion believed in, while concentrating on the next stage of women's public leadership in Hollywood: the guilds.

By 1938, McCall had entered the top tier of guild membership, working alongside Charles Brackett and Sheridan Gibney to force the producers to agree to a contract. On June 7, 1938, screenwriters were given official protection to unionize under the Wagner Act, but they had to decide whether the guild or the Screen Playwrights would be their official union. MGM was "the pivotal studio in the writers' war." [44] Not only did it employ twice as many writers as the other studios, but also more of its writers were women, and many of them, though overlooked by historians, were political. McCall's presence at MGM meant that she could organize the undecided writers to side with the guild in 1938. They did. [45] When, smarting from their defeat at the election, the Screen Playwrights and producers threatened to take the action to court, the Paramount antitrust suit was filed on July 20. The producers would blame their writers for their eventual defeat in 1948, a defeat that forced the deaccession of studio theater holdings and put an end to

Hollywood's media dominance. However, the studio heads would have their revenge with another, and more lasting, blacklist that would claim the careers of some of Hollywood's most prominent and political writers, including McCall.

But for now, McCall and the guild were entering their most powerful phase. In early 1939, she maintained relationships with high-ranking members of the Screen Actors Guild to keep the writers' union struggle in the public eye. Prominent SAG members Lucile Webster Gleason and James Cagney were frequent dinner guests at the McCall-Franklin home. McCall wrote the first Screen Guild Show play, *Can We Forget*, for friend Bette Davis, Robert Montgomery, and Basil Rathbone, which aired on WABC in January 1939.[46] That year, the "very militant" McCall would meet frequently with MGM's Eddie Mannix and Y. Frank Freeman, head of Paramount, to push for the closed shop and formal recognition of the union (finally obtained in March 1939). Freeman initially refused to negotiate, and McCall would quip, "Is Y. Frank Freeman a rhetorical question?" The two would publicly clash again in 1940, when, as acting president of the guild in Sheridan Gibney's absence, she defended the European and British émigrés who were coming to Hollywood in search of a new life against Freeman's xenophobic remarks ("We should take care of Americans first," he proclaimed).[47] In the spring of 1941, with American involvement in the war approaching, she and the executive committee forced a blanket pay raise from $40 to $125 a week for all writers with the threat of a strike. Writer Boris Ingster remembered Freeman going "insane" at some of those early meetings.

Although the guild had voted unanimously in favor of the seven-year contract on June 18, 1941, the producers wouldn't officially sign for several more months.[48] With the producers still stalling on points of the contract and a strike more than a possibility in the winter of 1941–42, many of the guild's left-wing members advocated a wage freeze to show wartime solidarity—including McCall's future vice president, Lester Cole. Moderate elements in the guild were strongly opposed to what effectively was "freezing the contract" for the duration before anything had been formally signed. When the producers offered the New Deal minimum wage of $125 a week before the freeze was proposed, Cole, Dalton Trumbo, John Howard Lawson, and Ralph Block had, as Richard Maibaum would remember, "egg on their faces." McCall's moderate group of guild leaders took control (the Far Left had lost their advantage with their support of Russia following the 1939 pact with Germany and the invasion of Finland).

McCall and Charles Brackett were particularly close. Both were from influential New York families, well educated, and intellectually subversive.

Brackett, though he appeared to be conservative in manner, dress, and politics, believed as fiercely in the union as McCall. Between them, they worked out a way of having moderates unable to attend guild meetings give their proxy votes to get the wage rise. The legions of poor writers who had worked on $40 a week for years were ready to vote for McCall a year later when she ran for president. Eddie Mannix, McCall's New York Irish friend, fellow Motion Picture Relief executive committee member, and now employer, was a useful ally in these negotiations and helped defuse the antiguild Freeman and Harry Warner.

McCall's move to MGM was professionally rewarding in more than one way. When Eddie Knopf assigned her Wilson Collison's *Dark Dame*, she brokered it into one of the studio's most lucrative franchises. Jean Harlow had a big success with Collison's *Red Dust* in 1932, scripted by McCall's conservative adversary in the Screen Playwrights, John Lee Mahin (it was said Mahin was Budd Schulberg's model for the servile, producer's boy-writer protagonist in *What Makes Sammy Run?*). Studio executives begged Collison to write more stories in this vein, but, as McCall sniffed, "He sold them two stories that were exactly the same . . . there was always the big, rough, tough guy who didn't want to get married and the girl who looked and talked like a floosie but had a heart of gold."[49] By 1938, Harlow was dead, but the search for a successful formula went on. McCall was brought in to work on a project that, without Harlow, was distinctly B in quality; this was no *Dramatic School*. But it meant that McCall could do whatever she liked with Collison's flimsy script titled "Broadway to Wyoming." Producer Jack Ruben and McCall "were in such a small way of business that no one paid us the slightest attention, and we had great fun. We used to read the scenes over to each other and laugh and laugh." Reworked and retitled, *Maisie* (a nod to the warm-hearted maid "Mazie" from *Craig's Wife*) was turned by McCall into the sleeper hit of 1939. As Louella Parsons remarked, *Maisie* is "the surprise movie of the year, a picture that no one on the MGM lot knew or even cared was being made and which is better than the majority of pictures."[50]

While MGM didn't care who played Maisie, Ruben allegedly refused to hire just anybody and said, "This is a part for a comedienne. Comedy is very hard to play."[51] Ann Sothern wanted a career reboot after playing a succession of sweet young things. As an article in the MGM *Studio News* noted, "18 months ago, after 8 years of assorted ingénue roles in which she had little more to do than look nice while the hero rescued her, or the comedian used her as a stooge, she announced that she never would play another straight leading role in motion pictures." She had married Roger Pryor and dropped out of Hollywood until a good part came along.

Maisie was her salvation. Said Sothern, "I've had the time of my life playing these different characters. Maisie the honkytonk girl who found love in the wide open spaces was such a far cry from straight leading roles that I reveled in her."[52]

As the tough-talking showgirl, Sothern embodied the modern American pioneer woman who had every curveball thrown at her, but dodged each one with wisecracks. McCall's Maisie was no damsel in distress. Like many women who came of age in the Depression, she was after money and men in that order, and might have done quite well as a studio executive, remarking that she understood two languages: "English and double-talk."[53] Whether in the Congo or the equally wild American West hunting for gold or a new man in Reno, Maisie was a global phenomenon, and like James Bond in the 1960s and 1970s, each adventure in the franchise rebooted from zero with a tasty new Maisie-man for her female fans. And they were legion. *Photoplay* profiled the impact it had on American women by 1941, who wrote in droves to Ann Sothern, asking her advice on love, career, and marriage![54]

Maisie Ravier may have been a distillation of the never-say-die, working-class Depression-era woman of McCall's generation, but she was also very much McCall's alter ego (figure 4.5). As McCall stated in an interview, "When writing, I literally step into Maisie's gaudy garb and go sailing through adventures with her. . . . I know her as well as I know myself."[55] McCall gave the interview surrounded by Maisie memorabilia, including a statuette made by her husband Dwight Franklin, showing Sothern as Maisie, signature red fingernails, heavily laden charm bracelet, and suitcase in hand, in search of more adventures. According to McCall, Mary Anastasia O'Connor, stage name Maisie Ravier, was an Irish American Brooklyn native with a prizefighter and a cop for uncles and a father who drank too much. "She made her stage debut at 4 playing *Ja-Da* on the accordion and imitating Al Jolson on roller skates. She has been in show business ever since, taking the jobs as they came."[56] Sothern became one of the biggest stars of the 1940s playing Maisie, and her comic timing, the result of endless hours of practice alone and with McCall as an audience, made the "trenchant and humorous lines of Mary C. McCall Jr." some of the best-known one-liners during the war years.[57]

But *Maisie* is known for another reason in the lore of the guild. In 1946, SWG president Emmet Lavery would write a letter to *New York Times* critic Bosley Crowther, criticizing him for taking seriously director Lewis Milestone's comments about *A Walk in the Sun* (1945), where he alleged, "The book was my script."[58] Crowther had completely ignored Robert Rossen's contribution as the screenwriter, and Lavery cited it as just another example of critics and directors trying to take credit from writers as film authors.

Figure 4.5 McCall with her alter ego, Maisie, 1942

"This is not the first instance of such treatment accorded to screen writers," Lavery continued. "Mary McCall Jr., past president of the Screen Writers' Guild, still blanches at the memory of a review written about one of the *Maisie* series, described as 'an otherwise dull picture relieved only by Miss Sothern's bright quips.' Is it necessary to point out that the quips were the work of the screen writer and were not ad-libbed by Miss Sothern?"[59] McCall would later acknowledge the studio directors were not that bright: some, she sniffed, "shot whatever you wrote, including the typographical errors."[60]

McCall wrote the first three *Maisie* films without assistance, but friend Betty Reinhardt was later brought in and could master McCall's string of gags and one-liners so well even Sothern was fooled by who wrote what. McCall, who always felt guilty Reinhardt never got "the recognition that she deserved," mentored her at the guild and was thrilled when Zanuck assigned her to adapt Vera Caspary's *Laura* in 1943.

Maisie is wise to men from the beginning ("Oh, just another guy who thinks blonde hair means a green light")[61] and is prepared for them to let women down. To her, men are as replaceable as cars, and, like cars, there's a new model coming around every minute. As she tries to tell one love-struck matron: "Oh, he's a kind of special job. A *de luxe* model of what he is—white wall tires, two horns and fog lights, but leaving out the gadgets—it's the same old car! You'd have a great six months. And when I say six months, I'm allowing for shrinkage. Three's nearer."[62]

Maisie is usually introduced at the beginning of the story hunting for an elusive showbiz job. Always down to her last dime, it's when she's backed into a corner that things start happening: "My friend, life has prepared me for a right upper-cut—and a double cross. But up to now, I never been caught off balance." But Maisie's attitude is simply, "When Heaven forgets to protect the working girl, she has to do the best she can on her own."[63] When a destitute sharecropping family feels bad about her helping them out on the road, she even takes a poke at the New Deal: "Listen, I'd like to have a dime for every dollar I've got on credit! It's a wonder I haven't got a government job!"[64] Many of her stories were set in the West, mythical place for fresh starts and a pioneering attitude, but Maisie never finds any heroes from a dime novel out there: "If you take my advice, you'll scram out of here—where the spaces are wide open and the minds are narrow. They can give my share of it back to the Indians."[65]

With *Swing Shift Maisie* (1943), her work moved from show business to aircraft defense plants, and in the OWI review of McCall's script, writer Lillian Bergquist praised "the now renowned showgirl" for her patriotism. She continued, "Maisie, in her own way, can set an example to all Americans—and especially to those millions of young women who are so urgently needed in all our war industries."[66] The film was "timely as well as vastly amusing"[67] for critics and audiences, and certainly resonated with McCall's other documentary and feature work for the war, starring women, including *Reward Unlimited* (1944), a film she developed as head of the Hollywood branch of the War Activities Committee.

Maisie's string of wisecracks and indestructibility reflected what McCall herself needed in order to get through the early 1940s. She was head, not only of the guild, but of Hollywood's War Activities Committee (shortly before her election as guild president she was in line for heading Lowell Mellett's Hollywood office for the OWI's Bureau of Motion Pictures but was not given the job since "Mellett said the job shouldn't be given to anyone who has been associated with the film industry"),[68] the Hollywood Democratic Committee (where she would meet and dine with idol Eleanor Roosevelt at Congresswoman Helen Gahagan Douglas's house in 1944), the Labor Management Committee, and several other political and charitable organizations (figure 4.6). At the War Activities Committee, she coordinated and commissioned cross-studio shorts, including a Tess

Figure 4.6 McCall with Eleanor Roosevelt, 1944

Slesinger–Frank Davis script (*What If They Quit?*, Twentieth Century-Fox); David O. Selznick's nurse's aide story, set to coincide with the release of the women's home-front drama *Since You Went Away*; and RKO's war bond drive short, *Ginger Rogers Finds a Bargain*, slated for WAC (Woman's Army Corps) release.

McCall's two OWI/WAC film commissions for MGM, *Box Office Maisie* and *Reward Unlimited*, were also aimed at female audiences. *Reward Unlimited*, directed by Jacques Tourneur, focused on the Cadet Nurse Training Corps as part of a major recruitment push.[69] Writer Garson Kanin supported McCall's efforts to make more documentary shorts about women in defense jobs and the armed services, and contacted the women's division of SPARS (US Coast Guard Woman's Reserve) about the possibility of arranging a guild interview with its director, Dorothy Stratton.[70] Kanin, whose wife, actress and writer Ruth Gordon, was a friend of McCall, had already helped Katharine Hepburn find work narrating a film about women in defense jobs written by Eleanor Roosevelt, *Women in Defense*.[71] McCall's *Maisie* short was tied in to *Swing Shift Maisie*, which was a big hit.

But this wasn't all she was up to during her first term as guild president. McCall also laid the cornerstone for the Motion Picture Relief Fund country house in the San Fernando Valley. She was vice president of the organization, and a few years before, had built upon Mary Pickford's early efforts with the studios to pay in a small fraction of employees' salaries toward a fund for retired or otherwise unemployed studio workers (who said Hollywood was a hard-hearted town?). MGM executive Eddie Mannix was also involved in the organization, and the two workaholic Irish Americans developed a sound relationship that would pay dividends for the SWG in 1941–42 when McCall negotiated with Mannix and his less cordial producer colleagues over the writers' contract.

Later during her presidency, she and guild attorney Morris Cohen went to Washington, DC, to negotiate wartime pay increases above and beyond the minimum wage (the increases had been guaranteed by the contract). The industry-wide committee involved actors, producers, and writers. When producers proposed to go along with a potential five-year wage freeze, McCall remembered, "I sucked air" and waited for "some of these handsome actors with good voices" to "come awake and say something," but they "didn't say a bloody word."[72] McCall then said baldly, "The Screen Writers Guild could not go along with this because a contract is a two-way street and if one party, for any reason, is unable to fulfill his part of the bargain, the bargain is off."[73] The producers caved in the face of her threat and were forced to ask permission to increase wages from the Roosevelt administration. This added another black mark to McCall's record, as far as the execs were concerned. But, as she remembered, her writing colleagues "were pleased with me," and the guild happily "draft[ed] Mary McCall Jr. for a second term as president."[74]

Writers had never had so much clout in the industry, and as far as the majority of members were concerned, McCall could do no wrong in her first two terms as president. As she prepared to give the Academy Awards for screenwriting in March 1943, the year *Mrs. Miniver* and MGM swept the event, she looked over the crowd with a triumphant gleam in her eyes and quoted the famous lines from the Bible, "In the beginning was the Word."[75] Columnists remembered it as the best speech of the evening.[76] It was a strong reminder to Hollywood's members that their industry would stand or fall by its story material, and that writers, the last major filmmaking branch to secure a union contract, were powerless no longer.

She may have been Hollywood's most influential woman during the war years, but McCall should also be remembered as one of Hollywood's most capable screenwriters. McCall's wartime choice of writing assignments reflected her shrewd understanding of the dynamics of gender, ethnicity, and power in wartime Hollywood. Perhaps one of her biggest successes was *The Fighting Sullivans* (1944), released through Darryl F. Zanuck's studio and directed by old Warner Bros. friend Lloyd Bacon. The independent producer was relatively new to the game: Sam Jaffe. McCall had known him for years; her agent, Mary Baker, was his partner at the Jaffe Agency. Together, they negotiated a deal that gave her $15,000 up front plus 5% of the producers' profits if they used 75% or more of her script. They took it all, and as McCall revealed in *Screen Writer* magazine, it was the most she had ever made on any film and set a new benchmark for writers' earnings.[77]

Jaffe recognized that this real-life story of Irish immigrant heroism was an ideal project for McCall, not only as a prominent Irish American screenwriter, but also as head of the War Activities Committee and Screen Writers Guild. But the subject matter was touchy: five young brothers (only one of whom had finished high school) were all killed aboard the same ship at Guadalcanal. The story had been all over the papers, and as McCall later said, "I do not think to watch a small child run over by a steam roller is drama; I think it's disgusting. You want to turn your face away."[78] But then she discovered that what did make the story dramatic was the durability of this average, working-class family unit: "These young men had so lived in their country and in their family that when their time came to die and when the parents and the young wife and the small baby learned the news that the five were gone, they were able to rise and fill a heroic frame without losing a step."[79] So McCall's most famous war picture only covers a few minutes of combat training and action.

She began *The Fighting Sullivans* by contrasting the solemn and frequent baptism ceremonies for the five boys with the rough language, noise, and overburdened clotheslines of the Sullivan house several years later. The focus of the film is on the life of a "full-blooded mongrel family," with eight people competing for one bathroom, a father perpetually cutting himself shaving, gang fights, black eyes at first communions, and smoking corn silk. If Tom Sawyer had had four brothers and a sister, they might have been like the Sullivan kids. And though the boys outnumbered the girls in the house, life lessons on fair dealing and becoming adults came from both the mother and father. The Sullivan boys live and die together, refusing to leave one injured brother before their ship explodes, but one Sullivan sibling remains: the only girl, Genevieve. Originally, in both the opening and closing sequences of the script, McCall noted that Gen enlisted as a WAVE and is in uniform in the final shots of the launch of the Sullivan destroyer.[80]

McCall's next war project for MGM developed some of these plot lines. *Keep Your Powder Dry* (1945) was McCall's idea (working title: *Woman's*

Army), developed at the request of the War Department to boost WAC recruitment, and belongs to a cluster of women's war films released during the height of McCall's influence. A variation on the male wartime "buddy" drama, the focus was on surviving training camp to become officers before being shipped overseas. Although Larraine Day's, Lana Turner's, and Susan Peters's characters remained in a training camp for the duration of the film, unlike Claudette Colbert's combat veteran in Paramount's *So Proudly We Hail* (1943) and Ann Sothern and Ella Raines in *Cry Havoc* (1943), McCall went to great lengths to show women from military families and female officers mixed in with the clueless glamour gal who learns the value of hard work and a profession. Agnes Moorhead's efficient lieutenant colonel is modeled on Mary Servoss's Captain McGregor in *So Proudly We Hail*, but McCall's script shows far more scenes of women managing the war from the home front and at army training facilities. McCall's script also takes far more swipes at male officers running conventional wars. As Val (Turner) complains, "Who was it said an army travels on its stomach?", another recruit responds, "Some general who rode a horse!"[81] Later, when the trio spot a broken down officer's jeep, Val sneers, "The chief of staff can't fix his car. He's waiting for mamma to come fix it."[82] The women are told to get it working after the chief of staff and general are unable to identify the parts of their engine. After a quick consultation, the jeep is up and running.

OWI script readers remained worried about the unflattering depiction of the American home front, with its hoarders, racketeers, and the back-stabbing army recruit (Larraine Day) jealous of Turner's WAC and determined to prevent her from becoming an officer. As OWI reader Sandy Roth commented, "At a time when women all over the world are serving the United Nations war effort, the story's presentation of American women at war could mislead overseas audiences as to the real nature of their contribution."[83] McCall was far less interested in presenting a perfectly united and patriotic home front by 1945 and wanted to show a range of women persuaded to cooperate. As she knew all too well, collaboration was never easy. By the end of the film, all of the WACs are unified in their effort to win the war, but the wartime coalition between the media, the film industry, and the government was not always smooth.

Although McCall would publicly defend Hollywood from smear campaigns from outsiders (particularly in her response to Marcia Winn's *Chicago Tribune* exposé in 1943), she continued to battle political groups on the extreme right intent on muzzling the unions. In the spring and summer of 1944, she and her fellow guild members were faced with the Motion Picture Alliance for the Preservation of American Ideals. President of the

MPA Sam Wood, William Randolph Hearst, and other conservative film-makers had been accusing liberal organizations and unions of "subversive activities." In the summer of 1944, McCall and other prominent Hollywood Democrats launched a "counterattack" from the Hollywood Women's Club, organized by the Emergency Committee of Hollywood Guilds and Unions. Fellow writer Oliver H. P. Garrett drew attention to the similarities between the MPA's public statements and those of Hitler. McCall focused on the attacks on Hollywood unions and "flatly accused MPA members of union-busting intentions." She was widely quoted in the national press: "We don't believe union-busting is an American ideal."[84]

The Emergency Committee united liberal workers across the industry and included the Brotherhood of Electrical Workers, Screen Cartoonists, the Screen Publicists Guild, the Society of Motion Picture Film Editors, the Story Analysts Guild, the Brotherhood of Carpenters and Unions, the Songwriters Protective Association, and the Screen Writers Guild. But protection of the unions, a fundamental policy of the New Deal, was under threat. As attacks increased from the likes of Cecil B. DeMille, McCall, with her mid-Atlantic, Roosevelt-esque drawl, responded on radio broadcasts, the champion of the Hollywood Left.[85]

One of McCall's characters in *Keep Your Powder Dry*, a young bride (Susan Peters) who joins the WACs when her husband is sent overseas, becomes an officer only to learn that her husband has been killed in action. She tells her girlfriends, "I just feel that right now, nothing's important, except doing the best you can—whatever happens. Sticking to it. Not quitting. Lots of people—ordinary people—taking a job and not running out on it."[86] This was McCall's philosophy, but the number of committees she belonged to or chaired was daunting even by her standards. She was one of the most visible and vocal women in the industry in the first half of 1944, recently divorced, and newly remarried to army officer, David Bramson, then serving overseas in Italy. She was also pregnant. On August 4, 1944, *Daily Variety* noted that she had resigned as president of the guild. At that time she was six months pregnant, but back in 1934–35, she had managed to work hours before she gave birth to twins and went back to work soon afterward. Was she forced to resign—a working, married, divorced, and now remarried-to-a-younger-man mother of three? It was a very sensitive time for the unions, but also one of the guild's last successful and unified periods. Her longtime ally Charles Brackett was not able to take over for her as he was serving as president of the Academy of Motion Picture Arts and Sciences, and that left Vice President Lester Cole.

Cole represented the guild's communist faction, and with increasing attacks on the Roosevelt administration, concerns about the Soviet alliance, and the strident MPA, the Screen Writers Guild was looking vulnerable. Though McCall's extensive Washington contacts gave her and the guild some measure of protection from conservative Republicans and HUAC when she sounded off about Hearst and union busting, Cole was not so skilled or well protected a negotiator. He also resented McCall's power within the guild. Years later, Cole's misogyny manifested itself when he described his election to the presidency "following the pregnancy of Mary McCarthy" [sic].[87] His attempt to diminish McCall's importance later in life revealed classic gendered resentment of a powerful woman. McCall had always inspired a range of emotions in her male colleagues, from antipathy and fear to friendship and loyalty. As daughter Mary-David Sheiner recalled, some of her mother's colleagues would playfully address McCall as "Sir" on the phone and at meetings. Anti-communist informants expressed their hostility a year later, in August 1945, when the FBI noted that according to one industry fink, "McCall had been active in communist front organizations, especially those having to do with women."[88] While McCall's "maiden" speech as guild president hadn't been overtly feminist, her war work for the War Activities Committee and her scripts about working girl Maisie Ravier revealed her commitment to expanding women's independence in the workforce—during and after the war. Shortly before her resignation, as she led her colleagues in an attempt to defend the Hollywood unions from attacks by the newly formed MPA, members of the Emergency Committee of Hollywood Guilds and Unions pledged to work with producers "in reabsorbing returning Hollywood servicemen and women."[89] McCall vowed this was one major industry where women's employment gains were not going to be purged with the peace.

Despite her resignation, McCall returned to work only a few months after the birth of her fourth child, Mary-David, in November 1944. On March 2, 1945, the *Hollywood Reporter* noted that McCall had been elected chairman of the Council of Hollywood Guilds and Unions. It was she who worked with the National Labor Relations Board to side with the radical alternative to IATSE, the strikers of the Conference of Studio Unions and Local 1421 picketing Warner Bros. It was a tricky situation, not only because it split the Left (the Communist Party members of the guild were abiding by a wartime no-strike pledge and would not support the strikers), but also because had McCall and other trade unionists gone with their first instinct and initially gone on strike with the CSU, the writers would have violated the guild's minimum basic agreement with the producers by siding with the other union.[90] McCall could sense the danger to Hollywood's labor movement through right-wing efforts to smear New Deal liberalism with communism. FBI informants reported that in the period since she resigned the presidency, "there had recently developed . . . considerable opposition to the pro-communist leadership."[91] Friend Emmet Lavery had assumed leadership of the progressive-moderate majority in the guild, and he would take over the presidency in 1945, with McCall later serving as his vice president from his second term in 1946.[92] To an extent, McCall was his mentor, and they shared a commitment to the Screen Writers Guild that trumped any political alliance. Things would stand or fall for them, not over HUAC's disputes with the Hollywood Ten, but over the threat posed by the Taft-Hartley Act (1947).

Briefly, however, writers united regardless of political affiliation to mourn the death of Franklin Roosevelt. The Roosevelt administration's labor policies were responsible for the guild's victories in securing a contract, and McCall was a conspicuous supporter of Roosevelt in the 1944 election.[93] Shortly after the president's death in the spring of 1945, MGM producer Dore Schary wrote to the secretary of the Hollywood Writers Mobilization, Pauline Lauber, asking McCall to write a speech for an event at the Hollywood Bowl. She, Helen Deutsch, Emmet Lavery, Francis Faragoh, Ring Lardner Jr., and Dalton Trumbo were among those members of the Hollywood Writers Mobilization approached to write speeches in tribute. Two years later, this work put her under scrutiny for communism; Jack B. Tenney's California Legislative Committee investigating un-Americanism claimed that the Hollywood Writers Mobilization was "100 percent pro-Communist controlled."[94] Although never specifically under investigation by the FBI, her file, opened when she was elected president of the guild in 1942, grew with her anti-MPA work, in spite of the fact that she did not belong to the Committee for the First Amendment, refused to publicly support the Hollywood Nineteen or other calls for the Screen Writers Guild to defend the Hollywood Ten. She did, however, continue to support the rights of unions, speaking in March 1947 at the Olympic Auditorium in Los Angeles in protest against the recent "attacks on labor."[95]

Political tensions exploded over the summer; forty-three names were added to HUAC's list as it opened investigations into alleged communist infiltration of Hollywood. Some were friendly witnesses; others—many of them screenwriters—were not. Ten would be cited for contempt of Congress and were given yearlong jail sentences. On November 25, 1947, the president of the Motion Picture Association of America, Eric Johnston, publicly fired the Hollywood Ten. But the battle wasn't over for McCall, Lavery, and the Screen Writers Guild. The issue for McCall was not saving a few screenwriters from jail time, but the survival of the guild itself. The Taft-Hartley Act stated that labor union leaders had to sign affidavits proclaiming their non-communist affiliation or lose the protection of the NLRB in labor disputes. Furthermore, should disgruntled members on the right break away from the guild, angered at any gestures of protection for communist members, Taft-Hartley would encourage them to break the power of the writers' hard-won company union. Only those non-communist-declaring groups would make the ballot for a new union, so outraged members of the Left fleeing the guild would have no protection at all and wouldn't even be eligible on a ballot. Should the guild members not declare themselves, then the guild couldn't even be on the ballot. Writers would be back to the days of the Screen Playwrights, when no contract existed and secretaries were paid more than screenwriters per week. This was why for so long McCall and past presidents had safeguarded the political affiliations and names of guild members. She, Lavery, James Cain, and other members of the board of executives offered to sign loyalty oaths that they were not communists, as a way of protecting the rest of the members. The alternative was the loss of the guild's legal status as a union and all McCall and her colleagues had fought for to obtain the contract.

As Lavery put it in a confidential Screen Writers Guild memo, "Is it too much, under all these circumstances, to ask our brethren of the far Left to sit out one waltz? To give the Guild every chance to protect itself in the event of another bargaining election? To put Guild policy, for a few months, or a year perhaps, above one's personal political policy?"[96] It was a question of temporary "strategy" to keep the wider gains of the guild safe, he argued. However unconstitutional Taft-Hartley was, it had been approved by Congress and was now the law of the land. Lavery had an especially tough time that fall and winter. His new play, *Gentleman from Athens*, was in rehearsal in New York when Lela Rogers claimed on the radio that it was communist propaganda. Though Lavery would sue her and eventually win, the play died a quick death on Broadway while he was in the middle of PR radio shows defending the guild from charges of subversion.[97] McCall, as his vice president, had remained in Hollywood, managing the guild's day-to-day affairs. Both stood down from their offices soon after, worn out by the thankless task of being moderates in the middle of a political shooting range. They continued to maintain a foothold in the industry, running again for the board of governors in 1948 along with a suite of other moderate writers, including Jane Murfin.[98]

For a while, at least, Lavery's and McCall's measures seemed to have worked to protect the majority of guild members. The writers' contract remained in place, though Lavery's claim, "we took the blows from both sides and today we have a guild stronger than it has ever been before," was only half right.[99] But McCall was facing her own personal reckoning.

In 1948, after four years at a $3,000-a-week salary at Twentieth Century-Fox and fifteen as a SWG organizer and leader, her studio career was in serious trouble. Fox did not renew her contract and no other offers were forthcoming. Hedda Hopper put items in her column stating that McCall was creating her own production company with new husband David Bramson, but nothing developed but rumors.[100] Her last major production with Fox, *Dancer in the Dark* (1949), a musical with a clumsy, nonsinging, nondancing, and, as far as McCall was concerned, nonacting Betsy Drake, was unpleasant. But even as work assignments evaporated, McCall's commitment to the union was paramount, and she continued to work with labor management committees to supervise disputes over credits.

Despite McCall's best efforts, the blacklist gained momentum, affecting the careers of many of her female colleagues and friends. Lillian Hellman was named a communist by the American Legion in 1949; Jean Muir, whom McCall had known since her early days in Hollywood, was similarly slandered in *Red Channels* and was fired from her job on NBC's *Aldrich Family* in 1950. A reenergized HUAC continued to call screenwriters to testify in 1951. That summer, guild members, their backs to the wall, begged McCall to take over its leadership. In November, she was elected a third time. Doris Gilbert, who began her career during McCall's second term as president writing women's war pictures (*Ladies Courageous*, 1944), wired McCall that she "couldn't be happier you're the president and I was right."[101] In a guild photo shoot commemorating her third term, McCall played up her "Sir" alter ego, posing in her office with her books, big desk, faithful St. Bernard, men's tweed jacket, and exaggerated calabash pipe (figure 4.7). The fun and games did not last. Her final term in office was marred by a credit dispute with the head of RKO, Howard Hughes, nephew of her old adversary on the MPA, Rupert Hughes.

Guild and communist writer Paul Jarrico had signed a contract with Hughes for *The Las Vegas Story* (1952), wrote it, and was denied final credit due to his political affiliation. This was in violation of a fundamental right of the guild, won in 1941–42, to arbitrate and award screen credit on all productions. Hughes did try to buy Jarrico off behind the scenes, but McCall threw the weight of the union at him. As she remembered, "I did not intend to permit Mr. Hughes to trample on a labor agreement with muddy tennis shoes."[102] McCall sent Hughes a strong letter stating that RKO was in breach of the SWG contract and that "this is clearly a labor dispute. It does not involve the political beliefs of Mr. Jarrico, however repugnant they might be to you or us."[103] But he and RKO took the case to court, and predictably, given the prevailing political climate, the guild lost

Figure 4.7 McCall aka "Sir," as Screen Writers Guild president, 1951

its case and the right to appeal to the California Supreme Court. According to the court, Jarrico's political beliefs were in breach of his contract on moral grounds. By 1953, the contract McCall had fought so hard to secure was rewritten to enable producers to deny credit to communists. But by then, McCall had resigned. Although Republic hired her to write a feminist western starring Ella Raines, *Ride the Man Down* (1952), and her wartime military contacts helped her with the background on *Thunderbirds* (1952), her career in Hollywood was over. To add salt to the wound, Twentieth Century-Fox denied her credit for writing Marilyn Monroe's dialogue in *There's No Business Like Show Business* (1954). With typically black humor, McCall later quipped, "She needs dialogue?"

To her dying day, it was McCall's grim belief that Hughes gave her name to his FBI contacts and had her blacklisted. Despite McCall's suspicions, however, Hughes should not receive sole credit for blacklisting her. It was her long-term commitment to the writers' union, her willingness to take stands, strategize, and compromise that ended McCall's career in Hollywood. Myron C. Fagan listed her as a fellow traveler in *Red Stars in Hollywood* back in 1950.[104] Already facing poverty in the summer of

1951, she wrote directly to J. Edgar Hoover, stating that she was "against both Communism and Fascism and was for Democracy."[105] Together with Sheridan Gibney, Charles Brackett, and Lavery, she claimed she was "among the middle-of-the-road people who believed sincerely in the principles of collective bargaining and craft unions, and who were willing to take the boredom and hard work of attendance at guild meetings and of office-holding in the guild."[106] Hoover responded personally but unhelpfully, stating that she was not a subject of any investigation and should "use your own good judgment" as to how to proceed with employers. Fagan, who had described her as "a female of the species," displayed a misogyny found in contemporaneous FBI reports drawing attention to the alleged communist elements in women's organizations. While few Hollywood news items contained any condescending rhetoric about McCall and other professional female writers from the 1930s through the war, the attitude and tone began to change beginning in the late 1940s.

She was out of the industry and virtually penniless by 1953. In the hope of getting assignments in television, McCall even testified before the California State Committee in 1954, refusing to take the Fifth Amendment, stating baldly that she "hated" communism, but declining to name names.[107] Her friend Charles Brackett wrote a letter to the California State Committee in 1954, in which he recalled, "Of all the fighters on our side, of all the ardent and aware anti-communists, Mrs. Bramson was the most ardent and the most effective."[108] Calling her his "right hand in the fight," he praised her for continuing the struggle when she became president of the guild. "That it should be necessary to write this letter for anyone with her magnificent public record shocks me profoundly," he wrote. Although the committee exonerated her, the FBI acknowledged that she was not a communist, and the press in Hollywood and nationally gave her sympathetic coverage, she remained blacklisted by the producers who had once made hundreds of thousands of dollars on her scripts.

She scratched out a living in the television industry, but several years later McCall was still being targeted by Fagan's right-wing organization. In the California Legislature's eleventh report of the Senate Fact-Finding Subcommittee on Un-American Activities, members discussed "The Case of Mary McCall" as a separate item. The committee members agreed with her criticism of Fagan and his ilk, deploring this particular manifestation of witch-hunting. *Daily Variety* went out of its way to exonerate her, but Hollywood producers did not offer her any pictures.[109] In 1960, a decade after serving his term in prison for contempt of Congress and continuing to write for Hollywood under false names, Dalton Trumbo would be back in the fold, receiving full credit on *Spartacus* (1960). But McCall, outspoken woman, political moderate, and defender of the Hollywood studio and guilds system, was not an appropriate "hero" for the postblacklist era.[110]

Never a communist, she pulled no punches in her dislike for guild members such as Trumbo: "My own feeling about persons who shout their virtues and disclaim their sins of which nobody responsible has accused them, is that they protest too much. And my feeling about members of the Communist Party is that they would not hesitate for a second to lie under oath, except when they know there's enough evidence in the hands of the investigators to convict them of perjury. Under those circumstances, they prate about the First Amendment, or run for the border."[111] Unlike Trumbo, Lester Cole, and even her cantankerous colleague Lillian Hellman, McCall respected and had publicly defended the Hollywood studio system, and had pledged herself to work within the industry to improve basic working conditions for writers and all members of the guilds and unions. Although it is perhaps understandable that some producers would want to destroy her career in revenge, historians' and critics' marginalization of McCall in favor of an almost exclusively male cast of valiant and vocal Hollywood lefties is more unsettling. Those same journalists and historians who lambast studio-era Hollywood for institutionalized sexism are even more guilty by omission than the industry that once respected, quoted, and feared Mary C. McCall Jr.

CHAPTER 5

Controlling the Cut

I'd rather do this kind of work all night than spend an hour scrubbing a floor.
Barbara McLean, 1939[1]

"Women are better at editing motion pictures than men."[2] So began an early 1941 article on "the only living person ever to edit DeMille": Anne Bauchens. Bauchens had just collected her Oscar for work on the action-filled *Northwest Mounted Police* (1940); a few years earlier, the year the Academy of Motion Picture Arts and Sciences created the award category in editing, she had been nominated for *Cleopatra* (1934). Bauchens's bald and uncompromising statement was not based on any subjective commitment to "feminism," the journalist insisted. "It's based on experience and a rather close observation. And, what's more, Cecil B. DeMille agrees with her." She had been cutting his pictures since 1918 (*You Can't Have Everything*) and would remain with him through *The Ten Commandments* in 1956. But though Bauchens's opinion of editing talent was "objective," she claimed that it was women's greater emotional development that made them better editors: "'Women are generally more sensitive than men. . . . And I've noticed that in editing a picture, just as in seeing one, men hold themselves aloof—they're more objective than women."[3] This emotional distance from the film limited men's dramatic sense of narrative and their creative risks with style. In order to write the language of film, an editor could not hold herself at a distance.

More than any other profession in Hollywood, editing demanded total immersion in the film medium. Studio-era Hollywood's top female editors understood that the emotional, intellectual, and physical demands of filmmaking knew no limits. Whether through shooting additional close-ups and footage, remaining on the set and in postproduction longer than anyone else, or sitting alone for hours in the editing room, studying, cutting, and running the celluloid through their fingers day and night (sixteen-hour workdays, six-day weeks, and working through the night were routine),[4] Hollywood's most influential female editors wrote and spoke about the profession as a true calling and commitment.

While writers, designers, executives, actresses, publicists, and press-women could divide their lives among work, family, union, political campaigning, and social life, with varying degrees of success, female editors lived and breathed for the studio. Few married outside their profession; even fewer had children. Unlike Hollywood's women in the Screen Writers Guild, female editors were not particularly politically active or prominent in the management of the Motion Picture Editors Guild, and of the 520 members of the Hollywood community accused of communism by the FBI, only one was an editor, assistant cutter Jeanne Turner.[5]

Many of the key female editors active in the studio era from the 1930s through the 1960s began their careers in the silent era. Certainly, women worked as film editors from the origins of filmmaking: Rose Smith began working for Griffith at Biograph and would edit *The Birth of a Nation* (1915) and *Intolerance* (1916), two of the masterworks of the silent era. Booth also had her start working with Griffith, before moving to MGM, where she would eventually control the studio's entire feature output and serve as associate producer. Veteran Viola Lawrence learned her trade at First National before establishing herself as Columbia's most respected cutter. Jane Loring and Blanche Sewell both started out acting in the silents before changing careers, while Dorothy Arzner would transition from editing Valentino's bullfighting scenes in *Blood and Sand* (1922) to directing. For young Bobbie Pollut, editing was a family business. Her father ran a film laboratory in the E. K. Lincoln studio in New Jersey, and she worked there during her summer vacations, cutting negatives and patching release prints. A few years later, she moved to the West Coast as Barbara McLean.

These women cultivated strong working relationships with their studio heads, who, in some cases, trusted their judgment on the entire range of feature output. From the mid-1930s, producers actively campaigned on their behalf for Academy Award nominations. Until recently, Barbara McLean, "Hollywood's Editor-in-Chief" according to the columnists,[6] was the most-nominated editor in the Academy of Motion Picture Arts and Sciences' history, nominated seven times (for *Les Misérables*, 1935; *Lloyd's of London*, 1936; *Alexander's Ragtime Band*, 1938; *The Rains Came*, 1939; *Song of Bernadette*, 1943; *Wilson*, 1944; and *All About Eve*), and winning for the Fox presidential biopic *Wilson*. Another editor who worked at Fox from 1942, Dorothy Spencer, was nominated three times, for *Stagecoach*, *Decision Before Dawn* (1951), and *Cleopatra* (1963). Booth won the 1936 award for *Mutiny on the Bounty* (1935); Adrienne Fazan was nominated for *An American in Paris* (1951) and won for *Gigi* (1958). Alma Macrorie was nominated for *The Bridges at Toko-Ri* (1955) and longtime Columbia editor Viola Lawrence for the musicals *Pal Joey* (1957) and *Pepe* (1960).

Producers also promoted their editors by arranging favorable interviews and feature articles, particularly during the 1930s, the high point for women's Academy nominations.[7] Women were crucial in publicizing the industrial and artistic importance of editing in Hollywood and became the public face of the profession.[8] They responded with unflinching loyalty. For Margaret Booth and Barbara McLean, the studio era's two most famous editors, MGM and Twentieth Century-Fox were "home," and the studio was a "family" one "loved" without reservation.

Yet, despite their fame within the industry and the syndicated press in the 1930s and 1940s, Booth, Bauchens, Lawrence, and McLean are obscure footnotes in Hollywood history. As female editors, they are doubly "invisible" in the director-driven agendas of contemporary film criticism. In her lively effort to bring attention to female writers in Hollywood, *Script Girls*, critic Lizzie Francke has dismissed the work of female editors: "Sewing up films in a dark room under the judicious eyes of the director obviously limited their participation in the story-telling process."[9] Other scholars and critics have persisted in seeing only a handful of celluloid seamstresses working behind the scenes, with some claiming only eight women worked as editors during the 1930s.[10] But there were far more than this.

Fragments of the Society of Motion Picture Film Editors and Motion Picture Editors Guild union records give some indication of the substantial numbers of women in the profession. The following women obtained membership in the guild from 1937 to 1949: Barbara McLean, Sylvia Reid, Monica Collingwood, Hazel Marshall (the "inventor" of Hollywood's oldest stock footage library at Paramount),[11] Dorothy Spencer, Mary Steward, Florence Leona Lindsay, Margaret Booth, Ida Jaediker, Lora Hays, Virginia Boland, Marjorie Fowler, Verna MacCurran, Iris Rainsberger, Virginia Lively Stone, Laura Jackson, Betty Lane, Lela Wetzel, Evelyn Kennedy, Erma Levin, Jill Vandenburg, Margaret Harfield, Jeanne Rochlin, Dena Levitt, Kay Rose, Eve Newman, Joyce Breeze, Virginia Gardner, Bettie Biery, Marguerite Sokolow, Rosemarie Hickson, Geraldine Lerner, Anna Kanis, Reva Schlesinger, Sally Flint, Beatrice Connetta, Mary Manfra, Alice Kellor, Wanda Rotz, Roma Crowder, Viola Brown, Mili Bonsignori, Angeline Sweeney, and Irene Bazzini.[12] The records are certainly not complete: Members Bauchens,

Lawrence, Fazan, Eda Warren, Alma Macrorie, Irene and Eleanor Morra, Frances Marsh, Judy Barker, Lucille Jelik, Helene Turner, Kay Fitzgerald, Lela Simone, Lucille Tanner, and Caroline Ries are not recorded, and original papers, transferred to databases in the 1970s, are fragmentary at best. But this is more than the "handful" of female editors syndicated journalists and popular historians insist worked in the studio system.

Although a number of the women listed above did not receive screen credit for their work, others did. Many of the top box-office and critical successes of the Hollywood studio era were edited by women: *The Merry Widow* (1925), *Chicago* (1927), *Our Dancing Daughters* (1928), *The Big House* (1930), *The Sign of the Cross* (1932), *Mutiny on the Bounty*, *Captain January* (1936), *Camille* (1937), *Only Angels Have Wings* (1939), *Jesse James* (1939), *The Wizard of Oz* (1939), *I Married a Witch* (1942), *My Sister Eileen* (1942), *Song of Bernadette*, *Frenchman's Creek* (1944), *The Bishop's Wife* (1947), *Twelve O'Clock High* (1949), *The Snake Pit*, *In a Lonely Place* (1950), *All About Eve*, *Singin' in the Rain*, *Gigi* (1958), *Elmer Gantry* (1960), and *Cleopatra* to name only a fraction.

As the partial list indicates, women were not assigned to productions aimed primarily at female audiences. Occasionally, as with Columbia's prestige project *Craig's Wife*, a studio's publicity releases would emphasize its commitment to women calling the shots in filmmaking by highlighting an almost exclusively female crew (in this case, Dorothy Arzner's direction, McCall's writing, Russell's acting, and Viola Lawrence's editing).[13] However, as journalist Amy H. Croughton noted in 1937:

> These women film editors by no means confine their work to society dramas. Margaret Booth, for instance, edited *Mutiny on the Bounty* before tackling *Romeo and Juliet* and *Camille*. Jane Loring has edited several of Katharine Hepburn's pictures. Barbara McLean is responsible for the editing of *A Country Doctor* and *Lloyd's of London*. Irene Morra edited two Shirley Temple pictures and then switched to a football film, *Pigskin Parade*. Eda Warren turned from editing the gay *Paris in Spring* to the grim picture of Chinese revolution, *The General Died at Dawn*.[14]

Croughton indicated that Hollywood supported men and women editors equally, not only through gender-blind film assignments, but also by making credit attribution more rigorous. Things had changed for the better since the silent era. In the 1920s, editors were often uncredited, "seeing credit for their cleverness go to directors, actors, and photographers."[15] Anne Bauchens was one of these, Croughton pointed out, a DeMille veteran, who for years was responsible for "bringing order out of the chaos of film that he shoots in producing his great spectacles."[16]

But with the death of the studio system in the 1960s, things changed. McLean was approaching retirement and Booth, though she won a lifetime achievement award in 1978 and would continue to edit until 1982 (John Huston's *Annie* featured clips from her work on *Camille*, 1937), was not receiving the public attention she had during Hollywood's golden age. Instead of focusing on women, press articles on editing interviewed men such as Ralph Winters (who received an Academy Award for *Ben-Hur*, 1959, a film Booth actually cut). In one such interview, Winters mused on the relative anonymity of editors (male and female): "No one should be conscious of a cut."[17] Toward the end of the article, journalist Gene Handsaker acknowledged, as if surprised, "A few editors are women." But he named Spencer, Fazan, Bauchens, and McLean, women who had their start in the industry decades ago. Younger female cutters—such as sound editor Verna Fields (*El Cid*, 1960), Anne Coates (*Lawrence of Arabia*, 1962), Dede Allen (*Bonnie and Clyde*, 1967) and Thelma Schoonmaker (*Who's That Knocking at My Door*, 1967)—weren't even mentioned. By the 1960s, popular history had relegated influential female editors to another era.

However, it is no accident of history that this shift coincides with the rise of popular and academic film criticism reliant on Andrew Sarris's director-focused theories of screen authorship. The concept of the director's primary authorship of a film eliminated an important period in the studio era when writers, producers, actors, and editors assumed and were awarded authorship within a collaborative system of production. Although directors have become more hands-on in the editing room since the end of the studio era, studio-era film editors were not mere technicians carrying out the vision of the director.

From the late 1920s, editors were on the set when shooting started and frequently put a rough cut together with little or no input from the director. Often the second editor's rough cut became, with a few minor changes, the final cut seen by audiences.[18] Nancy Naumburg's collaborative portrait of Hollywood film production, featuring essays by sixteen key professionals, came about because, she argued, "The technique of the American film is the most highly developed and most widely imitated . . . [but] few people outside of the industry are familiar with it." A year before Anne Bauchens's essay on editing was published in Naumburg's book, *The Plainsman* (1936) had again earned the veteran editor critical attention and was one of the biggest box-office draws of the year. Despite working for arguably Hollywood's best-known director-producer, Bauchens downplayed the control directors had over the final cut: "While a few insist on cutting their own pictures . . . they are very scarce."[19] It was far more common in the 1920s and 1930s for directors to simply leave the cutting to the editors and producer.

At Twentieth Century-Fox, Zanuck's directors John Ford, Gregory La Cava, and Henry King would leave after the final take and avoid the editing room so that Barbara McLean could get down to work. As she recalled of her years with Zanuck, "I've always been pretty fortunate in being able to put the picture in the first cut as I saw fit."[20] Though arguably a skilled director or cinematographer could make the editor's job of selecting the "best" shots easier, as often she was "presented with a mass of film, evidently shot at random, from which [s]he must piece together a smooth, pictorial story."[21] In an in-depth article on McLean in 1939, journalist Hubbard Keavy explained the job of the editor:

> The cutter has to make sense out of all the stuff the director shoots, eliminating loose ends and poorly-made scenes, switching his continuity, simplifying the story and speeding it up, giving it rhythm and otherwise trying to make the picture so good that you and I won't squirm and get restless when we see it.[22]

McLean's summary of editing was essentially that it involved "making filmed matters seem better than they are."[23] Neither the director nor the producer seemed to figure in the equation except as rather undisciplined coworkers the editors had to put up with. So much for the auteur theory.

There are obstacles in reconstructing the careers and influence of editors, male or female, for sadly, the extant production materials are not particularly helpful. The studio archives, once avoided by left-leaning critics and cultural historians ideologically suspicious of the corporate capitalist studios but star-struck enough to interview directors John Ford, Orson Welles, and Alfred Hitchcock, have been key in adjusting historians' awareness of the limitations of traditional genre studies and director-based auteur frameworks. Yet for women in certain branches of the industry and feminist film historians, this has been only a partial victory. While the Howard Gotlieb Center at Boston University was instrumental in acquiring the papers of actresses such as Bette Davis, Myrna Loy, and Janet Gaynor, and more recently, the Academy of Motion Picture Arts and Sciences's Margaret Herrick Library continues to add major collections for Katharine Hepburn and Eva Marie Saint, the papers of nonacting female filmmakers are relatively scarce. Editors—both men and women—did not save their papers after they retired; Booth's papers at AMPAS are scanty and focused on the last few years of her career with Ray Stark, and McLean destroyed hers. During their lifetimes, major universities did not approach these women for the purchase or donation of their papers, and instead focused on acquiring the work of famous men: Cecil B. DeMille at Brigham Young University and Darryl F. Zanuck at the University of Southern California. Ironically, though Jeanie Macpherson's and Sonya Levien's prominent roles as screenwriters emerge through DeMille's and Zanuck's extant papers, memos, and story conferences (again, transcribed and edited by female secretaries and production assistants), cutting notes and continuities are not part of these collections (although, on occasion, Zanuck's script conference notes indicate that editors McLean and Dorothy Spencer were present and involved in routine decision-making about rewrites and retakes).[24] Studio cutting continuities—for example, the material housed in the Turner-MGM Script Collection at the Academy of Motion Picture Arts and Sciences Library—tell us nothing about how editing decisions were arrived at and are merely brief, anonymous transcripts of shots.

In some cases from the 1940s, younger directors such as Fred Zinnemann (*The Seventh Cross*, 1944) and George Stevens (*I Remember Mama*, 1948) chose to preserve their own handwritten editing notes in order to control the final cuts of their films (which were in turn solicited and preserved in the Academy of Motion Picture Arts and Sciences Library), but unlike many of their contemporaries, they represent director-editors who took charge of a rough cut beginning in the late 1940s when directors pushed to extend their control over the final cut. During the 1930s and early 1940s, producers and writers would develop a project, and once it was passed on to a director, an editor would do a rough cut and then take general direction from a producer and a supervising editor. These supervising editors had control over an entire studio's feature output, and from 1936, Margaret Booth worked in this capacity for the industry's wealthiest studio, MGM. McLean and Lawrence would also work as supervising feature editors for many years at Fox and Columbia, yet historians have not considered how much these studios' "house styles" are actually indebted to the creative control of their female supervising feature editors.

While some historians have pointed out how well Britain's David Lean and Robert Wise did transitioning from editing to directing, and Dorothy Arzner also worked as a cutter before becoming a full-time director, no one remembers Jane Loring. A former silent actress, Loring first met Katharine Hepburn while editing *Alice Adams* (1935) and continued to edit her films at RKO. The two maintained a lifelong friendship that was acknowledged in the columns.[25] Always versatile, she codirected Hepburn in *Break of Hearts* (1936),[26] wrote treatments for *The Seventh Cross*, *Dragon Seed* (1944), and other high-profile films, and worked as Pandro Berman's associate producer and editor at MGM in the 1940s. Berman, overshadowed by Selznick at RKO, was nonetheless an intelligent and capable producer, and he and Loring deserve considerable credit for the maverick Hepburn's early and most assertively feminist works. The range and depth of Loring's work survives in the Turner-MGM Script Collection at the Academy library, but she appears as one of many collaborators on the scripts (and an uncredited editor) rather than as a named auteur (while, in contrast, Howard Estabrook's and John Huston's scripts are organized under their own collections). Today, Loring is remembered only in Hepburn's memoirs and biographies as one of Hollywood's "top cutters."[27]

The few important traces that survive indicating the industry's more complex attitude toward female editors in the studio era are trade paper and syndicated press articles, interviews with women active in the industry, the rare collaborative film history, star memoirs, and oral histories. Looking closely at these sources reveals a group of women who had potentially more impact on the development of Hollywood's film language than any other filmmaking or professional branch. At a production level, supervising editor Margaret Booth was arguably as influential as Irving Thalberg. Her colleague and friend at MGM, Blanche Sewell (figure 5.1), was known as one of the best editors in the business. Anne Bauchens created the "DeMille look" over five decades, and Irene Morra was one half of a winning combination with director David Butler at Fox, Paramount, and Warner

Figure 5.1 MGM studio portrait of its two top editors, Margaret Booth and Blanche Sewell, 1934

Bros., producing dozens of hits including *Sunny Side Up* (1929), *Bright Eyes* (1934), *The Littlest Rebel* (1936), *Dimples* (1936), *Road to Morocco* (1942), *The Time, the Place, and the Girl* (1946), *Calamity Jane* (1953), and *The Girl He Left Behind* (1956).[28]

But it is through the perspective of Barbara "Bobbie" McLean that the power of studio-era Hollywood's editors truly emerges. McLean's oral history, conducted just after her retirement in 1970, remains the most extensive source on editing in the studio era, and ironically was only commissioned as part of the American Film Institute's Darryl F. Zanuck Research Project to preserve the reputation of the mogul. But "Bobbie" was more than the pretty young girl at his elbow, taking notes in the darkness as he watched the rushes; she was the woman who shaped Twentieth Century-Fox's film style from 1935 to 1969, providing continuity among the production eras of Zanuck Senior, Spyros Skouras, Buddy Adler, and Richard Zanuck.

Twenty-one-year-old Barbara McLean and her husband Gordon, a special effects technician, left her father's film lab and moved to the West Coast in 1924. She took a job at the Fox Studios on Western Avenue in Los Angeles, and then, when she'd learned everything from the head of the lab, Henry Goldfarb, applied for "a better job" at First National down the road in Burbank. Editor Harold Young, who would work for Alexander Korda, first as an editor (*The Private Life of Helen of Troy*, 1927) and then as a director (*The Scarlet Pimpernel*, 1935), hired her as his assistant. It was there at United Artists that she learned to synchronize music on the early Colleen Moore–Gary Cooper war picture *Lilac Time* (1928), working under Alexander Hall: "We did it with a stopwatch. . . . Oh, it was a mess," she remembered.[29] McLean loved the technical challenges of mixing sound and images, and remembered with a laugh that they were still synching the film when it opened, completing a little bit each day, but "The people who went to see the picture about three weeks later saw all the sounds"— without a synchronizer for the soundtrack, they had to stretch the intertitles to cover the gaps.

Ironically, when her future boss Darryl Zanuck and Warner Bros. took over First National in the fall of 1928, she was fired and went to work with Mary Pickford and Sam Goldwyn at United Artists. It was here among a cohort of independent production companies that she developed a close relationship with Pickford, learned the value of the close-up, and experimented on her own with technique. The introduction of sound gave editors more power than directors over the development of the cut. In the silent era, directors often cut their own negatives, using an assistant to take direction and expedite the process. Editors worked as technicians and glorified filing clerks, but the good ones learned their trade through watching directors. This was, for example, how Margaret Booth remembered learning to cut—by watching director John Stahl, until one day, when Stahl "couldn't get a sequence the way he wanted," he looked at a rough cut Booth had been practicing on with the outtakes and used that instead in the final cut.[30] However, with the addition of the dialogue and music soundtracks, sound effects, and later color, editing became far more "arduous" and complex. Many directors didn't have the time, patience, or skill to edit with the soundtrack. Also, the studio production system had changed by the late 1920s, so that it became less efficient to allow maverick directors to rack up miles of footage and cut by themselves (like the notorious Erich von Stroheim, famously reined in by Thalberg, the man who created Margaret Booth's job as supervising editor at MGM). Now, in the financially straitened 1930s, producers worked first in consultation with writers, then directors, and then editors. The Society of Motion Picture Film Editors—later the Motion Picture Editors Guild—would form in 1937 and agree on minimum wages and overtime bonuses with the producers,[31] but already the Academy was recognizing the value of editing through the creation of the award.

Amid this upheaval, McLean worked as an assistant editor on Pickford's first sound picture, *Coquette* (1929), where, as she recalled, seven cameras were used to photograph the courtroom sequence. At one point, she cut a word from the soundtrack that Pickford didn't like: "Well, you'd think I had performed a brain operation. . . . Oh, everybody thought I'd done something wonderful, taking out the word 'red.'"[32] Working with sound and image tracks made things more complicated than they had been for silent editing, but McLean relished the technical challenges and loved the fact that in the early 1930s "I could get to every department and do everything, even to do a good deal of working on music. . . . You'd go on the scoring stage when they'd do the music, to see what he would be doing. You were there watching out for your own good. You know, to know how everything was going to fit. Each thing you learned a little more."[33] Later, departments formed and the work was more compartmentalized and constrained by unions, but McLean's more free-wheeling, collaborative experience at Pickford's studio and her own early musical training gave her an appreciation for editing as a kind of musical composition and scoring. It was this inner "rhythm," she and Margaret Booth would argue, that gave editing the power of an art.

McLean remembered her period with Pickford with affection: "This was a very close company." At Pickford's studio, collaboration worked on two levels: people worked for each other and with each other, often doing several jobs at once without complaint. As McLean recalled, "If the script girls that worked on the set were sick, the assistant editor would run on the set and take notes."[34] Artistic hierarchies did not exist on the set, even with someone of Pickford's status at the helm. According to McLean, Pickford also dressed the sets and made sure the editors had tea while they worked. And because the younger woman didn't have a car, Pickford "used to pick me up and take me home every night. . . . When she left to go on her vacation, she'd send me a little note saying how wonderful it was that she could leave the picture in such good hands."[35] It was not the last time that a producer would leave Bobbie in charge of the cut.

According to McLean, independent production companies, first at United Artists and later at the breakaway Twentieth Century, created a unique, family environment that defined her studio work experience. And though she would remember Zanuck and Sam Goldwyn affectionately for their ability to forge a family environment at their studios, it all derived from Pickford's matriarchal production company, spirit of collaboration, and equal treatment of workers: "When you worked for these independents, when you worked for Mary Pickford, it was a whole family. . . . When, at four o'clock in the afternoon, her maid would come up with a cup of tea for you and some little cookies, and take them right to the cutting room for you, because she always had that. It was like the whole family, so naturally you worked like mad because you loved every bit of it. You loved them, and you wanted the picture to be great, and you didn't mind how hard you worked."[36] McLean's portrait of the matriarchal studio environment resonates with Mary C. McCall Jr.'s own defense of the studio system in the 1940s. And though Zanuck and Goldwyn were hardly anyone's idea of mother hens, McLean argued that their work style mimicked Pickford's.

Although much of post-studio-era historiography has given producers and moguls a bad reputation, McLean's oral history is imbued with a sense of collaboration and mutual support. In 1933, while she was working on her first picture for Zanuck's Twentieth Century Pictures, *The Bowery* (to be released through United Artists), the editors went on strike over pay. As she recalled, production manager Ed Eberle "didn't want to hire me back, because I'd been on strike." But colleague Alan McNeil went to Zanuck and told him to rehire her because she "had worked on the balance of the picture." Zanuck, hearing only the name "Bobbie," said, "'Get him back, get him back,' thinking I was a boy."[37] McNeil kept quiet and got her back on the picture. Zanuck "didn't know me from a hole in the wall," but rather than keep her head down, McLean quickly gained a reputation for speaking out at Twentieth Century and later Twentieth Century-Fox. Because of the confusion over the strike, director Raoul Walsh was missing some footage on *The Bowery*. As she was telling Walsh about the missing film and the need to reshoot, Zanuck roared up in his car, fresh from a polo match. Walsh conferred with him and called her over to the car: "Bobbie, come here and tell Darryl what you just told me." She was direct. Reshooting was "necessary to the picture." Walsh may have used the pretty blue-eyed brunette to soften the blow about the costs of reshooting, but Zanuck, to his credit, respected her judgment and called actor Wallace Beery back to the set.

Sometime later, McNeil had her accompany him to the projection room while Zanuck viewed the rushes with the editor. McNeil was supposed to take note of Zanuck's comments and discuss things with him, but he never wrote anything down and, as McLean stated, "would forget it or something." When Zanuck complained later, "Why don't you do what I told you to do?" McNeil tried blaming McLean. McLean, tired of being ignored and pushed over on the other side of the room behind a tiny desk, was livid. "Now look, Alan, don't you pass the buck to me," she shot back across the room. "I can't hear what Mr. Zanuck tells you. Now, if you can't remember it, don't you blame it on me."[38] As McLean recalled tartly, "From there on, Zanuck would yell the notes out so I could hear them. I suppose that's how he finally discovered that if I could hear, then we would do the changes." McLean's grit won her the right to cut the well-named *Gallant Lady* (1934) herself. It was her first sole credit.[39] Bobbie, a fine sailor in her rare moments away from the editing room, celebrated by christening her new craft *Gallant Lady*. Zanuck valued people who could get the job done, and McLean supplanted McNeil and other male editors at Fox as Zanuck looked at the day's rushes.

Even before they moved from the lot at United Artists (Twentieth Century) to the new Twentieth Century-Fox studios in 1935, McLean was fundamentally changing the way all of the company's pictures were edited. She went over to work at the new Fox lot two months before the rest of the employees, and when she found out that the studio had Movietone (which had the soundtrack on the film strip), she went straight to Zanuck asking that this be changed so they could run image and sound on separate tracks. "I told him that he wouldn't be able to see his picture the way he had been seeing it over at United Artists, because it wasn't on separate picture and track . . . you can do much more when you have separate picture and track. You can run it over a close-up, and you can do anything with it."[40]

Zanuck preferred this flexibility and delegated McLean to change the film and fix tracks before operations really got underway. With separate picture and track, McLean was able to put a cut together with all her own sound effects two days after shooting finished—even for a film as complicated as the historical disaster epic *In Old Chicago* (1937). She laughed later, remembering the headache of orchestrating the Chicago fire and Tyrone Power's love life: "I don't know how I ever did it, when I was the department head at Twentieth Century-Fox."[41] Her technological acumen ended up saving production time and money, making her Zanuck's ideal employee.

As her studio's chief cutter in the 1930s, McLean often functioned like an associate producer for the studio's output. For as much as Zanuck liked to get his own way and exert his vision on each film, so did McLean. She didn't simply transcribe Zanuck's desires. "When you got an idea, he would listen to you," she insisted.[42] She would argue with him over keeping a sequence the way she liked it, and "all you had to do is give him some kind of an idea . . . and he'd think about it later and say, 'O.K., leave it alone.'"[43] They even flipped a coin when they couldn't resolve a conflict and of course, she won. "Nine out of ten times I was right," she insisted.[44] But she also had subtle ways of influencing Zanuck. When she left Goldwyn for Fox in the early 1930s, she took with her a small music library that she had built up over time from working on her other pictures. "When you are working in the cutting room or as a film editor, you have little pieces of music left over from other pictures. You have a little library all your own."[45] She was putting the chase in the sewers together for *Les Misérables* for Zanuck to see, and as it was silent, she added her own sound effects and music "so it wouldn't be so dull." Though Alfred Newman was "mad" at her for infringing on his territory as music director, Zanuck "thought it was great." She continued this practice throughout her career, with riveting results. Many of the evocative sound bridges covering cuts away from close-ups in *Twelve O'Clock High* are her work.[46] For Bobbie, having the key sound effects and additional music prepared for her rough cuts protected her editing style, which used a lot of close-ups: "Very often if you have a lot of close-ups back and forth for dramatic purposes, and you don't have something in there to play, they'll say, 'What have you got so many cuts for?' You say, 'If you put the music in, it'll dramatize it.'"[47]

It is often assumed that editors in the Hollywood studio system were not on the set; their work began in postproduction. But Bobbie liked being on the set throughout production and would take her own "script notes."[48] She adored one of Zanuck's top actors, George Arliss, who would meticulously rehearse his films from start to finish. McLean would sit on the set and watch, script in hand, mentally cutting the film as they progressed. Over at MGM, Greta Garbo also knew the value of a good editor who understood the star's overall performance; Margaret Booth was one of the few people the star would talk to on the set of her MGM pictures, journalists reported.[49] Garbo, with her flawlessly feminine face but the broad shoulders, big feet, and awkward hands of a Swedish farm girl, may have recognized that close-ups were her strong suit on screen. And editors, far more than directors, understood their value.

McLean had been advocating more close-ups for top stars since working with Pickford. On *The Affairs of Cellini* (1934), when director Gregory La Cava "left to go to Europe or someplace, on another picture or something . . . Zanuck let me retake the close-ups."[50] McLean "knew exactly where to use them," and for Zanuck, she was the obvious choice. McLean acknowledged "it was not very much," but she loved being in control on the set. As she recalled, "I told the assistant director, Freddie Fox, where I wanted them and how I wanted to use them, and told him what to do. So he made about twenty close-ups of Connie Bennett to cut into the picture. That was my first at directing."

Margaret Booth became very familiar with this scenario at MGM. As she remembered in the mid-1970s, L. B. Mayer would order retakes on any areas she didn't like in a studio film, and while she was on the set, she frequently went down to the soundstage and said, "I need a close-up. I can't cut that footage unless I have a close-up to replace it."[51] McLean believed firmly that audiences demanded close-ups, particularly in love scenes, and it was personal drama, far more than spectacle, that drove public interest in photoplays. As she explained *Suez* (1938), the romantic epic story of Ferdinand de Lesseps,

> The terrible sand storm, which sweeps everything before it, is the dramatic highlight of the picture. . . . In cutting it, we must retain the spectacle and the terror and yet the story with the necessary close-ups must be kept going at a good pace. Storm or no storm, there must be no slackening in the personal drama between Tyrone Power, Loretta Young, and Annabella.[52]

But it wasn't just close-ups that editors demanded and often shot on the set. As Anne Bauchens revealed in 1937, while "different directors and producers work differently with their editors," all editors had influence on the set. They were instrumental in getting directors to shoot scenes from multiple angles. She argued that the "protection shots" editors called for and sometimes directed were used "to give variety to the telling of the story."[53] Bauchens defended directors who shot multiple takes and versions, and disliked directors who camera-cut, saying, "You can never be sure exactly which of these will best tell your story until you have cut it one way and then, if it does not look right, tried it another."[54] Yet obviously, Bauchens's preference for more film inevitably gave her and her editing colleagues more creative control over the final cut. Speaking in 1970, McLean pointed out that it was the director's job to give the editor the raw material to achieve the kind of rhythm necessary for good storytelling. She explained, "They do shoot everything in one long take from beginning to end, but you intercut it."

Edmund Goulding was a director who liked to shoot everything in one take. "You had to sit on the set with him in case you wanted him to cover it. He liked the flow of the whole scene, and I'd say, 'You'd better cover it. You'd better make a close-up.' He'd say, 'Well, you tell me where you want it.'"[55] McLean went on to dismiss the newfangled long takes favored by continental directors: "They do them a lot of them in one bit, but half the time the scene doesn't hold up. When it appears on screen, it dies the death of a dog, it's so darned dull. Even if you just have a cut in it, it's better . . . you can just drop in one close-up without hurting it."[56] While directors shot the script, lazily shooting one uninterrupted sequence, editors found a rhythm in the contrast of images.

When asked to articulate what motivated their judgment, and how film editing translated as a language to the audience, McLean, Bauchens, and Booth had similar reactions: it was intuitive and based on their long experience of cutting a variety of work. Bauchens acknowledged that editors assembled scenes according to the script, but "each shot expresses a different phase of emotion or interest." In general, long shots were for information or spectacle, medium shots were to enhance clarity and the audience's relationship with the actors, and, while it was useful to focus on individual elements, it "is not always necessary" to narrate moments of emotional intensity with "a close-up of a face."[57] In contrast, Booth and McLean were more drawn to close-ups. It was John Stahl's advice Booth would remember fifty years later. "He said, 'Always play it in the long shot unless you want to punctuate something.'"[58] But as with music and poetry, different film genres had their own forms within which a good editor could experiment with thousands of feet of footage and dozens of different takes. For a comedy like Harlow's *Bombshell*, Booth chose "such a fast tempo" that there wasn't "a sprocket hole in between each line of dialogue." That was the way she "loved" to cut.

Whether through calling for or directing close-ups and protection shots on the set, these top female editors of the 1930s were proving not only that their work was not confined to the editing room, but also that they functioned as directors and producers. Booth, perhaps the most powerful editor during the studio period, worked as an assistant producer from 1936. The

MGM Studio Club News was a lively source of monthly information about the studio's employees, ranging from executive secretary Ida Koverman to the legions of secretaries and script girls who formed softball teams and regularly played each other in competitive "league" matches. Booth, it noted, "one of our ace cutters, has recently been advanced to the position of assistant producer." It went on to describe her rise to power within familial terms: "Practically born with a pair of scissors in her hand, Margaret has been brought up with the picture business and will prove a valuable factor in her new job."[59] When Booth gave her oral history interview with film historian Rudy Behlmer in 1990, she didn't mention this, only noting her promotion to supervising editor in 1936. But in her interview with another woman, fellow editor Irene Kahn Atkins, Booth was more revealing of the extent of her power, admitting that she had control over "all the dailies from everybody's pictures at MGM," and could get L. B. Mayer to order directors to reshoot anything she did not like.[60]

Booth owed her career to Irving Thalberg, who put her in charge of the studio's most prestigious films. She became so individual and skilled in her cutting that Thalberg assigned her to new directors to protect them from potential incompetence and help them to develop their style. She cut George Cukor's first picture and handled Lionel Barrymore's one effort, *The Rogue Song* (1930). But Thalberg also wanted her to turn director when she was working for George Cukor on *Camille* (1937) and pressured her to do this shortly before his death. Other former male editors had made the transition, as had Paramount's documentarian, Frances March, and former RKO editor Jane Loring. But even with Thalberg's support, Booth declined, and later explained her decision: "I enjoyed what I was doing. And I said, 'I want to be the best, if I can, at that.'"

While it is tempting to read her rejection of directing in gendered terms, with Booth internalizing her subservience as an editor and accepting the gendered hierarchies of direction and creative control, the more logical and ironic motivation may have been her emulation of Irving Thalberg's approach to film authorship. The man most responsible for the look of MGM's releases from the late 1920s to his death in 1936 never liked putting his name on any picture's credits.

But Thalberg also worked so heavily on scripts under his control he could also have been credited as a screenwriter. The same applied to Booth, who wrote part of *Mutiny on the Bounty* and, throughout her career, would work with directors during production, writing new scenes when her viewing of the rushes indicated that there were gaps or problems with the existing storyline. Her work with Sidney Franklin on *Command Decision* (1949), for example, shows just how much power she had in transforming a film regardless of existing writers or directors. Booth not only reworked the opening scenes and changed dialogue, but also altered scenes by calling for multiple close-ups and protection shots for added clarity.[61] Her colleague Jane Loring worked in a similar capacity for Pandro Berman. As his "assistant producer," Loring not only did extensive treatments and dialogue rewrites, but also supervised the first and final cut with assistant editors.

This collaboration between editors and producers was the norm during the 1930s and early 1940s, but Zanuck and McLean's association was special.[62] Many of Zanuck's archived comments on tightening aspects of scripts or planning a particular sequence were influenced by his conversations with McLean, who was often looking at the script the moment Zanuck had assigned the director. Zanuck recognized McLean's gifts and, as he pushed the idea of his youthful and innovative studio and employees, actively campaigned for McLean's nominations for Academy Awards in the studio's first decade (figure 5.2). McLean, though proud of being Hollywood's "Editor-in-Chief," was intrigued by Booth's and Loring's career developments, admitting in a 1947 Fox studio newsletter that her "ambition" was "to become a producer."[63] However, this "promotion" would very

Figure 5.2 Barbara McLean, fresh from another Academy Award nomination, 1938

likely have put an end to her record of the most Oscar nominations in editing. It was only in the mid-1950s, her record secure with a win for *Wilson* and another nomination for *All About Eve*, that McLean was acknowledged associate producer on *Seven Cities of Gold* (1955).

Journalists in the 1930s often mentioned Zanuck's and McLean's shared commitment to their work. Zanuck's favored film of the moment was referred to as "his baby," while McLean's dislike of housework and preference for demanding professional work were seen as part of a shared work ethic in Hollywood that cut across and blurred gender lines. "All film workers, when they get into the heart of something, are seized with a sort of hysteria which causes them to work excessive hours," said Hubbard Keavy. But she was well compensated by Zanuck: time and a half for Sundays, double for holidays, and bonuses for more than sixteen hours in a day. McLean was also presented as a successful *married* woman working, whose husband also worked in film and "understood" her commitment to her work. That journalists, studio publicists (presumably with Zanuck's backing), and McLean were invested in presenting McLean as a happily married woman fulfilled by her creative and administrative work, long hours, and $200-a-week paycheck presents a different picture of attitudes toward married women working in the Great Depression.

While editors' insistence on using more close-ups of key stars in features arguably bolstered the studios' reliance on the star system, and could make or break actors' careers by cutting their footage,[64] McLean should also be remembered as the one responsible for making Tyrone Power a star. When Zanuck couldn't make up his mind to cast Don Ameche or Power in the main part of *Lloyd's of London*, he asked Bobbie's advice. To her, Power was "more dashing" in those fancy clothes. Zanuck told Bill Goetz, "Tell Henry [King] that Bobbie made up my mind for me."[65] Zanuck spent a lot of money promoting Power as the studio's new star, and the surest way to make that happen on screen was for Bobbie to shoot whatever close-ups she wanted of him. He asked her advice on everything from script to costumes, and when it came to costumes, she enjoyed manipulating all the men in the projection room. "Being the only woman, I'd get my way. . . . I was just like the female audience."[66]

Booth occupied a similar role at MGM. Cukor relied on Booth since she cut his first picture in 1930. Although Cukor had a solid reputation as a women's director, who would talk with his stars between takes to "'keep them at a pitch,'"[67] he encountered some resistance from Ingrid Bergman, who resented this close collaboration on the set of *Gaslight* (1944). While Cukor withdrew, it was Booth who "complained" that Bergman was "underacting" in the rushes. Screwing up his courage, Cukor had it out with Bergman, who eventually realized that "actors have to listen."

One of McLean's most important revelations about her work was that with many directors, and especially for her long collaboration with Henry King (over thirty pictures), she would be on the set even before shooting started, script in hand, discussing things with the director, but also disagreeing with him and often getting him to shoot the scene her way. "I'd read the script and if I didn't like something about the script, I'd discuss it with him, and he'd tell me how he was going to do it."[68] It was safer for King to agree with McLean because Zanuck always deferred to her judgment. Recalling her work with King, McLean acknowledged:

> We used to have some little arguments. I'd spend a lot of time on the set and sometimes he would say, "I'm going to do so-and-so-and-so-and-so." I'd say, "You are?" He'd say, "Now what's the matter?" I'd say, "Well, gee . . ." and I'd give my opinion on something. And he'd say, "Now, don't get me all off the track." I'd say, "Well, you asked me and I'm telling you."[69]

McLean didn't wheedle or gently suggest or use her eye-fluttering feminine charms. As in her memories of working with Zanuck, she shot straight from the hip, with no apologies, and her colleagues and boss could take it or leave it. The straight-talking New Jersey woman had the southern-born, gentlemanly King in her pocket after their first picture. She would work on all his films, and King was so dependent on her judgment he got paranoid when she wasn't on the set: "Every time I didn't show up on the set, he'd think there was something wrong with the film."[70] Their collaboration lasted through three decades, and "at the end of the picture he's always kiss me on the head and say, 'Well, you've done it again. . . . Sometimes I don't know where you find the film to put on the screen because I don't remember having shot some of them.'"[71] It was all of those extra protection shots and close-ups, evidently!

But McLean hadn't wanted to do their first film, *The Country Doctor* (1936), which told the story of the famous Dionne quintuplets. McLean had wanted to cut Frank Lloyd's *Under Two Flags*, an exciting period war picture, and resented being stuck with a film about babies. McLean was a beautiful, petite brunette and was understandably popular with all of her male colleagues, but she was hardly the home-and-babies type. That material just bored her. Zanuck said, "Oh my goodness, Bobbie, you're a woman. You can understand these little babies,"[72] and McLean fumed. While she didn't mind well-meaning journalists drawing occasional attention to her gender as a way of opening up the profession as a possibility for other women, she wanted her work to push boundaries for what was considered "women's work." Biopics, historical dramas, disaster epics, adventures, westerns, war pictures—these were fine. But babies?

She did the film, albeit grudgingly. It ended up being amusing and a quick assignment, but happily, Zanuck did not make a habit of assigning her to things male executives assumed were "women's pictures." She laughed that "naive" Henry King and Joseph Mankiewicz understood "women's pictures" and romance more than she did.[73] One of her all-time favorite assignments was the historical epic *In Old Chicago*, where she was in her element coordinating the massive amounts of footage and sound effects. Journalists would joke that McLean height-wise "is the smallest film editor at Twentieth Century-Fox and cut its biggest picture."[74] But with more Academy Award nominations than any other editor at the close of the decade, she didn't need platform heels to put down any man on the Fox lot who tried to patronize her.

McLean's influence on Fox's product on so many levels makes a strong case for her "authorship" on key film texts such as *Jesse James*, *Song of Bernadette*, *Wilson*, *A Bell for Adano* (1945), *Twelve O'Clock High*, *The Gunfighter* (1950), and *All About Eve*. More traditional auteur critics who've noticed these patterns in Twentieth Century-Fox's continuity editing such as Jonathan Rosenbaum smugly dismiss it as Fox's "corporate signature."[75] Yet, given McLean's and other successful women filmmakers' comments on their attitudes toward working for the studios, McLean embraced the idea of studio collaboration. For Rosenbaum, a "corporate signature" was a slight on film styles determined by those other than directors (in Fox's case, a woman). According to this approach, artistry is reserved solely for directors (men) who receive all the creative credit in the film histories.

The ultimate critic's "auteur," John Ford, used to claim that his pictures were "editor proof" because he shot so little footage there was only one way—his way—to cut them. When interviewer Tom Stempel reminded McLean of this old story, and asked her about it, she replied, "No, I never found that."[76] In terms of editorial oversight, Ford was no different than King or any other director with whom she worked (McLean had experience working on Ford's *Arrowsmith* [1931] for Goldwyn and later *Tobacco Road* [1941] for Zanuck).

She was fairly terse about Ford, however, and Ford's sexism toward her protégé, assistant cutter Mary Steward, may have been the reason. Along with McLean, Spencer, Sylvia Reid, Monica Collingwood, Hazel Marshall, and Florence Leona Lindsay, Steward was one of the original charter members of the Editors Guild in 1937 and was assistant cutter on *Drums Along the Mohawk* and *The Grapes of Wrath*. As with McLean, part of her job involved going on the set to call for protection or close-ups if she felt the scene wasn't adequately covered. Ford disliked interference and used a demeaning tactic to curb her editorial power on the set. Interviewed in 2012, she would remember: "Every time I went to the set or out on location for business, Mr. Ford would always yell, 'Bring Mary's gam box'—that's 'gams' as in 'legs'—and they'd put an apple box on the ground in front of me. Then he'd tell me I had to stand on it and turn around two times before I could open my mouth. I just wanted to get back to work."[77]

No wonder McLean preferred working for Henry King, a director well known for supporting women's careers in Hollywood (including Ginger's mother, screenwriter Lela Rogers) and who would have been appalled by this sexist behavior. Ironically, Ford's other two acclaimed masterpieces, *Stagecoach* and *My Darling Clementine* (1946), were edited by a woman, McLean's colleague Dorothy Spencer. In some sense, Ford's status as a lone auteur rests on dismissing the important work of the women who edited his films.

But during the postwar era, Hollywood's production hierarchies began to shift. More and more, producers ceded creative and administrative control to directors. Even with Zanuck's continued support in the early 1950s, McLean found that there were far more conflicts as directors got more hands-on in the editing room. Although she liked Joseph Mankiewicz, she mused that the auteur frequently "falls in love with his own film" and loses his ability to communicate with others—something Bette Davis would also argue later in life.

Looking at the rushes, she would argue with directors, "It doesn't tell me that. You want *me* to tell *me* what *I* think about it?" As she remarked to Stempel, when she questioned directors point blank, "They'd look at me as if I was crazy."[78] While McLean avoided making the cinematic contest of wills a gendered one, her resentment of a male director telling a female editor and audience member what to think is quite apparent. Film historians remain wedded to the idea that directors such as Mankiewicz did all his own editing on *All About Eve* even when Mankiewicz himself revealed in an interview that McLean cut the picture without him at her elbow.[79] Though slowly, some are accepting the role Zanuck played in trimming excess in scripts and on screen, few have heeded former Fox producer and film educator Kenneth Macgowan's words in *Behind the Screen*:

> Whatever a director may contribute to the editing of a film, the cutter never gets the credit he deserves. . . . Editing holds a unique place in the development

of the motion picture as an art. Writing and directing, acting and photography, set design and sound recording, all existed before the birth of the film. These skills were merely adopted and adapted. Editing was born in and of the movies. Without it, the motion picture would never have become the art it is today.[80]

It was the rise of the long take over the technique of continuity editing that upset McLean most about 1950s auteurism. Yet in the early 1950s, at work on the set of *The Snows of Kilimanjaro* (1952), McLean worked out a revolutionary way of transforming the combination of narration and flashbacks to eliminate lap dissolves "as an introduction to the past."[81] The film was just "straight cutting" from start to finish. According to Macgowan, this dissolve-free cutting was one of the great stylistic innovations in the 1950s, something he credited to both King and McLean, though McLean remembers it as her own idea: "With Zanuck's blessing," she took all of her lap dissolve signs out of her rough cut and "asked Zanuck for additional close-ups of star Gregory Peck to handle the transitions." Zanuck said, "'You get the ones you want, and go and tell Henry King that you need some close-ups of Gregory Peck. Tell him what you want.'"[82] Nearly twenty years had passed, but she still called the shots at Twentieth Century-Fox.

That year, McLean was acclaimed one of the Hollywood film industry's "creative brains," profiled in *Vogue* alongside director George Stevens, composer Alex North, and her Fox colleague, cinematographer Leon Shamroy.[83] Actress and photographer Jean Howard took McLean's picture as she cut the studio's latest biopic, *Viva Zapata!*, directed by Elia Kazan (1952). Though the diminutive brunette did not look out-of-place in the fashion magazine, journalist Allene Talmey revealed that she was not just a pretty face. McLean's studio "pays her more than the $30,000 a year the country pays Vice-President Barkley."

McLean was amused by how little the hotshot Method director Elia Kazan knew about filmmaking. Exploring the rhythmic possibilities of one scrap of footage in *Viva Zapata!*, she duped and reduped and blew up some shots of rocks being smashed, creating "a whole sequence out of it."[84] Kazan had no clue how she'd done it. Astonishing the younger "professionals" amused her. Aging auteur Michael Curtiz also made her and Zanuck laugh when he tried to tell McLean how to do dubbing on *The Egyptian* (1954). But things weren't as fun as they used to be. Although Zanuck was enthused with the new widescreen techniques pioneered by his studio, she was bored to death by the long takes in *The Robe* (1953) that she felt were a natural result of widescreen film. McLean continued to supervise all of the cutting at the studio and to work on Zanuck's personal productions, while briefly transitioning to producing in the mid-1950s, working in collaboration with her second husband, director Robert Webb. After Zanuck's departure, she worked as Buddy Adler's assistant, but disliked the added burdens of administrative work.

At MGM, Margaret Booth would seek some administrative respite working with producer Ray Stark. During the 1960s, she maintained a measure of power in shaping his "personal" productions such as *The Night of the Iguana* (1964). Booth's years of experience and firmness were daunting to Stark, who tried to respond to her editorial vision (rigorous cutting of excessive footage and emphasis on explosive close-ups) by listing each one of their ideas and separately attributing it. His typed cutting notes could be summarized by one comment: "I don't agree, but I have no definite idea."[85] Booth had strong opinions on all sequences and usually got her way. Her distress over Ava Gardner's unflattering close-ups and the film's abrupt ending were reflective of her long-held beliefs in photographing female stars to their best advantage and having some kind of narrative closure.[86] These were things she tried to teach to the young school of editing talent at the studio, but the days when editors called the shots at the studios were over. In 1968, she left MGM to work with Stark's Rastar production company, primarily as editor and associate producer. Her last film credit was as executive producer of *The Slugger's Wife* (1985).

It was telling that when the Academy began considering recognizing Booth with a Lifetime Achievement Award, it was the CEO of MGM, producer Frank Rosenfelt, who proposed the award, acknowledging that "For 32 years, from 1936 until 1968, Miss Booth helped determine the shape and final form of nearly every film produced by this studio."[87] But Academy president Howard Koch solicited letters of support from *directors*, including William Wyler and George Cukor and George Sidney. Cukor and Sidney were generous, with Cukor stating, "I myself had the enormous benefit of MB's expertise, her sharp perception, and her generous help,"[88] and Sidney concurring, "I am one of the large legion of filmmakers who have been enriched by her generous talents."[89] But it was former editor David Lean, mentor and employer of female editors including Marjorie Saunders (*Brief Encounter*, 1945) and Anne Coates (*Lawrence of Arabia*), who understood the real dynamics of authorship in the industry and the myth of the "great director":

As an ex-editor I can't resist pointing out that even with her brilliant record, her greatest achievements are probably unsung and certainly unpublicized—for editors' best work is generally done on the worst pictures. I see a fantasy set-up of Maggie standing in the centre of that proverbial cutting room floor knee-deep in thousands of feet of ham, self-indulgence and bad story telling accompanied, on sound track by wailings, angry protestations and cries of "Butcher!!" Some butcher. And I would love to see you honour her.[90]

In her later years, Booth developed quite a reputation as a mentor and champion of younger editors, both men and women. At a time when editing's creative powers and the role of women in the technical aspects of filmmaking had declined, Booth was a reminder of Hollywood's golden age, when true cinematic collaboration reigned at MGM. In a way, when the industry and film historians "mourn" Thalberg, they miss the point. MGM never lost the taste and judgment and artistry associated with his era, because MGM didn't lose Margaret Booth until 1968.

One of the claims feminist historians often make about mid-century working women is that they were a minority "out for themselves," and did not support the networks of other women necessary for the development of women in the profession. To a certain extent, one might assume this to be true for studio-era Hollywood's editors. Many began in the silent period as part of a wider cohort of female editors and hung on through the sound, Depression, war, and postwar eras by focusing exclusively on their individual careers. Their punishing, round-the-clock hours meant they had little time for guild politics largely controlled by men, and even less time to cultivate friendships among their female colleagues.

Although extant membership data indicates that when the guild was founded in 1937, 14 out of 130 members were women (11%) and numbers climbed steadily through the mid-1950s to around 18%, contemporaneous journalists often focused on one editor such as McLean or Lawrence or Sewell, claiming she was the industry's only "top cutter" or one of a few female editors.[91] Their pioneering individualism was stressed in articles and interviews, giving an impression of a great artist working alone with almost godlike powers. Back in 1933, in his column on MGM's women, Arthur Brisbane noted, "At a small side table in the lunch room of a big movie picture lot sit two young women, very businesslike, eating too rapidly and talking hard." Another of MGM's hardworking women, Ida Koverman, pointed them out as "the two best 'cutters' in the business": Blanche Sewell and Margaret Booth. Brisbane writes of the titanic tasks they faced each day cutting "the miles" of film like the mythological Fates with life-or-death control over a studio's output.[92]

To an extent, top female editors collaborated with journalists in these workaholic studio portraits: in interviews, Booth and McLean highlighted their studio-centered lives (neither had children, and twice-married McLean stuck to attractive fellow filmmakers as mates).[93] As Hubbard Keavy noted of McLean, "She puts in about sixty hours a week, not because her contract says so, but because she wants to."[94] In 1970, McLean still enthused about her high-powered schedule: "I was so happy about it. It was wonderful, because you wanted to work. I worked awfully hard. . . . We used to work Christmas and New Year's." Zanuck was her role model: "Zanuck always used to work all the time at night. He's always worked nights."

Ironically, in embracing some traditionally masculine "pioneer" traits such as hard work and toughness, these women appear to align themselves with the mostly masculine collective of the studio rather than their collective political identity as women in the 1930s and 1940s, and its subsequent refraction in Second Wave feminist discourse. Yet, for many Equal Rights Amendment feminists working during the studio era, gender equality was truly achieved when women were able to do their work well, without asking for special treatment or being metaphorically patted on the head for making it in a man's world. In blatantly ignoring the differences, Booth, McLean, and their colleagues proved that Hollywood was not a man's world and that hard work, mental toughness, and professionalism were not inherently masculine. But, as with their colleagues Ida Koverman and Edith Head, these female editors saw the studio as home, and the barriers between professional and private life collapsed into memories of a collaborative "family" workplace.

Sadly, feminist film historians seem to find it difficult to acknowledge women's impact on the editing profession without diminishing film editing as artistically second-class "feminized labor"—or cinematic "sewing." In her oral history, McLean presented a case for editing as a form of intense artistic control, extending to every component of pre- and postproduction. But, while she resisted attempts to see the profession as feminine or subservient, she also refused to highlight her gender as aberrant within the professional system of Hollywood. She replied bluntly to interviewer Tom Stempel's question about why there had been so many top female editors: "Why? Because you have to be good or you wouldn't get there."[95] No one was turning her into a statistic to hurt the system that gave her and her female colleagues a chance. As far as she was concerned, the studio system offered women the best chance for workplace equality, and that's why she remained unflinchingly loyal to Zanuck and Fox through the years. She did not see herself as a pioneering feminist actively pushing barriers for women within a male-dominated system, but rather as a filmmaker who thrived within a collaborative environment that accepted and honored her work regardless of gender.

Though her coworkers and colleagues respected her, ironically it was Hollywood journalists of the poststudio era who wanted to diminish her abilities. After her death in 1996, a *New York Times* journalist interviewing Stempel wanted to know if Zanuck and his editor had had an affair because of their years of round-the-clock work. Stempel, one of the few Fox historians who recognized her creative impact at the studio, was outraged. It was typical of most critics to see any woman within the company as sexual fodder for the great mogul. In her oral history, McLean saw her young self as one of the Zanuck family. Shortly after Zanuck let her direct some of *The Affairs of Cellini*, she met Mrs. Zanuck and remembered, "Darrylin was about two or three years old. I felt like part of the family."[96] And she recalled that while Zanuck would always ask her professional opinion about actors, costumes, and scenes in the films in addition to editing issues, he also respected Mrs. Zanuck's judgment.

Although in many histories of the studios, Zanuck and Fox are cast as hypermasculine manufacturers of macho entertainment, Zanuck employed more female editors than other studio heads and had a strong record of hiring female writers and focusing on films with female protagonists. After leaving the Warner Bros. patriarchies, it is significant that Olivia de Havilland (*The Snake Pit*), former MGM queen Myrna Loy (*Cheaper by the Dozen*), and Bette Davis (*All About Eve*) all found success working with Zanuck.

Bobbie McLean excelled in an environment where the majority of her coworkers were men, but, apart from her early dust-ups with Alan McNeil, she didn't indicate there was any overt sexism. Her colleague, first cutter Dorothy Spencer, came to Fox in early 1942 after working for a variety of studios and edited some of the studio's most prestigious postwar films, including *A Tree Grows in Brooklyn*; *The Ghost and Mrs. Muir* (1947); and *The Snake Pit*.[97] Spencer's assistant was a man, John Ehrin, who by 1943 had worked at Fox seventeen years to Spencer's two. Although in the early 1940s, Hector Dods was the company's overall supervising editor (including shorts and news), he had no control over McLean's work with Zanuck, and Bobbie was head of the feature editorial department, looking over her colleagues' work with Zanuck and later Buddy Adler. But, like Booth at MGM, McLean disliked the added control of hiring, accounts, and administration.

When she was interviewed at the height of Second Wave feminism, Booth also seemed uncomfortable with the assumptions Irene Kahn Atkins wanted to make about editing as a less-valued form of creative labor, or "women's work." She replied, on her guard: "I really can't say why that was. It just seemed like girls took to that at that time."[98] However, she quietly nurtured other young editors such as Dede Allen (*Bonnie and Clyde*) just as McLean promoted Mary Steward at Fox during the 1930s and 1940s and mentored Fox screenwriter Nunnally Johnson's daughter

Marjorie when she decided to become an editor.[99] These women may not have been conventional "pioneering" auteurs, but they were true organization women, viewing the studio system as a negotiable artistic hierarchy where their perspectives shaped the language of Hollywood film. "Sewing," Ms. Francke? Hardly. McLean may wear white gloves in her famous 1952 portrait in *Vogue*, but only because she handled the film. In most cases, she and her colleagues could cut it how they saw it during the studio era, director or no director.

CHAPTER 6

Designing Women

It takes a woman to design for a woman.

Sylvia Weaver, 1942[1]

In 1940, journalist Bettina Bedwell observed that "Hollywood fashions for years were the production of a man-dominated world." Men controlled the business of women's clothes, and "there wasn't a woman to sass them back."[2] But, she continued, "The Hollywood I'm discovering belatedly is a fashion center in which women designers are getting to be a big power. And it is my firm conviction that there is enough feminine designing talent in this town to feed a very big, and ever-growing demand for modern styles." While Edith Head and Irene Saltern were her key names, Renie Conley, Dolly Tree, Vera West, and Natalie Visart were also named as the Hollywood designers of the future. Other style commentators such as Sylvia Weaver and Sandra Smythe noted that in a town where "the working girl is queen," it was women who really knew how to dress working women in and outside the studios.[3]

More than any other female designer, however, Edith Head was invested in promoting herself as "the only woman style creator who has managed to survive as head fashion designer in any major studio in Hollywood," a peer of Travis Banton, Adrian, Orry-Kelly, Robert Kalloch, and Edward Stevenson. Interviewers of the time often followed Head's lead, omitting the Paramount designer's two female competitors, chief Twentieth Century-Fox designer Gwen Wakeling and Universal's Vera West. Wakeling was brought out from New York and received a great deal of attention in the 1930s designing Loretta Young's and Shirley Temple's clothes. West had directed Universal's costume department years before Head became a force at Paramount.[4] But it was Head's frequent interviews and syndicated fashion column that set her apart both from the female colleagues she ignored and from her male competitors.

Head had competition from more than Wakeling and West as Hollywood's top female designer. From the early 1930s to the end of the studio era in the late 1950s, women were equally represented as the industry's top costume designers. In addition to Head, Renie, Tree, Visart, Wakeling, Irene Lentz Gibbons, and West, there were Adele Balkan, Marjorie Best, Bonnie Cashin, Ethel Chaffin, Coco Chanel, Marjorie D. Corso, Lucia Coulter, Kay Dean, Mary Kay Dodson, Eloise, Margaret Furse, Mary Grant, Elizabeth Haffenden, Dorothy Jeakins, Anna Hill Johnstone, Barbara Karinska, Rita Kaufman, Kathleen Kay, Marion Herwood Keyes, Muriel King, Norma Koch, Ruth Morley, Helen A. Myron, Kay Nelson, Mary Ann Nyberg, Sheila O'Brien, Rosemary Odell, Alice O'Neill, Adele Palmer, Natacha Rambova, Leah Rhodes, Helen Rose, Irene Saltern, Irene Sharaff, Helen Taylor, Sophie Wachner, Claire West, Mary Wills, and Yvonne Wood.

The five-dollar-a-week sketch artists, fitters, and dressmakers were almost exclusively female. During her tenure at Paramount in the 1930s and 1940s, Head managed over two hundred women and men in her department. Unfortunately, before union records, only a few names were mentioned in memoirs and oral histories. Some of the more famous were Leah Rhodes, who began as Orry-Kelly's sketch artist and assistant before replacing him in 1943; Willa Kim, brought over from Broadway as a Paramount sketch artist; Head's assistant, Adele Balkan (who designed a number of things Travis Banton took credit for); seamstresses Ilse Meadows and Sheila O'Brien (the latter rose to become Joan Crawford's personal designer and a leading force in the creation of the Costume Designers Guild); *Rear Window* sketch artist Grace Sprague; and Edith's Head's loyal assistant, Pat Barto. With the end of the studio system, the position of the costume designer virtually disappeared—indeed, columnist Hedda Hopper viewed the decline and downsizing of the costume departments as a primary indication of the end of the studio system.[5] Although Thea van Runkle, who began as a sketch artist for Jeakins and Renie, managed to remain a presence in the 1960s and 1970s by associating with a self-styled "classic" Hollywood star, Faye Dunaway (*Bonnie and Clyde*; *The Thomas Crown Affair*, 1968), she was the exception to the new rule.

Unlike the directing and stunt professions, where numbers of women declined from the early 1920s through the end of the decade, the position of the Hollywood costume designer, and in particular, the female designer, became more influential, particularly at the wealthier studios. In the late teens and early twenties, women such as Triangle designer Peggy Hamilton, Goldwyn's Sophie Wachner, her replacement Ethel Chaffin, Paramount's Claire West (who began working for Griffith), and Universal's Lucia "Mother" Coulter laid the foundations for studio wardrobe departments. Star Mae Murray was instrumental in bringing her favorite designers, Maude Marsh and Kathleen Kay, to the MGM lot, but by and large, male designers such as Erté and Norman Norell handled the big pictures with Gloria Swanson and Renée Adorée. In the mid-1920s, with the formation of FBO (later RKO), Warner Bros., and Columbia, designers Walter Plunkett, Orry-Kelly, and Edward Stevenson and later Robert Kalloch (who was the first contracted head of costume for Harry Cohn) established their studios' wardrobe departments.

While it is tempting to see the larger, pre-1920 studios with their strong cohort of women in opposition to the post-1920, male and organization man-dominated studios as oppositional gender models for design employment, RKO and Columbia later supplemented their costume departments with prominent female designers such as Muriel King (initially hired to design Katharine Hepburn's wardrobe at the star's request), Irene Lentz Gibbons (supported by many Hollywood women who wore her work off camera), and Leah Rhodes (who, from 1943, worked within the more male-dominated world of Warner Bros.). At Darryl F. Zanuck's Twentieth Century-Fox, a number of women managed the costumes and handled the studio's prestige output, including Wakeling, Wood, Renie, and Cashin, who designed Gene Tierney's signature working-woman wardrobe for *Laura* (1944). Zanuck fired Helen Rose in the 1930s, but rehired her for a year in 1943. But it was Wakeling who was heavily publicized as a superstar at the youthful studio, and in 1936 she became the first female designer to win the silver trophy given by the Association of American Apparel Manufacturers of Los Angeles. Known as Hollywood's "foremost woman designer,"[6] she remained one of the most visible designers through the early 1950s, when she won a shared Oscar for *Samson and Delilah* (1950) with Edith Head and Dorothy Jeakins.

After Lucia "Mother" Coulter left for MGM in 1924, Universal hired Vera West as its chief designer. She held the position for twenty years, creating memorable period work for Irene Dunne in *Show Boat* (1936) and Marlene Dietrich in *Destry Rides Again* (1939), but as David Chierichetti has pointed out, West lacked the support of the studio to hang onto its top projects, and actresses such as Deanna Durbin and Dunne abandoned her work for Howard Greer, Gilbert Adrian, and Walter Plunkett.[7] West committed suicide shortly after resigning her position in 1947 due to alleged blackmailing scandals involving her first husband. Although Adrian's shadow loomed large over MGM, the studio had a cohort of prominent female designers, and by the 1940s, Irene and Helen Rose had taken over. In the 1920s and early 1930s, Paramount was controlled by Howard Greer and later Travis Banton, but in 1938, it became the exclusive domain of Edith Head.

The late 1930s and early 1940s represented not only the period of greatest influence for female designers in Hollywood, but also were Edith Head's most important career years. In many ways, Head defines women's work in studio-era Hollywood costume design. Not wanting to look like any ordinary seamstress, she refused to sew in public or give demonstrations, leading many critics to assume she had never learned.[8] Yet she also understood what the average woman wanted to wear and wrote many articles on the importance of a practical wardrobe. Though instrumental in establishing the Academy Award in costume design in 1949 and developing the Costume Designers Guild in 1954, she was not the organization's first president (that was Howard Shoup)[9] or the first recipient of the costume design Oscar (that honor was Dorothy Jeakins's). Through carefully crafted studio publicity and syndicated columns, Head built a formidable image as Hollywood's most influential designer. However, many looked upon her as a formidable organization woman, but not as a creative force. Unfortunately, some historians of Hollywood costume design have made similar judgments about Irene Lentz Gibbons, West, and Wakeling, claiming they lacked the brilliance and originality of Adrian, Banton, and Greer, but that other women, stars, and second-string actresses favored their work. As Dale McConathy remarked of Irene, the successor to Adrian at MGM, "Her designs may not have had much flair, but the stars inevitably felt flattered by her attention and comfortable with her professionalism."[10] While costume design historians' comments occasionally diminish the talents of women designers, press of the time lacked this gender bias and praised men and women in the profession equally. There is a sense, nevertheless, emerging from the thousands of articles on Head published in her lifetime, that she and many of her colleagues were true organization women using a system of self-obsessed women to enhance their own power. In Head's case, she certainly got results—a record number of Oscars and nominations for costume design and a studio contract with Universal from 1968 to 1975 after she left her career of nearly forty-five years at Paramount.

When Head took over costume design at Paramount, Dorothy Jeakins was a little-known sketch artist. During her long tenure at the studio, the older designer learned what it meant to work for a studio family. She looked after hundreds of mostly female employees in her department for decades. Though she didn't get along with all the women she worked with, Head was known for her diplomacy and loyalty to the Hollywood system. Jeakins, in contrast, did not want to belong to any studio family and was unafraid of clashing with her female star "clients." From the beginning, she preferred to work for directors on a freelance basis. While Head remained anchored to Hollywood, Jeakins did not need Hollywood. She frequently designed for the stage and for television. While Head herself was dedicated to making fashion work for ordinary working women with limited finances, Jeakins saw costume as humanity's second skin, a collaborative endeavor reflecting life's poverty, struggle, complexity, and search for beauty. In many senses, Jeakins's rise in the postwar era indicated a change in the relationship between the Hollywood system and its female designers and fans. That change was decline. Jeakins was emblematic of new Hollywood, the Hollywood of the auteur. She was a director's designer, but her intellectualism, her fame, her commitment as a female designer in what she viewed as a man's world, would all have been impossible without the groundwork created by Edith Head and the studio system. It is this tension between stardom and collaboration, the powerful and the ordinary, that defines the history of Hollywood and American women's liberation through dress and a quest for realism on and off screen.

Edith Head entered the picture business when she read a news item in the paper saying that Paramount's new chief of design, Howard Greer, needed another sketch artist. She was disillusioned with her current job and her marriage. Charles Head was a salesman for the Southern Californian Refined Metals Company and an alcoholic who did not share his wife's passion for design. A native Angelino who spoke fluent Spanish thanks to her Mexican governess, Head had been a brilliant student, earning a B.A. from the University of California–Berkeley and an M.A. from Stanford University with a focus on Romance languages. In spite of her academic attainments, she only became a teacher at Hollywood Girls' School, and while Cecil B. DeMille's daughters were among her pupils, Head was earning "a bare living wage." Her art school background (she studied at both the Otis Art Institute and the Chouinard Art School in Los Angeles in order to keep ahead of her students) got her a job at the studios, but in addition to finding it difficult to sketch the human form (she preferred landscapes), Head disliked sewing. Greer may or may not have been aware that most of Edith's sample sketches were the work of her more precocious students, but she was hardworking, adaptable, and chic, and for several years, he promoted her career.

In 1928, Greer, weary of working within the confines of a studio system, left to form his own couture shop. His assistant, the gifted and flamboyant Travis Banton, replaced him. Head quietly took over Banton's position as assistant and in ten years would replace him as chief of design (but, as she recalled, at a much smaller salary). While working as second designer under Banton, she handled Clara Bow, the studio's recalcitrant free spirit who wouldn't wear what Banton told her to, second-string stars such as Gail Patrick and Dorothy Lamour (for whom she designed the landmark sarong in 1936), and freelancer Barbara Stanwyck, who, before meeting Head, had been famously uninterested in clothes. During this time, Head developed a reputation for being unfailingly cooperative with colleagues, building solid working relationships with a range of female stars from Mary Martin to Carole Lombard. But when Banton's increasingly erratic personal behavior became too much for Paramount's financially conscious executives to bear, he reportedly left "to pursue freelance work" in March 1938.

David Chierichetti alleges that Paramount executives searched for several months for a male replacement for Banton before grudgingly appointing Head, and that the press paid little attention to her promotion.[11] However, extant press coverage reveals another story. A news clipping from *New York Women's Wear* dated March 29, 1938 (and preserved in Head's own scrapbooks) announced that Head had been "elevated to head designer" following Banton's "resignation" that month.[12] Head had come a long way from her days as a $35-a-week sketch artist.

Although it would be several years before she would pull in the top $750-a-week salary, in 1938 she was earning $200 a week as Paramount's number one designer. Journalists covered the story as a major gain for women in the industry, for Head became without doubt Hollywood fashion's most influential woman. As Lon Jones in the *Sun News* wrote, "One of the very real success stories in Hollywood is not about any famous movie star, but of a very courageous woman who fought her way to the top in a career that has been traditionally a man's."[13] Journalists continued to promote Head as a role model for young women, with her initiative, drive, and salary. She advocated designing as "among the most interesting careers any girl could follow," and discussed the time commitment, the creative versatility, the historical knowledge, and the will to work around the clock on a dozen different projects. In many ways, Head was the ultimate organization woman who created her own female-dominated empire within Paramount Studios, one that extended her influence to millions of American women. Diplomatic and adaptable though she appeared, Head was determined that her name alone would dominate the Hollywood fashion world.

In a separate profile by Nancy Naumburg in 1939, Head was presented as a tough, resilient working woman who, after "tiring of domestic duties," found her calling through the studio system. "When she entered the department, no woman designer headed her department," Naumburg noted. "Today two do, and the number of women designers in other studios is increasing."[14] Naumburg's coverage included basic advice on how women could follow Head's path, by going to design school and getting a studio job. For however remarkable Head was, journalistic coverage always positioned her as a role model for young working women who would continue to "open up" and shape the film industry; she wasn't simply a one-of-a-kind individualist who was out for herself.

In the spring of 1941, Head's career was profiled again to coincide with graduation days across the United States. "With graduation just around the corner, future career girls are on the alert tracking down straws in the wind with which to start feathering their respected nests." Given how popular design was as a career for women, Head's life story was presented "with the fond hope that it will inspire some would-be designer to realize her dream of success."[15]

Although Head's admiring press coverage was often at the expense of her other female designer colleagues, she certainly promoted other women at Paramount, including Dorothy O'Hara, who was appointed the studio's assistant designer in 1943. However, she kept the names of her female sketch artists from the public until Paddy Calistro started working on her biography and oral history project, *Edith Head's Hollywood* (1983).[16] By the late 1940s, journalists reported Head earned "as much in two weeks as she made in a year of school teaching, directs a large corps of sketch artists, wardrobe women, seamstresses and cutters—sometimes running as high as 200, depending on the picture—and supervises all details of fashions, including jewelry and accessories, worn by even bit players and extras appearing in Paramount productions."[17] Though she ran a tight ship in her department, Head, like so many other prominent women and men in the film business, viewed the studio as "home." As she stated proudly in the early 1960s, she and longtime studio mates such as Bing Crosby felt more like brother and sister than colleagues.[18]

Historian Rebecca Arnold has pointed out that American designers were leaving Parisian influences behind in the 1930s and developing an independent, uniquely American sportswear style; however, New York–based designers were still made to feel inferior to Europeans in the press.[19] Head, as a Hollywood designer, had to contend with Paris's entrenched power as the center of creative design and influence and New York's reputation as America's one style oasis. The West Coast, by comparison, was considered frivolous and provincial. During the 1930s and 1940s, Head set to work restoring the industry's and her own reputation. On the one hand, she defended her work in Hollywood as more nuanced and demanding than traditional design; it involved research and budgetary restrictions unknown in the ateliers of Paris. She explained, "There's a budget for every picture, and a poor girl story gets a poor girl budget, rich girl, rich, etc."[20] During the silent era, notorious for its exaggerated and gaudy styles, film designers had reputations for outrageous demands and extravagance. As one journalist characterized a silent-era style conference: "Cut it out in the back and down the front. Add a feather boa and get her on the set."[21] Head was grateful that Natalie Visart handled most of DeMille's epics at Paramount in the 1930s, for she was appalled by his over-the-top bad taste.

But in the increasingly female-dominated world of studio-era Hollywood, things changed. Designers worked with the script, and the outlandishly expensive designs of the silent era were gradually replaced by a combination of studio frugality and feminine demand. Realism mattered, not only in a world where writing and socially conscious pictures were attracting more critical and box-office attention, but in a postproduction world where female fans wanted to wear what they saw stars dressed in on and off screen. Head designed with the film's realism and overall effect in mind: "The designer gets the script of a story she's going to dress and has to learn the character and action as boundaries for the clothes to be worn."[22] From the beginning, she asserted, designers were collaborators in a system.

While she admitted that she and other Hollywood designers were responsible for bringing anachronistic trends from period pictures into modern fashion, Head was not happy about this. She preferred the clean, strong lines of modern women's clothes and advocated the freedom of women's sportswear: "Sportswear is the solution to modern living. . . . You can take sportswear and 'stretch it,'" she argued.[23] While serving under Banton, she had been assigned to many of the period pictures he disliked. When she took over at Paramount, she focused instead on the future of women's dress. In her syndicated fashion column, she described her designs for Paramount's top female stars in "modern" pictures. Evening gowns and wraps were always a part of these columns, but Madeleine Carroll, Paulette Goddard, and Mary Martin were reportedly dressed first and foremost in simple, tailored suits and sports ensembles.[24] Though part of the Hollywood glamour industry, in interviews, Head was at pains to reach American women directly and make film fashion trends accessible and affordable, whether through advocating sportswear and shirtwaist dresses or showing how to transform her ermine wraps and gold lamé gowns into white velveteen and crepe renditions.[25]

But she was not involved simply in suggesting adaptations of the latest screen trends that could be easily whipped up at home on a sewing machine. In the 1930s, Head also produced a line of her own autographed models for New York department stores. "Styled by Hollywood," these street and party-wear ensembles were marketed for Eighth Avenue clientele, allegedly bringing the average young woman the "vivacity" and "glamour" of an original Head design with the "serviceable" qualities of the new Celanese taffeta.[26] Already the Edith Head signature, always accompanied by the serious, unsmiling photo of her with her Louise Brooks bob, meant originality and accessibility.

She also advised working women not to be afraid of ignoring trends that were too time-consuming and inappropriate (as she dismissed the pompadour hairstyles advocated by Paris in the late 1930s: "Not at the movies or over the typewriter—it just doesn't seem right").[27] Hollywood's working women, from secretaries to stars, had to have a wardrobe that accommodated their long workdays and dinner dates with boyfriends, husbands, and colleagues, and no one knew better than Edith Head how to make work look glamorous and navigate the "danger" of "women at work" from eight till five and beyond.[28] The "danger" was no longer about the crumbling gender divides in the workplace or the single and married women who made up 25%-30% of the US workforce, but how those women, entrenched in their career lifestyles, could appear stylish, immaculate, and untouched by the pace of public life. "Career girl" fashions would become the focus of many Hollywood style op-eds, with Head and Irene at MGM doing some of the more high-profile work.[29]

The war in Europe caused Head and other designers and journalists to reconsider Hollywood's influence on fashion, and Head argued that the film industry had the potential to shape fashion due to the increased realism of its film stories. "The general story trend in the industry is leaning toward a more legitimate, less madcap theme. Our screen heroines are now normal, average, every-day girls and women instead of overdramatized, synthetic sirens."[30] The average women were working and taking an active part in modern life: "We are glorifying stenographers, salesgirls, waitresses and practically every type of woman, up through the young married sets to debutantes, heiresses and dowagers. But every heroine will be dressed smartly, appropriately, and sanely."[31] Like Bette Davis, Head welcomed the trend in modern realism in film stories as a way of freeing women from confining life narratives and clothing.

Ironically, this trend toward realism, accompanied by the studios' more general financial conservatism in the late 1930s and 1940s, favored the careers of women designers over the industry's key male designer-stars. While her predecessor at Paramount, Travis Banton, had been responsible for designing some of Marlene Dietrich's more outlandish costumes, when Head succeeded him as first designer, she promoted herself as a designer for the studio's younger, more homegrown cohort of stars who dressed for the real world. More widely in the industry, in contrast to designers such as MGM's Adrian, Head designed not simply for the star on screen, but for the legions of American working women who wanted glamour without compromising their independence or pocketbook. As David Chierichetti reveals, Adrian, who had spent lavish amounts of MGM's money in the Depression making Garbo look gorgeous, "knew his era was over" when George Cukor famously rejected all of his wardrobe designs for the star on *Two-Faced Woman* (1941) and directed him "to make simple garments like those Garbo wore in her private life."[32] Unfortunately, Adrian's replacement as head designer by a woman, Irene, is also viewed as part of the "end" of Hollywood glamour and creativity, reinforcing a gender bias in the historiography. Yet, with these two women heading the two richest studios' costume departments, American women had their strongest advocates for working women's fashion.

Budget-conscious and efficient Head, in addition to being "a producer and director's dream," was able to restyle Barbara Stanwyck on and off screen with a wardrobe most American women could affordably adapt for themselves. Stanwyck, more than any other actress, was Head's muse in the late 1930s and 1940s and key to her vision of practical American women's fashion. Though the two had worked with each other many times in the 1930s, it was only for *The Lady Eve* (1940) that Head was able to design a smart and sexy wardrobe for Stanwyck that developed the story and set the fashion trends for the next few years.

When in 1941, several of the industry's key designs were on public display, the press juxtaposed Adrian's "unusual" wedding gown for Katharine Hepburn in *The Philadelphia Story* (actually a very slight revamp of the original design by Valentina in the Broadway production) with Head's sporty nautical trouser suit for Barbara Stanwyck in *The Lady Eve* (figure 6.1).[33] The contrast was startling on more than one level. Hepburn looks away from the camera, the epitome of delicate femininity in trailing chiffon (a stark contrast with her usual brash masculine attire), while Stanwyck stares back at the camera, hand in her pocket, in the ultimate American *sports luxe*

Film, Custom Designers to Display Styles Feb. 13

KATHARINE HEPBURN wears an unusual wedding gown designed by Adrian.   BARBARA STANWYCK displays a nautical slack suit designed by Edith Head.

Figure 6.1 Katharine Hepburn in Adrian and Barbara Stanwyck in Head, 1941

that nicely dovetailed with her athletic, outdoor-loving, off-screen image. Stanwyck adored Head; they were both hardworking, serious women, and basically shy. As Stanwyck remembered, "I had Edith Head's name written into every contract, no matter what studio I was working for."[34] From that moment, a historic partnership was born.

One of Head's key achievements with Stanwyck was in rethinking American women's fashion with a strong regional and ethnic component.

Stanwyck's bolero jackets, toreador trousers, gold braid detailing, and serapes took the country and Head back to their roots. As the stepdaughter of a mining engineer, young Edith spent her childhood in remote sections of the southwestern deserts with Mexican American and Native American children as her companions. One of the few Hollywood people to speak fluent Spanish, she could work better with Paramount's many Mexican American seamstresses.[35] Her birth parents were both Jewish, and Head was allegedly self-conscious enough about her heritage to emphasize her Mexican upbringing and keep her hated drunkard ex-husband's goyish name to ward off any anti-Semitic attacks on her career. In 1948, a prominent article on her career even alleged that Head's mother was Mexican.[36]

Although very few biographies mention her ethnic roots, in every press tribute to her, Head was sure to include a nod to her upbringing in the Southwest and the simplicity of line and naturalness of color native to that region: "Miss Head's childhood background has left its mark in her love for primitive colors, choice of fabrics, and simple lines. She adores homespuns and hand-woven materials and uses them at every opportunity."[37] As Lester Geiss commented, "Few designers have as thorough a grounding in the art traditions of the American continent." But though she enjoyed "pioneering" Hopi and Navaho design and style elements like the wraparound, she wanted to be the dominant American designer "adapting" these aspects for a predominantly Anglo public. Without knowledge of her upbringing, one might mistakenly assume that like any imperialist with a good racket, she resented other designers competing for this creative territory, and by 1943, was feeling "'bitter' about the way certain American exploiters have been acting in Mexico."[38] However, Head was deeply committed to reinvigorating American design with Latin and Native American style, and often gave interviews to Mexican newspapers and journals about fashion and Hollywood's interest in cultivating a relationship with a broader "American" fashion network.[39]

In 1941, Head was a key participant in the California "Fashion Futures" event, a major fashion show at the Ambassador Hotel sponsored by the Los Angeles and San Francisco Fashion Groups, featuring seventy-five models and including designs by her colleagues Renie and Vera West. Press coverage emphasized the number of Hollywood women involved, and in the publicity Head was pictured contemplating one of her sketches, draped with fabric, flanked by Renie and Marie Miller.[40] Intended as a showcase for "California originals as indicative of America-inspired world fashion trends," it linked private and film industry designers, offering a second fashion base alongside New York for American design. While male designers like Milo Anderson still aimed for impossible glamour (with diamond garters on his cancan dress), Head instead went back to her and California's roots and the Latin American–inspired fashion of *The Lady Eve*, showing two "Mexican boy guayavera jackets" that would soon sweep the nation in women's fashion.[41]

The show, covered on air by Hedda Hopper, who was well known for trumpeting the achievements of women behind and in front of the camera, had its origins in the summer of 1940, when journalists speculated about Hollywood taking Paris's place as a leading fashion city. Most designers, including Walter Plunkett, initially dismissed the idea, arguing that Hollywood could suggest individual things, but designers worked nine to five and had little time for making their own collections. Others such as Milo Anderson and Vera West thought that collectively, with the help of a costume designers' guild, Hollywood designers might manage to contribute a few pieces each and do an annual show. Head recognized that with Paris occupied by the Nazis, "if average American women are to have new fashions this year they'll have to get most of them from the screen."[42] However, she was against seeing Hollywood or anywhere else as a fashion "capital": " 'Why any one center? Why not ideas from all over America, gathered in at some important headquarters like New York?" she responded diplomatically. "Hollywood will always be an important source of ideas—but Hollywood designers have a real job on their hands and you can't do two jobs well.' "[43] In another interview, Head was more direct, saying flat out that while it might have potential, "Hollywood is not now a true fashion center."[44] The "problem," she argued, was that Hollywood designers had to "handle the gangster opuses, the hillbilly flickers, and all the other dreary chores."[45] She had designed collections for public consumption, but it was a mammoth task alongside overseeing Paramount's design output.

Her criticism may have spurred the industry to action. A year later, faced with the sponsorship of the California fashion industry and with the backing of the studios and the honorary patronage of four New York fashion editors (Louise Macy of *Harper's Bazaar*, Margaret Case of *Vogue*, Aimee Larkin of *Collier's*, and Winifred Ovitte of *Women's Wear*), Head could not resist showcasing her talents. It paid off; the show coincided with Paramount's renewal of her contract as its top designer for a third year in a row (with a salary increase).[46] And given her diplomatic handling of the New York–Hollywood style battle in 1940, the New York Museum of Costume honored her (and colleagues Dolly Tree, Irene Lentz Gibbons, Irene Saltern, Howard Greer, Travis Banton, Edward Stevenson, Avis Caminez, and Jack Huston) as "one of ten outstanding Hollywood designers" at a reception in 1942.[47]

Adrian, who had rashly backed Hollywood over New York as the new fashion capital of America and had since left MGM,[48] was not invited. In the winter of 1943, it was announced that the New York Costume Designers Guild invited Head as "guest of honor" at its annual fashion show to be held in January.[49]

The Los Angeles show and the attention from New York's fashion guilds may have made her Hollywood's ambassadress of costume design, but Head was not always a compliant booster of her own industry. She complained in interviews about the time involved in having to "create styles that will show our stars off to the best advantage—styles that will compensate for their various beauty and figure faults."[50] Head managed to convey that Hollywood designers worked harder than Paris designers, their jobs demanded more versatility, and they also had to deal with imperfect models! As she commented, "Stars are like other women. They like to wear certain styles, whether they suit them or not. It is my job to modify their tastes to suit their personalities and to make them happy in the clothes I design for them."[51]

Occasionally Head betrayed her exasperation with her female stars: "The easiest person to dress," she commented, "is the girl who admits she knows nothing about clothes and doesn't look in the mirror while being fitted, leaving it all to the designer and her assistants."[52] Women were even more of a challenge since they often refused to subordinate personal glamour to the demands of the film. Head commented, "Actresses know what they want. They want a certain neckline, a certain material, a certain color, a certain style." Yet "They like to wear stylish clothes even if the character they are playing is living in a shack along the river bank and has never been in a department store in her life."[53] Later in the 1940s, she took a swipe at Hollywood's top women, with Gene Handsaker reporting that she had taken the different anatomical features of nine actresses "to form the perfect dummy."[54] On their own Diana Lynn, Stanwyck, Dietrich, Lamarr, de Havilland, Young, Lizabeth Scott, Veronica Lake, and Mona Freeman might not be perfect, but Head could cut out their figure faults and make something ideal!

Most of the time, however, press coverage presented her work as a close and happy collaboration with a series of female stars. Some of this, it must be admitted, she invented. Head claimed that because she knew Claudette Colbert's personality—her likes and dislikes, her preferred color palette and styles—she could quickly sketch any wardrobe for her with the help of the script. Colbert actually disliked Head, and after Banton's departure, brought Irene in to design all her personal costumes while Head handled the supporting cast. However, this didn't make the papers. Instead, Head emphasized, "conferring" with the star in the early stages of sketching the wardrobe was essential. "'I'm not always a dictator. . . . The stars I dress— Carole Lombard, Claudette Colbert, Dorothy Lamour—have a lot to say about their clothes.'"[55] In her interviews, Head never talked about working with actors—it was the women's fashion that interested her, period.

In 1925, when she was just starting out as a screen designer, she was photographed showing one of her *Wanderer* sketches to Greta Nisson.[56] These consultations between designer and star remained a feature of production as the studio era developed. Ten years later, Head even "welcomed" the opinion of pint-sized Virginia Weidler, who took "an avid interest in everything involved in the making of motion pictures."[57] Head's relationship with Weidler harkened back to the sound partnership between Shirley Temple and Fox's Gwen Wakeling in the 1930s. As journalists noted, "Shirley Temple is aware of the fact she sets the clothes fashions for practically all the little girls in the world so, rather than make any mistake, she will not appear in anything that Gwen Wakeling does not pass on."[58] In such cases, the actresses and designers were pictured together in a "style conference," emphasizing the friendly and informal collaborations that defined women's work in Hollywood. Other female stars helped their favorite designers by wearing their work off camera—both Janet Gaynor and Joan Crawford did this for former seamstress Sheila O'Brien, helping her to make the leap into major studio design.[59]

But though Head would later say that Audrey Hepburn's curveless figure would be "the reward that comes to a designer after years of horse operas," her favorite women to work with were mature actresses Gloria Swanson and Bette Davis. Of Swanson, Head would rave, "She knows as much about clothes as I do. It's like working with another technician in your own field."[60] Head would remark that Davis "is the only actress I have ever met who can be objective about clothes. She can put aside her own dislikes and immerse herself in the requirements of a part. The only demand Bette makes is 'I have to be able to move in this costume.'"[61] Head had designed a number of Davis's films over the years and, though she was busy on several productions leading up to 1950 (including *Samson and Delilah*, for which she would share an Academy Award with Wakeling and Jeakins, and *Sunset Boulevard*), persuaded Davis to have Joseph Mankiewicz hire her for Margo Channing's wardrobe. When the famous "bumpy night" cocktail dress didn't fit Davis's bust properly and began to slide off her shoulders, the actress merely laughed at the mortified Head and pulled the neckline lower, saying, "'Don't you like it better like this, anyway?'"[62] Davis, always a rule breaker, knew the attraction of casual disarray.

But as a studio collaborator, Head had to work with cameramen and art directors "to be sure her costumes fit in with the set backgrounds." Directors were sometimes harder to please than the stars, often cherishing purely personal likes for certain fabrics or colors. As one journalist commented, Head "claims the men are harder to please about frocks stars wear in pictures than the stars themselves. . . . All have favorite colors and would have them in every frock if they had their way."[63] Head's challenge was "to please all and still stick to her original design—no easy task."[64] She didn't look like one given to compromise, with her dark glasses, grim smile, and plain black business suits, yet her organizational skills and ability to negotiate with Hollywood egos helped to maintain her position as Hollywood's most powerful designer.

Although during the 1930s, Head had advocated simple, chic professional silhouettes for the working woman, she drew the line at women in uniforms. As she remarked in 1942: "I have always thought that military uniforms for women were in bad taste as men see enough uniforms in the field. At home, in the boudoir, they're looking for femininity." Gwen Wakeling concurred. "Men who have been in army camps don't want to come back on leave and find their wives and sweethearts done up in clothes that are modified versions of the uniforms they've been wearing. . . . Don't take any chances with your femininity in fashion! The slick, chic look is no more!'"[65] Suits weren't out, necessarily, but needed to be dressed up so they were distinctly different from men's attire. The gender neutrality that had been changing women's fashion over the past few years had to be finessed given the added grimness of war.

Even though women were doing the same jobs as men during the day, at night things had to be different. As Wakeling continued, "When your soldier beau comes back on leave—by all means *park* your uniform and get into something pretty for him . . . remember that no course in mechanics or anything else is sufficient excuse to wear nails with chipped polish or to let your hair go!'"[66] Some women rejected Wakeling's and Head's strictures, however. As Evelyn Bailing wrote in response to their article, "Didn't you rather overdo the glamour in your style story . . . I know from my own experience that after-work hours aren't just a succession of movies, parties, bowling, and dancing. What about sorting laundry bundles, slicking up the apartment, shopping for food, pressing blouses, and all the rest? Besides, do American girls *have* to have glamour to be sold on the idea of doing patriotic war work?"[67]

Head believed that glamour had been redefined by women's growing role in society. What was once "extravagant . . . is out today" and was replaced by the concept of a well-dressed, well-groomed, confident woman.[68] Hollywood's female designers didn't feel they were compromising the gains women had made in equality and employment opportunities in the 1930s by advocating a feminine silhouette and design. On the contrary, women were empowered by such difference, and female designers could truly come into their own by reaffirming femininity as an inspiration to themselves and their soldier love-interests. As journalist Sylvia Weaver commented, "Only a woman designer, seeing the war from a woman's eyes and feeling it with a woman's heart, can really give the best sartorial guidance to American women in the achievement of this inspirational dress, is Edith's belief." Weaver continued, "And it is notable that the great designers of women's clothes, expressed in terms of their lives and times, have been women. The '20s had Lanvin, the '30s had Schiaparelli. Whom shall the '40s bring forth?"[69] Head was the top name.

Despite her position in Hollywood, Head was careful not to appear too much of a fashion dictator. For Stanwyck's role as a doctor in *You Belong to Me* (1941), Head "made a survey of women doctors" and responded to their preference for simple tailoring, "not mannish in any sense," and "pretty and flattering" evening wear.[70] However, this did not depart very much from her long-term interest in catering to "any successful woman in business."[71] In handling *Tender Comrade* (1943), the studio pushed Head further to adapt her ideas about women in uniform. It was Head's second of several pairings with Ginger Rogers, an actress who throughout her career epitomized the American working woman. Journalists noted that in the film, Ginger Rogers plays a war worker "in an airplane factory" who "earns a good wage," and they covered Rogers's jumper slacks with slashed pockets, multiple cotton blouses, and wool gabardine trench coats as a "smart" and "practical" dress code.[72] The outfit was even approved by the defense council of the aircraft industry as suitable for the real war workers. Again, Head went to the source for inspiration, spending several days with the women working at the Kaiser shipyards, forging an effective relationship with other working women that added to her already formidable public profile.[73]

Off screen, stars continued to find their own freedom in Head's designs regardless of the designer's feelings about androgyny in dress. In 1943, Ingrid Bergman liked Head's twill ankle button commando trousers for Gary Cooper in *For Whom the Bell Tolls* (1943) so much she asked the designer to make some for her own use off the set.[74] The trousers were perfect for the cycling-mad Bergman, who wanted trousers with enough pockets so she could ditch her purse and still bring lipstick, keys, and money along for the rides! A journalist noted that, in the film, Cooper had used the series of pockets down the side for grenades and wire cutters.

Head understood that her career-long interest in making clothes that all working women could wear from season to season, from stars to secretaries, set her in good stead with her public, and that the war would only improve her position. She became a strong advocate for simplicity; small, hardworking, but feminine wardrobes; ethnic influences (when they saved cloth like the short bolero jacket); and even slacks.[75] She was embarrassed about her involvement in creating Ginger Rogers's $35,000 mink dress for former designer-turned-director Mitchell Leisen's *Lady in the Dark* (1944; planned before the US War Production Board issued order L-85 in March 1942 to cut down on the amount of cloth used in women's clothing), and said film fashion could no longer tolerate these extravagances, which were hangovers from the silent era when even cowgirls would wear white fox chaps and chiffon blouses! According to press releases, Head "was only now beginning to recover from her exertions of years past."[76] But she would go still further, arguing, "L-85 was the greatest boon that ever came to the fashion designers in Hollywood. . . . It banished super-luxury and brought us all down to earth. Today we create sensible styles for women—the kind they can actually wear. How well I remember the day when we would swirl fox skins around the hem of a secretary's dress, or put a white satin uniform on a trained nurse. Now we hold to stark realism."[77]

In her assessment, Head was perhaps overly harsh on the industry, which had turned to realism in a great many of its genre films by the early 1930s (enforced certainly by the financial restrictions of the Great Depression), but she was also unfair to her own efforts to forge links between women's fashion and the screen. But always a shrewd politician, she knew public recognition and endorsement of government initiatives would only enhance cooperation between her industry and the OWI. She was also right about *Lady in the Dark*. Neither she nor Rogers liked the director's complaints that Rogers's executive work-wear looked unbearably severe and somber, and Rogers hated the heavy mink dress and other equally fanciful and ridiculous dream-sequence costumes she had to wear.[78] The story of a career-obsessed fashion editor who needed a psychological cure in the form of romance and Ray Milland appealed to neither designer nor actress.

By the mid-1940s, Head had become so formidable a force in the design industry that Paramount planned her biopic. Press releases claimed Paramount executives planned a "top budget" production "glamorizing the career" of the designer, and writers had Rogers, who had played the notorious fashion magazine editor in *Lady in the Dark*, in mind to play Head.[79] But a modern biopic of a famous woman, however much she embellished the studio's image (and one not in any need to be "cured" by romance!), was too much for Paramount.

Ironically, it was Head's rival at MGM, Helen Rose, who supplied the idea for a film about women's role in the fashion world, *Designing Women*, several years later. Rose's 1953 story focused on a young working girl, immigrant Frenchwoman Lizette, whose ability to sketch fabulous costumes in her spare time is exploited by a shady boyfriend. He makes the deals and pockets 90% of her earnings. He sells the sketches to a couturier, "Mlle. Julienne," who in reality is middle-aged Marcus Bonet, who "figured no one would pay much attention to a fairly successful runt of a Parisian tailor named Marcus Bonet. So he invented the fabulous and mysterious Mlle. Julienne and voila! He has one of the most prosperous salons in New York."[80] Eventually, Bonet realizes who is really doing the creative work and hires Lizette, who in turn gets a job for her girlfriend Trixie as "a style commentator."

Admittedly a lightweight working-girl success story, Rose's narrative nonetheless pointed out the gender exploitation and hierarchies in contemporary fashion. On the one hand, unknown, impoverished women are coming up with all the ideas and being exploited by a network of men. On the other, the expectation for a top designer is that he be female. The film, in this form, was sadly never realized, and instead, despite Vincente Minnelli's protestations to the contrary,[81] *Designing Woman* (1957) became a thinly veiled remake of George Stevens's historic pairing of Katharine Hepburn and Spencer Tracy in *Woman of the Year* (1942), with Hepburn's Dorothy Thompson / Tess Harding journalist degenerating into Marilla (Lauren Bacall), a jealous designer and one half of a lackluster marriage. In spite of the negative images the film generated about "famous" women in the workforce, in contemporary star and lifestyle magazines, Head's own marriage to another studio employee Bill Ihnen was represented as happy and contented. Both were focused on their comfortable, ranch-style home away from the studio, and the couple cherished a life apart as something both had earned through years of hard work.[82]

But the failure of the Head biopic and Rose's commentary on costume design indicated that the world of Hollywood design had changed fundamentally from the 1930s and 1940s. Although Banton's and Adrian's departures enabled women to rise to the top of the Hollywood fashion world, Hollywood costume design underwent other shifts. There is some feeling among costume design historians that the establishment of a union in 1937 (the Motion Picture Costumers, IATSE Local 705) with minimum pay scales and firmly defined jobs and hours prevented young designers from rising to the top through hard work and experimentation with different jobs. Certainly, Head, Wakeling, Visart, West, and Irene all emerged in the nonunionized past when they could put the extra time in to get ahead.[83] (This sentiment certainly emerges in Barbara McLean's account of film editing in the 1930s.) In spite of the fact that the Academy Award for Costume Design and the Costume Designers Guild were established by Sheila O'Brien (chief designer for former SAG star Joan Crawford) and Head during the late 1940s and early 1950s as a way of raising Hollywood's design profile, these agencies tended to favor established names.

More familiar to histories of Hollywood costume design is the impact of Dior's 1947 New Look, where Head and other Hollywood designers were caught "unprepared" for the shift from practical glamour to feminine illusion (generated by a coterie of French *men*). Head, however, could hardly have been said to be sitting on her laurels in the spring of 1947, when Paramount staged one of the biggest shows at New York's Waldorf-Astoria Hotel. It was a true couture fashion show, with day and evening designs from Paramount's latest films "all created by Edith Head," who served as commentator at the show.[84]

Head's show has been forgotten, ignored in the wake of excitement generated by press eager for a return of Continental masculine control over the industry (top female designer Coco Chanel, once aligned with Hollywood, was beset by postwar claims of Nazi collaboration and only returned as a force in England during the 1950s). Yet Head quickly recovered, and even dared to criticize the Paris-inspired New Look and the trend away from modest practicality and toward bust-baring naughtiness: "You aren't stylish anymore unless you look like a peep show."[85] Adapting her philosophy, she designed wardrobes for Grace Kelly in the early 1950s that would bring buzz back to Hollywood fashion trends while paying tribute to the clean lines and practicality of the working woman (Kelly's lime-green two-piece suit and overnight case in *Rear Window*, are among the most memorable examples and hallmarks of the professional wear made famous by Anita Colby).

As one profile attested shortly after she received her sixth Oscar, Head continued to change "a starlet's whole personality," with the "cool detachment" of "a scientist."[86] But, significantly, Head reached back to the 1930s for her definitive women, changing the 1950s nobody into a replica of Carole Lombard. She still advocated women taking an honest, practical look at themselves and their career and personal needs before shaping their wardrobes in her direction, but found the raw material coming out of Hollywood increasingly uninspiring.

However, there was another movement within Hollywood costume that was less about controlling trends and taste. It was Dorothy Jeakins's approach to design that in many ways hearkened back to the strengths of studio collaboration and the achievements of Walter Plunkett in period design. While Head had often publicly condemned period costume design as a waste of her talents, under Jeakins, a new power and intellectualism linked Hollywood with the wider world of theater and art.

Plunkett was known as the master of period costume. One of the most educated and urbane of men, strikingly handsome, charming, and—though he escorted and enjoyed close friendships with many women—openly gay, he was the favorite designer of Katharine Hepburn, Ginger Rogers, Greer Garson, and Elizabeth Taylor. He had honed his craft at RKO in the 1930s, designing period gowns for Hepburn, Irene Dunne, and Ann Harding. Selznick appreciated Plunkett's research ethics, sense of fabric, and meticulous design for women's costumes, and would hire him without question to handle his masterpiece *Gone with the Wind* (though he would later criticize Rhett Butler's suits; like Edith Head, the designer was not particularly interested in men's clothes). Plunkett understood color and character with a subtlety few could match.

Although he grew close to many of his stars, Katharine Hepburn was Plunkett's lifelong friend and muse.[87] He appreciated her quirky taste in menswear off screen and, in her frequent excursions to Broadway, would always send wires and flowers when he could not be in the front row for opening night. Portrait artist Paul Clemens would pay tribute to the Plunkett-Hepburn partnership in the late 1940s when he painted Hepburn as Lutie, her character in the nineteenth-century melodrama *The Sea of Grass*, her personal favorite of her film pairings with Spencer Tracy (Hepburn sometimes signed her notes and letters to Tracy "Lutie"). Plunkett's dark velvet traveling dress fit Hepburn's long lean back and silhouette like a glove.

He remained one of the most successful freelance designers through the 1950s, but worked primarily for MGM on elaborate period work for Greer Garson (*That Forsyte Woman*, 1949), Lana Turner (*Plymouth Adventure*, 1950; *Diane*, 1955), and Elizabeth Taylor (*Raintree County*, 1956). But MGM's glossy costume dramas were not the kind of work he had once loved doing for *Gone with the Wind*, where the designs were not always about stunning glamour, richness, and bandbox-new perfection, but also about chronicling a way of life, war, and survival for women. He liked clothes to look lived in. It was Dorothy Jeakins, more than other designers, who possessed something of Plunkett's seriousness and his commitment to film as a social document. Though Jeakins was not always so successful at gaining the affection of her female stars (Olivia de Havilland, extremely loyal to Edith Head, clashed with Jeakins's assertiveness over *My Cousin Rachel*, 1952, and Marilyn Monroe also rejected her work on *The Misfits* in favor of

Rita Hayworth's former designer, Jean Louis),[88] Jeakins made her lasting professional friendships with directors.

In many ways, Jeakins was the polar opposite of Edith Head. While Head had a stable, even privileged childhood, Jeakins, the daughter of a Danish immigrant mother (who also designed women's gowns) was raised in poverty in a series of foster homes after her father abducted her, at the age of five, from her mother. While Head disliked sewing and sketching the human form, Jeakins was a born artist and a seamstress with remarkable appreciation for fabric and color. Teachers encouraged her gifts for drawing and took her to visit a costume house, which transformed her life and decided her career. She was one of three California students to win a state scholarship to the Otis Art Institute, where instructors Lucy Billings and Frederick Monhoff encouraged her, and *Los Angeles Times* publisher Harry Chandler contributed $30 a month for her art supplies and living expenses.[89] After a three-year stint with the Federal Art Project, she worked as a background painter for the Disney Studios at $16 a week. Her close friend Tyrus Wong worked there as an artist (he was responsible for the Asian-inspired look of *Bambi*, 1942), and the two of them, never with enough to eat, would "put our dimes together" and "share our meals."[90]

She also worked as a sketch artist at Paramount (designing Beatrice Lillie's clothes for *Doctor Rhythm*, 1938). In 1940, still struggling financially, she began working as a fashion illustrator for I. Magnin's in Los Angeles to supplement her income. She could have been a model at the famed department store where many of Hollywood's stars including Greta Garbo shopped. A statuesque six feet, slender, with high cheekbones, widely spaced eyes, and a magnificent head of dark hair twisted in a crown at the top of her head, Jeakins was hard to miss, even by Hollywood's standards. She had an attitude to boot, allegedly referring to the small, wall-eyed Head as "that little dressmaker." After her husband, Fox publicity chief Raymond Dane, left her to raise her two young sons alone, she continued to work as a single mother for Magnin's, when one day in 1947 her drawings impressed Twentieth Century-Fox art director Richard Day. He introduced her to Victor Fleming, who was directing Ingrid Bergman in Walter Wanger's independent production of *Joan of Arc* (1948).

Fleming had been unhappy with noted New York costume designer Madame Barbara Karinska's work. He liked Jeakins, a fellow California native, straight away. Hard-working, shy, and awkward in social situations, Jeakins was plainspoken and brilliant. She grasped the historical aspects of the Maxwell Anderson script and the production's need for simplicity and authenticity. The director fired Karinska, hiring the untried Jeakins in her stead. Although terrified at having to handle a major production alone, she did a phenomenal amount of work, meticulously copying historical notes on every aspect of French medieval design, sketching minutely with multiple swatches, and supplementing her work for Fleming with photographs of contemporaneous images.[91] Her "workbook" was a stark contrast to the way Head functioned (figure 6.2). Head habitually did a rough sketch and then had a sketch artist reproduce her design (uncredited) for director, star, and producer to scan. Jeakins loved involving herself in the dyeing and weathering of fabrics, and produced multiple sketches and notes to help cutters and fitters. Though her designs for Bergman's Joan were stunning in their simplicity, she was equally drawn to court and military costumes, spending her time lavishly on supporting players and extras.

Her work won the newcomer the first Academy Award for Best Costume Design in early 1949, a fact that infuriated veteran Edith Head (who had to wait a year for *The Heiress*, 1949, to win her an award). Head's open dislike didn't faze Jeakins. After Fleming's untimely death in 1949, she went to work for the exacting Cecil B. DeMille, who enjoyed bullying his female designers—Head included—and would share the third Oscar for design with Head and Gwen Wakeling for *Samson and Delilah*.

Jeakins had, as she put it, a "Dickensian" youth. She was a ragamuffin child, grew up "without supervision," begging for handouts, spending lonely weekends in the public library researching costume and textiles,

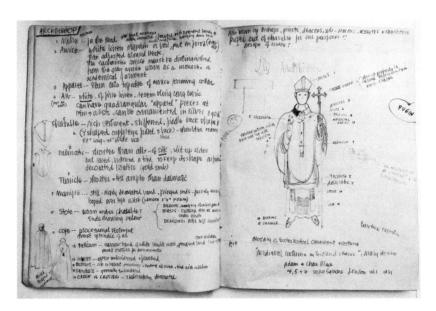

Figure 6.2 Dorothy Jeakins's workbook for *Joan of Arc*, 1948

making her own designs for innumerable imaginary productions. As she remembered,

> I used to run around Los Angeles on street cars or walk vast distances to get to the public library to take a book out or just to be alone and read and look at art books. The first year at Otis I only had the scholarship, I had no support from my father (who had left several years before); and I was unable to accept the scholarship unless I worked as a servant after school and weekends; and I did this.

Although lacking any stable support network as a child and young woman, she did not seek to replace it with a Hollywood studio family when she attained success in 1948. She was, as she recalled, infused with the rich cultural and political moment of 1930s Los Angeles, creating a network of like-minded friends from many ethnic and racial backgrounds: "The feeling about Roosevelt in those days, and what was happening to the country, was terribly exciting. And it was exciting to be poor. I have walked many a mile in Los Angeles to save a 5 cent car-fare expense."[92] Instead, after her initial success with *Joan of Arc*, Jeakins struck out boldly on her own, refusing to sign a contract from the beginning, supplanting Plunkett as the most successful freelance costume designer in Hollywood history (with twelve Academy Award nominations and multiple awards).

Jeakins was a self-taught intellectual, with an appetite for all aspects of art and design. Technically proficient, she was the first to design the second-skin nude nylon and silk mesh suits that helped eliminate seams and wrinkles in nude swimming scenes for Janet Leigh and Debra Paget in the Cinemascope *Prince Valiant* (1953).[93] She found a silk gauze for Audrey Hepburn's ethereal role as Rima in *Green Mansions* (1959) that hadn't been made since 1910.[94] Hepburn, who shared the designer's dedication to locating period fabric, adored Jeakins and asked her to do the costumes on *The Unforgiven* (1960). Unlike Head, who would have shuddered at the thought of designing for a "horse opera," Jeakins relished the challenge of recreating the American frontier period. Though Hepburn is still popularly known as a fashion icon, she loved roles where modern fashion was not the primary concern (*The Nun's Story*, 1959, where she spent most of her time swathed in a black habit, was her favorite production). As Agnes McKay noted of Jeakins's work for Hepburn on *Green Mansions*, "Some designers are content to create beautiful clothes-of-the-moment, but not so Dorothy Jeakins, who revels in any sort of fashion challenge that takes her off the beaten path."[95]

Although Jeakins fought DeMille's appallingly bad taste (he made Paulette Goddard wear high-heeled moccasins in *Unconquered*, 1947, believing women should wear high heels "at all times"), she got on well with the normally cold William Wyler (*Friendly Persuasion*, 1956), did some sheer and sexy designs for Shirley Jones in Richard Brooks's *Elmer Gantry* (figure 6.3), and was a kindred spirit with John Huston. They both reveled in the marginal and sometimes threadbare community of the artist (Huston had started as a painter in Paris before returning to Hollywood), and Jeakins's deep respect for the script and for Huston's storytelling abilities won him over. They worked together from *The Unforgiven*, *The Misfits*, *The Night of the Iguana*, and *Reflections in a Golden Eye* (1967) until *The Dead* (1987), the final work of their careers.

But though Jeakins loved collaborating with some directors, she remembered in the 1970s that she was often too shy to ask for credit in a world she saw as dominated by men. Her superb freelance work for *High Noon* (1952) was uncredited thanks to Stanley Kramer.[96] As she stated, "My first impression of a movie studio was a place where women had to be subservient. All the executives and all the key jobs were held by men. . . . Altogether it struck me a woman was expected to be seen and not heard." Here, Jeakins

Figure 6.3 Jeakins's sketch for Shirley Jones in *Elmer Gantry*, 1960

is clearly ignoring women such as Head, Wakeling, O'Brien, and Rose, who held positions of leadership in her field, and this slight testifies to the rivalry that existed between established and younger female designers. Snubbing the system was her own way of escaping from any hierarchy controlled by other women. But, as her own success was founded on Fleming firing another woman—Barbara Karinska—in *Joan of Arc*, Jeakins's career was in some sense built on the ashes of the female-driven studio system and on the increased power of the male director.

Jeakins admitted that from the beginning her work "had to stand on its own," and she was by nature "different" and "sharp-tongued," as opposed to the more diplomatic women around her. She got along without Hollywood and insisted that in the 1970s workplace "women are much more recognized for their abilities," but admitted that "ironically there are fewer opportunities" in Hollywood given the decline in annual feature film production.[97]

To a certain extent, it is worth asking whether Jeakins should be identified as primarily a Hollywood designer. She refused to belong to the system or be a contract designer, and yet, by the time she attained success, very few designers—with the exception of Edith Head—were working exclusively on studio contracts. More than any other designer, she mastered all trades in costume design, working in fashion, advertising, theater, television, and film. She loved working for Anatole Litvak on the acclaimed 1957 televised production of *Mayerling* starring Audrey Hepburn and Mel Ferrer and again, stressed the importance of research long before she actually began sketching he designs: "When I am home on the West Coast, my principal source of material is the library at UCLA. In New York I use the public library."[98] That same year, she recreated Annie Oakley's wardrobe for Mary Martin in the NBC-TV special *Annie Get Your Gun*, which aired on Thanksgiving. Again, in press interviews, Jeakins emphasized the act of designing for Mary Martin as a collaborative process. But while Head's alleged meetings of the minds only manifested themselves in staged photo-shoots, Jeakins elaborated with the press: "I did the sketches here in California and mailed them to Mary Martin in New York. We had a marvelous correspondence flashing back and forth for a while. I glued the letters on the back of each sketch!"[99]

Her theatrical work at the Stratford Shakespeare Festival (*Romeo and Juliet*, 1959) and for UCLA, where she designed for Dorothy McGuire (*Winesburg, Ohio*, 1958), Nina Foch (*The Three Sisters*, 1960), and Katharine Ross (*King Lear*, 1964), were all deeply satisfying experiences.[100] She took time off her busy film career in 1961, spending an entire year on a

Guggenheim fellowship to study classical Japanese theater costumes at the behest of Rico Lebrun. She returned with an exhibition of sketches. Later, in 1967, she was appointed chief curator of textiles at the Los Angeles County Museum of Art, and throughout the 1960s her sketches appeared in design exhibitions in Los Angeles and Santa Barbara. While other designers floundered following the collapse of the studio system, Jeakins was always in demand. Far more than Head, she was a director's rather than a star's designer. By the 1950s, the power of female stars had arguably diminished. Jeakins, though not always working amicably with female stars, got on well with auteurs and actors. She laughed that Sean Connery (*The Molly Maguires*, 1970) was the only star to ever send her a fan letter about her work. Jeakins survived the Hollywood system as a woman by subtly adapting to the new production forces operating in 1950s Hollywood. The big, splashy historical films continued into the 1960s, and Jeakins designed some of these last gasps of the studio production system, among them *Hawaii* (1964), *The Sound of Music* (1965), *Finian's Rainbow* (1968), *Catch-22* (1970), and of course Martin Ritt's *Molly Maguires*.

It was during the making of *The Molly Maguires* that Jeakins was interviewed about her career. The interview later appeared on network television as an educational outreach program. Jeakins explained the role of the costume designer: "Our part of it is identity establishing—it is the final skin on the actor—it tells you what you're looking at. . . . It's how you read what you are looking at. . . . It's the transmission of the story through one means."[101] Jeakins acknowledged that as an intellectual challenge she preferred "the study of the past" and period pictures. "I love to tell the story of America. . . . Each story is influenced by social change and by many conditions pressing in from the outside." In another article she argued that like politics, fashion was "a force,"[102] and that both reflected and shaped social and cultural developments. Her own historical research and work in period design gave her a sense of humor and detachment about the urgency and ego that propelled modern fashion.

In a letter to journalist Marshall Berges, she argued that her own work as a designer had to serve not only her creative outlets and the art of good design, but also the idea, the realism of the film. She mused, "Sometimes it is better for me to serve the assignment in terms of what is right for it [rather] than in terms of what is original. No matter how pedestrian or drab or commonplace the subject may be it must be true. Choice and taste and wit and honesty can be brought even to the commonplace. . . . What I do must relate to a made experience. . . . a designer is a bringer-to-life. Films must be human."[103]

Her dedication to recreating the realistic dress and economic conditions of nineteenth-century Pennsylvania miners in *The Molly Maguires* was intensely rewarding because the collaborative project in realism and humanity was a political act. She worked from February to July 1968 with Ritt, but emphasized that she worked as part of a team. "Nothing is done alone in this world by anyone and I am always aware of the fact that . . . I am fortunate that I have marvelous people to work with." Jeakins described her career as "a we experience" in which dressmakers, cutters, and fitters worked as a collective. She went on to say that although she had "the authority to get the effect that I wish for," "no one in this world is so self-involved or so creatively total in the commercial connotation that they can say 'I did it.' It's impossible; it's a way we did it." For her, "It's a constant education and it never ends with me." Jeakins's comments on the working-class, collaborative nature of the film were intended to mirror the left-wing Ritt's story of labor unrest in the Pennsylvania mines. For both Jeakins and Ritt, the film production was an attempt to replicate the creative excitement of the New Deal's cultural moment and the history of the American labor movement in the nineteenth century. And yet Jeakins remained dismissive of studio-era Hollywood's collaborative system and her own female colleagues.

When film historian and director of the State Historical Society of Wisconsin's cinema archive Tino Balio began to develop the film collections, he approached a number of writers, directors, and actors. His two most important acquisitions for costume design and women in Hollywood were the papers of Edith Head and Jeakins. Balio seems to have identified designer donors based simply on their number of Academy Awards. Head was still working at Universal round the clock and was difficult to reach. Jeakins, in contrast, replied promptly to his letters and was helpful to his support staff. Typically for Head, many of Jeakins's sketches for *Samson and Delilah* and *The Ten Commandments* were in Head's papers before the authorship issues were rectified years later.

Though rivals, both Head and Jeakins represent the twin achievements of women in studio-era Hollywood costume design. While Head claimed the limelight and built an empire for herself at Paramount, paradoxically stressing her connection with the average woman, Jeakins remained an independent, experimental, and intellectual designer, embracing realism of the period design rather than the temptations for display and glamour. Both survived the studio system. One is remembered as a towering queen of Hollywood costume design; the other is comparatively ignored. One was a company woman who relished the company of powerful women;

the other was a New Deal artist and free-spirited Cinderella who relished the collaborative artistic practice and needed no fairy godmother to design her dress. Appropriately, in the press, Jeakins rarely dictated what women should wear in public and private life. Head's project to educate the working woman in her wardrobe choices was, for Jeakins, an exercise in the control of the individual. But few of Hollywood's women could afford to be as courageous as Jeakins. In kissing Hollywood goodbye, the women who worked for the American film industry lost their greatest cultural advocate.

—

CHAPTER 7

Last Woman Standing

Pinkie: Fadiman said she's the number two dame in the country . . . next to Mrs. Roosevelt.

Phil: So they're giving them numbers now—like public enemies.

Woman of the Year, 1942

On September 11, 1973, Katharine Hepburn sat down with talk show host Dick Cavett, "just as you'd expect," in her trademark white yachting trousers, frizzy hair, and complete disregard for crossing her legs.[1] Over two nights and three hours of airtime on ABC, the "charmingly direct and blunt," "radiant" star "got off more good lines" than most networks had in a season.[2] Early in the interview, he asked her whether she was inspired to carry posters for the contemporary women's movement. Without hesitation, she said no. "We did that a very long time ago. And it is a strange situation because women and men are simply not the same at all. . . . Women unfortunately have to bear the children. And what are you going to do with them? . . . There are men and then there are women like me who have lived like men."

The star, caught up in her blunt polarities, seemed unaware, in contrast to her own mother Kit Houghton Hepburn and Hollywood colleague Bette Davis, that the right to vote did not guarantee equal rights and the decision to have children did not compromise a woman's serious commitment to her career. Hepburn's mother gave birth to and raised six children while working tirelessly for the First Wave feminist movement, and she continued to campaign for birth control and awareness of venereal disease until her death in 1951. Davis formed solid networks of working women in Hollywood and combined the challenges of motherhood and career independence during the late 1940s and 1950s. But, in contrast, as Hepburn admitted in her interview with Cavett, personally and professionally, "I didn't know how to support someone. I was out for myself."

During her own interview with Cavett back in 1971, Bette Davis had generously recognized the worth of rivals and colleagues Joan Crawford and Hepburn, but the latter brushed off any comparisons between herself and the Queen of Hollywood, merely saying, "She was very good." In her interview, Hepburn created a gendered opposition between feminism and its network of women and the rarified club of individual achievement where men and Katharine Hepburn were members. This egotism in pure form gave her the courage to survive the studio system and established the fantasy of the narcissistic, post-studio-era Hollywood star. But this formula only worked for Hepburn. The troubling question remains: In uncritically celebrating Hepburn as a feminist icon and lambasting studio-era Hollywood as a misogynist industry, have the post-studio-system media "professionals" and public turned on the American business that was once most inclined to promote women's careers?

Today, when the media puts studio-era Hollywood and feminism together, the answer is usually Katharine Hepburn.[3] But during her career at RKO and MGM, she did not discuss women's issues regarding equal pay, career opportunities, or political equality. However, she did state flatly in 1933, "I intend to speak my mind when I please, despite movie traditions,"[4] setting her independence against the Hollywood establishment. She remained uninterested in working with other Hollywood women or in recognizing the advantages of promoting women's careers and freethinking through its publicity networks and presswomen. Unlike Bette Davis and Carole Lombard, she did not actively promote the careers of her female colleagues and admitted more than once that she took a part she did not want so that some other actress wouldn't get it. Her theft of *Morning Glory* (1933) from Constance Bennett is perhaps the best-known example.

It's true this competitive nastiness drove more than one Hollywood woman's career. Actresses' feuds were legendary: Bette Davis and Miriam Hopkins fought over roles (but Davis agreed to carry Hopkins's proxy vote at the odd SAG meeting), and Davis and Joan Crawford allegedly fell out off camera over Franchot Tone. Yes, Franchot Tone; they both got over him. Louella Parsons and Hedda Hopper were sworn enemies—except where Harriet Parsons's career was concerned. Women writers were not always that supportive of each other; Zoe Akins publicly claimed women "weren't fitted for careers" even though her success as a novelist and screenwriter obviously disproved it.[5] Sonya Levien, who started out as a lawyer and First Wave feminist before turning screenwriter, claimed to one Fox production executive in 1928 that she had "a horror of the female scenarist," and sympathized if he "had your fill of the poisonous species" after interviewing several other candidates for a writing job.[6] However, during the production of *Kidnapped* (1938), she went toe-to-toe with boss Darryl F. Zanuck when he tried to supplant her and junior colleague Eleanor Harris by awarding two do-nothing male writers top screen credit. [7] She and Harris had written 75% of the script, and in those days, there was no Screen Writers Guild or Mary C. McCall Jr. to pursue producers over credit disputes. But Zanuck listened to Levien, and the credits were changed to reflect the women's authorship.

While other Hollywood women might stick their necks out for female colleagues more readily when their own careers were affected, Hepburn was known for simply sticking her nose in the air. She was consistently dismissive of the Hollywood system and her more glamorous and successful colleagues (she only grew friendly with Judy Garland when the latter's career was on the skids), and sniffed at Second Wave feminism and female solidarity. Though invited to attend Dorothy Arzner's DGA tribute in 1975, she declined, using the occasion to send a telegram congratulating the director but slamming the studio era as a time "when you had no right to have a career at all."[8] Arzner didn't necessarily feel that way; as she put it, "No one gave me trouble because I was a woman. Men were more helpful than women."[9] But Hepburn always defined herself in opposition to the Hollywood system. On one level, the star endures as a product of American myths about pioneering individualism, the Hollywood star system, and the studio-era film industry's ambivalent investment in strong women. But if, as historian Nancy Cott has argued, "pure individualism negates feminism because it removes the basis for women's collective self-understanding or action,"[10] then Hepburn was no feminist.

Though in their memoirs, filmmakers from Frances Marion to Ginger Rogers charged the Hollywood studio system with sexism that financially crippled them and intellectually constrained their work, the men responsible for launching Hepburn's career deliberately crafted her as a feminist star. They seemed to have done this against her will: Hepburn's rejection of the press and rudeness toward her Hollywood colleagues sabotaged what could have been a potentially influential feminist campaign within the film industry. As Pandro Berman remembered, "She had a little bit of a chip on her shoulder about Hollywood."[11] But Hepburn's own strategies of career survival from 1939 profited from the demise of the studio system and the diminishing choices available to women on both sides of the camera. If there is only one Katharine Hepburn, it was because she intended to be the last woman standing.

In 1932, few thought Hepburn would last beyond her first picture for RKO, among them director George Cukor, who, when he saw her get off the train in Pasadena, took one look at her bizarre traveling clothes (designed by the innovative Elizabeth Hawes), shiny, freckled face, and red hair and realized he'd "made the most terrible mistake." Writer Adela Rogers St. Johns remembered, "As long as I live I will never forget the first day she appeared on the lot. . . . Several executives nearly fainted. Mr. Selznick swallowed a chicken wing whole."[12] In a variation of Bette Davis's treatment by Universal, RKO was in a state of total "consternation" over their latest acquisition.[13] She hadn't come cheaply, either. Although Universal had picked up their new contract player in 1930–31 for the standard $400 a week, Hepburn was expensive. Her agent Leland Hayward had seen to that.

Hers was one of the first college-educated voices heard on American screens. But Katharine Hepburn was an even rarer case: she was a second-generation college-educated woman. Her mother, Katharine Martha "Kit" Houghton, was also an alumna of the elite Seven Sisters Bryn Mawr (B.A.) and Radcliffe (M.A.) and had her own career as a suffrage and birth control campaigner. When Hepburn's parents weren't working, they pushed their daughter to read Shakespeare, Shaw, and Ibsen. She and her older brother Tom loved the theater, and Tom wanted to go on the stage rather than follow his domineering father in a medical career. In the spring of 1921, he was fifteen and his sister thirteen. Already he was under pressure in the overachieving Hepburn household. His father was "making plans" for him to enter Yale as a medical student that fall. His mother, sensing the strain, sent the two older children to New York for some relaxation and a theater excursion with one of her former Bryn Mawr classmates, lawyer Mary Towle. They saw Pavlova dance and went to the movies. The night before they were to have returned home to Hartford, Tom committed suicide.

Young Kate, who was close enough to her brother to shave her head in solidarity at age nine and demand to be called "Jimmy" by friends and family, absorbed Tom's dreams with her own. Though her grades and concentration were erratic through home schooling and college, she had decided on a theatrical career. Several Broadway walk-ons and melodramatic firings later, she had one success in *The Warrior's Husband* (1932) and gave in to the debonair agent Leland Hayward's offers of an RKO contract. The role of Antiope in *The Warrior's Husband*, opposite Colin Keith-Johnson's statuesque Theseus, had pretensions to classicism and was a high-toned variation on the battle of the sexes. "They didn't like me until I got into a leg show," she later quipped in 1967.[14]

In 1932, RKO production chief David O. Selznick saw his strange new star as a force and inspiration to other young women in Hollywood, and was at pains to cast her in a film directed by Dorothy Arzner and written by playwright and novelist Zoe Akins: *Christopher Strong* (1933). Selznick tried to create a community of like-minded women in a single film, but it was not a happy production for Hepburn, who was already notorious for her imperious behavior. Even with Arzner, whom she admitted years later to admiring, there was "a competitive rivalry."[15] Harry Cohn's efforts to create a similar community with *Craig's Wife* coworkers Rosalind Russell, Mary McCall, Viola Lawrence, and Arzner worked better in 1936.

Throughout the early 1930s, Hepburn emulated Greta Garbo, wearing slacks and Salvation Army menswear castoffs and ducking the press. The press tried pushing her as an American version of the Swedish star. Curiously, the two women shared the same types of friendships: Garbo's closest female companions were not potential rivals (other actresses), but rather those who could directly support her career (writers Salka Viertel and Mercedes de Acosta). Hepburn's equivalents in the 1930s were editor-director-associate producer Jane Loring and friend-cum-secretary and American Express heiress Laura Harding. When she did appear in public, it was on the margins of Hollywood society with a mixture of gay men and women. Although she got along well with former Broadway director George Cukor (also a friend of Garbo) and the urbane Walter Plunkett, she quickly developed a reputation for aloofness or downright rudeness among her female peers. When the equally outspoken Tallulah Bankhead tried to make friends with her, Hepburn refused, and, when in the company of Cukor, persisted in referring to Broadway's top actress as "your friend Miss Bankhead."[16]

Yet, early in her career, Hepburn started a following among certain educated, wealthy women. In 1934, her Bryn Mawr teachers and fellow students were amazed that the Katharine Hepburn they knew was now "The Katharine Hepburn." They certainly hadn't expected a great actress. "If asked, her chums might have said, 'Oh, she'll probably marry.'"[17] But the young women she left in her wake now all wanted to emulate her—particularly in her off-screen penchant for "patched trousers" that drove RKO execs to distraction.[18] "The description of Katharine Hepburn's college dress as 'casual' might well fit campus fashion today at Bryn Mawr," one journalist opined. One faculty member lamented, in that respect, they've all "gone Hepburn." While her star-struck competitors and the working women who went to see her films dressed as fashionably as their paychecks allowed as a buffer in a competitive job market, Hepburn and the well-heeled, educated young women like her could afford to turn their backs on Hollywood-inspired dictates on female glamour. As Hepburn laughed in one of her rare early interviews, "It's no wonder the report got around that I have 16 million dollars. They thought no new actress would dare go about Hollywood dressed as I was, without that backing."[19]

Sometimes her eclectic style on and off screen won her attention from New York fashionistas who, in 1933, put Hepburn on a best-dressed list alongside Garbo and Gloria Vanderbilt. As one style guru put it, "Miss Hepburn is perfect in sports things and even her evening things have the casual look of sports clothes."[20] At the time, she was occasionally appearing in the pioneering "working woman" designer wear of Elizabeth Hawes. But more often, she made casual sartorial choices. Her scruffy New England fisherman's sweaters and worn yachting sneakers—even the famed combination of mink coat and blue jeans immortalized on the RKO backlot—indicated, as biographer Anne Edwards once put it, an intellectualized "take-me-as-I-am-or-go-to-hell" attitude that many could quietly admire but only a few dared to copy. Although some of Hepburn's unique star appeal was in not "going Hollywood," whether she liked it or not, Pandro Berman at RKO followed Selznick's original instincts and crafted her as a distinctly feminist icon in the 1930s. She played variations on the rich, educated career woman, from aviatrix Lady Cynthia Darrington (*Christopher Strong*) to Mary Stuart (*Mary of Scotland*).

Before he left RKO for MGM, Selznick promoted Jane Murfin, Sarah Mason, Zoe Akins, and Wanda Tuchock as studio writers. He and Berman also worked with Zoe Akins on Hepburn's Academy Award–winning turn in the Broadway-breakthrough film *Morning Glory*. Murfin, Tuchock, and Mason contributed to the adaptation of Louisa May Alcott's *Little Women* (1933), which starred Hepburn in a definitive early role as Josephine ("Jo") March, a liberated nineteenth-century woman who works as a teacher and writer. With the exception of her first film, Howard Estabrook's adaptation of Clemence Dane's *A Bill of Divorcement* (1932), all of Hepburn's early work was scripted by women: Jane Murfin wrote *Spitfire* (1934), Murfin and Mason wrote *The Little Minister* (1934), Mason was one of the writers of *Break of Hearts* (1935), Jane Murfin and Dorothy Yost did *Alice Adams* (1935), and Gladys Unger wrote the ill-fated *Sylvia Scarlett* (1936). Even Estabrook had a reputation as a writer of strong women's material. When he was assigned to *A Bill of Divorcement*, he was fresh from winning his Academy Award for adapting Edna Ferber's pioneer-woman saga *Cimarron*, the role that shot Irene Dunne to fame and an Academy Award nomination.

But, after starring in these pictures, in the late 1930s Hepburn was famously labeled "box office poison" by a group of male exhibitors (along with a list of other actresses who played strong female roles, including Marlene Dietrich, Dolores Del Rio, Luise Rainier, Mae West, Joan Crawford, Kay Francis, and Greta Garbo).[21] While listing Dietrich, Del Rio, Rainier, and Garbo indicated American exhibitors' Depression-era xenophobia, West had strikes against her because she wrote her own material and refused to conform to male-authored and enforced censorship strictures. Crawford was a noted union leader of SAG (and Rainier and Del Rio were also known liberals),[22] and Francis was a public embarrassment to Warner Bros. given her complaints about their trite scripts. Hepburn was rude, rich, and educated—perhaps, for some men, the most dangerous woman of all. One of the roles that contributed to her contentious screen status was *A Woman Rebels*, a manifestation of Hollywood's overlooked commitment to the liberated woman.

A Woman Rebels was one of several RKO films edited by Hepburn's close friend Jane Loring, who would go on to be a screenwriter and associate producer at MGM with Pan Berman. Although Berman loved Loring's editing on *Alice Adams* (1935), which did much to focus audience sympathy on Hepburn's lonely, awkward heroine, director George Stevens resented Loring's relationship with Hepburn, and Berman and would ban her from the set of *Quality Street* in 1937. It didn't do anything to improve the film; audiences stayed away from Stevens's film in droves. Loring's work on *A Woman Rebels* is uncredited, as was the work of story editor Marjorie Dudley, who was instrumental in promoting the novel as "an excellent vehicle for Hepburn."[23]

Netta Syrett's original novel, *The Portrait of a Rebel* (1930), narrated the life of Pamela Thistlewaite, a pioneering journalist and advocate of women's suffrage in England who had an illegitimate child, passed it off as her niece, fell in love with married and unmarried men, but discarded them all in the interests of the women's movement. Dudley was ecstatic about the property, writing of Pamela's crusades in journalism: "She becomes the rage. Her bookshop is a smart salon. It is Bohemia. It is a secure haven of the enlightened female and the advanced male. It is here that the New Woman is discussed, and that suffrage is launched."[24] Here, it seemed, was an opportunity to look in depth at a woman who flouted social and political conventions on a big scale, providing a role model for future generations of women.

A Woman Rebels was part of the studios' long-term reliance upon women's historical fiction as "prestige" story material. Many studios and independent producers were drawn to this type of material; the production costs were high risk, but epic romance, heroism, and spectacle paid off in an era that was dominated by female audiences wanting female-driven narratives.[25] Only Warner Bros. continued to focus its historical offerings on Paul Muni and the lives of great men—at least until Bette Davis pushed herself into top stardom with *Jezebel* (1938), *The Private Lives of Elizabeth and Essex*, and *All This and Heaven Too* (1940). During the 1930s, arguably the height of Hollywood's interest in lavish period dramas, producers purchased a wide variety of historical material, ranging from popular biographies and history to best sellers and widely read articles in major journals like the *Saturday Evening Post* and the *Ladies' Home Journal*. In addition to Syrett's book, the studios bought the work of Edna Ferber (*Cimarron*, 1931; *So Big*, 1932; *Show Boat*; *Come and Get It*, 1936); Fannie Hurst (*Imitation of Life*, 1934, 1959 and *Back Street*, 1932, 1941); Elizabeth Madox Roberts (*The Great Meadow*, 1931); Rachel Field (*All This and Heaven Too*); Margaret Mitchell (*Gone with the Wind*); Pearl Buck (*The Good Earth*); and Edith Wharton (*The Age of Innocence*; *The Old Maid*). Many of the writers in the top salary brackets adapting these and other historical properties were women, including Lillian Hellman, Frances Goodrich, Sarah Mason, Anita Loos, Frances Marion, Mary C. McCall Jr., Marguerite Roberts, Tess Slesinger, Jane Murfin, and Jeannie Macpherson. But, as with editing, women were not always assigned to women's films. Anita Loos could write one top disaster action film of the 1930s (*San Francisco*) and Bobbie McLean could edit another (*In Old Chicago*), but the "single standard" worked both ways in Hollywood. *A Woman Rebels*, like many other top female-oriented films in development during the second half of the 1930s and early 1940s—including the top-grossing *Gone with the Wind* and *Kitty Foyle*, and Hepburn's *The Philadelphia Story* (1940) and *Woman of the Year* (1942)—was scripted by men.

RKO's contract writer Larry Bachmann, veteran John Twist, Allan Scott, Anthony Veiller, and Ernest Vajda all worked on the script, though in an initial production memo by Cliff Reid to production executive Merian C. Cooper, Claudine West, Sarah Mason, and Jane Murfin were all suggested as writers, with Bette Davis as a possibility as Hepburn's illegitimate daughter who carries women's liberation into the next generation. As Reid wrote, "It is my opinion that in this story we have an opportunity, with the proper treatment, to bring about a picture that could be comparable to *Little Women*. Its wide appeal to women, together with its foreign market value, is exceptional."[26]

Yet Pam Thistlewaite was no quaint and tomboyish Jo March. She gets a job on the *Ladies Weekly Companion* and shakes things up with an editorial headed, "The New Women! A Woman is Queen of England! But no woman is allowed to have an intelligent profession." Later she gives major lectures on women's rights, and the screenwriter Ernst Vajda was at pains not to belittle the suffragettes: "Note: This is not a comic suffragette meeting. None of the women present is dressed in the exaggerated suffragette style. They are serious, eager, fine ladies."[27] Vajda's scripted speech for Pamela is unprecedented in its commitment to women's equal rights:

> The position of women in the world must be changed. Women must be better educated! Why should women of brains and intelligence be condemned to an idle, useless existence? Why shouldn't the professions be thrown open to properly qualified women who wish to practice them? A woman today is not admitted to the bar—to the hospitals—to a physician's profession. . . . It will be changed. Our enemies say that we, the new women, represent the height of recklessness, daring, and audacity. . . . Let them say so. We, the pioneers of a new freedom, will go ahead on our own road, scorned, ridiculed, ostracized, but with the vision of a different world ahead of us. In our vision, we see a happier world, a changed world, changed by the help, the brains, and the intelligence of the new woman: free lord of herself, and equal with men in everything.[28]

But it was either too extreme—or too lengthy—for RKO, and the scene was cut, replaced by a montage of press headlines, Hollywood's normal solution for compressing historical time. Curiously, the cutting continuity would end on the faintly humorous comment of Pamela's husband, played by Herbert Marshall, "These modern women are so weak—aren't they?"—removing the final lines of the script, which alluded to Pamela's career plans: "I hope you have packed all those speeches of yours, because I imagine the women in America are having their troubles too." Scripted connections between the British and American women's movements (and extratextual connections between Katharine Hepburn, Hepburn's mother Kit Houghton, and Pam Thistlewaite) were potentially too controversial for the studio, and Hepburn had no interest in breaking one of her privacy rules to publicize the film. *A Woman Rebels* did succeed in flouting Production Code guidelines on adultery, and Pamela remains a crusading feminist of the last century. But the film, "openly on the side of a liberated life for women," was not popular and lost over $200,000 at the box office.[29]

However tempting it may be to see the failure of *A Woman Rebels* as a sign of American audience's general disapproval of women's rights and equality, the issue is more complicated. One critic endorsed the feminist material, but slammed the director Mark Sandrich, a musical comedy director, as "out of his element."[30] Ginger Rogers usually had more to do with Sandrich in her films with Fred Astaire at RKO and remembered the director's misogyny and put-downs of her dancing decades later.

Audiences may have had more of a problem with Hepburn than the material. Her acting skills aside, Hepburn, with her hoop skirts and educated Anglicized drawl, never looked like she had to work for anything, including women's rights. She was one of the outside contenders for Selznick's Scarlett O'Hara in the late 1930s, and had she played the never-say-die Irish American belle with a good head for business, perhaps she could have salvaged something of her independent persona earned from the early success of *Morning Glory* and *Little Women*. However, RKO's resident working woman was her rival, Ginger Rogers. And in 1937, shortly after *A Woman Rebels*, RKO offset Hepburn's unpopularity with Rogers's charm in a story about women working on Broadway during the Depression, Edna Ferber and George Kaufman's *Stage Door*. Hollywood reporters expected fireworks at the very least. When the star pairing was announced, "The studio found out that all revolutions were not confined to Spain."[31] Some expected one of the actresses to go on suspension rather than work together. But the film was a comic success, with the likes of Ann Miller, Lucille Ball, Eve Arden, and Rogers trading wisecracks in their derelict boarding house. Off camera, Hepburn got along with no one save her on-screen mentor, Constance Collier, who would later become her ego-booster and acting coach in the late 1940s. Future television executive Gail Patrick, like Hepburn one of the few college-educated performers in Hollywood, recalled,

> Kate Hepburn just hated Ginger Rogers. It was pure green envy. Ginge was everything Great Kate wasn't. The crews loved her [Ginger] and hated Kate for the airs she put on. And Ginge at the time was a bigger box office star than Kate. And can I add a better *natural* actress? I mean she had no training but she was so wonderful. . . . With Great Kate every take was the same. She never took direction and she walked around with that haughty air.[32]

While popular Hollywood histories often include stories about women only to indicate their real or invented bitchiness with their fellow actors, Hepburn, on stage and on screen, was not known as an ensemble player. Unlike Bette Davis, she wrote no articles for screen magazines on career, love, and lifestyles, but would occasionally agree to interviews with prominent critics in order to promote her most recent production or to make the odd snide comment about Hollywood. Though raised by one of America's most prominent First Wave feminists, it's hard to gainsay that "Katharine of Arrogance" was out for herself. Interestingly, Ginger Rogers, however much she disliked Hepburn personally, was raised well by her old-fashioned single mother and feminist Lela, who worked as a successful screenwriter and entertainment critic before bringing her daughter west. When Hepburn appeared in an off-Broadway production of *Jane Eyre* in 1937, Rogers sent her a telegram of congratulations (which Hepburn kept all her life).[33] Adulation, evidently, was acceptable.

While Hepburn played queens of literature (*Little Women*) and history (*Mary of Scotland*), early in her career, Rogers more often was assigned anonymous working girls (her famous attempt to play Elizabeth to Hepburn's Mary in Ford's *Mary of Scotland* amused director John Ford but infuriated Hepburn, who wanted a "real" stage actress like Florence Eldridge to play opposite her). Clara Bow, Jean Harlow, Joan Crawford, Bette Davis, Barbara Stanwyck, and Rosalind Russell all played variations of the working-class career woman during the 1930s, but Ginger Rogers played three of these women for RKO in 1939 alone, including dancing and fashion icon Irene Castle (*The Story of Vernon and Irene Castle, Fifth Avenue Girl, Bachelor Mother*). As she recalled in her autobiography, she spent the first ten years of her career fighting for equal pay in her pairings with Astaire (Hepburn, in contrast, was making more than President Roosevelt at $50,000 a picture!). After a three-year hiatus from questions of suffrage and equality, the studio seemed ready to give those anonymous working girls of the 1920s and 1930s the historical treatment in *Kitty Foyle* (subtitled the "natural history of a woman"). Rogers was the ideal female star to market a story of gender and class struggles in America.

While Ernest Vajda's script hadn't caricatured women fighting for equal rights back in 1936, Dalton Trumbo's "prologue" played to the misogynist mob and stereotyped the majority of *Kitty Foyle*'s suffragettes as unattractive spinsters. As he describes them at a rally, "They are very grim. Most of them are old and hatchet-faced. Some of them are fat, others are inordinately skinny. They wear suits, still quite close to the pavement but shorter than in our previous scene. Gone are the flamboyant plumed hats of the past. Now they wear businesslike, hideous ones. Many of them wear spectacles."[34] His heroine is the only attractive woman in the group: though silent (to conform with the 1900 to 1920 cinematic time period), she is a wife and mother who joins the movement after having children and goes back to work—traveling by streetcar.

In contrast to Hepburn's Pam Thistlewaite, working-class Irish Kitty (Rogers), who works, romances married men, and aborts her child-out-of-wedlock in the novel (finessed as a more acceptable stillbirth onscreen), is not a crusader for women's rights. Instead, she climbs her corporate ladder steadily, her eyes on dates, free dinners, and romance. Though in an early draft, Kitty's childhood friend Molly says that she won't get married after high school ("I'm going to finish college and then I'm going to get a job and lead my own life. Men are so bossy, don't you think?"),[35] this subversive comment was cut from Trumbo's subsequent drafts. Another writer, Robert Ardrey, had an even more provocative take on women's work, as when he planned an exchange between Kitty and Molly about the lack of time modern women have for dreaming about the future in the workplace:

> Talk about the pioneer woman of the covered wagon, at least she knew where she was going. Look at the modern woman of the covered typewriter. She does-n't even know what she wants. You know what we are, Molly? We're sharecrop-pers, that's all. We're sharecroppers in the dust bowl of business.[36]

Given that women made up 37% of the unemployed and only got 19% of the work relief jobs during the Depression, it was easy to see why some women viewed the New Deal as a *raw deal* for women.[37] Ardrey's comment was too politically close to the mark for comfort and never made it to the final script either.

But a few years earlier, Rogers was able to acknowledge the impact of the Depression on working women. As her character Jean Maitland remarks in *Stage Door*, for actresses, "There's always a Depression." Three years later, in RKO's final cut, Kitty does indeed seem "weak" in comparison to Hepburn's nineteenth-century crusader and even the gutsy Jean. In her work as a New York cosmetics executive, Kitty is slightly unpleasant in her willing manipulation of women (made more insidious by Christopher Morley and two other men writing the novel and scripts). Male executives reading the galleys were bewildered that a man had written the book, yet Kitty's comments, transcribed by Ardrey, articulate Hollywood's compli-cated reconstruction of "empowered" modern women: "I make my living now by trading on women's herd instincts, and I can see how useful it is for them to think they're exercising their own choices when actually they're simply falling in line with what some smart person has doped out for them."[38] Needless to say this revealing comment was not used in Trumbo's script! Christopher Morley's choice of first-person narration for *Kitty Foyle* created an elaborate confidence trick that Hollywood willingly replicated, manipulating the established market for women's history, film, and liter-ature, while anchoring it firmly to a script written by men who indicated that while women were undoubtedly capable in the workplace, their ulti-mate goal was heterosexual romantic fulfillment.

Though David O. Selznick sponsored many female screenwriters early in his career, and even in 1938, his advice to Sidney Howard and his other *Gone with the Wind* writers was to keep to Margaret Mitchell's narrative as much as possible and to "avoid trying to improve on success,"[39] Dalton Trumbo, Casey Robinson, and Donald Ogden Stewart, and many other prominent male producers and writers were increasingly responsible for rewrit-ing women's stories within these romantic confines. By 1938, Hepburn realized, after several years of rocky stardom, that being RKO's resident feminist and prickly and imperious loner would ruin her career. Either her roles or her personality would have to change. When she returned to screens two years later, competing with Rogers's ethnic working girl at the 1940–41 box office, both her scripts and screenwriters had changed.

Initially, RKO's decision to assign men to write Hepburn's films did nothing to improve her box-office draw. *Stage Door* did well thanks to Rogers's popularity, but even *Bringing Up Baby* (from a story by Hagar Wilde but adapted by Dudley Nichols) and *Holiday* (made while she was on loan to Columbia), now considered classics by film scholars and fans, did mediocre business. After being labeled box-office poison, she bought out her Hollywood contract for $22,740 and returned to New York.[40] Hepburn made no new friends in Hollywood when she contributed to an interview on censorship in motion pictures. Speaking of the issues facing contemporary Hollywood films in September 1939, she stated, "I made a lot of money, but in Hollywood you get $9,000,000 times what you're worth. I was never a great draw. I was overpaid." She continued, "The films are too amiable, and that does not make for excitement. Censorship becomes a terrible cross. Here we have all manner of thrills in our daily life, but it is never used for story material. If you eliminate sex and eliminate politics what have you left?"[41]

Hepburn was fortunate that the New York Theatre Guild was run by fellow Bryn Mawr alumna Theresa Helburn, who was willing to take a chance on Hepburn's lackluster Broadway career. But Hepburn's high-stakes attempt at a Broadway comeback made no great contribution to her image as a feminist: a comedy of remarriage among the rich and famous, it was one of those amiable, fluffy dramas ideally suited to the Hollywood she criticized with such contempt. Playwright Philip Barry's tailor-made play was "indifferent, yet pleasant," according to John Mason Brown in the *New York Post*.[42] As Broadway critics recognized, without Hepburn's star reputation, the play "could hardly support its own weight."[43] It was about a bored, rich Mainline heiress named Tracy Lord who can't make up her mind which man to marry—her wealthy ex-husband (Joseph Cotten, on loan from Orson Welles) or two versions of "the people's choice," a reporter (played by a young Van Heflin) and a nouveau riche businessman-turned-political hopeful (Frank Fenton). But with production design and lighting by renowned color expert Robert Edmund Jones and gowns by Valentina ("designed to give a soft, feminine allure to tall, angular Miss Hepburn"),[44] she was given star treatment.

As she prepared for the role, Hepburn gave every indication of relinquishing her Hollywood career. She remarked to critic Helen Ormsbee of the *New York Herald Tribune* that she preferred the stage to motion pictures: "It's the same as acting in pictures only it's a million times harder," Hepburn explained. "In pictures . . . if there is a speech you haven't done very well, you say, 'Wait a minute. Let me go back and try it again.' Then you shut your eyes, get into the mood, and make a fresh start. But on the stage you can't have a second chance. The play keeps moving along and you must move with it." She continued, "Whether I'm working in pictures or the theater, I act emotionally; but in the theater you must go into every feeling right in front of everybody. Besides, the stage demands more of you in the way of ensemble work. In pictures, acting is broken into small snatches— often scenes for two people or scenes in which you're alone." Although she acknowledged that "picture acting is more egotistical, particularly if you are a star," she denied that she liked an environment where "everything is arranged to pamper your playing." She dismissed Hollywood, reaffirming that her stage work "is the only thing I've done that has given me any feeling of real achievement. At last I've taken a step in the direction I have been wanting to go. A film career is all right, but it is the theater that I have been aiming at for years."

Although while in Hollywood she had displayed little interest in the running of the Screen Actors Guild, she became quite active in a labor strike in the summer of 1939 involving all actors in film, theater, and vaudeville. Helen Hayes, Miriam Hopkins, Jean Muir, Binnie Barnes, Tallulah Bankhead, Sophie Tucker, Olivia de Havilland, and Peggy Wood joined her in Atlantic City for the American Federation of Labor's annual meeting. Tucker had gotten into trouble with the rest of the actors' unions that belonged collectively to the 4A (all overseen by the AFL). Her American Federation of Actors formed an alliance with stagehands (IATSE), breaking the tradition of all-actor unions. Actors in the 4As and SAG were threatening a strike if the AFL didn't outlaw the charter and keep actors separate within their own union. Journalists reporting on the event noted with some surprise "the acute intelligence" with which these glamorous women discussed labor questions. "Today a star . . . must be learned and active in social economic, and labor problems," Mark Barron concluded.[45] Hepburn made one of the speeches at the meeting, and luckily a strike was averted.

Hollywood publicity from the 1930s had usually mentioned her education and wealthy background as a daughter of "a Houghton from Boston," and press coverage of the stage version of *The Philadelphia Story* was no exception. But her political opinions were also a matter of public interest, and in 1940, Hepburn made radio appearances in support of Roosevelt's re-election. As one critic noted, "She is also one of the most intellectual women of her day, interested in serious problems of the war and economics, the sort of person in this respect that Eleanor Roosevelt is, and Dorothy Thompson and Clare Booth." Already the press seemed to anticipate her new role for *Woman of the Year*. Evidently she was also one of the richest women in the public eye: "Miss Hepburn is not only giving her salary and her profits this week as part owner of *The Philadelphia Story* to the Canadian Red Cross but she is sorry anything was said about it." "I wouldn't think of doing anything else," the patrician Hepburn remarked.[46] Unlike Davis and many of her Hollywood peers, Hepburn was not an ERA supporter, believing that poorer women not born with the advantages of the Boston Houghtons could not afford the tough demands of equality with men.

Although during the run of *The Philadelphia Story*, Hepburn may have given the impression she was through with Hollywood, she was no fool. Even before Barry had finished the play, she had bought a 25% stake and was already collecting impressive royalties each week from the gross receipts.[47] Once the play was officially declared a hit by the eastern press, she parlayed her stake into a $175,000 offer from MGM for the film rights, with $75,000 for her to star and to join the MGM "family"[48] in a long-term contact. They shot the film quickly in the summer of 1940. With Cary Grant getting top billing over his former RKO costar and, in the opening silent sequence, having the satisfaction of grabbing her famous face and throwing her to the floor, as one critic pointed out, it was a modern version of *The Taming of the Shrew*.[49] Audiences and critics were pleased with Hepburn as a chastened rich bitch, and it was one of the top-ten hits of 1940.

Her return to Hollywood as a mature thirty-three-year-old star was something new in a business where second chances for over-thirty non-blondes were as scarce as hen's teeth, to use Hedda Hopper's expression. Recruiting her was, to a certain extent, even more financially risky for MGM than hiring union organizer Mary McCall in the writing department. But for the first couple of years, Hepburn was not only more diplomatic with the press, but also provided her own scripts, negotiating with Mayer for *The Philadelphia Story* and then helping to write and sell Ring Lardner Jr. and Michael and Garson Kanin's *Woman of the Year*, a barely concealed biography of top foreign correspondent and radio commentator Dorothy Thompson, for the then-unheard-of amount of $211,000.[50] In 1939, Thompson sold an American pioneer story about Jefferson, Hamilton, and Betsy Brown "in one of the most quickly completed story transactions on record," and Mayer allegedly had been interested in Thompson's life story for several years.[51] So the young writers knew how to maximize demand and save him the costs of having to pay her exorbitant story rights.

Hepburn's friends, mostly in the writing department, were urbane, left-leaning easterners (Donald Odgen Stewart, Garson Kanin, Ruth

Gordon, and Ring Lardner Jr.) contemptuous of Hollywood and soon under investigation by HUAC (in fact, Lardner's name allegedly had to be concealed until the *Woman of the Year* deal was struck because Kate Corbaley's replacement, story editor William Fadiman, had vowed that the SWG troublemaker would never be hired by MGM).[52] It didn't help that Lardner's first wife had publicly roasted Mayer's son-in-law in *I Lost My Girlish Laughter*. Although Hepburn could have pushed for producer's status at this stage, she did not, and used her rare feminine charm on L. B. Mayer. It worked for a while; Mayer really thought the notorious RKO shrew had been tamed by MGM's money. In the postwar climate, both would miscalculate, and it was Hepburn who compromised.

But MGM's *Woman of the Year* was an achievement in women's filmmaking as well as Hepburn's career. Most fans remember it as the film that started the Tracy-Hepburn partnership, a relationship in which she had second billing on screen and off and relinquished control of her independent image in the interest of a safe, on-screen marriage. *Woman of the Year* still has connections to the old Hepburn image. It's certainly a stark contrast to her final film with Spencer Tracy, made well after the end of the studio system, *Guess Who's Coming to Dinner* (1967), in which Tracy is the newspaper editor and journalist and she is just the well-dressed wife. Even in 1957's *Desk Set*, she was the librarian and he the genius. That same year, journalists noted the irony that Dorothy Thompson now "writes a column about cooking."[53] "How are the mighty fallen," to quote Philip Barry!

Back in 1942, things were different in Hollywood and in American journalism. Hepburn worked closely with her team of young writers. Just as in her own life, Tess Harding, like Dorothy Thompson, the second biggest woman in the country, has a close female relative who arguably has done more than she for women's rights. At one point, when her marriage to mediocre sportswriter Sam Craig begins to fail, the two women discuss the conflicts between marriage and career. Her Aunt Ellen (Fay Bainter) asks, "What is it you want so much you're willing to toss your personal life over for it?"[54] Tess responds with surprise, "Why, my work! And, anyway, I didn't toss it over—he did. The only thing I ever insisted on was that my job came first." She continues, "Ellen—if you're going to tell me a women's place is in the home and her highest reward is a pat on the back from her husband, I'm going to be sure one of us has gone crazy." But Ellen is not to be persuaded by absolutes: "Now why should I say anything like that? I've been fighting in the woman's movement all my life. Not that I always understood it fully—just as you apparently still don't." For Ellen reveals that she is lonely and that she has nothing to look forward to in spite of her public achievements.

Surprisingly, though the script indicates the special conflicts that affect women who want love and a career, Kanin and Lardner deny that women have to choose or that they have to stop working after marriage (at the time, both men had equal partnerships with a writer-actress [Gordon] and novelist, though Lardner would divorce Schulman). When Tess tells her estranged husband Sam that she is going to quit her job, he responds, "If you gave up your work, well, you'd stop being you. What you do—what you are—is part of you and I'm in love with it—just the way I am with everything else about you. And now you want to give it all up for—well, for no reasons at all I can see. . . . I can't tell you how glad I am you want to be my wife, but there's no reason to give up your job for it. I want to be your husband—and I'm not giving up my job."[55]

Sadly, this speech was replaced by an ending dictated by George Stevens where Hepburn goes back to her average husband and abases herself in the kitchen. It was another modern version of *The Taming of the Shrew*, and as with *The Philadelphia Story*, Hepburn's talents as a producer were demurely concealed behind the MGM logo. As one critic summarized, "After their marriage, their opposite personalities cause them to clash—with Sam believing a woman's place is in the home and Tess thinking she has a right to continue with her career. It takes several jolts, plus some sly work by her husband, to teach Tess what it means to be a real woman."[56] The role of compliant wife was one she continued to play, with slight variations, through the decade—usually opposite Tracy. Though fewer of her films with Tracy had any input from female writers, the adaptation of Pearl Buck's Chinese resistance story *Dragon Seed* (1944) saw her briefly reteamed with Murfin and Marguerite Roberts, who would later write an adaptation of Conrad Richter's *The Sea of Grass* for her. And of course, actress-screenwriter Ruth Gordon would pen two of the more popular Tracy-Hepburn pairings, *Adam's Rib* (1949) and *Pat and Mike* (1952), which had more explicitly feminist storylines, with Hepburn working as a successful lawyer and Babe Didrikson-esque sports star.

Although she cultivated a good relationship with L. B. Mayer, during her tenure at MGM, Hepburn rubbed Hollywood's prominent presswomen the wrong way. Alice Hughes, recipient of her rudeness when she tried to approach the star "about speaking on behalf of Russian War Relief," only got somewhere when she mentioned Hepburn's recent film (and that she was "a lot more charming" on screen than in person). Hepburn immediately warmed up when her career and that of Spencer Tracy's were under discussion, but as far as Hughes was concerned, Hepburn was top of only one list: "the most un-cooperative star of all time."[57] In April 1947, Hedda Hopper noted that when she dropped by MGM, she found Hepburn with

Frank Whitbeck, the studio's director of publicity and exploitation. "Making no effort to conceal her freckles," Hopper admitted with some vinegar, "she looked perfectly natural. Her costume consisted of a pair of slacks, a white sweatshirt, a sports jacket, and a baseball cap. On her it looked good. But on any of our top ten best-dressed women it would have been horrible."[58]

But it was Hepburn's political looks that really irritated Hopper. After five years at MGM, where she had played a succession of lackluster "wives," "La Hepburn," the columnists noted, had evolved into "quite a leading Democrat in Hollywood." She also seemed to be one of the few female stars unafraid of aging and remaining political. In the summer of 1947, Leonard Lyons reported that she "was offered a stereotype role in a picture, the kind of role she played when she first arrived in Hollywood." Hepburn was said to have replied, "I'm too old, too tired, and too rich." But she was not too tired to argue with Fox actress Gene Tierney (*Leave Her to Heaven*, 1945; *The Ghost and Mrs. Muir*) at a party. Both were daughters of wealthy Connecticut families, but resemblances stopped there. When the younger actress tried to stop the argument by declaring, "I'm a conservative," Hepburn quipped, "A conservative at your age? God help you."[59]

It was Hepburn who would soon be in trouble. She and MGM friend Judy Garland (introduced to each other in 1945 by Hepburn's *Undercurrent* director and Garland's current husband, Vincente Minnelli) spoke at a rally for Progressive Party candidate and New Dealer Henry Wallace in May 1947 at the Gilmore Auditorium. The postwar backlash against the Left was underway, and Wallace's supporters were prevented from hiring the more usual Hollywood Bowl for the event. Although "Republicans in the picture colony" advised Hepburn not to go, fearful she would be labeled a communist, they later admitted, "She did a whale of a job."[60] How could she not, when Dalton Trumbo wrote her keynote?[61] "Silence the artist and you silence the most articulate voice the people have," she told the twenty-seven-thousand-strong crowd in her pink dress ("How could I have been so dumb!" she later laughed at her sartorial faux pas).[62]

Garland was more simple and succinct, and urged the crowd, without help from any speechwriter, "Before every free conscience in America is subpoenaed, please speak up!" But Hepburn was in far more trouble, and with the House Un-American Activities Committee gaining momentum in September, columnists were predicting Hepburn would be one of the stars subpoenaed for her Wallace speeches.[63] A few weeks later, Sam Wood singled her out for attending a meeting where it was alleged $87,000 was raised by Communist Party members. Although he did not say Hepburn was a communist outright, he sneered that she "didn't go to the Boy Scouts" that evening.[64] These weren't the kind of front-page headlines she needed, and Hepburn "declined to comment" on Wood's allegations.[65] Nevertheless, she headed the list of stars scheduled to speak out against the HUAC hearings, among them Ethel Barrymore and civil rights activist Rita Hayworth.[66] Following the October 23 testimony of Gary Cooper, director Leo McCarey, Robert Montgomery, and writer Fred Niblo Jr., who all alleged some degree of communist propaganda at work in the Screen Actors Guild or in film scripts, Hepburn was among a list of star members of the Committee for the First Amendment who signed a letter of protest against the Washington committee's attempt "to smear the motion picture industry."[67] The signatures of younger stars Ava Gardner, Dorothy McGuire, and Marsha Hunt appeared alongside those of more noted liberals Myrna Loy and Paulette Goddard.

Interestingly, although lists of accused writers normally included Dorothy Parker, Niblo included only one woman among his twenty-eight branded names: former Brooklyn reporter-turned-Fox writer Marian Spitzer (*The Dolly Sisters*, 1945; *Look for the Silver Lining*, 1949). She was promptly blacklisted. Spitzer only returned to television in the 1950s, writing for the *Loretta Young Show*. But in the winter of 1947, Hepburn was definitely in the cold at MGM, with Hedda Hopper taking calculated aim: "It wouldn't surprise me if Metro cancels Katharine Hepburn for that fine actress, Margaret Sullavan. Maggie never got the parts she deserved at Metro, and that is the reason she didn't make more pictures."[68] That really was twisting the knife. Sullavan may have lost the roles during the 1930s, but she had snagged Hepburn's former lover, Leland Hayward.

But in April 1948, while journalists noted the ongoing differences between Mayer and stars Hepburn and Garland over their "political affiliations" (memory of the notorious Wallace rally died hard), they argued that these didn't seem to have negatively impacted the stars' careers. Garland had three films on the books, and with Frank Capra's production *State of the Union* (1948), Hepburn "stepped into the best role she has had in years."[69] But Hepburn had to compromise to get this role. Mayer had offered her no films for several months. Press reported that she had agreed to stop her "politicking" when "the studio objected to her Wallace talks."[70] She did not attend the "Women for Wallace" lunch or the National Council of Arts, Sciences, and Professions cocktail parties in New York, and when Wallace made another Los Angeles visit in May, Hopper noted with asperity that only William Wyler, Anne Revere, and "that great patriot, Charles Chaplin" entertained him: "Lucky for Katharine Hepburn that she was out of town."[71] Wallace's campaign was very supportive of women entering politics, and press in 1948 noted there were forty-four women in fifteen different states "who are seeking important legislative posts under the Progressive Party banner."[72] Hepburn's absence was notable. Only Lillian

Hellman continued to speak in support of Wallace and to "discuss issues of the national presidential campaign" in 1948.[73] But by then, Hellman had kissed her lucrative career as one of Samuel Goldwyn's top writers goodbye, preferring to maintain her political independence and anchoring her reputation firmly to Broadway.

But Hepburn's pledge of silence and willingness to compromise her political principles for her job didn't win her long-term favor. She just got to play the wronged wife of a bloated political hopeful (Spencer Tracy) who preferred behind-the-scenes romps with Angela Lansbury's young, ambitious Washington glamour girl. Though her friends Ruth Gordon and Garson Kanin wrote *Adam's Rib* with her and Tracy in mind as sparring married lawyers (the script was heavily influenced by Constance Bennett's turn as a defense lawyer in *Smart Woman*, 1948), the film, shot in the early spring of 1949, would be Hepburn's last at MGM for a few years. In the midst of Judith Coplon's trial for espionage that June, a secret report from an FBI informant dated April 24, 1947, was made public. It named Ruth McKinney, Dorothy Parker, Paul Robeson, Fredric March, Florence Eldridge, and Canada Lee as Communist Party members and fellow travelers. The report coincided with the release of the 1949 report of the California Un-American Activities Committee, which named Congresswoman Helen Gahagan Douglas, Charles Chaplin, Frank Sinatra, Lena Horne, Anita Whitney, John Huston, and Hepburn, among hundreds of others. Interestingly, while actors Gene Kelly and Gregory Peck denied their ties to the Communist Party, Huston dismissed the report as "a vicious campaign of slander," and Sinatra, plainly furious, called it "the product of liars," Hepburn, the only woman asked for comment by the press, "refused to 'dignify' the accusation with a reply."[74] A week later, Louella Parsons reported that Hepburn was leaving for New York to revive her Broadway career. The journalist remarked, with more than a little irony, that Hepburn "no longer finds Hollywood films 'stimulating.'"[75] Hepburn knew how seriously her career had been damaged and that a New York respite might help recover her box-office pull. A few years later, Lena Horne wasn't so lucky. Fed up with the racism and limited parts available, she left Hollywood, though admitting she still had some lingering affection for MGM—as represented by Hepburn. "I love that gal," she admitted to reporters.[76]

By the late 1940s, many of the women who had figured prominently in Hollywood ten years back had disappeared. It became increasingly clear that Garbo had retired for good. Shirley Temple, the top box-office star of the 1930s, had grown up, lost her hold on the public, and despite press rumors, did not resurface as a producer. Another box-office star, writer-actress Mae West, increasingly the target of an all-male cen-sorship board in the 1930s, gave up trying to get her scripts past by the completely male-run Production Code Administration in 1943. Motorcycle-riding rebel Margaret Sullavan went back to Broadway, and after her brief stint as a producer, so did Constance Bennett. Before Hepburn left for New York, she attended Ethel Barrymore's 70th birth-day party, given by her old friend George Cukor. Barrymore was known for her liberalism, but still managed a successful Hollywood career free-lancing, appearing in Dory Schary's *Farmer's Daughter* (1947), Harriet Parsons's *Night Song*, David Selznick's *Portrait of Jennie,* and Darryl Zanuck's ambitious racial melodrama, *Pinky*. As Hepburn and Garland gathered around one of Barrymore's portraits, Hepburn's former costar and Broadway headliner, Billie Burke, joined them. An enterprising photographer snapped an unforgettable portrait of two mature stars at challenging points in their career, paired with older women who had moved to more marginal roles (figure 7.1). But where was the future for women in Hollywood?

By then, prominent women writers who had made their careers in the silent era, including Anita Loos, Frances Marion, and Jeanie Macpherson, had left Hollywood, retired, or died. The next generation of female writers to leave Hollywood left because of the blacklist. Unlike actresses, writers usually lacked the financial resources to tell the studios to go to hell. It was either television or the wall. Poverty with four kids, as Mary C. McCall Jr. found out, was bitter. Once the most famous writer in Hollywood, she couldn't afford to send her daughters to her alma mater, Vassar, thanks to the blacklist. But if you were a well-known actress, even if you were a known Democrat, a woman still had a few options. You could recast your past, like Joan Crawford, and get your anti-communist press connections to make you over in the columns. You could leave Hollywood for Europe (voluntarily, not because you'd been subpoenaed) and follow the "Don't call us, I'll call you" routine favored by Ava Gardner, Paulette Goddard, and Olivia de Havilland. You could work for the United Nations, if you were Myrna Loy. You could keep working, be nice to your colleagues, and brazen it out—but only if you were Bette Davis. Or, if you were Katharine Hepburn, you could kiss Hollywood goodbye twice in one lifetime and live to tell the tale.

Hepburn may have given the impression she alone was in control of her career, but again, it was Theresa Helburn and the Theatre Guild who came to her rescue. Hepburn spent the fall and winter in New York rehearsing Shakespeare's *As You Like It*. The production opened at the Cort Theatre in

Figure 7.1 Katharine Hepburn with Judy Garland and Billie Burke at Ethel Barrymore's 70th birthday party, 1949

late January. Though Hepburn had played a brief scene from *Romeo and Juliet* opposite Douglas Fairbanks Jr. in *Morning Glory*, Rosalind was her first bonafide Shakespearean role. According to the press, "After seven years of velvet bondage in Hollywood, Katharine Hepburn has returned to the stage in Shakespeare's *As You Like It*." Hepburn commented, "Good new plays are hard to find. Hollywood is all right, but working there gets repetitious and monotonous. I wanted to do a stage play. About 10 months ago I took my courage in my hands and told the Theatre Guild I would do *As You Like It*." In another one of life's great ironies, it was Hepburn's legs, well-known since her days from *A Warrior's Husband*, that were the crowning attraction of her boyish Rosalind rather than her diction. "Her gams are as good as her iambics,"[77] one critic quipped. Later that spring, several weeks into her run as Rosalind (which received good but not glowing notices), she gave another interview to Louella Parsons in a major effort to salvage her Hollywood career. Although when Parsons interviewed her, Hepburn claimed she was "loving every minute of her experiences this time on the stage," the star defended Hollywood. "I love living in Hollywood. It's an easier life and when people say there's a big gulf between the stage and the screen, they don't know what they are talking about. There really is not very much difference and there should be less. They should be closer together."[78] What a difference ten years makes to one's opinions.

But shortly after Hepburn's retreat to Broadway, she was approached by John Huston to star opposite Humphrey Bogart in an adaptation of C. S. Forrester's World War I adventure, *The African Queen* (1952). Huston planned to shoot in Africa, something unprecedented even for him, and the two stars agreed, Hepburn enthusiastically and Bogart, who disliked travel, with some misgivings. Both stars and director had been burned by their liberal political commitments over the past few years. All of them had been forced to recant their criticism of HUAC.

Hepburn had more in common with Bogart than with any of her other leading men. Humphrey DeForest Bogart came from a wealthy New York family. His mother had made him a star as a baby—Maud Humphrey was one of the most successful illustrators of the early twentieth century, and her husband, Belmont DeForest Bogart, was a doctor like Hepburn's father (and far less well known to the public than the mother, as well). Both coped with depression in their families—Bogart's sister developed manic depression following an extended labor, and Hepburn still lived with the effects of Tom's suicide and the suicide of her maternal grandfather. Both had a reputation for being acerbic to the press. As one journalist recalled of Bogart, "His quotes to the press were often rude but never dishonest. If he didn't like you he told you . . . if you bored him he was rude."[79]

Hepburn and Bogart mirrored and complimented each other in ways she and Tracy never could, and although "Bogie" and "Katie" had known each other casually for years, in Africa they discovered they were kindred spirits. As Bogart remarked upon his return to Hollywood, "I've more admiration for Katharine Hepburn than any other woman I've met in my life."[80] Although she represented the wealthy, educated, and seemingly prim woman he knew from his youth ("her type has always irritated me"), she relaxed in Africa, becoming the "messiest-looking" missionary opposite his "drunken bum." Their rejection of Hollywood glamour and off-screen contempt for the crass and craven nouveau riche establishment united them.

He even made her the star of his article, "African Adventure," describing her as a "fearless woman" when she took only a 16 mm camera to photograph a large wild boar family in the jungle.[81] She was fifteen feet away from death, and Bogart was "frozen but fascinated" while Hepburn, who "communicated no fear," calmly filmed. "In a desperate situation," the action star admitted, "I'll take Katie before Huston—or myself—any time." It was Bogart who first coined the phrase "A Remarkable Woman" to describe her. With Bogart, Hepburn could play Rose Sayer as an old-style feminist in the mode of Emmeline Pankhurst, Eleanor Roosevelt, and especially her mother, who had died of a heart attack in March before her daughter left for Africa. Unlike Tracy, Bogart wasn't threatened by her strong personality and could toss his urbane toughness aside and show gifts for "Chaplinesque" comedy and broad humor few had guessed at. They were equals on screen and off. Set in the early years of the war when suffrage was still a hotly debated issue for both British and American women, Hepburn had a chance to return to the roots of her RKO stardom and her mother's generation's fire to craft a character equally matched with her costar's. But by 1951, a film in which the male and female protagonists shared danger, action, and dialogue in equal measure could not be made in Hollywood. *The African Queen* was one of a kind even among independent productions: to paraphrase Nancy Cott, it was the ultimate expression of cinematic individualism, which was, unlike Davis's run of top-grossing films for Warner Bros. or McCall and Ann Sothern's *Maisie* franchise, not tied to a wider community of like-minded films and women's audiences.

Moreover, *The African Queen* made a break with Hepburn's cycle of films with Spencer Tracy. *Woman of the Year* publicity shots follow the film's *Taming of the Shrew* narrative trajectory, and often show Hepburn looking up at Tracy or kneeling before him (figure 7.2). Even in *Adam's Rib*, in which the two had played married lawyers ostensibly on an equal educational and financial footing, Tracy had the last word in the picture and top billing. Correspondence from Hepburn's friend and drama coach Constance Collier at the time she was making *The African Queen* indicates the chauvinism that defined the Tracy-Hepburn relationship: "Spencer is in fine form and has a new MGM script from Kanin . . . Mike and something," he had told Collier. The script, by Ruth Gordon and Garson Kanin, actually gave Hepburn top billing for once: it was *Pat and Mike* (1952). Tracy did not want her to go to Africa at all. As Collier noted,

> Spence is terrifically excited about the new picture you and he are to do. He has to hurry back, because he has got to get another picture done, before you start with him, which he expects to be in October. He really is very happy about it and

Figure 7.2 Hepburn looking up at Spencer Tracy, *Woman of the Year*, 1942

said if only they had made up their minds sooner at MGM you would never have had to go to the Belgian Congo and do this picture.[82]

But while Tracy remained unsympathetic toward Huston, Bogart, and Hepburn's project and despondently "longed" for Hepburn's letters, Collier recognized when she saw the rushes in London how wonderful the film would be. While Tracy and Hepburn's photographic publicity—even from the beginnings in 1942—showed her at his feet looking up to him, with Bogart, things were equal (figure 7.3). There was a single standard flying on *The African Queen*, and it was a brave gesture to make in 1951–52, when HUAC and an anti-communist screed like *Red Channels* were still destroying

Figure 7.3 Hepburn and Humphrey Bogart pulling an equal share of the burden, *The African Queen*, 1952

the lives of outspoken men and women, among them Hepburn writer Marguerite Roberts and theatrical colleague Jean Muir. The cast and crew reveled in their freedom from Hollywood: "All her life Katie has been making up her own mind about what she can and cannot touch, and it's a rare thing to argue her out of a decision," one reporter noted.[83] The great irony was of course that Sam Spiegel had to buy the property from Warner Bros. The studio had originally intended it for Bette Davis![84]

Bogart would win an Oscar for his portrayal of Charles Alnutt, the drunken riverboat captain who is persuaded by Rosie to build torpedoes and ram a German patrol boat in British East Africa. Hepburn would be nominated for best actress, but lost to Vivien Leigh, who played one of the classic female victims of modern drama, Blanche Du Bois (*A Streetcar Named Desire*, 1951), a depressing inversion of her most famous southern belle, Scarlett O'Hara. But just as the success of *The African Queen* proved to Huston and his coworkers that filmmakers didn't need the Hollywood studios to produce a successful film for an international market, so the triumph of playing Rosalind and making *The African Queen* on location proved to Hepburn she did not need Hollywood as much as it needed her. Tracy, crippled with ill health from years of drinking, unfortunately did need what was left of

Hollywood's studio support system; he was too erratic an alcoholic to survive the physical and mental demands of the stage. Hepburn returned to the studios only when his demands prevented her from remaining in New York. If she had been too old and rich to bother with playing silly ingénues a few years back, in the 1950s, when Davis was financially suffering for remaining within Hollywood, Hepburn proved she didn't need it.

In 1952, she fulfilled another of life's ambitions by playing the leading role in George Bernard Shaw's *The Millionairess*. She had watched a few years before while Olivia de Havilland failed on stage in *Romeo and Juliet* and in Shaw's *Candida*. She kept de Havilland's bad reviews as reminders of what *not* to do. Broadway critic Brooks Atkinson had been withering: "a lovely lady with good motives who unfortunately lacks experience in acting on the stage."[85] As Collier sniffed, "You can't get away with the arrogance of choosing Shaw and Shakespeare to experiment with for a first venture. If she had only had enough sense to play a small modern comedy . . ."[86] But Collier was just the sort of friend Hepburn needed to fuel her theatrical ambitions. Collier took shots even at Vivien Leigh and husband Laurence Olivier's Shakespearean tour, and of interloper and name thief Audrey Hepburn's performance in *Ondine*, Collier wrote, "I suppose they all fell in love with her (not on account of her acting) and everybody is going to the theatre, but I have not met one person who likes it. As Cecil [Beaton] says, it is a gorgeous bore."[87]

In the mid-1950s, an equally rewarding experience with David Lean in Italy (*Summertime*, 1955) and an Australian tour with the Old Vic and friend Robert "Bobby" Helpmann got her away from Hollywood again. International crowds gathered to cheer the star on. Outside of the Hollywood bubble, something had mellowed her toward the press, and she was polite enough now to accept bouquets from admiring children and to exchange quips with hard-drinking Australian reporters (autographs were still banned, however). As usual, the articles discussed her clothes. When she got off the plane in Brisbane, "Miss Hepburn wore slacks, stout tan shoes, and a gabardine coat, with a careless wisp or two or hair blowing in the soft breeze." Helpmann, reporters noted, "was a complete contrast in a neat and conservative dark suit, and with his hair carefully brushed."[88] A couple months later in Perth, reporters noted, "Exclamations of 'She's just the same as she looks in her pictures,' and 'She doesn't look a bit different off the screen,' could be heard in the crowd." It was the younger generation, perhaps surprisingly, who loved her most. As one reporter noted, "A special greeting came from Katharyn Foote (9), of Como, who leaned over the heads of the crowd from her father's shoulder to present Miss Hepburn with a bunch of Australian wildflowers." As it wasn't an autograph request,

Hepburn took the flowers, "and the crowd clapped and cheered." Katharyn admitted that "she was not a Hepburn fan until quite recently, but she became enthusiastic after listening to her elder sister talk of the actress."[89]

The adulation from younger women continued as she aged. Two years after Tracy's death, she won her record third Oscar for playing Eleanor of Aquitaine in *The Lion in Winter* (1968), a stagey but riveting contest of performances from her and Peter O'Toole (who played the patriarch in the dysfunctional Plantagenet family). She didn't attend any of her four Oscar ceremonies, but in 1969, she had an excuse: she was on stage again playing another "big operator," Coco Chanel, on Broadway. Hepburn kept her fan letters, and one of them, from a young Cindie Lovelace, captures the appeal Hepburn had for her younger fans:

> Mummy raised us in the film tradition of Katharine Hepburn, Spencer Tracy, and Humphrey Bogart. The day the first mention of your forthcoming lead in *Coco* appeared . . . I took my lunch break to go to the Hellinger. . . . Anyway, I took Mummy; we sat in the fifth row—and I doubt either of us has ever been happier. . . . I'm going to law school next year, and hope I'll be as great a woman lawyer as you were in that role![90]

To the younger generation who had not lived through her long conflicts with Hollywood and her female colleagues, Hepburn became an image, an attitude, and an inspiration. For many years, she had symbolized the woman who didn't need Hollywood anymore than she needed glamour or studio-era feminism. When those contexts and frames of reference began to vanish for American audiences in the late 1960s, Hepburn appeared in stark relief as one of America's great individualists.

Perhaps Miss Lovelace did become a lawyer thanks to Hepburn's role as a defence attorney in *Adam's Rib*. But, ironically, with Spencer Tracy's death in 1967 and the slow press leak of her long-time status as his companion, cook, secretary, and cop (in as much as she monitored his alcohol consumption), the star also appealed to droves of women who put their men above their careers and collected the dubious rewards of domestic conformity and professional widowhood. While Bette Davis had consistently embraced her career and the Equal Rights Amendment through the 1970s and early 1980s, Hepburn's off-screen compromises positioned her better with an American public increasingly ambivalent about the status of working women but always susceptible to a self-sacrificing love story. It was no accident in 1970, when the popular women's magazine *McCall's* named her its first "Woman of the Year," it was "as woman, not actress."[91]

EPILOGUE
The Cellophane Wall

In her memoirs published in the mid-1970s, screenwriter Anita Loos recalled that sixty years earlier, director D. W. Griffith hired a certain "A. Loos" to write his silent photoplays, and he kept the writer on the studio payroll even when she turned out to be a teenager in pigtails and a sailor suit. There was no sexism if you did your job, she said flatly: "Note to Women's Lib: I need never have signed my name 'A. Loos.'"[1] Loos loved working in Hollywood, especially the Hollywood of the 1930s and early 1940s that she remembered with such hilarity in *Kiss Hollywood Good-By*. With her pixie cut and rail-thin, off-the-rack figure, love of fashion, gossip, travel, and hard work, Loos defied any stereotypes leveled at Hollywood's working women. However, in her adaptation of Clare Booth Luce's *The Women*, made in Hollywood's "golden year" of 1939 for MGM, Loos was more than happy to slam New York's empty-headed Ladies-Who-Lunch set, whose idea of a hard day's work was three hours at the hairdresser's. Loos had many women friends in the motion picture business, one of whom was Katharine Hepburn. While the retired memoirist kissed Hollywood goodbye in the 1970s with sadness and regret, the still-active Hepburn was happy to see it buried.

But many other studio-era women agreed with Loos that the Hollywood system supported their careers and enabled them to succeed regardless of gender. Between 1924 and 1954, Hollywood was, more than any other American business enterprise, enriched by women: women's pictures, women audiences and fans, and women filmmakers. It was not the classic patriarchy supervising the post-silent-era disempowerment of women so dear to film theorists and historians from the 1970s—because even classic patriarchs such as Sam Goldwyn acknowledged in print that "Women Rule Hollywood."[2] Molly Haskell and other critics have pointed out the strong women stars who dominated screens in the 1930s and 1940s, but women also ruled occasionally, but very prominently, behind the scenes.

Nearly two dozen women worked as producers or associate producers between 1930 and 1954—not the three (Harrison, Van Upp, and sometimes Parsons) mentioned by journalists.[3] There weren't eight women working as film editors in the studio system, but—at my most recent count of numbers between 1937 and 1947—over sixty.[4] And a few of these women determined the way their studios' or production companies' feature outputs looked for decades. Women were a quarter of all Screen Writers Guild members, but today make up only 13% of employed Hollywood writers.[5] During the studio system, women were elected to the executive committees of SAG, the Academy's board of governors, and the Motion Picture Relief Committee. They chaired or ran the War Activities Committee, the Hollywood Canteen, and the Women's Press Club. During the Great Depression and war years, top Hollywood actresses earned more money than President Roosevelt, and off the set, they exerted their political voices in the syndicated press and on the radio. Paramount's Edith Head told American women what to wear, and Anita Colby told them how to do everything else. Kay Brown pushed her reluctant boss to buy *Gone with the Wind*; years later, it is still the most widely read American novel and the biggest domestic box-office hit of the twentieth century. In the 1950s, Brown engineered the return of Hollywood's fallen idol, Ingrid Bergman, outwitting both the American public's fickle moral judgments and Bergman's husband's distain for Hollywood. Story veteran Eve Ettinger had the foresight to put Buddy Adler and Daniel Taradash together, making *From Here to Eternity* the only film to equal *Gone with the Wind*'s Oscar tally at that time. In today's Hollywood, men dominate film franchises, but from 1939 and through the war, Mary C. McCall Jr. gave American women Maisie Ravier, a heroine as durable as Scarlett O'Hara. Ida Koverman managed the studio most associated with women's pictures—MGM—and gave American women their two most swoonable stars: Clark Gable and Robert Taylor. The geniuses of the system were not just men.

Were these women feminists? They believed in equal rights, hated socially constructed gender definitions, loved their work, and recognized that men could sometimes be greater allies in their career struggles than other women. Did their commitment to equal rights mean that they lost awareness of their shared experience as women? Not at all. Hollywood's women were very aware of the importance of their identities as women in the workforce. Virginia Van Upp might have sniffed at Gene Kelly's praise for her ability to write a good man's part in a "female" musical, but the industry was dominated by films catered to women audiences—musicals among them. Van Upp's coworker on *Cover Girl*, Anita Colby, made a successful career as a beauty and technical executive by doing something she stated flatly her male colleagues could not. Even Bobbie McLean laughed that she got her way on decisions on casting and costume design—areas supposedly outside her domain as top feature editor—because she represented the women's point of view at Twentieth Century-Fox. Hollywood's women knew the value of the woman's perspective in the boardroom, the pressroom, in writers' meetings, and in screening rooms. They also knew the value of exploiting their physical appearance to get their way on the set or in a meeting. As Joan Harrison remarked: "Being a girl helps in business."[6]

They helped each other up the ladder when they could—and Hollywood's presswomen did the rest, plugging career and family successes in the columns. Most believed in the tenets of Alice Paul's Equal Rights Amendment, and this sits uncomfortably with some entrenched feminist historians who see Republican, business class, Equal Rights terminology as antithetical to feminism. But most women in late 1930s and 1940s Hollywood united behind ERA principles regardless of political party; they saw each other's shared goals as women, even if they voted for different parties or worked for different studios at different jobs. For many studio-era Hollywood women, bluntly refusing to recognize gender differences or overt misogyny in the Hollywood workplace was a way of staying true to their core beliefs in equality and their essential resilience in a system they loved. This "refusal" did not mean that they weren't appropriately political or "good" feminists.

Though she would joke about "Women's Lib" in a 1971 interview, Bette Davis proclaimed the Equal Rights Amendment "the most important thing in the world." During the 1970s and early 1980s, Davis, together with colleagues Dorothy Arzner, Margaret Booth, and Ruth Gordon, was honored with awards for her Hollywood career—but the accolades were bitter (figure E.1). No Women in Film Crystal award could make up for the diminishing number of women working as writers, editors, producers, and directors in Hollywood—or for the final defeat of the Equal Rights Amendment (figure E.2). During her heyday as Hollywood's top female star, Davis's brand of practical feminism was the ideological glue enabling her to genuinely get along with Republican women such as Hedda Hopper and Helen Hayes. But her comments on the ERA are also a key to explaining why Hopper routinely praised Democrat Ida Lupino in her column,

Figure E.1 Margaret Lindsay (*standing*) reads telegrams of congratulations for Arzner, flanked by McCall, Arzner, and Francine Parker, 1975

Figure E.2 Carmen Zapata, Davis, Booth, and Ruth Gordon at the Women in Film Crystal Awards, 1983

why Frederica Maas sought out Dorothy Hechtlinger for coffee and commiseration, why the MGM script girls knew they could still keep their jobs after marriage and children, why Constance Bennett gave young writer Dorothy Kingsley her first big break on her radio show, why Cohn promoted Parsons, Van Upp, Deutsch, and Manson to producer, why Selznick trusted Kay Brown's judgment on *Gone with the Wind*, and why Zanuck and Thalberg promoted McLean's and Booth's careers beyond any other editor.[7] These women weren't simply dutiful daughters or yes-women. They may have worked for the producers or executives in their studios, but they "called them as they saw them." They were nobody's girl Fridays. Because in Hollywood, these women weren't only good, they were the best at what they did. And because of the Hollywood system, the best women sometimes got the job and kept it.

There are problems with the representation of studio-era women's experience in Second Wave feminist historiography and in feminist film history. At a popular level, mostly top Hollywood stars are recklessly endorsed as "pioneers" and "feminists"—Katharine Hepburn's media myth is perhaps the most potent example. On the other hand, historians have tended to marginalize or dismiss the evolving discourse of feminism and employment gains made by women in Hollywood between 1924 and 1954. Grisham and Grossman's work on Lupino, Judith Mayne's on Arzner, and Emily Carman's on freelance actresses of the 1930s remain exceptions, but are limited by the popular and academic obsessions with director-auteurs and glamorous stars. When we do get broad-based attempts at women's employment in Hollywood, as in Erin Hill's tellingly named *Never Done*, women's work in the studio system is presented as key but underpaid and usually unrecognized drudgery, setting the pattern for women's continued disempowerment in the film industry to this day. It's a depressing narrative without a solution. But things were neither so simple nor gloomy.

McLean, Head, McCall, Davis, Harrison, Hopper, and many other Hollywood women's portraits of the collaborative rather than patriarchal model of the studio system are perhaps the most controversial and difficult concepts of all for film historians and the public to face. Recognizing that the Hollywood studio system helped to foster and sustain women's careers between 1924 and 1954 means a radical rejection of two ideologies that have held sway over American film and cultural history for decades: the "great man" theory of authorship that has dominated film history and criticism since the 1960s, and the wider assumption that things for women in Hollywood have improved—if slowly—over time, due to our vague faith in "progressive" history. Today, women trying to break into the industry are told that although things are difficult and women are certainly not represented equally in the creative professions, the overall situation has improved since the big bad studio days, and they should be grateful for the changes. "Bunk!" as Bette Davis would have said.

In 1970, Davis contrasted the star system of her early career, when "the studios built our careers with care and bought vehicles or created them especially for us," with the situation in contemporary cinema. "The directors are the stars nowadays," she observed. "They have taken over pictures and use them to demonstrate their own virtuosity. I think that's bad for the business." Like Bobbie McLean, she stated flatly, "If you notice what a director is doing, then he's not a good director. . . . For all its abuse, the studio system was pretty damn good for a lot of us."[8]

Mary C. McCall Jr. also defended her business back in 1943, and got heckled by Hepburn's friend Donald Ogden Stewart and the Hollywood Left for her pains. But, considering that women were better represented and empowered in Hollywood at the time than in any European or American political system, there was no question for McCall where her first loyalties lay. She was too moderate to be the kind of writer dear to the Hollywood Left, and she and her colleagues were not the kind of feminists late twentieth-century and early millennial historians have wanted them to be. As she used to say, "When the revolution comes, you can put me up against a cellophane wall and shoot at me from both sides." It's a good one-liner, but shouldn't be an epitaph for the women of the studio era.

Hollywood's women are still in need of a revolution, but it's anyone's guess when it will come.

NOTES

ABBREVIATIONS

ATU	*Albany Times-Union*
AMPAS	Margaret Herrick Library, Academy of Motion Picture Arts and Sciences
AFI	American Film Institute
BDP	Bette Davis Papers
BDE	*Brooklyn Daily Eagle*
CT	*Chicago Tribune*
DOSP	David O. Selznick Papers
DJP	Dorothy Jeakins Papers
EHP	Edith Head Papers
HNC	*Hollywood Citizen-News*
HR	*Hollywood Reporter*
HGC	Howard Gotlieb Archival Research Center
HRC	Harry Ransom Center
KHP	Katharine Hepburn Papers
LAE	*Los Angeles Examiner*
LAT	*Los Angeles Times*
MPD	*Motion Picture Daily*
MPH	*Motion Picture Herald*
NYEP	*New York Evening Post*
NYLPA	New York Library for the Performing Arts
NYP	*New York Post*
PI	*Philadelphia Inquirer*
SAG	Screen Actors Guild
SWG	Screen Writers Guild
WCFTR	Wisconsin Center for Film and Theater Research
WGAW	Writers Guild Foundation Archive, Writers Guild of America West

INTRODUCTION

1. Hubbard Keavy, "Tact, Patience, Ingenuity and Nest Egg Entres to Movie Industry Aspirants," *Utica Observer* (February 12, 1939): 6C.
2. *The 1943 Film Daily Yearbook of Motion Pictures* (New York: Film Daily, 1943), 590.
3. Hedda Hopper, "Looking at Hollywood," *LAT* (August 28, 1946): A2.
4. *Film Daily Yearbook*, 588.
5. Ibid., 593.
6. Eileen Creelman, "Samuel Goldwyn Plans a Picture about the Young People of Soviet Russia," *New York Star* (December 2, 1942): 39.
7. Louella Parsons, "Notes from Filmland: The Famed *Haircut* Can Be Screen Play," *ATU* (May 27, 1935): 18.
8. Carl Rollyson, *Lillian Hellman: Her Life and Legend* (New York: St. Martin's Press, 1988), 78.
9. *Film Daily Yearbook*, 609.
10. Ibid., 589–90.
11. Ibid., 602; "Women at the Helm," *Jamaica Long Island Daily Press: Screen and Radio Weekly* (1937): 13.
12. *Film Daily Yearbook*, 603.
13. Ibid., 608.
14. Ibid., 597.
15. Ibid., 600.
16. Ibid., 629–31.
17. "Women at the Helm," 13.
18. Ettinger's postwar cocktail parties were a staple of Hollywood's rich and powerful. See Louella Parsons, "In Hollywood," *ATU* (July 8, 1949): D8; Parsons, "Hollywood," *ATU* (November 9, 1949): 10; "Louella Parsons Says," *ATU* (April 7, 1951): 12; Parsons, "*On the Beach* Cast Loaded," *ATU* (September 24, 1958): 21. Ferguson became a full-time publicist in 1933 after she retired from filmmaking. See Parsons, "Louella Parsons Says," *ATU* (July 25, 1951): 6.
19. "Screen Actor's Guild Reorganized," *LAE* (October 4, 1933): 1. For the purposes of this book, the current guild syntax, Screen Writers Guild and Screen Actors Guild, are used in place of contemporaneous variants, i.e. the Screen Writers' Guild and Screen Actor's Guild (unless directly quoted).
20. SAG minutes, October 4, 1933, Screen Actors Guild archives, Los Angeles, CA.
21. *HR* (October 9, 1933).
22. *Film Daily Yearbook*, 673.
23. Ibid., 648.
24. Bob Thomas, "Film Capital Is Girls' Land of Opportunity in Variety of Callings," *Binghamton (NY) Press* (January 10, 1948): 12.
25. "The Hollywood Writers Report and TV Staffing Brief," March 2016, 59 pp., p. 12, WGAW.
26. The WGAW Women's Committee, "Employment Statistics for Male and Female Writers, Television and Feature Films," May 1984, 19 pp., WGAW; "Women's Job Statistics Oct. '73–Sept. '74," Newsletter, Writers Guild of America, West (December 1974): 1, WGAW.
27. *Film Daily Yearbook*, 675.
28. Ibid., 651.
29. Ibid., 656–57.
30. Ibid., 653.
31. Ibid., 643.

32. Society of Motion Picture Film Editors and Motion Picture Editors Guild records, Motion Picture Editors Guild archives, Los Angeles. My thanks to Lisa Dosch for this material.

33. Mary Steward quoted in Edward Landler, "Post-production Pioneers: The Guild's Earliest Members," *Editors Guild Magazine* 1, no. 5 (September–October 2012).

34. Hubbard Keavy, "Hollywood Screen Life," *Poughkeepsie Daily Eagle* (June 19, 1934): 6.

35. David Robb, "Female Cinematographers a Rarity in Hollywood," *Deadline Hollywood* (September 23, 2015), deadline.com; Read Kendall, "Around and About in Hollywood," *LAT* (June 17, 1938): 17; Patricia Clary, "Movie Notables Show Various Talents," *Rochester (NY) Democrat and Chronicle* (November 23, 1949): 9.

36. "In Hollywood . . . Women Win Executive Jobs," *Saratoga Springs Saratogian* (September 29, 1943): 1.

37. Elsa Maxwell, "Elsa Maxwell's Party Line: The Man I Love," *NYP* (July 10, 1944): 8; "Ann Dvorak Says American Women Should Be Drafted," *Syracuse Herald-Journal* (October 14, 1943): 16.

38. "Film Writers Honor Miss Davis and Hope," *ATU* (December 15, 1941): 8.

39. "Hollywood Yearbook," *American Weekly* (September 25, 1955): 8–9.

40. Marcia Winn, "City of Magic, Fantasy and Filth: It's Hollywood," *Chicago Sunday Tribune* (July 2, 1943): 1; Winn, "Hollywood Vice Swallows 300 Girls a Month," *Chicago Daily Tribune* (July 26, 1943): 9; Winn, "Blackmail King in Hollywood: Anything Goes," *Chicago Daily Tribune* (July 27, 1943): 7.

41. "Mary C. McCall Challenges the Chicago *Tribune*'s Charges of Corruption," *Motion Picture–Hollywood* (November 1943): 34–36, 84–85, 88.

42. J. E. Smyth, "A Woman at the Center of Hollywood's Wars: Mary C. McCall Jr.," *Cineaste* 41, no. 3 (Summer 2016): 18–23.

43. Compare Bob Thomas, "Film Capitol Is Girls' Land of Opportunity in Variety of Callings," *Binghamton (NY) Press* (January 10, 1948): 12, to Bosley Crowther, *The Lion's Share* (New York: E.P. Dutton, 1957); Andrew Sarris, *The American Cinema: Directors and Directions, 1929–68* (New York: Da Capo, 1968); David Bordwell, Kristin Thompson, and Janet Staiger, *The Classical Hollywood Cinema* (New York: Columbia University Press, 1985).

44. Keavy, "Hollywood Screen Life," 6.

45. Lois W. Banner, *Women in Modern America: A Brief History* (New York: Harcourt Brace Jovanovich, 1974), 256.

46. Keavy, "Tact, Patience, Ingenuity," 6C.

47. Some of the more famous stuntwomen in the 1930s were Helen Thurston, who doubled for Hepburn; Aline Goodwin, Hazel Hash, and Lila Finn, who all doubled for Vivien Leigh's Scarlett; ace fencer Betty Danko; and Polly Burston. See Florabel Muir, "They Risk Their Necks for You," *Saturday Evening Post* (September 15, 1945): 27–35, which lists Thurston, Frances Miles, Danko, Nellie Walker, Jeanne Criswell, Evelyn Smith, Mary Wiggins, Aline Goodwin, Ione Reed, Vivian Valdez, Loretta Rush, and Opa Ernie.

48. Associated Press, "Women Find Opportunities in Hollywood," *Elmira Star Gazette* (January 29, 1948): 23.

49. "Communists in Hollywood Raise $87,000," *Schenectady Gazette* (October 21, 1947): 3.

50. Herman A. Lowe, "Congress Shies at Passing Legislation to Aid Women," *Philadelphia Inquirer* (June 23, 1950): 27.

51. "Artists Seek Soviet Amity," *New York PM* (November 14, 1945): 16.

52. *Washington Star*, "She Put Nixon on the Map," *Olean Times Herald* (July 14, 1980): 28. See Sally Denton, *The Pink Lady: The Many Lives of Helen Gahagan Douglas* (London: Bloomsbury, 2012).

53. Danny Reitz, "What Kind of Freedom Does He Like?," *Olean Times Herald* (July 9, 1979): 28.

54. Terry Ramsaye, *A Million and One Nights* (New York: Simon & Schuster, 1926); Benjamin Hampton, *History of the American Film Industry from Its Beginnings to 1931* (1931; New York: Dover, 1970); Lewis Jacobs, *The Rise of American Film* (New York: Harcourt, Brace, 1939); Leo Rosten, *Hollywood: The Movie Colony, The Movie Makers* (New York: Harcourt, Brace, 1941); Arthur Knight, *The Liveliest Art* (1957; New York: Macmillan, 1978).

55. Rosten, *Hollywood*, 362.

56. Crowther, *Lion's Share*, 271.

57. Note that the first edition's dust jacket blurb on Crowther's *Lion's Share* begins with the Screen Directors Guild's decision to award its first Critics Award to Crowther.

58. MGM Directory, August 1934, Leslie Bohem Collection, USC Cinematic Arts Library, Los Angeles, CA. My thanks to Ned Comstock for locating this document.

59. Laura Mulvey, "Visual Pleasure and Narrative Cinema," *Screen* 16, no. 3 (1975): 6–18. See Judith Mayne, *Directed by Dorothy Arzner* (Bloomington: Indian University Press, 1995) and Therese Grisham and Julie Grossman, *Ida Lupino: Her Art and Resilience in Times of Transition* (New Brunswick, NJ: Rutgers University Press, 2017).

60. Cari Beauchamp, *Without Lying Down: Frances Marion and the Powerful Women of Early Hollywood* (Berkeley: University of California Press, 1998); Eileen Whitfield, *Pickford: The Woman Who Made Hollywood* (Lexington: University of Kentucky Press, 2007); Marina Dahlquist, *Exporting Perilous Pauline* (Urbana: University of Illinois Press, 2013); Hilary A. Hallett, *Go West, Young Women!* (Berkeley: University of California Press, 2012); Jane Gaines et al., *Women Film Pioneers Project*, https://wfpp.cdrs.columbia.edu.

61. Karen Ward Mahar, *Women Filmmakers in Early Hollywood* (Baltimore: Johns Hopkins University Press, 2006); Mark Garrett Cooper, *Universal Women: Filmmaking and Institutional Change in Early Hollywood* (Urbana: University of Illinois Press, 2010).

62. Hallett, *Go West, Young Women!*, 99; Gaines et al., *Women Film Pioneers Project*.

63. Dee Brown, *The Gentle Tamers: Women of the Old Wild West* (Lincoln: University of Nebraska Press, 1958); Glenda Riley, "Frederick Jackson Turner Overlooked the Ladies," *Journal of the Early Republic* 13, no. 2 (1993): 216–30; Riley, *The Female Frontier* (Lawrence: University of Kansas Press, 1988); Riley, *The Life and Legacy of Annie Oakley* (Norman: University of Oklahoma Press, 1994).

64. Andrew Sarris, *The American Cinema: Directors and Directions, 1929–1968* (New York: Da Capo, 1968); Cheryl Robson and G. Kelly, eds., *The Celluloid Ceiling: Women Film Directors Breaking Through* (London: Supernova Books, 2014).

65. William Chafe argues the late 1930s were the "nadir" of the women's movement, in *The American Woman* (Oxford: Oxford University Press, 1982), 132.

66. Susan Ware, *Holding Their Own: American Women in the 1930s* (Boston: Twayne, 1983), 88.

67. Stephanie Coontz, *The Way We Never Were* (New York: Basic Books, 2000), 158–59.

68. Ware, *Holding Their Own*, 88.

69. Nancy Cott, *The Grounding of Modern Feminism* (New Haven: Yale University Press, 1987), 4, 231–32; Genevieve Parkhurst, "Is Feminism Dead?," *Harper's Magazine* 170 (May 1935): 735–45.

70. Ware, *Holding Their Own*, 49–50.

71. Jane Allen, *I Lost My Girlish Laughter* (London: Faber & Faber, 1938), 8.

72. Robin Coons, "Hollywood Sights and Sounds," *Niagara Falls Gazette* (May 11, 1944): 19.

73. Rollyson, *Lillian Hellman*, 78.

74. Lillian Hellman, Bloomgarden Theater, 1951, Playwright Lecture Series Recordings, NYLPA.

75. Lizzie Francke, *Script Girls* (1994; London: BFI, 2000), 42–43.

76. Cott, *Grounding of Modern Feminism*, 276.

77. "Business, Professional Women, Tired of 'Protection,' Vote in Convention for Their 'Rights,'" *Courtland Standard* (July 24, 1937): 1.

78. Ware, *Holding Their Own*, 110.

79. The only adequate coverage of her writing career is by critic Marsha McCreadie, *The Women Who Write the Movies* (New York: Citadel Press, 1996).

80. Jay Jorgensen, *Edith Head* (New York: Running Press, 2010); Samantha Barbas, *The First Lady of Hollywood: A Biography of Louella Parsons* (Berkeley: University of California Press, 2005); Jennifer Frost, *Hedda Hopper's Hollywood: Celebrity Gossip and American Conservatism* (New York: New York University Press, 2011).

CHAPTER 1

1. Mel Gussow, "In a Brutally Frank Interview, Bette Davis Says, 'I'm Amazed I'm Not Dead—after the Life I've Endured,'" unmarked press clipping, March 1977, Scrapbook 88, BDP, HGC.

2. Whitey Stine and Bette Davis, *Mother Goddam: The Story of the Career of Bette Davis* (New York: Hawthorn Books, 1974), 6–7; Charles Higham, *Bette* (New York: Macmillan, 1981), 42. One of the earliest and most detailed versions is in an unmarked press clipping, Adela Rogers St. Johns, "The Hollywood Story," *American Weekly, ATU* (1951): 7, 7132.pdf, fultonhistory.com.

3. "Bette Davis Credits Many for Helping Her to Top," *Jezebel* press book, 1938, 4, box 5, BDP, HGC.

4. Jim Tully, "Bette Davis," *This Week in Lowell*, May 8, 1936, box 1, folder, BDP, HGC.

5. Martha Martin, "Queen Bette: Voted '40's Top Movie Actress, She Hopes to Do Better," *Sun News* (February 4, 1940): 6.

6. Ida Zeitlin, "Bette Take a Bow," typescript (1938), box 1, folder 2, BDP, HGC.

7. Ruth Rankin, "The Golden Goose Reaches Thirty," *Photoplay* (August 1938): 10–11, 84.

8. Zeitlin, "Bette Take a Bow."

9. Hedda Hopper, "My Own Super-superlative Academy Awards," *Photoplay* (March 1941): 24–25, Scrapbook 44, BDP, HGC.

10. Unmarked press clipping, *Movie Radio Guide* (1941), Scrapbook 34, BDP, HGC. See also "We Like You," *HCN* (December 24, 1941): 12.

11. Bette Davis with Bill Davidson, "All About Me," *Collier's* (November 25, 1955): 100, box 2, folder 7, BDP, HGC.

12. "Bette Davis Has Narrow Escape from Ingenue Role," *Bordertown* press book (1935), p. 8, NYPLA.

13. Zeitlin, "Bette Take a Bow."

14. Grace Grandville, "The Almost Perfect Face," *Long Island Daily Press, Screen and Radio Weekly* (1936): 6.

15. David, Chierichetti, *Edith Head* (New York: HarperCollins, 2003), 86.
16. George Hurrell to Mark Vieira, June 27, 1988, *Hurrell's Hollywood Portraits* (New York: Harry N. Abrams, 1997), 176.
17. Virginia Vale, "Stardust Movie & Radio," *Harlem Valley Times* (March 26, 1936): 11.
18. Bette Davis with Bill Davidson, "All About Me," *Collier's* (December 9, 1955): 37, box 2, folder 7, BDP, HGC.
19. Martin, "Queen Bette," 6; *Look* Magazine Secret Poll of 30 Correspondents; Exhibitors' Polls, 9/10 of 1940 moneymakers, 8/10 of 1941 moneymakers, Scrapbook 34, BDP, HGC.
20. Jack Smalley, "One Year with Oscar," *Photoplay*, 55–56, 96–97.
21. Bette Davis, "Where Did You Get That Hat?," *Screen Guilds' Magazine*, vol. III, 2 (April 1936): 14.
22. "Bette Davis Has Narrow Escape from Ingenue Role," *Bordertown* press book (1935), p. 8, NYLPA.
23. "Bette Davis Tells Girls How to Win Career in Films," *Boston Sunday Advertiser* (April 5, 1936), box 2, folder 7, BDP, HGC.
24. Zeitlin, "Bette Take a Bow."
25. Helen Hayes to Bette Davis, September 2, 1937, box 1, folder 1, BDP, HGC.
26. "Strike Threat Facing Giant Film Industry," *Amsterdam Democrat and Recorder* (May 1, 1937): 1; "Craftsmen of Studios Ready For Conflict," *Buffalo Courier-Express* (May 11, 1937): 3; "Movie Studios Fear Violence in Strike," *BDE* (May 1, 1939): 2; Howard Heffernen, "Screen Actors Make Guild Film Force," *Rochester (NY) Democrat and Chronicle* (June 11, 1937): 29.
27. Chuck Cochard, "Hollywood Star-Lites," *Rogersville Review* (November 21, 1935): 7.
28. Bette Davis with Bill Davidson, "All About Me," *Collier's* (November 25, 1955): 28, box 2, folder 7, BDP, HGC.
29. See Emily Carman, *Independent Stardom: Freelance Women in the Hollywood Studio System* (Austin: University of Texas Press, 2016), 48–52, 69–78.
30. Stine and Davis, *Mother Goddam*, 76, 77–82.
31. Bette Davis to Jack Warner, June 21, 1936, in Rudy Behlmer, ed., *Inside Warner Bros., 1935–51* (New York, Viking, 1985), 27–28.
32. Lloyd Pantages, "I Cover Hollywood," *ATU* (August 22, 1936): 6.
33. Bette Davis with Bill Davidson, "All About Me," *Collier's* (November 25, 1955): 100, box 2, folder 7, BDP, HGC.
34. Ibid.
35. Kirtley Baskette, "*Gone with the Wind* Indeed!," *Photoplay* (March 1937): 21–23, 102.
36. Smalley, "One Year with Oscar," 96.
37. Bette Davis, "The Actress Plays Her Part," in Nancy Naumburg, ed., *We Make the Movies*, 117–30 (New York: W. W. Norton, 1937).
38. Ibid., 117.
39. Ibid., 120, 122, 121.
40. *Life Magazine* (January 23, 1939), box 2, folder 7, BDP, HGC; Sonia Lee, "Beloved Hussy," *Radio Guide* (March 2, 1940), Scrapbook 33, BDP, HGC.
41. Paul Muni, "The Actor Plays His Part," in Naumburg, ed., *We Make the Movies*, 131–42, 142.
42. *Life Magazine* (January 23, 1939).
43. Bette Davis to Mr. Ferris, June 21, 1937, box 1, folder 1, BDP, HGC; Thomas Schatz, " 'A Triumph of Bitchery': Warner Bros., Bette Davis, and *Jezebel*," in

Janet Staiger, ed., *The Studio System*, 74–92 (New Brunswick: Rutgers University Press, 1994).

44. Sonia Lee, "Beloved Hussy," *Radio Guide* (March 2, 1940), Scrapbook 33, BDP, HGC.

45. "Rooney, Davis, Voted Film King, Queen," *Los Angeles Daily News* (January 22, 1940). Readers of the *Daily News* and fifty-four other papers elected Davis queen of Hollywood: Rooney polled 38,290 from fans, and Davis got 68,723.

46. Lee, "Beloved Hussy."

47. Louella Parsons, "News From Film City," *ATU* (August 25, 1943): 6.

48. Mike Mann, "Radio Chatter," *Knickerbocker News* (September 13, 1944).

49. Harold Heffernan, "In Hollywood," *Long Island Star Journal* (March 27, 1946): 8.

50. Bob Thomas, "Olivia Leads Quiet Life in Gay Paree," *Long Island Star-Journal* (August 1, 1961): 8.

51. UP, "Round About Hollywood: Olivia de Havilland Keeps Her Private Life Her Very Own," *BDE* (October 20, 1939): 22.

52. "Bette Davis Does Not See Husband During Filming," *Bordertown* press book (1935): 6, NYPLA.

53. Nancy Seely, "Famous Custody Battles: Ann Harding," *NYP Daily Magazine* (September 11, 1964): 43. See also "Miss Harding to Take Daughter East," *HCN* (November 30, 1937): 3.

54. Seely, "Famous Custody Battles."

55. Robert McIlwaine, "Bette Davis's Fight for Happiness," *Picture Play* (January 1940): 29, Scrapbook 33, BDP, HGC.

56. Sonia Lee, "Leigh-Donat Win," *Movie-Radio Guide*, March 16, 1940, says that Bette "named" the Oscars.

57. "Mrs. Roosevelt Speaks Out," *Poughkeepsie Daily Eagle* (July 7, 1933): 6.

58. Hart Seymore, "Carole Lombard Tells 'How I Live by a Man's Code,'" *Photoplay* (June 1937): 12–13, 78.

59. Marian Young, "Best Personality in a City Full of It Is Bette Davis," unmarked clipping, Scrapbook 34, BDP, HGC.

60. "Dionne Quints, "'Too Many' for Her, Bette Davis Says," *Syracuse Herald-American* (November 5, 1939): sec. 2, p. 8.

61. Eleanor Roosevelt to Miss Bette Davis, Luncheon Invitation, January 13, 1940, Scrapbook 33, BDP, HGC.

62. "*Watch on the Rhine* Opening at the Buffalo," *BCE* (October 8, 1943): 10.

63. Hedda Hopper, "The Nicest Women in Hollywood—and Why!" *Photoplay* (June 1941): 26–27, 108.

64. Rosalind Rosenberg, *Divided Lives: American Women in the Twentieth Century* (New York: Hill & Wang, 2008), 110.

65. Unmarked press clipping, 1941, Scrapbook 34, BDP, HGC. There is only one paragraph (128) in *Mother Goddam* on her election and resignation—four sentences in total! See also mention in *BCE* ("John Golden as Producer of Hits," November 16, 1941): sec. 6, p. 5.

66. "Bette Davis Elected New Academy Head," *HCN* (7 November 1941): 1; "Bette Davis First Woman to Head Coast Academy," *MPD* (November 10, 1941): 9.

67. "Bette Davis Head of Film Academy," *MPH* (November 15, 1941): 54.

68. Unmarked clipping, "Punched," Scrapbook 34, BDP, HGC.

69. Louella Parsons, "Bette Davis Quits Academy in Row Over Dropping Awards," *ATU* (December 29, 1941): 7.

70. James Francis Crow, "British Fighting Men Granted Leave to Do Roles in Pictures," *HCN* (December 24, 1941): 6.

71. "Editors Named on Film Awards," *HCN* (December 22, 1941): 12.

72. "Bette Davis Quits as Academy Prexy," *Film Daily* (December 29, 1941): 1; "Bette Davis Resigns Post as Academy President," *HCN* (December 26, 1941): 1.

73. William R. Weaver, "The Hollywood Scene," *MPH* (January 3, 1942): 41.

74. Hedda Hopper, "My Own Super-superlative Awards for 1941," *Photoplay* (March 1942): 42–43.

75. "Hollywood's War Effort," *Hollywood* (January 1943): 22–23.

76. Elizabeth Wilson, "The Hollywood Canteen," *Liberty Magazine* (January 23, 1943): 26–27.

77. Davis's *Photoplay* column ran from January to June 1943, but she continued to give more interviews and contribute stand-alone articles to other journals. For more on Davis's war bond tours, see Kathryn Cramer Brownell, *Showbiz Politics* (Chapel Hill: University of North Carolina Press, 2014): 65–71.

78. James Hilton, "Salute to the Hollywood Canteen," *Photoplay* (November 1943): 38–39, 84.

79. Red Kann, "On the March," *MPH* (November 6, 1943): 16.

80. Hedda Hopper, "My Own Super-Duper-Dilly Academy Awards," *Photoplay* (April 1943): 28–29.

81. Louella Parsons, "Stars at War!" *PI* (1943).

82. Jerry Asher, "Hedy Lamarr's Lowdown on Love," *Screenland* (May 1944): 20–21.

83. Sgt. John Whitehead, "Hollywood Canteen," *Los Angeles Radio Life*, December 13, 1942, Scrapbook 45, BDP, HGC.

84. See for example, Cal York, "Inside Stuff," *Photoplay* (January 1943): 8–9, where Bogart is seen washing dishes in one photo.

85. Adela Rogers St. Johns, "Hollywood Has Changed!" *Photoplay* (March 1943): 36–37, 86–87.

86. "Agents, Unions Go to Bat for H'Wood Canteen," *Film Daily* (January 5, 1944): 1, 3.

87. Unmarked press clipping, "Canteen Heads Have Row Over Mixed Dancing," Scrapbook 45, BDP, HGC. See also "Bette Davis Overrules Objection to Mixed Couples Dancing," *Pittsburgh Courier* (January 16, 1943): 21.

88. Sherrie Tucker, *Dance Floor Democracy: The Social Geography of Memory at the Hollywood Canteen* (Chapel Hill: Duke University Press 2014): 118.

89. "Guest Stars and Dramatic Shows," *New York Sun* (December 10, 1938): 22; John Chapman, "Hollywood," *BCE* (October 9, 1940): 7; James Francis Crow, "RKO-Radio to Star Michele Morgan in South Seas Film," *HCN* (December 16, 1941): 8; Sidney Skolsky, "This is Bette Davis—Funnily Enough," *NYEP* (1942).

90. *Hollywood Advertiser* (April 20, 1944), Scrapbook 45, BDP, HGC.

91. Bob Thomas, "Sights and Sounds From Hollywood," *Leader-Republican, Gloversville and Johnstown, NY* (August 22, 1945): 6.

92. Delight Evans, "The Editor's Page: An Open Letter to Bette Davis," *Screenland* (February 1944): 19.

93. Bob Thomas, "Tears Follow Turkey as Hollywood Canteen Locks Up For All Time," *Binghamton (NY) Press* (November 23, 1945): 89. It's amazing how little coverage biographers give Davis's work for the Canteen (Stine and Davis, *Mother Goddam*, 168–69 only).

94. Bette Davis, "Speech Material for War Workers," 3 pp., typescript, box 1, folder 2, BDP, HCN.

95. Bette Davis, "Bond Pitch for Defense Plant Seventh War Bond Drive," box 1, folder 2, BDP, HGC.

96. Davis's speech was delivered September 21, 1944, at a rally for Roosevelt where Henry Wallace and Orson Welles also spoke. Fredric March introduced her ("As Wallace Urged a Rebirth of Liberalism," *New York PM*, September 22, 1944: 12–13).

97. Bette Davis, "Roosevelt Re-Election Speech," September 1944, typescript, 3 pp., BDP, HGC.

98. Associated Press, "Film Celebrities Arrive in Capital for Parties," *BCE* (January 30, 1940): 8.

99. "Tenney Warns of Red Drive; Lists Many Hollywood Names," *HR* (March 25, 1947): 1, 10.

100. Jack Moffitt to Congressman Norris Poulson, April 11, 1947, p. 6, RG 233, National Archives, Washington, DC.

101. "Wall Street Rules Hollywood Production, Graham Charges," *Daily Variety* (July 7, 1947): 4.

102. R. P. Hood to Director, FBI, October 25, 1947, FBI Files, AMPAS.

103. Louella Parsons, "Hollywood," *ATU* (June 24, 1947): 8.

104. See Robert Presnell, Jr. "Censorship is Menacing Our Movies," *Glamour* (November 1948): 122–23, where he does all the pontificating, and Hunt merely leans on his arm in a photograph.

105. Louella Parsons, "In Hollywood With Louella Parsons," *ATU* (October 2, 1946): 12. See also Emily Leider, *Myrna Loy: The Only Good Girl in Hollywood* (Berkeley: University of California Press, 2012).

106. Marshall Stimson to Myrna Loy, March 15, 1948, box 8, folder 2, Myrna Loy Papers, HGC.

107. Richard Coe, "Myrna Loy Talks of UNESCO Role," *UNESCO News* (1950) vol. 3, no. 8, reprinted from the *Washington Post* (December 23, 1949), box 8, folder 2, Myrna Loy Papers, HGC.

108. Ibid.

109. See *Eleventh Report of the Senate Fact-Finding Subcommittee on Un-American Activities* (Sacramento: California State Legislature, 1961), 200.

110. Bette Davis with Bill Davidson, "All About Me," *Colliers* (December 9, 1955): 40, box 2, folder 7, BDP, HGC.

111. Jimmie Fidler, "Bette Has a Good Deal," *Nassau Daily Review-Star* (August 3, 1948): 11.

112. Hedda Hopper, "Miss Bergman Is Enthusiastic over Nun Role," *BCE* (November 29, 1944): 6.

113. Danton Walker, "Broadway Roundup," *PI* (July 22, 1944): 10.

114. Hedda Hopper, "Films of Past Based on Real Entertainment," *BCE* (November 20, 1949): 15.

115. Louella Parsons, "Hollywood," *ATU* (March 27, 1950): 4.

116. "Mrs. Roosevelt Tops Popularity Poll Here," *ATU* (December 17, 1946): 9; "Eleanor Roosevelt Tops World's 12 Smartest Women," *Binghamton (NY) Press* (December 30, 1949): 1.

117. Stine and Davis, *Mother Goddam*, 199.

118. Bette Davis, Handwritten Speech to the Democrats of Maine [1955], box 1, folder 2, BDP, HGC.

119. Bette Davis with Bill Davidson, "All About Me," *Colliers* (December 9, 1955): 46, box 2, folder 7, BDP, HGC.

120. Bette Davis, *This 'n That* (New York: Pan, 1987), 13.

121. Ibid., 60, 65.

122. Ibid., 63–64. According to Davis, her song, written by Joe Sherman with lyrics by George Weiss, "was written to answer" Richard Burton's recording "A Married Man" (Hugh Downs with Bette Davis, NBC Today Show, NBC Universal Media, February 22, 1965).

123. Davis, *This 'n That*, 66.

124. Pamela Fourzon, "Bette Davis: A Woman, a Feminist, a Humanist," *World Tribune* (6 April 1977): 7, Scrapbook 88, BDP, HGC.

125. Nancy Collins, "Bette Davis: 'You Can't Have It All,'" October 15–22, 1976, syndicated column, Scrapbook 88, BDP, HGC.

CHAPTER 2

1. Josephine Lowman, "Calls Mental Organization Women's Need," *BCE* (May 25, 1947): 11C.

2. Anthony Slide, *The Hollywood Novel: A Critical Guide to Over 1200 Works with Film-Related Themes or Characters* (Jefferson, NC: McFarland, 1994).

3. Most critics highly praised Allen's novel without identifying the author: "All Answers Are Contained in Jane Allen's *I Lost My Girlish Laughter*," *North Tonowanda Evening News* (May 14, 1938): 1; Don O'Malley, "New York Inside Out," *Auburn Citizen Advertiser* (May 4, 1938): 4. Leonard Lyons revealed Schulman's identity in his column, "The Lyons Den," *NYP* (March 26, 1938): 1.

4. Though Anthony Slide lists Jane Shore, a "professional writer" as coauthor with Schulman, none of the columns containing Schulman's name mentions Shore.

5. Jane Allen, *I Lost My Girlish Laughter* (London: Faber & Faber, 1938), 102–3, 37.

6. Ibid., 8.

7. Ibid., 13.

8. Ibid., 9.

9. Ibid., 37.

10. Ibid., 98.

11. Ibid., 110–11.

12. Jimmy Fidler, "In Hollywood," *Nassau Daily Review-Star* (January 13, 1940): 9; E. V. Durling, "On the Side," *ATU* (January 27, 1943): 6.

13. Walter Winchell, "On Broadway," *Binghamton (NY) Press* (January 24, 1937): 18; J. R., "New Books Passed in Review," *BDE* (May 27, 1938): 12.

14. "Author Is Dramatization Guest," *Daily Argus* (January 27, 1939).

15. As late as 1943, columnists complained that Hollywood hadn't filmed Allen's book. E. V. Durling, "On the Side," *ATU* (January 27, 1943): 6.

16. "Women at the Helm," *Long Island Daily Press: Screen & Radio Weekly* (1937): 13.

17. Eileen Creelman, "Katharine Brown, Selznick Story Head, Talks of *Intermezzo*; a Love Story," *New York Sun* (October 4, 1939): 30.

18. "Kay Brown, Obituary," *Independent* (January 31, 1995).

19. "The Camera Reports," *MPH* (May 21, 1932): 79.

20. "Kay Brown Joins Selznick," *MPH* (October 26, 1935): 93; Katharine Brown, contract, November 20, 1935, 7pp, Katharine Brown, Consolidated Legal Files, 1935-37, box 851, folder 18, DOSP, HRC.

21. "Kay Brown on Way Here," *MPD* (February 7, 1936): 11; "Kay Brown Gets Aide," *Film Daily* (January 7, 1938): 2.

22. "Selznick Years Set March 21," *Saratoga Springs Saratogian* (March 14, 1969): 6; "Amendment of Agreement of November 20, 1935," August 16, 1937, 4pp,

Katharine Brown, Consolidated Legal Files, 1935–37, box 851, folder 18, DOSP, HRC. By 1939, she was making $500 a week.

23. Helen Taylor, *Scarlett's Women* (New York: Virago, 1989); and J. E. Smyth, "Organization Women and Belle Rebels: Hollywood's Working Women in the 1930s," in *Hollywood and the Great Depression*, Iwan Morgan, ed., 66–85 (Edinburgh: Edinburgh University Press, 2016).

24. Rudy Behlmer, ed., *Memo from David O. Selznick* (New York: Viking, 1972).

25. See ibid., 137.

26. Creelman, "Katharine Brown," 30.

27. Leonard Lyons, "The Lyons Den," *NYP* (January 18, 1938): sec. 2, p. 1.

28. Whitney Bolton, "Monday Morning Gossip of the Nation," *Philadelphia Inquirer* (June 1, 1953): 19.

29. Ingrid Bergman and Alan Burgess, *Ingrid Bergman: My Story* (London: Michael Joseph, 1980), 80. While Selznick takes full credit for signing Bergman (Behlmer, *Memo from David O. Selznick*, 96), contemporaneous reportage states Brown discovered her.

30. Eileen Creelman, "Viveca Lindfors, Young Star from Sweden, Arrives under Contract to Warners," *New York Sun* (April 12, 1946): 21.

31. Bergman and Burgess, *Ingrid Bergman*, 236, 310.

32. Tony Stevens, "I Refuse to Grow Old," *Modern Screen* (November 1960): 44, 46, 63, 67.

33. "Kay Brown, Ex-Selznick, Has Two Other Offers," *Variety* (July 22, 1942): 6. See Memos, Kay Brown to Val Lewton, 27 January 1942, and Brown to Lewton, 5 March 1942, Kay Brown Story Files, box 159, folders 1 and 2, DOSP, HRC. The Amelia Earhart story, co-written by Jane Murfin, was later produced at RKO as *Flight for Freedom* (1943).

34. "Kay Brown Joins Goldwyn in East," *MPD* (July 14, 1943): 12; "Coast Flashes," *MPD* (August 3, 1943): 9; "Kay Brown Resigns as Goldwyn's Story Editor," *Film Daily* (July 27, 1944): 1.

35. Elsa Maxwell, "Elsa Maxwell's Party Line: Women in Films," *NYEP* (September 7, 1944): 12.

36. "Kay Brown Resigns as Goldwyn's Story Editor," *Film Daily* (July 27, 1944): 3.

37. "Miss Hechtlinger Leaves," *Variety* (July 14, 1943): 27.

38. Frederica Maas, *The Shocking Miss Pilgrim: A Writer in Early Hollywood* (Lexington: University Press of Kentucky, 2002), 237.

39. Dorothy Hechtlinger, Obituary, May 30, 1979, *Variety Obituaries*, June 6, 1979, vol. 8 (1975–79).

40. "Women at the Helm," *Rochester (NY) Democrat and Chronicle: Screen and Radio Weekly* (1937): 13.

41. Rudy Behlmer, ed., *Memo from Darryl F. Zanuck* (New York: Grove Press, 1995).

42. Jim Earie, "Information Please," *Action* 8, no. 11 (December 1947): 6–7. Richardson's department routinely employed other women, including the library's Ruth Fox, Gertrude Kingston, Ruth Swarzchild, Katherine Lambert, and Helen Webb.

43. Mary Duncan Carter, "Film Research Libraries," *Library Journal* (May 15, 1939): 404–7; Frances Richardson, "Previous to Previews," *Wilson Bulletin for Librarians* 12, no. 9 (May 1939): 589–92.

44. Julien Johnson, "Story Department," *Action* 9, no. 6 (August 1948): 3–5. But unlike at Columbia, RKO, and MGM, Fox's head of story was a man, Julien Johnson.

45. Molly Mandaville, Report and Comparison of book and script, October 22, 1955. 53 pp., *The Man in the Gray Flannel Suit*, production material, USC.

46. Molly Mandaville, Obituary, August 23, 1970, *Variety Obituaries*, September 2, 1970, vol. 7 (1969–74).

47. U.S. Congress HUAC Hearings, 1951–52, vol. 2 (US Government Printing Office, 1951–52), Statement of Eve Ettinger, 2076–89. See also E. G., "Four New Films Today," *New York Herald Tribune* (April 27, 1945): 14B; "Of Local Origin," *New York Times* (April 26, 1945): 26.

48. For a comprehensive list of Berkeley's named names, see "Names Listed by Writers in Probe on Film Reds," *LAT* (September 20, 1951): 8.

49. United Press, "38 Movie Writers Called Commies," *Long Island City Star-Journal* (April 2, 1952): 5.

50. See Associated Press, "Told of Having Red Ties," *New York Times* (April 2, 1952): 8; United Press, "38 Movie Writers Are Linked to Reds," *New York Herald Tribune* (April 2, 1952): 14; United Press, "38 of 900 Writers for Single Studio Linked to Reds," *Washington Post* (April 2, 1952): 8.

51. See Herbert Mitgang, "Transmuting a Touchy, Topical Tome," *New York Times* (June 14, 1953): X5.

52. "Three Quit CBS Story Dept . . .," *The Billboard* (September 5, 1953): 6; Edwin Schallert, "Charlton Heston Eager for Capt. Cook Break; Cooper Forms Company," *LAT* (September 22, 1954): B7.

53. HUAC (1951–52), Tunberg's testimony, 1834–56, 1840.

54. Nancy Lynn Schwartz, *The Hollywood Writers' Wars* (New York: iUniverse, 2000): 287.

55. "Plan Anti-fascist Rally to Greet Rankin, Smith," *California Eagle* (February 21, 1946): 4.

56. Thomas J. Foley, "Hollywood Writer Admits Red Role, Names 24 Others," *Rochester (NY) Democrat and Chronicle* (April 13, 1951): 12.

57. HUAC (1951–52), 1701.

58. Ibid., 1667.

59. Ibid., 1670.

60. Ironically, Roberts would return to the screen at Hal Wallis's behest in the late 1960s, to write *True Grit* (1969). John Wayne thought it was "the best script he had ever read." It was one of the most popular Westerns of all time, and won the anti-communist star his first and only Oscar.

61. Roby Heard, "Garbo—the Eternal Stranger," *Long Island Star-Journal* (August 9, 1954): 8.

62. Henry W. Clune, "Seen and Heard: The King," *Rochester (NY) Democrat and Chronicle* (April 28, 1963): 2M.

63. Hedda Hopper, *The Whole Truth and Nothing But* (Garden City, NY: Doubleday, 1962), 264.

64. Sidney Skolsky, "Taylor Modest—Best Draw," *Rochester (NY) Democrat and Chronicle* (September 16, 1936): 2.

65. Gordon Kahn, "The Real Robert Taylor," *PI* (December 13, 1936): 8.

66. Hopper, *Whole Truth*, caption 7.

67. Louella Parsons, "Child Star Is Found for *National Velvet*," *PI* (November 4, 1937): 18.

68. Jimmy Fidler, "In Hollywood," *Freeport Daily Review* (April 11, 1938): 9.

69. "The Lady Herself," *MGM Studio Club News* (November 14, 1938): 1, 3, 10.

70. "Death Claims Ida Koverman," *Los Angeles Herald* (November 25, 1954).

71. Hopper, *Whole Truth*, 265.

72. Arthur Hachten, "Mayer Family Entertained by Hoovers," *Syracuse Journal* (March 13, 1929): 14.
73. Patricia Dillon, "In Hollywood: Not Much Hope for John Gilbert," *Brooklyn Standard Union* (July 5, 1930): 7.
74. Elsa Maxwell, "Weekend Round-Up," *NYP* (September 11, 1943).
75. Hopper, *Whole Truth*, 269.
76. Clarence Sinclair Bull (1930), *Ida Koverman*, Charlotte Greenwood Collection, University of Southern California Cinematic Arts Library, Los Angeles, CA.
77. *Jamaica (NY) Long Island Daily Press* (1941).
78. Hopper, *Whole Truth*, 120.
79. Ibid., 124–25.
80. James Padgitt, "Judy May Call in the Press," *ATU* (June 22, 1950): 8.
81. "Women Execs in Hollywood," *BCE*, 1940, 4; Irene Thirer, "Ann Harding's Farewell to Hollywood Pictures," *NYP* (April 17, 1936): 17. Neuberger would later work for Brown at SIP before taking over as Vanguard's Eastern Story Editor in 1946.
82. "Death Claims Mrs. Corbaley, Screen Editor," *LAE* (September 24, 1938). Sam Marx eventually replaced her after her death in 1938.
83. Pete Martin, "I Call on Clark Gable," *Saturday Evening Post* (October 5, 1957): 24–25, 64, 66, 68.
84. Hubbard Keavy, "Hollywood Screen Life," *Poughkeepsie Daily Eagle* (June 19, 1934): 6; Louella Parsons, "Connie Planning Honeymoon in Venice," *ATU* (June 23, 1933): 26.
85. *LAE*, February 28, 1933.
86. Louella Parsons, "*Hamlet*: Critics' Views Sought by Producer," *Syracuse Journal* (June 24, 1935): 9.
87. Hedda Hopper, "Baking of GOP Laid to Plot of Democrats," *BCE* (July 1, 1944): 4.
88. Elsa Maxwell, "The Party Line," *NYP* (July 23, 1945): 12.
89. "*Gentleman's Agreement* and *Crossfire* among the Films Given Unity Awards for 1947," *New York Age* (February 28, 1948): 7.
90. "Hollywood Forms New GOP Group," *PI* (October 19, 1947): 6A.
91. Hedda Hopper, "Taylor Given Commie Role in New Picture," *BCE* (September 30, 1948): 14.
92. Hedda Hopper, "*Ice Follies* Feature to Be Put on Screen," *BCE* (September 14, 1950): 27.
93. Hedda Hopper, "Hedda Hopper's Hollywood: Upstate New York Tabbed for Film of *Devil's Disciple*," *BCE* (July 5, 1952): 5.
94. Hopper, *Whole Truth*, 278; *Variety Weekly*, Obituaries (December 1, 1954).
95. Bob Thomas, "Hollywood Happenings," *Amsterdam Evening Recorder* (January 18, 1955): 6.
96. Sidney Skolsky, "Hollywood Tintype: Her Face Is Her Fortune," *NYP Magazine* (March 23, 1943): 1.
97. Anita Colby, "Is It True What They Say about Kelly?" *American Weekly* (December 26, 1954): 7.
98. Lucille Ball, "Memories of a Side Street," *Parade Magazine* (March 22, 1959): 4. When "Lucy" bought RKO and transformed it into the Desilu lot, she turned Lela's former stage into a training school for future television hopefuls.
99. Lela Rogers, "Why Not Be Somebody?" *Photoplay* (May 1939): 17, 82–83.
100. "Triple Careerist," *HCN* (February 24, 1943): 5.
101. Walter Winchell, "The Man on Broadway," *Syracuse Herald-Journal* (March 29, 1943): 13.

102. "Anita Colby on Tour as *Cover Girl* Advance Man," *Showman's Trade Review* (January 29, 1944): 15.

103. Anita Colby, "Advice from a Cover Girl: All Women Can Star, but It Takes Will Power," *PI* (May 5, 1952): D25.

104. "Glamour Expert," *PI* (June 25, 1944): 14.

105. Harold Heffernan, "In Hollywood," *Long Island Star-Journal* (January 28, 1946): 12.

106. Margaret McManus, "TV Latest of Anita Colby's Many Careers," *Amsterdam Daily Democrat and Recorder* (July 13, 1961): sec. 2, p. 13. Ginsberg, like Cohn, wasn't fazed by promoting women to positions of executive power or working with female producers. After leaving Paramount in the mid-1950s, he would coproduce *Giant* (1956) with writer Edna Ferber.

107. Robbin Coons, "Hollywood Sights and Sounds," *Niagara Falls Gazette* (July 21, 1943): 6.

108. Hedda Hopper, "Ida Lupino Will Play in Early Autumn," *BCE* (April 9, 1947): 16. In this same column she mentions that Evelyn Koleman is Roy Rogers's publicist.

109. Inez Gerhard, "Star Dust," *Brookfield Courier* (April 1, 1948).

110. Louella Parsons, "Hollywood," *ATU* (May 13, 1947): 9.

111. "Elsa Maxwell's Week-End Round-Up," *NYP* (September 29, 1945).

112. Betty Clarke, "A Glamor Guide for Career Girls: Anita Colby Provides Some Advice," *Corning Evening Leader* (May 5, 1948): 7.

113. Ibid.

114. Hedda Hopper, "In Hollywood," *Elmira Star-Gazette* (October 6, 1948): 12.

115. McManus, "TV Latest," sec. 2, p. 13.

116. Anita Colby, "I Love Being a Bachelor Girl!" *American Weekly* (March 16, 1952): 15.

117. Colby, "Advice from a Cover Girl," D25.

118. Ibid.

CHAPTER 3

1. Louella Parsons, "Dorothy McGuire to Do 'Anna' Role," *ATU* (December 14, 1944): 20.

2. Maxine Davis, "Women Opponents of Equal Rights Amendment Called Amazons by Those Opposed," *Rochester (NY) Democrat and Chronicle* (February 5, 1929).

3. "Business, Professional Women, Tired of 'Protection,' Vote in Convention for Their 'Rights,'" *Courtland Standard* (July 24, 1937): 1.

4. Ibid.

5. Mary Padgett, "National Woman's Party Convenes Here Friday," *PI* (October 18, 1942): 6.

6. Associated Press, "Women Fight Equality Amendment," *Utica Observer* (August 19, 1943).

7. "Equal Rights Planks," *BCE* (July 28, 1944): 12.

8. "Salary for Men, Women Equalized," *HCN* (November 26, 1942).

9. Alice Hughes, "Woman's New York," *BCE* (January 20, 1944): 12.

10. Lois W. Banner, *Women in Modern America: A Brief History* (New York: Harcourt Brace Jovanovich, 1974), 256.

11. Women Total Quarter of GE Staff," *HCN* (November 16, 1942): 12; "Mama Won't Go Back Home after War, Parley Told," *HCN* (November 20, 1942): 1.

12. GNS, "Women's Party Fights for 'Equal Rights,'" *Saratoga Springs Saratogian* (April 18, 1944): 7.

13. James Marlow, "Women's Equal Rights Measure Appears Snagged," *Courtland Standard* (September 8, 1944): 5.
14. "Westchester Republican Women Adopt Equal Rights Measure," *Herald Statesman* (April 30, 1945): 11.
15. "Equal Rights Amendment," *Binghamton (NY) Press* (July 20, 1946): 6.
16. Adelaide Kerr, "New Group to Renew Fight for Women's Rights Bill," *Evening Leader* (September 11, 1946): 3.
17. "More Ambiguous Than Before," *Rome Daily Sentinel* (January 26, 1950): 6; "Equal Rights Amendment," *Binghamton (NY) Press* (February 7, 1950): 6.
18. "Little Theaters Valued as Film Training School," *NYP* (March 24, 1936): 7; Erskine Johnson, "In Hollywood," *Gloversville and Johnstown Morning Herald* (October 11, 1943): 2; George Phair, "Retakes," *Variety* (July 25, 1944): 2; Sidney Skolsky, "Hollywood Tintype: The Girl from Missouri," *Post Weekly Picture Magazine* (April 21, 1945).
19. John Truesdell, "In Hollywood," *Long Island Daily Press* (October 23, 1943): 19.
20. Victor Gunson, "Ginger Rogers, Who Always Believed, Most Successfully, in Taking a Chance, Takes Another, Producing Her Own Films," *Gloversville and Johnstown (NY) Leader-Republican* (August 17, 1945): 5.
21. Mary Morris, "Bette Davis," *New York PM* (March 1945): 13; Harold Heffernan, "Bette, as Producer, Decides Not to Waste Film," *Jamaica (NY) Long Island Daily Press* (March 8, 1945): 23.
22. Elsa Maxwell, "Elsa Maxwell's Party Line," *NYP* (September 21, 1945): 12.
23. "Old Film Custom, Teams in Movies, Gets a New Twist," *Brooklyn Eagle* (March 30, 1947): 30.
24. Irene Thirer, "*Paris Underground* Stars Producer Constance Bennett," *NYEP* (October 20, 1945): 15; Earl Wilson, "It Happened Last Night: Ratoff the Mohammedan Comes to Mount Parker," *NYP* (November 30, 1944).
25. Associated Press, "Constance Bennett Dies; Film Beauty of the 30s," *Albany Knickerbocker News* (July 26, 1965): 6A.
26. Thirer, "*Paris Underground* Stars," 15. See also Jane Corby's positive review, "Constance Bennett and Gracie Fields in *Paris Underground* at the Gotham," *Brooklyn Eagle* (October 20, 1945): 12.
27. Harold Heffernan, "In Hollywood," *Long Island City Star Journal* (October 6, 1945): 16.
28. Hedda Hopper, "Looking at Hollywood," *BCE* (September 6, 1943): 35.
29. Louella Parsons, "Kay Francis Going to Monogram Soon," *ATU* (July 14, 1944).
30. Paul Harrison, "They're Not Stars—They're Corporations," *Gloversville Morning Herald* (1936).
31. Mae Tinee, "Mae Finds Gold and Glory in Hollywood," *BCE* (December 10, 1933): 10.
32. Irene Thirer, "Mary Pickford Talks of Plans to Produce and Act Next Season," *NYP* (July 27, 1935): 11.
33. Harrison Carroll, "Mary Pickford Tells of Plan to Produce Film," *ATU* (July 2, 1933): D7.
34. Associated Press, "Miss Pickford Battles Jinx in New Film Firm," *Binghamton Press* (July 8, 1935): 14.
35. Thirer, "Mary Pickford Talks," 11.
36. "Laemmle Ends Movie Career 30 Years Long and Mary Pickford Begins Her Second as Producer," *Binghamton (NY) Press* (May 5, 1936): 16.
37. Louella Parsons, "Mary Pickford Offered $150,000 to Play Lead," *ATU* (July 9, 1937): 10.

38. Jimmy Fidler, "In Hollywood," *Jamaica (NY) Long Island Daily Press* (January 1941).
39. Louella Parsons, "Comedy Role Goes to Claudette Colbert," *PI* (July 27, 1943): 13.
40. Hedda Hopper, "Movie Studio Buys Writer's First Novel," *BCE* (May 11, 1945): 10.
41. Associated Press, "Mary Pickford Upheld in Suit over Contract," *Albany Evening Journal* (November 30, 1950): 4A.
42. "Mrs. La Cava Seeks $850 a Month for Son," *Los Angeles Evening News* (April 28, 1938), RG 233, HUAC Exhibits, Evidence, etc. Hollywood Blacklist, boxes 1–9, box 3, National Archives, Washington, DC.
43. *HCN* (April 26, 1938), RG 233, HUAC Exhibits, Evidence, etc. Hollywood Blacklist, boxes 1–9, box 3, National Archives, Washington, DC.
44. Bob Thomas, "Mary Pickford Planning to Sponsor Protégé," *Geneva Daily Times* (April 28, 1947): 3.
45. Louella Parsons, "Hollywood," *ATU* (January 19, 1948): 4.
46. Louella Parsons, "Hollywood," *ATU* (March 11, 1948): 23. That year, Claudette Colbert formed a new production company with Jack Skirball and Bruce Manning (they produced Ginger Rogers's 1946 *Magnificent Doll* when she was in the middle of her producer phase).
47. Louella Parsons, "Hollywood," *ATU* (October 18, 1949): 6.
48. Hedda Hopper, "Movieland's Sam Spade Readies New Cop Film," *BCE* (May 27, 1953): 11.
49. "Ida Lupino—Director," *BCE* (February 11, 1951): 7.
50. H. H. Duffy, "Young Entrepreneur," *Greenfield Recorder-Gazette* (1958): 12.
51. Hedda Hopper, "Hedda Selects Film Stars to Rise in 1950," *BCE* (January 1, 1950): 7C; Hopper, "Sally Forrest Cast for Role in *The Door*," *BCE* (May 12, 1951): 6.
52. Hedda Hopper, "Ida Lupino, Awaiting Sir Stork, Writes Film Story," *BCE* (January 30, 1952): 6.
53. See Ida Lupino, "New Faces in New Places," *Films in Review* (December 1, 1950): 17–19; Lupino, "Me, Mother Directress," *Action* 2, no. 3 (May–June 1967): 14–15.
54. Bob Thomas, "Ida Lupino Returns to Acting," *Greenfield Recorder* (October 15, 1970): 17.
55. Tim Snelson's *Phantom Ladies: Hollywood Horror on the Home Front* (New Brunswick, NJ: Rutgers University Press, 2014) is the only significant treatment of aspects of Harrison's career, but argues, rather bizarrely, that she had only a wartime career.
56. Joan Harrison and Philip McDonald, treatment *Rebecca* (June 3, 1939), 45pp, Barbara Keon, Script Development, *Rebecca*, 1936–46, box 492, folder 8, DOSP, HRC; Harrison contract, June 14, 1941, 7pp., box 896, folder 4, Consolidated Legal Files, Joan Harrison, 1939–44, DOSP, HRC. Harrison began working for Selznick for 20 weeks at $125 a week (Daily Report, to DOS, July 12, 1939), Barbara Keon, Script Development, *Rebecca*, 1936–46, box 492, folder 8, DOSP, HRC.
57. Hedda Hopper, "Looking at Hollywood," *BCE* (May 15, 1943): 21.
58. "Woman Boss," *NYEP* (April 16, 1943).
59. "In Hollywood," *Saratoga Springs Saratogian* (July 3, 1944): 1.
60. Alice Hughes, "Woman's New York," *Courier-Express* (March 15, 1946): 14.
61. Bob Thomas, "Producer Joan Harrison Knows How to Say 'No,'" *Knickerbocker News* (June 1, 1946): A3.

62. Erskine Johnson, "In Hollywood," *Gloversville (NY) Morning Herald*, (November 2, 1943): 2.
63. Gay Pauley, "Career Girl Must Retain Sex Appeal," *BCE* (August 3, 1957): 11.
64. John T. McManus, "Good up to the Last Drop," *PM* (August 24, 1945): 16.
65. Eileen Creelman, "The New Movie," *New York Sun* (November 22, 1944): 10; Creelman, "The New Movie," *New York Sun* (November 11, 1946): 16. The film nonetheless made over $500,000 at the box office (Richard Jewell and Vernon Harbin, *The RKO Story* (New York: Arlington House, 1982), 216).
66. Hedda Hopper, "Looking at Hollywood," *Jamestown Post-Journal* (January 9, 1945): 6; Eileen Creelman, "The New Movie," *New York Sun* (November 22, 1944): 10.
67. Harold A. Nichols, "Joan Harrison Says Good Jobs Awaiting Women in Hollywood," *Rochester (NY) Democrat and Chronicle* (January 15, 1961): 6F.
68. Ibid.
69. Bob Thomas, "Hitch's Joan Harrison Is Boon to Man's World," *Herald Statesman, Yonkers* (May 18, 1963): 7.
70. Ibid.
71. Nichols, "Joan Harrison."
72. Ed Misurell, "Murder Is Her Business: A Schoolgirl's Interest in Crime Formed the Basis of a Successful Career in Video for Joan Harrison," *ATU* (November 24, 1956): P-3.
73. Ibid.
74. Lloyd Shearer, "Gail Patrick: Happiest Woman in Three Worlds," *BCE* (April 26, 1959): 4.
75. Ibid.
76. Hubbard Keavy, "Tact, Patience, Ingenuity and Nest Egg Entres to Movie Industry Aspirants," *Utica Observer* (February 12, 1939): 6C.
77. Louella Parsons, "Songbird Will Play Opposite Rudy Vallee," *Syracuse Journal* (December 27, 1937) 10.
78. Whitney Bolton, "How a Working Set Is Created," *PI* (1938): 7.
79. "Writers Kept Busy by Studio," *Rochester (NY) Times-Union* (December 8, 1938).
80. Keavy, "Tact, Patience, Ingenuity," 6C.
81. Louella Parsons, "Deanna Durbin's Contract Brings Offer of $25,000," *Philadelphia Inquirer* (December 30, 1937): 8.
82. "Theaters Schedule New Films," *Rochester (NY) Times-Union* (February 24, 1941): 12.
83. Louella Parsons, "Chatter of Hollywood Stars," *ATU* (April 5, 1941): 15.
84. Jane Corby, "The Sound Track: Technicolor Makes Script Writing Easier, Says *Cover Girl* Author," *BDE* (March 26, 1944): 28.
85. Bob Thomas, *King Cohn* (1967; Beverly Hills: New Millennium Press, 2000), 234.
86. "Columbia Film Co. Signs Guild's Theresa Helburn," *BDE* (November 2, 1934): 24.
87. Lloyd Pantages, "I Cover Hollywood," *ATU* (July 31, 1934): 10.
88. Wilella Waldorf, "Theresa Helburn Back from Coast," *NYP* (September 3, 1935): 17.
89. Wilella Waldorf, "Theresa Helburn to Produce *Gentleman in High Boots* Soon," *NYEP* (September 12, 1935): 11.
90. James Francis Crow, "Ida Lupino Assigned to Destiny Drama of Women in Wartime," *HCN* (February 12, 1943): 4.

91. Dorothy Manners, "Hollywood," *PI* (August 15, 1946): 21. See also "Helen Deutsch Signs as Columbia Producer," *NYEP* (August 20, 1946).
92. "Screen Notes," *BDE* (August 20, 1946): 10.
93. Dorothy Manners, "Hollywood," *PI* (June 27, 1944): 15.
94. Louella Parsons, "Louella Parsons Column," *ATU* (September 19, 1944): 6.
95. "You Can Learn about Films from Her," *BDE* (December 17, 1944): 26.
96. Louella Parsons, "Dorothy McGuire to Do 'Anna' Role," *ATU* (December 14, 1944): 20.
97. Ibid.
98. "She's a Jill of All Trades," *BDE* (February 10, 1946): 26.
99. W. E. J. Martin, "British Rap US Movies," *BCE* (October 28, 1945): 4D.
100. Thomas (1967), 233.
101. "She's a Jill of All Trades," 26.
102. Irene Thirer, "Screen News and Views," *NYEP* (March 12, 1946): 28.
103. Louella Parsons, "Hollywood," *PI* (March 1, 1947): 13.
104. Louella Parsons, "Hollywood," *ATU* (September 6, 1947): 4. See also Hedda Hopper, "Looking at Hollywood," *Jamestown Post Journal* (March 26, 1947): 20.
105. Louella Parsons, "Hollywood," *ATU* (November 13, 1947): 20.
106. Louella Parsons, "Hollywood," *ATU* (January 8, 1948): 12; Parsons, "Hollywood," *ATU* (November 1, 1948): 22; Hedda Hopper, "Right Cross Top Role Goes to Montalban," *BCE* (March 10, 1949): 21.
107. Josephine Lowman, "Calls Mental Organization Women's Need," *BCE* (May 26, 1947): 11C.
108. Ibid.
109. United Press, "Rita Insists She'll Go Through with Divorce Plans," *NYP* (July 8, 1951).
110. Louella Parsons, "Sam Goldwyn Plans Trip to Samoa," *PI* (May 1, 1951): 27.
111. "Louella Parsons Says," *ATU* (October 25, 1951): 21.
112. "Germany Story to Be Filmed," *Rochester (NY) Democrat and Chronicle* (October 1, 1953): 35; Louella Parsons, "Gloria Swanson Arranges Nose Operation Here," *PI* (October 25, 1952): 12.
113. Dorothy Manners, "Hollywood: Red Skelton Teams with Ann Sothern," *PI* (November 24, 1953): 31.
114. "Germany Story to Be Filmed," 35.
115. "Hollywood Has Lots of Jobs for Women, Aside from Acting," *BDE* (November 12, 1953): 11.
116. Louella Parsons, "In Hollywood: Stack Signs Pact with Century-Fox," *ATU* (July 9, 1954): 6.
117. Louella Parsons, "Gregory Peck Sought for *Papa Married a Mormon*," *ATU* (November 2, 1955).
118. Hedda Hopper, "Looking at Hollywood," *Jamestown Post-Journal* (July 31, 1946): 14.
119. Louella Parsons, "Hollywood: News of West Coast Studios" (November 30, 1945), box 7, scrapbook, Dorothy Kilgallen Papers, NYLPA.
120. "Nellie Bly," *New York Woman* (October 7, 1936), box 7, scrapbook, Dorothy Kilgallen Papers.
121. *HR* (August 15, 1946). Kilgallen's 1940s breakfast radio show with husband Dick Kolmar was a huge success, and she of course would go on to become one of the best-known television personalities.
122. Harriet Parsons, "European Tour for Jeanette McDonald," *ATU* (July 1, 1931): 11; Harriet Parsons, "Fox Seeking 3 Players for Jungle Film," *ATU* (September 13,

1932): 13; Harriet Parsons, "MGM Buys *Three Comrades*, Erich Maria Remarque Novel: Studio Executives List Julie Haydon for Woman's Role," *ATU* (August 22, 1936): 6.

123. Harriet Parsons, "David Gets Leading Role in *Hollywood Hotel*, Based on Louella Parsons' Radio Program," *ATU* (July 5, 1937): 10.

124. Irene Thirer, "Screen News and Views: Femme Film Bosses? Studio Personnel Cooperates 100%," *NYEP* (May 12, 1945): 7.

125. "Harriet Parsons' Debut Picture," *Syracuse Herald-Journal* (August 12, 1942): 22.

126. Murfin worked as a writer and associate producer until 1935, when she made a well-publicized move to Goldwyn's Studios as simply a writer. She later returned to producing in the late 1940s. "Jane Murfin, Writer, Joins Goldwyn Staff," *BDE* (May 25, 1935): 5.

127. Louella Parsons, "Teresa Wright Gets *Enchanted Cottage*," *PI* (August 30, 1943): 20; Amy Croughton, "Scanning the Screen," *Rochester (NY) Times-Union* (September 2, 1943): 19.

128. Hedda Hopper, "Looking at Hollywood," *CT* (February 21, 1944).

129. Hopper, *Whole Truth*, 75.

130. Louella Parsons, "In Hollywood," *ATU Pictorial Review* (March 25, 1945): 7.

131. Thirer, "Screen News and Views: Femme Film Bosses?," 7.

132. Margaret Mara, "Producer of *Enchanted Cottage* Admires Femininity in Women," *Brooklyn Eagle* (May 8, 1945): 15.

133. Eileen Creelman, "Picture Plays and Players," *New York Sun* (May 14, 1945): 30.

134. "Whether Be a Brain or a Beauty," *Woman's Home Companion* (June 1946).

135. Louella Parsons, "Hollywood," *ATU* (March 18, 1949, and October 15, 1949): 8, 16.

136. Hedda Hopper, "Looking at Hollywood," *CT* (March 12, 1948).

137. Hedda Hopper, "Looking at Hollywood," *BCE* (February 14, 1944).

138. "*Green Danger* to Be Shown Aug. 7," *BDE* (July 29, 1947): 5.

139. Jack Lait Jr., "Hollywood," *BDE* (July 28, 1947): 5.

140. Louella Parsons, "Another Woman Will Produce Movies," *Rochester (NY) Democrat and Chronicle* (November 23, 1949): 9.

141. Jack Lait Jr., "Hollywood," *BDE* (July 28, 1947): 5.

142. Jane Corby, "Wanting Hard to Be Producer Is a Start Toward Being One," *Brooklyn Eagle* (August 1, 1954): 25.

143. Hal Boyle, "Mary Pickford, Now 60, Muses Back on Career," *Niagara Falls Gazette* (February 19, 1954): 5.

144. Louella Parsons, "Parsons on Parsons in New Role," *ATU* (August 30, 1955): 9.

145. Louella Parsons, "Star Producer Going into Television," *ATU* (November 12, 1956): 12.

146. Louella Parsons, "*Billie* Slated for Broadway," *ATU* (December 14, 1959): 6.

147. Louella Parsons, "Dolores Hart Gets Mink for Europe," *ATU* (June 13, 1961): 19.

148. Louella and Harriet Parsons, "Everything Roses for Janet Leigh," *ATU* (August 29, 1965): F2.

149. Harriet Parsons, "Ida Lupino Rarity as Director," *ATU* (November 28, 1965): F2.

150. Louella Parsons, "Newspaper Ad Started Nixon," *ATU* (August 2, 1960): 26.

151. Hedda Hopper, "Ambitious Girl Has Filmland Success Story," *BCE* (August 15, 1962): 31.

152. The show aired in early March 1956.

CHAPTER 4

1. Final Report and Ballot for the Annual Election of Officers and Executive Board, SWG, November 12, 1942, WGAW Executive Director Transfiles, series 7, box 18, SWG Records, 1921–54, WGAW.
2. McCall, interview, 1970, 37, private collection.
3. Minutes of Membership Committee, May 2, 1934, WGAW Executive Director Transfiles, series 7, box 66, SWG Records, 1921–54, WGAW.
4. Officers and Executive Members of the SWG, 4 pp., Art Arthur Re: Guild Library, January 12, 1948, Executive Board, Miscellaneous Correspondence, 1948–50, WGAW Executive Director Transfiles, series 7, box 16, SWG Records, 1921–54, WGAW.
5. Bob Thomas, "Film Capitol Is Girls' Land of Opportunity in Variety of Callings," *Binghamton (NY) Press* (January 10, 1948): 12.
6. Open SWG letter, October 23, 1935, Studio Deputies, WGAW Executive Director Transfiles, series 7, box 66, SWG Records, 1921–54, WGAW.
7. Mary C. McCall Jr., November 1942 speech, 8 pp., 1, Annual Meeting, November 12, 1942, WGAW Executive Director Transfiles, series 7, box 18, SWG Records, 1921–54, WGAW.
8. Ibid., 2.
9. Ibid.
10. McCall, "Let's Have a Motion Picture Kindergarten," *Screen Guilds' Magazine* (June 1935): 9.
11. Ibid.
12. McCall, November 1942 speech, 8.
13. Ibid.
14. Marsha McCreadie (*The Women Who Write the Movies* (New York: Citadel Press, 1996)), and more recently Barbara Hall, ("Jarrico V. Hughes," *Written By* 19, no. 5 (September–October 2015): 38–39) and Smyth ("A Woman at the Center of Hollywood's Wars: Mary C. McCall Jr.," and "The Mary McCall Years: When a Woman President Called the Shots at the Guild, Part 2," *Written By* 21, no. 5 (September–October 2017): 38–42, 62) have discussed aspects of her career.
15. McCall, "As Much as Mary McCall Bramson Knows about the Burkes and the McCalls," 19 pp., p. 12, private collection.
16. Ibid., 13.
17. Louella Parsons, "*Goldfish Bowl* Causes Stir at Warners, But It's Name of Film for Young Fairbanks," *New York American* (November 9, 1931): 10; Mary C. McCall Jr., *The Goldfish Bowl* (Boston: Little, Brown, 1932).
18. McCall, "As Much as Mary McCall Bramson Knows," 15.
19. Mary C. McCall Jr., "Sonnet for a Partnership," 1928, private collection.
20. Sheila Benson, interview by author, March 2016.
21. "Louella Parsons's Column," *ATU* (January 1, 1945).
22. McCall, "As Much as Mary McCall Bramson Knows," 15.
23. Ibid., 16.
24. McCall, interview, 3.
25. Ibid., 4.
26. Mildred Martin, "Camera Angles: *Craig's Wife*," *Philadelphia Inquirer* (October 18, 1936): 12.
27. Archer Winsten, "*Craig's Wife* Shown Up at Radio City Music Hall," *NYEP* (October 2, 1936): 19.
28. "Feminine Technical Crew Works on *Craig's Wife*," *NYP* (September 19, 1936): 9.
29. Martin, "Camera Angles," 12.

30. McCreadie, *Women Who Write the Movies*, 120.
31. McCall, interview, 3.
32. Ibid.
33. Ibid.
34. McCall, WGAW tribute, 1978, *WGAW News* (June 1978).
35. McCall, interview, 28.
36. Schwartz, *The Hollywood Writers' Wars*, 73.
37. Ibid., 96.
38. Ibid., 101; McCall, *Screen Guilds' Magazine* (February 1937): 7.
39. Donald Ogden Stewart, *Screen Guilds' Magazine* (March 1937): 18.
40. Schwartz, *The Hollywood Writers' Wars*, 69.
41. Patrick McGilligan, "Dorothy Kingsley: The Fixer," in *Backstory 2: Interviews with Screenwriters of the 1940s and 1950s*, ed. Pat McGilligan (Berkeley: University of California Press, 1991), 120.
42. Frances Marion, *How to Write and Sell Screenplays* (New York: Covici-Friede, 1937).
43. Both Meredyth and Jeanie Macpherson were founding members of the Academy of Motion Picture Arts and Sciences in 1927 (Pickford was the other female founder). Schwartz, *The Hollywood Writers' Wars*, 19.
44. Ibid., 128.
45. "Screen Guild Wins: Elected to Represent Film Writers in Hollywood," *New York Sun* (June 29, 1938): 17.
46. Jo Ranson, "Radio Dial Log," *Brooklyn Eagle* (January 17, 1939).
47. Louella Parsons, "Hollywood at Odds over Foreign Talent," *ATU* (August 11, 1940): D5.
48. Schwartz, *The Hollywood Writers' Wars*, 172–73.
49. McCall, interview, 23.
50. Louella Parsons, *San Francisco Examiner*, June 21, 1939. See Arthur Pollock, "Twin Bright Comedies Come to Do Us Good," *Brooklyn Eagle* (June 23, 1939): 11.
51. McCall, interview, 25.
52. "Ann Sothern Sticks to New Resolution: No 'Straight' Roles," *MGM Studio News* 6, no. 27 (November 7, 1939): 12, box 4, folder 65, Harold Bucquet Papers, AMPAS.
53. McCall, *Maisie*, M218 (January 19, 1939), 120 pp., p. 24, Turner-MGM scripts, AMPAS.
54. Marian Rhea, "Maisie's Remedies for Heartaches," *Photoplay* (June 1941): 34, 84–85.
55. "Finds Her Maisie Thoroughly Real," *Brooklyn Eagle* (August 2, 1942): E5.
56. Ibid.
57. Herbert Cohn, "*I Take This Woman* Shown at Music Hall," *Brooklyn Eagle* (February 16, 1940).
58. Emmet Lavery, "Writers and Critics," *Screen Writers' Guild Bulletin* (February, 1946): 34.
59. Ibid., 34–35.
60. McCall, interview, 28.
61. McCall, *Big Hearted Maisie*, later *Swing Shift Maisie,* June 23, 1942, S3114, p. 1, Turner-MGM scripts, AMPAS.
62. McCall, *Congo Maisie*, C-1172 (July 19, 1939), 116 pp., p. 93, Turner-MGM scripts, AMPAS.
63. McCall, *Gold Rush Maisie*, C1179 Selection of Changes out of Mary McCall OK script, October 27, 1939, changes dated November 27, 1939, and December 2, 1939, from Mary C. McCall Jr., 8C and 8D, Turner-MGM scripts, AMPAS.

64. Ibid., 63.
65. McCall, *Maisie*, M218, p. 90, Turner-MGM scripts, AMPAS.
66. Lillian Bergquist, Report *Swing Shift Maisie*, November 25, 1942, 2 pp., RG 208, box 3527, OWI Film Analysis, National Archives, College Park, MD.
67. Chester Bahm, "The Week in Theaters," *Syracuse Journal* (June 5, 1943): 21.
68. Leonard Lyons, "The Lyons Den," *NYEP* (November 2, 1942): 53.
69. John C. Flinn (secretary to McCall) to Lance Heath, PR committee of the MP industry, November 26, 1943, and 5pp. report on activities, December 30, 1943, box 20, folder 365, Motion Picture Association of America World War II Records, War Activities Correspondence, 1943–44, AMPAS.
70. Lt. Lea Burke to Mary C. McCall Jr., August 27, 1943, Government Agencies, WGAW Executive Director Transfiles, series 7, box 289, SWG Records, 1921–54, WGAW.
71. Irene Thirer, "Screen News and Views," *NYEP* (December 10, 1941): 1.
72. Mary C. McCall Jr., oral history, SWG (August 21, 1979): 4, WGAW.
73. Ibid.
74. Leonard Lyons, "The Lyons Den," *NYEP* (November 13, 1943): 14.
75. McCall, oral history, 6. The awards were held March 4, 1943.
76. Sidney Skolsky, "The Week in Review," *HCN* (March 6, 1943): 4.
77. McCall, "Facts, Figures on Your Percentage Deal," *Screen Writer* 1 (June 1945): 32–35.
78. McCall, interview, 30.
79. Ibid.
80. McCall, *The Sullivans*, August 27, 1943, 19, box 1, folder 32, Lloyd Bacon Papers, AMPAS. The real Genevieve Sullivan ended up serving twenty-one months in the WAVES to avenge her brothers.
81. McCall, *Woman's Army*, May 15, 1944, K76, 124 pp., p. 37, Turner-MGM Scripts, AMPAS.
82. Ibid., 55.
83. Sandy Roth, Report on *Woman's Army*, August 8, 1944, RG 208, box 3520, OWI Script Review, National Archives, College Park, MD.
84. "Guilds Attack Hearst-Based Film Alliance," *New York PM* (July 2, 1944): 17.
85. "Replies to De Mille," *Daily Variety* (July 23, 1945): 5.
86. McCall, *Woman's Army*, 119.
87. Lester Cole, *Hollywood Red* (New York: Ramparts Press, 1981), 201.
88. Mary C. McCall, FBI report, WFO 100-22248, Activities, p5, b2, b6, b7C, b7D, Mary C. McCall Jr Confidential FBI File, FBI, Department of Justice, Washington, DC.
89. "Guilds Attack Hearst-Based Film Alliance," *New York PM* (July 2, 1944): 17.
90. Schwartz, *The Hollywood Writers' Wars*, 221–27.
91. FBI compilation report, March 4, 1955, p4, b6 b7c, McCall Confidential FBI file, The report was at pains to note that McCall had never been under investigation by the FBI, but that FBI informants, including a prominent MGM screenwriter (very likely Rupert Hughes, uncle of Howard Hughes, or James Kevin McGuinness) accused her of being a fellow traveler.
92. "Screen Guild Elects Progressive Slate," *Los Angeles Eagle* (November 21, 1946): 22.
93. McManus, "Speaking of Movies: Who's for Dewey, Who's Who for FDR," *New York PM* (September 22, 1944): 20.

94. "Leftish Ghost-Writing Told on Coast," *Rochester (NY) Democrat and Chronicle* (November 4, 1947): 14; "Coast Probe Hits Pro-Red Writers," *Philadelphia Inquirer* (November 6, 1947).

95. FBI compilation report, March 4, 1955, p8, b2 b7D, McCall Confidential FBI file.

96. Emmet Lavery, "Sitting Out the Waltz" [1947–8], confidential memo to SWG Members, 3pp, box 26, folder 5, Alva Bessie Papers, WCFTR .

97. Louella Parsons, "Million Dollar Damage Suit Filed Because Film Story Gets Communism Label," *Rochester (NY) Democrat and Chronicle* (September 18, 1947): 12.

98. *Billboard* (May 8, 1948): 22.

99. Emmet Lavery to SWG Membership, November 1949, 9pp., 8, WGAW Executive Director Transfiles, series 7, box 293, "Communications to Member 1949," SWG Records, 1921–54, WGAW.

100. Hedda Hopper, "Marion Cooper, John Ford to Make New Argosy Film," *BCE* (May 6, 1948): 14.

101. Doris Gilbert to Mary C. McCall, November 23, 1951, Executive Board, President, 1945–51, Executive Director Transfiles, series 7, box 16, SWG Records, 1921–54, WGAW.

102. McCall, oral history, 9.

103. McCall to Hughes, March 27, 1952, Executive Board of SWG, WGAW; see Barbara Hall, "Jarrico V. Hughes," 38–39.

104. Myron C. Fagan, *Documentation of the Red Stars in Hollywood* (Hollywood: Cinema Education Guild, 1950), 86.

105. McCall to Hoover, August 29, 1951, McCall Confidential FBI file, FBI.

106. Ibid.

107. "Rather Be Dead Than Red, Says Script Writer," *Albany Knickerbocker News* (July 28, 1954): 10A.

108. Charles Brackett, copy, undated letter [1954], box 20, folder 2, Charles Brackett Papers, AMPAS.

109. "State Legislature Punctures Some of Fagan's H'Wood Red Charges," *Daily Variety* (June 14, 1961): 3.

110. McCall didn't even feature as a supporting player in the biopic *Trumbo* (2015), so the regressive political narrative persists.

111. McCall to Hoover, August 29, 1951, McCall Confidential FBI file.

CHAPTER 5

1. Hubbard Keavy, "Film Cutting 60 Hours a Week Tops Housework, Avows Woman," *BCE* (May 21, 1939): 13.

2. "Woman Editor of De Mille [sic] Working on 37th Film," *Brooklyn New York Daily Eagle* (June 22, 1941): E8.

3. Ibid.

4. Barbara McLean, "An Oral History with Barbara McLean," conducted by Tom Stempel, Darryl F. Zanuck Research Project, AFI, 1971, 108.

5. "Summary of the Communist Infiltration into the Motion Picture Industry," July 15, 1949, 1/E/VIII, 45 FBI file no. 100-HQ-138754, FBI File on Communist Infiltration-Motion Picture Industry (COMPIC), https://archive.org.

6. "Shows of the Week," *Erie County Independent* (Hamburg, NY) (December 29, 1938): 3.

7. One out of three editors nominated in 1934 was a woman (McLean); in 1935 two out of six nominees were women (Booth and McLean), one out of six in 1936

(McLean), one out of five in 1938 (McLean); and two out of five nominated films had female editors in 1939 (Spencer and McLean).

8. Hubbard Keavy, "Hollywood Screen Life," *Poughkeepsie Daily Eagle* (June 19, 1934): 6.

9. Francke, *Script Girls*, 1.

10. Ally Acker, *Reel Women: Pioneers of the Cinema, 1896 to the Present* (New York: Continuum, 1993), quoted by Myrna Oliver, "Barbara McLean: Groundbreaking Film Editor," *LAT* (April 2, 1996).

11. Michael Kunkes, "Tales from the Vault: Guild Librarians' Stock Is Rising," *Editors Guild Magazine* 29 (March–April 2008): 2, editorsguild.com.

12. Society of Motion Picture Film Editors and Motion Picture Editors Guild membership records, 1937–49, Motion Picture Editors Guild archives, Los Angeles, CA.

13. "Feminine Technical Crew Works on *Craig's Wife*," *NYEP* (September 19, 1936): 9.

14. Amy H. Croughton, "Film Editor's Role Growing in Importance: More Women Employed as Cutters," *Rochester (NY) Times Union* (May 10, 1937): 11.

15. Amy H. Croughton, "Scanning the Screen," *Rochester (NY) Times Union* (September 17, 1935): 15.

16. Ibid.

17. Gene Handsaker, "Writing with Scissors," *Binghamton (NY) Press* (August 12, 1967): 10.

18. For editors on the set, see "*Grand Hotel*," *NYEP* (February 23, 1932): 6.

19. Anne Bauchens, "Cutting the Film," in Nancy Naumburg, ed., *We Make the Movies* 199–215 (New York: W. W. Norton, 1937), 199.

20. McLean, "Oral History," 15.

21. Croughton, "Film Editor's Role Growing," 11.

22. Keavy, "Film Cutting 60 Hours," 13.

23. Ibid.

24. See, for example, *David and Bathsheba* (McLean, 1950) and *Lydia Bailey* (Spencer, 1952) conference notes, Twentieth Century-Fox Papers, USC Cinematic Arts Library, Los Angeles, CA.

25. Chuck Cochard, "Hollywood Star-Lites," *Rogersville Review* (November 21, 1935): 7.

26. "Hepburn Stars as Composer in Suburban Film," *Binghamton (NY) Press* (August 2, 1935): 20; "Joan Crawford Stars in *No More Ladies*," *Long Island Daily Press* (July 5, 1935): 17.

27. Katharine Hepburn, *Me* (New York: Ballantine Books, 1996), 144, and Anne Edwards, *A Remarkable Woman* (New York: Morrow, 1984), 138, 147.

28. "Hollywood Has Lots of Jobs for Women, Aside from Acting," *BDE* (November 12, 1953): 11.

29. McLean, "Oral History," 3.

30. Irene Kahn Atkins, "Margaret Booth: Interview," *Focus on Film* 25 (1976): 51–7, 52.

31. "Film Cutters, Studios Reach Union Accord," *HCN* (November 16, 1937): 4.

32. McLean, "Oral History," 5.

33. Ibid.

34. Ibid., 6.

35. Ibid., 7.

36. Ibid., 8.

37. Ibid., 10.

38. Ibid., 11.
39. According to Julien Johnson, McLean named her boat *Gallant Lady* and sailed it herself. McLean loved sailing, which Johnson felt was "another expression of her vigor and self-reliance," "The Assembly Line," *Action* IV, 4 (April 1943): 3–6, 4.
40. McLean, "Oral History," 20.
41. Ibid., 26.
42. Ibid., 43.
43. Ibid., 52.
44. Ibid., 54.
45. Ibid., 16.
46. Ibid., 27.
47. Ibid., 17.
48. Ibid., 13.
49. Paul Harrison, "The Day's Newsreel in Hollywood: Garbo Laughs Out Loud and Requests Rhumba Music," *Albany Evening News* (September 8, 1936): 20.
50. McLean, "Oral History," 14.
51. Kahn Atkins, "Margaret Booth: Interview," 53.
52. "Shows of the Week," *Erie County Independent* (Hamburg, NY) (December 29, 1938): 3. See also Joseph W. La Bine, "Behind the Hollywood Stage: *In Old Chicago* Typifies the Preparatory Operations Underlying This Immense Business of Making a Modern Movie," *Friendship New York Weekly Register* (December 30, 1937): 2.
53. Bauchens, "Cutting the Film," 200.
54. Ibid., 204.
55. McLean, "Oral History," 41.
56. Ibid., 39.
57. Bauchens, "Cutting the Film," 204.
58. Kahn Atkins, "Margaret Booth: Interview," 52.
59. *MGM Studio Club News* 1, no. 12 (December 1936): 1.
60. Kahn Atkins, "Margaret Booth: Interview," 53.
61. *Command Decision*, C-1121, "Notes and Added Scenes," June 7, 1948, Turner MGM Script Collection, AMPAS.
62. See J. E. Smyth, *Reconstructing American Historical Cinema* (Lexington: University Press of Kentucky, 2006).
63. "The Hand That Rocks the Cradle," *Action* VIII, 8 (August 1947): 10.
64. "Women Behind the Screen," *LAT* (April 28, 1940); Jean Howard, "Barbara McLean," *Vogue* (February 1952).
65. McLean, "Oral History," 23–24.
66. Ibid., 51.
67. Quoted by Emanuel Levy in *George Cukor: Master of Elegance: Hollywood's Legendary Director and His Stars* (New York: William Morrow, 1994), 154.
68. McLean, "Oral History," 36–37.
69. Ibid., 48.
70. Ibid., 48–49.
71. Ibid., 48.
72. Ibid., 22.
73. Ibid., 65, 78.
74. "Women at the Helm: Screen and Radio Weekly," *Rochester (NY) Democratic Chronicle* (1937): 13.

75. Jonathan Rosenbaum, "The Cutting Edge," *The Movie*. http://www. jonathanrosenbaum.net/1982/07/the-cutting-edge/.
76. McLean, "Oral History," 44.
77. Mary Steward to Edward Landler, "Post-production Pioneers: The Guild's Earliest Members," *Editors Guild Magazine* 1, no. 5 (September–October 2012).
78. McLean, "Oral History," 113.
79. Sam Staggs, *All About "All About Eve"* (New York: St. Martin's Press, 2000), 160–73, which offers contradictory accounts of whether director, producer, or editor did the real working shaping the film. Joseph Mankiewicz is quoted as saying he let McLean do her work (162).
80. Kenneth Macgowan, *Behind the Screen* (New York: Dell, 1967), 422.
81. Ibid., 419.
82. McLean, "Oral History," 48.
83. Allene Talmey, "13 of Hollywood's Creative Brains," *Vogue* (1 February 1952): 182–87, 234–35.
84. McLean, "Oral History," 86.
85. Ray Stark to John Huston, February 17, 1964, *The Night of the Iguana*, p. 2, folder 436, John Huston Papers, AMPAS.
86. Ibid., 6 and 7.
87. Frank E. Rosenfelt to Howard Koch, October 19, 1977, box 4, folder 16, Margaret Booth Papers, AMPAS.
88. George Cukor to Howard Koch, November 4, 1977, box 4, folder 16, Margaret Booth Papers, AMPAS.
89. George Sidney to Howard Koch, November 3, 1977, box 4, folder 16, Margaret Booth Papers, AMPAS.
90. David Lean to Howard Koch, November 10, 1977, box 4, folder 16, Margaret Booth Papers, AMPAS.
91. These early percentages are based on only fragmentary guild evidence, since many top editors' guild cards are not recorded in their databases. The true numbers of women editors during this period would be considerably higher. Keavy, "Film Cutting 60 Hours"; Anne M. McIlhenney, "Filmland Rambles," *BCE* (June 22, 1941): sec. VI, p. 5; "Women Execs in Hollywood," *BCE* (1940): 4. To this day, IMDB and other Internet sites persist in requoting an erroneous 1990s article alleging that only eight women worked as editors during this period.
92. "Arthur Brisbane's Comment," *BCE* (March 3, 1933): 1.
93. Margaret Booth, oral history conducted by Rudy Behlmer (1991), 16, AMPAS.
94. Keavy, "Film Cutting 60 Hours."
95. McLean, "Oral History," 120.
96. Ibid., 14.
97. Julien Johnson, "The Assembly Line," *Action* 4, no. 4 (April 1943): 6.
98. Kahn Atkins, "Margaret Booth: Interview," 53.
99. As Marjorie Fowler, she went on to edit *Separate Tables* (1958) and *Elmer Gantry* (1960).

CHAPTER 6

1. Sylvia Weaver, "Wardrobe Should," *Akron Beacon Journal* (February 8, 1942), press clipping, scrapbook, EHP, WCFTR.
2. Bettina Bedwell, "Hollywood's Women Stylists Are Prominent," *CT* (September 22, 1940), scrapbook, EHP, WCFTR.

3. Sandra Smythe, "Workaday Clothes Should Reflect Common Sense in Style, Coloring, and Accompanying Accessories," *Akron Beacon Journal* (August 31, 1941), scrapbook, EHP, WCFTR.

4. Sara Day, "By Women for Women: Feminine Fashions," *Jamaica (NY) Long Island Daily Press* (1937): 12, partially undated clipping, 5854.pdf, fultonhistory.com; Rita Swann, "Style Trend away from Military Seen by Expert," unmarked press clipping, [1940], scrapbook, EHP, WCFTR.

5. Hopper, *Whole Truth*, 132.

6. "Young Designer Is Awarded Silver Trophy for Her Art," *Peekskill Evening Star* (May 1936): 6.

7. David Chierichetti, *Hollywood Costume Design* (New York: Harmony Books, 1976), 163.

8. Norma Lee Browning, "She Garbs Hollywood," *Chicago Sunday Tribune, Grafic Magazine* (June 13, 1948): 5, 20.

9. The Costume Designers Guild, established in 1954 at the urging of Joan Crawford's key designer, Sheila O'Brien, had thirty designer members and eight associate sketch artists when it began (it was a more exclusive version of IATSE Local 705). Other prominent members included Head, Helen Rose, and Jean Louis (see Erskine Johnson, "Designer Explains New Trend of Stars," *Saratoga Springs Saratogian* [January 12, 1954]: 1). Ironically, even though O'Brien was an advocate for unionization, at the same time she was one of the most exclusive of Hollywood designers, working for Crawford and advocating the star's "natural flair for glamor" that other women could never attain. Patricia Clary, "Crawford Holds to Glamor," *Rochester (NY) Democrat and Chronicle* (June 14, 1950): 14.

10. Dale McConathy with Diana Vreeland, *Hollywood Costume* (New York: Harry N. Abrams, 1976), 178.

11. Chierichetti, *Hollywood Costume Design*, 58.

12. "Travis Banton, Head Designer at Paramount Studios, Resigns," *New York Women's Wear* (March 29, 1938), scrapbook, EHP, WCFTR.

13. Lon Jones, "From School Teacher to Famous Fashion Designer," *Sun News-Pictorial* (November 3, 1938), scrapbook, EHP, WCFTR.

14. Nancy Naumburg, "Women Don't Always Act," [1939] unmarked press clipping, scrapbook, EHP, WCFTR.

15. Lester Hartley Geiss, "Designer Edith Head Began as Art Teacher," *Kansas City, (MO) Journal* (May 27, 1941), scrapbook, EHP, WCFTR.

16. "Made Junior Designer for Paramount Pictures," *New York Women's Wear* (July 7, 1943), scrapbook, EHP, WCFTR.

17. Browning, "She Garbs Hollywood," 5, 20.

18. Edith Head, "I Dress the Stars," *Motion Picture* (April 1960): 30–33, 57–58, 58.

19. Rebecca Arnold, *The American Look* (London: I.B. Taurus, 2009): 4–5, 28–29, 79–80.

20. Bettina Bedwell, "Hollywood's Women Stylists Are Prominent," *CT* (September 22, 1940), scrapbook, EHP, WCFTR.

21. Katherine Vincent, "Hollywood Fashions," *New York Herald-Tribune* (September 16, 1940), scrapbook, EHP, WCFTR.

22. Ibid.

23. Helen P. Wulbern, "Edith Head Rates Sportswear First as Style Solution to Modern Living," *New York Women's Wear* (August 19, 1943), scrapbook, EHP, WCFTR.

24. Edith Head, "Hollywood Designer Lauds Simple Mode," unmarked press clipping [1940], scrapbook, EHP, WCFTR.
25. Margaret Follin Eicks, "Hollywood Designer Copies Expensive Costume for Little," *Boston Transcript* (September 22, 1940), scrapbook, EHP, WCFTR. See also Edith Head, "California Contributing to World's Style Chic," *LAT* (September 18, 1940); Bettina Bedwell, "Golden Girl of the West is Tops in Hollywood Fashions," *New Orleans States* (October 15, 1940), all scrapbook, EHP, WCFTR.
26. *Women's Wear Daily* (October 6, 1937), scrapbook, EHP, WCFTR.
27. Gwen Walters, "Hollywood Fashion News," *Photoplay* [1938], 9, 19, scrapbook, EHP, WCFTR.
28. Sandra Smythe, "Workaday Clothes Should Reflect Common Sense in Style, Coloring, and Accompanying Accessories," *Akron Beacon Journal* (August 31, 1941), scrapbook, EHP, WCFTR.
29. "Business Girl Modes Created in Hollywood," *Milwaukee Journal* (September 27, 1942), scrapbook, EHP, WCFTR.
30. Edith Head, "Screen Mode Accents Hips," unmarked press clipping [1939], scrapbook, EHP, WCFTR.
31. Ibid.
32. Chierichetti, *Hollywood Costume Design*, 32.
33. "Film, Custom Designers to Display Styles Feb. 13," *LAE* (February 3, 1941), scrapbook, EHP, WCFTR.
34. Edith Head and Paddy Calistro, *Edith Head's Hollywood* (New York: E.P. Dutton, 1983), 44.
35. Chierichetti, *Edith Head*, 15–16.
36. Norma Lee Browning, "She Garbs the Great of Hollywood," *Chicago Sunday Tribune* (June 13, 1948): 5, 20.
37. Mari Lucas, "Designer Has Magic Touch of Simplicity," unmarked press clipping [1941], scrapbook, EHP, WCFTR; Lester Hartley Geiss, "Designer Edith Head Began as Art Teacher," *Kansas City (MO) Journal* (May 27, 1941), scrapbook, EHP, WCFTR. See also "Edith Head Stars Pan-American Theme in Film Costumes," *New York Women's Wear* (March 23, 1943), scrapbook, EHP, WCFTR.
38. Helen P. Wulbern, "Edith Head Rates Sportswear First as Style Solution to Modern Living," *New York Women's Wear* (August 19, 1943), scrapbook, EHP, WCFTR.
39. Canta Claro, "Hollywood en Close-Up" (1944), 22, EHP, WCFTR; G. R., "Secreto de la Elegencia," *Mexico Cinema*, undated clipping, 98, EHP, WCFTR; Alvaro Alfareda, "De Charla con la Disenadora de las Estrellas de Hollywood," unmarked press clipping, scrapbook, EHP, WCFTR.
40. "Fashion Show Readied," *HCN* (February 12, 1941), scrapbook, EHP, WCFTR.
41. Alice Hughes, "No Hint of Budgets or Inhibitions in California's Fashion Futures," *NYP* (February 14, 1941): 11.
42. Associated Press, "New Films Will Stress Fashions," *Albany Knickerbocker News* (July 15, 1940): 4A.
43. Jessie Henderson, "Nazi Occupation of Paris May Make Hollywood New Capital of Fashion World," *Philadelphia Bulletin* (August 27, 1940), scrapbook, EHP, WCFTR.
44. Bettina Johnson, "Will Hollywood Take Over Fashion Spotlight with Paris Out of Picture? No! Says Expert," *Akron Beacon Journal* (September 3, 1940), scrapbook, EHP, WCFTR.

45. Ibid.
46. "Edith Head Renewed," *Hollywood Variety* (February 10, 1941).
47. "Reception to Honor Hollywood Designers," *New York Sun* (May 14, 1942), scrapbook, EHP, WCFTR.
48. Molly Hollywood, "Film Colony, N.Y. Battle to Set Styles," *LAE* (September 21, 1941), scrapbook, EHP, WCFTR.
49. "Notes of the Studios," *New York Sun* (December 21, 1943): 22.
50. Johnson, "Will Hollywood Take Over."
51. Lon Jones, "From School Teacher to Famous Fashion Designer," *Sun News-Pictorial* (November 3, 1938), scrapbook, EHP, WCFTR.
52. Joan Gardner, "Designers Jump L-85," *Hartford Courant* (August 1, 1942), scrapbook, EHP, WCFTR.
53. Head, "I Dress the Stars," 58.
54. Gene Handsaker, "Hollywood Sights and Sounds," *Niagara Falls Gazette* (November 3, 1948): 34.
55. "Film Fashion Designer No. 1 Gets Lots of Criticism—from Men," unmarked press clipping [1938], scrapbook, EHP, WCFTR.
56. Unmarked *Photoplay* clipping [1925], scrapbook, EHP, WCFTR.
57. "Style Conference," November 2, 1936, unmarked press clipping, scrapbook, EHP, WCFTR.
58. Lloyd Pantages, "I Cover Hollywood," *ATU* (March 5, 1936): 18.
59. "Friendly Token," *Rochester (NY) Democrat and Chronicle* (October 2, 1938): 8D; "Joan Dons Wow Duds Off Screen," *Binghamton Press* (November 27, 1949): 11C.
60. James Bernard Luber, "Paramount's Edith Head Talks about Fashion and Women," *Highland (IL) News Leader* (September 13, 1950): 14.
61. Head, "I Dress the Stars," 58.
62. Head and Calistro, *Edith Head's Hollywood*, 93.
63. Jones, "From School Teacher."
64. Ibid.
65. Sylvia Weaver, "Wartime Styles," *St. Paul Pioneer Press* (January 18, 1942).
66. Dorothy Manners, "World at War Likes Its Women Gay," *Los Angeles Herald-Express*, unmarked press clipping, scrapbook, EHP, WCFTR.
67. "War Glamour," *Des Moines Look* (July 27, 1943), scrapbook, EHP, WCFTR.
68. Ibid.
69. Sylvia Weaver, "Wardrobe Should," *Akron Beacon Journal* (February 8, 1942), press clipping, scrapbook, EHP, WCFTR.
70. "Edith Head Develops Wardrobe Ideas in Barbara Stanwyck Role," unmarked press clipping [October 9, 1941], scrapbook, EHP, WCFTR.
71. Ibid.
72. "Edith Head Designs Film Garb Checked for Workability," October 14, 1943, unmarked press clipping, scrapbook, EHP, WCFTR.
73. "Hollywood Fashions Becoming Sensible," *New York Times* (February 1, 1944), scrapbook, EHP, WCFTR; Hedda Hopper, "Looking at Hollywood," *BCE* (August 23, 1943): 19.
74. "Pants Ideal for Cycling," unmarked press clipping, scrapbook, EHP, WCFTR.
75. "Fashion Seals Ruffles Doom," *Portland Oregonian* (January 3, 1943); "Actress Believes Feminine Frills Out for Duration," *HCN* (January 19, 1944); "Slacks Comfortable for Housework," *Boston Traveler* (February 23, 1944), scrapbook, EHP, WCFTR.

76. Frederick C. Othman, "Movie Clothes Now Realistic," *New York World-Telegram* (November 12, 1943), scrapbook, EHP, WCFTR. Price estimates on this dress range from $5,000 to $35,000.

77. "Hollywood Fashions Becoming Sensible," *New York Times* (February 1, 1944), scrapbook, EHP, WCFTR.

78. Ginger Rogers, *Ginger: My Story* (New York: HarperCollins, 1991), 253–55.

79. W. E. J. Martin, "Of New Shows," *BCE* (April 9, 1944): 5D; Jimmy Starr, "Studio Will Film Life of Stylist," *Los Angeles Herald-Express* (February 8, 1944), scrapbook, EHP, WCFTR.

80. Helen Rose and Milton P. Kahn, "A Designing Woman," October 20, 1953, 6 pp., Turner-MGM Scripts D-503, AMPAS.

81. Vincente Minnelli, Memos, *Designing Woman*, box 13, folder 243, Vincente Minnelli Papers, AMPAS.

82. Edith Head: Her Sunshine Route to the Bright Lights of Hollywood," *California Stylist* (July 1954): 64–77. See "Edith Head at Home: Her Favorite Role," 76–77.

83. Chierichetti, *Edith Head*, 31, 33–34.

84. "Jackie Cooper Wins Film Lead," *Brooklyn Eagle* (January 15, 1947): 7.

85. United Press, "Says U.S. Women Are Turning Into Bunch of Strip-Teasers," *Brooklyn Eagle* (March 1, 1949): 3.

86. Cynthia Lowry, "Hollywood Designer Changes Starlet's Whole Personality," *Binghamton (NY) Sunday Press* (September 4, 1955): 5B.

87. Walter Plunkett to Katharine Hepburn, December 24, 1936, box 25, folder 7, KHP, NYLPA.

88. Jay Jorgenson and Donald Scoggins, *Creating the Illusion: A Fashionable History of Hollywood Costume Designers* (New York: Running Press, 2015), 301.

89. Dorothy Jeakins, oral history interview by Betty Hoag, June 19, 1964, Archives of American Art, Smithsonian Institution, Washington, DC.

90. Ibid.

91. Dorothy Jeakins, *Joan of Arc* workbook, 1948, US Mss, 42AN, box 1, folder 11 DJP, WCFTR.

92. Jeakins, interview.

93. Aline Mosby, "'Nude' Bathing Scenes Aren't, Even for Camera Long-Shots," *Brooklyn New York Daily Eagle* (August 19, 1953): 9.

94. Agnes McCay, "Path of Fashion Leads Movie Designer to 'Safari' into Wilderness of Jungle," unmarked press clipping, box 14, folder 3, DJP, WCFTR.

95. Ibid.

96. Jorgensen and Scoggins, *Creating the Illusion*, 300.

97. Marshall Berges, "Dorothy Jeakins," *LAT* (October 31, 1976): 35.

98. Ed Misurell, "TV's Dorothy Jeakins Is a 'Spectacular' Designer," *ATU* (March 30, 1957): P-3.

99. "Let's Go to *Annie Get Your Gun*," *Co-Ed* (November 1957): 36–37, box 14, folder 3, DJP, WCFTR.

100. Judith Crist, "*Romeo and Juliet* Opens Stratford Drama Season," *New York Herald Tribune*, undated clipping box 14, folder 3, DJP, WCFTR; Betty Barrett, "She Sets the Stage for Immortal Bard at Theater in Stratford," *Hartford Courant* (July 5, 1959): E1.

101. Dorothy Jeakins, tape 519a, June 1968, DJP, WCFTR.

102. Arlene Creed, "Fashion a Force," *LAE*, box 14, folder 3, DJP, WCFTR.

103. Dorothy Jeakins to Marshall Berges, October 1976, 4 pp., p. 2, box 14, folder 4, DJP, WCFTR.

CHAPTER 7

1. Rick Du Brow, "Hepburn Absolutely Perfect during Cavett Performances," *North Tonawanda Evening News* (October 4, 1973): 19.
2. Ibid.
3. See Andrew Britton, *Katharine Hepburn: Star as Feminist* (New York: Columbia University Press, 2008); Radhika Sanghani, "Why Katharine Hepburn Is Still a Feminist Icon," *Daily Telegraph* (September 22, 2016).
4. "Bouquet Hollywood," *Photoplay* (February 1933): 92.
5. Francke, *Script Girls*, 39.
6. Levien to Chandler Sprague, March 20, 1928, box 25, HM 56335, Sonya Levien Papers, Huntington Library, San Marino, CA.
7. Larry Ceplair, *A Great Lady: A Life of Sonya Levien* (Lanham: Scarecrow Press, 1996), 92–93. Unfortunately Levien wasn't around when Zanuck took Harris's pet project, *Brigham Young* (1940), and gave credit to Louis Bromfield and Lamar Trotti. Harris, though a studio insider (her father was screenwriter Ray Harris) retaliated by suing the studio (*Harris v. Twentieth Century-Fox Film Corporation*, District Court, S.D. New York, 1942 and 2nd District Circuit Court of Appeals, 1943), demanding a halt to exhibition until she was given credit. She lost the suit (this was the pre-guild contract era) and her career in Hollywood for taking punitive action outside the studio system.
8. Katharine Hepburn to Dorothy Arzner, January 22, 1975, box 7, folder 15, Dorothy Arzner Papers, Performing Arts Special Collections, UCLA.
9. Karyn Kay and Gerald Peary, "Interview with Dorothy Arzner," in Claire Johnston, ed., *The Work of Dorothy Arzner: Towards a Feminist Cinema* (London: BFI, 1975), 23.
10. Cott, *Grounding of Modern Feminism*, 6.
11. Michael Freedland, *Katharine Hepburn* (London: W. H. Allen & Co., 1984), 31
12. Edwards, *A Remarkable Woman*, 86.
13. Behlmer, *Memo from David O. Selznick*, 43.
14. Lee Israel, "Last of the Honest-to-God Ladies," *Esquire* (November 1967).
15. Edwards, *A Remarkable Woman*, 102.
16. Gavin Lambert, *On Cukor* (New York: G.P. Putnam's, 1972), 99.
17. "Katharine Hepburn Amazes Bryn Mawr by Her Stardom," *PI* (February 26, 1934): 4.
18. Seymour, "Hollywood Fashions," *Photoplay* (April 1933), 62.
19. Mary Temple, "She Stole His Best Scenes," *Photoplay* (January 1933): 82, 116–17.
20. Associated Press, "Who Are Ten Best Dressed?" *Albany Evening News* (June 15, 1933): 6.
21. Harry Brandt, "Box Office Poison," *Independent Film Journal* (May 3, 1938).
22. Elizabeth Yeaman, "Luise Rainier's Future at Metro Pondered," *HCN* (November 27, 1937): 6.
23. Marjorie Dudley, *A Woman Rebels*, Synopsis, June 30, 1933, 11 pp., RKO S393, Collection 3, Performing Arts Special Collections, UCLA.
24. Ibid.
25. Samuel Goldwyn, "Women Rule Hollywood," *New Movie Magazine* (March 1935): 18–19.
26. Cliff Reid to Merian C. Cooper, January 12, 1934, RKO S393, Collection 3, Performing Arts Special Collections UCLA.
27. Ernest Vajda, *A Woman Rebels*, March 16, 1936 script, 202 pp., p. 125, RKO S393, Collection 3, Performing Arts Special Collections, UCLA.

28. Ibid., 127–28.
29. Richard Jewell, "RKO Film Grosses: 1931–1951," *Historical Journal of Film Radio and Television* 14, no. 1 (1994): 57; Jeanine Basinger, *A Woman's View: How Hollywood Spoke to Women, 1930–1960* (Middletown, CT: Wesleyan University Press, 1993), 49.
30. Norbert Lusk, "Thumbnail Reviews: *A Woman Rebels*," *Picture Play* (January 1937): 58.
31. "Ginger Rogers, Katharine Hepburn," *Photoplay* (February 1937): 38.
32. Gail Patrick, interview by James Bawden [1979], http://www.classicimages.com/films_of_the_golden_ages/article_39f84018-cfc0-11e3-b0b4-001a4bcf887a.html.
33. Ginger Rogers to Katharine Hepburn, December 24, 1936, box 25, folder 8, KHP, NYPLA.
34. Trumbo, *Kitty Foyle*, revised continuity, August 13, 1940, box 1, folder 20, Milton E. Pickman Papers, Performing Arts Special Collections, UCLA.
35. Trumbo, *Kitty Foyle*, first draft continuity, June 1, 1940, box 719, RKO Collection 3, Performing Arts Special Collections, UCLA.
36. Robert Ardrey, *Kitty Foyle*, treatment, February 17, 1940, 12, box 720, RKO Collection 3, Performing Arts Special Collections, UCLA.
37. Rosenberg, *Divided Lives*, 114.
38. Notes on *Kitty Foyle*, February 3, 1940, box 720, RKO Collection 3, Performing Arts Special Collections, UCLA.
39. Selznick to Sidney Howard, January 6, 1937, in Behlmer, *Memo from David O. Selznick*, 145.
40. RKO Radio Pictures Correspondence, TS 1996-018, box 1, folder 7, NYPLA.
41. Paul Harrison, "Hollywood Writers and Actors Take Crack at Acting," *Albany Knickerbocker News* (September 12, 1939): 6A.
42. John Mason Brown, "Katharine Hepburn in *Philadelphia Story*," *NYP* (April 1, 1939): 8.
43. John Anderson, "*Philadelphia Story* Bought in by Guild," *New York Journal and American* (March 29, 1939).
44. "Katharine Hepburn in Frilly Clothes Triumphs in New Play," *Life* (March 1939), undated press clipping, box 35, folder 30, KHP, NYLPA.
45. Mark Barron, "Glamour Shed in Labor War," *PI* (August 20, 1939): 9; Associated Press, "Actors Carry Union Fist Fight to AFL Sessions" and "'To Be or Not': ABC of Unions' Tangle," *ATU* (August 9, 1939): 5.
46. Main Johnson, "Katharine Hepburn, Hatless, Tramps Fields, Defying Rain: Famed Actress, Staunchly Pro-British, Is Strong Roosevelt Backer," *Toronto Daily Star* (October 15, 1940), box 25, folder 30, KHP, NYPLA.
47. *The Philadelphia Story* contract, January 19, 1939, box 35, folder 26, KHP, NYLPA.
48. *The Philadelphia Story* contract, January 19, 1939, box 35, folder 26, KHP, NYLPA.
49. Chester Hahn, "*Philadelphia Story* with Katharine Hepburn Is Season's Smartest Comedy," *Syracuse Journal* (December 7, 1940): 9; "Theater Review," *BCE* (January 25, 1941): 9.
50. Edwards, *A Remarkable Woman*, 194.
51. Anne M. McIlhenney, "Interference by Children's Aid Fails to Irk Katharine Hepburn," *BCE* (October 18, 1940): sec. 5, p. 6; "Dorothy Thompson Flies

to Hollywood to Sell New Story," *MGM Studio News* 6, no. 27 (November 7, 1939): 2, folder 65, Harold Bucquet Collection, AMPAS.

52. Edwards, *A Remarkable Woman*, 187.

53. *Lockport Union-Sun and Journal* (September 4, 1957): 6.

54. Michael Kanin and Ring Lardner Jr., original short story for *Woman of the Year*, box 21, folder 275, KHP, AMPAS.

55. Original short story for *Woman of the Year*, box 21, folder 275, 89 pp., KHP, AMPAS.

56. "*Woman of the Year* Feature for Buffalo," *BCE* (February 20, 1942): 10.

57. Alice Hughes, "Woman's New York: Katharine the Great (Hepburn Declared Not Same Off Stage," *Courier-Express Daily Pictorial* (April 10, 1945): 10.

58. Hedda Hopper, "Communism to Be Target of New Films," *BCE* (April 12, 1947): 15.

59. Leonard Lyons, "Actors Are Fliers," *Post-Standard* (July 25, 1947): sec. 2, p. 11.

60. "Under the Dome," *New York Post Standard* (June 8, 1947): 1. Incredibly, Kathryn Cramer Brownell's *Showbiz Politics* (2014) makes no mention of Hepburn's notorious support of Wallace.

61. Schwartz, *The Hollywood Writers' Wars*, 256.

62. Ibid.; Edwards, *A Remarkable Woman*, 252.

63. Drew Pearson, "Another Glamour Probe," *Alfred Sun* (September 25, 1947).

64. Associated Press, "Communists in Hollywood Raise $87,000," *Schenectady Gazette* (October 21, 1947): 3; Associated Press, "$87,000 Raised for Red Cause in Hollywood, Says Producer," *Rochester (NY) Democrat and Chronicle* (October 21, 1947): 1.

65. Associated Press, "Moffitt Testifies Hollywood Only Place Where Reds Have Been Strongly Resisted Here," *Courtland Standard* (October 21, 1947): 1.

66. Associated Press, "Defense Scheduled in Film Red Probe," *NYEP* (October 25, 1947): 5. She was also mentioned in other articles in protest groups including Paulette Goddard, Marsha Hunt, Dorothy McGuire, and Myrna Loy. George Sokolsy, "These Days," *Kingston Daily Freeman* (October 24, 1947): 4.

67. "Rejected Red-Tinged Movie Scripts, Cooper Tells Un-American Probers," *ATU* (October 24, 1947): 3.

68. Hedda Hopper, "Hollywood," *BCE* (December 5, 1947): 10.

69. Erskine Johnson, "Orson Picks Spot for Rita's Death Scene," *Saratoga Springs Saratogian* (April 20, 1948): 1.

70. Ruth Brigham, "Cockney Fans' Lingo Baffles Joan, Barbara," *BCE* (June 1, 1948): 15.

71. Hedda Hopper, "Bing, Wellman Have New Film in Father's Day," *BCE* (May 20, 1948): 24.

72. Mary Padgett, "21 Women Candidates on Wallace Ticket Feted," *PI* (July 26, 1948): 2.

73. "Artist, Writer to Speak at Wallace Rally," *Albany Knickerbocker News* (October 27, 1948): 10-B.

74. Associated Press, "California Lists Famed in Report on Communism," and "Actors Deny Red Labels as Absurd," *Lockport Union Sun Journal* (June 9, 1949): 1.

75. Louella Parsons, "Circus Head and DeMille Plan Movie," *PI* (June 14, 1949): 27.

76. Erskine Johnson, "Lena Horne Explains Hollywood Walkout," *Saratoga Springs Saratogian* (July 26, 1951): 1.

77. William F. McDermott, "Katharine Hepburn," Souvenir Program, *As You Like It*, P2, box 18, folder 6, KHP, NYLPA; *Life* clipping, undated, "*Life* Congratulates Katharine Hepburn," [1950], 47, box 17, folder 11, KHP, NYLPA.

78. Louella Parsons, "In Hollywood," *Pictorial Review* (March 19, 1950), box 17, folder 11, KHP, NYLPA.

79. Robert C. Ruark, "Tribute to Bogie," *Post-Standard* (January 29, 1957): sec. 2, p. 13.

80. Erskine Johnson, "Bogart Praises Katie after African Film," *Saratoga Springs Saratogian* (October 5, 1951): 1.

81. Humphrey Bogart, "African Adventure," *American Weekly* (August 31, 1952): 8. This story is often retold in memoirs, with John Huston playing Bogart's role.

82. Constance Collier to Katharine Hepburn, May 28, 1951, box 3, folder 18, KHP, NYLPA.

83. "To Katie Hepburn, Africa—Flies and All, 'Marvelous,'" *BDE* (February 10, 1952): 29.

84. Edwards, *A Remarkable Woman*, 266.

85. Brooks Atkinson, "Candida," *New York Times* (April 23, 1952), box 3, folder 25, KHP, NYLPA. The folder is filled with Olivia de Havilland's poor reviews.

86. Constance Collier to Katharine Hepburn, April 26, 1952, box 3, folder 25, KHP, NYLPA.

87. Constance Collier to Katharine Hepburn, March 7, 1954, box 3, folder 30, KHP, NYLPA.

88. "Kate Arrives: Picture of the Week," *Courier Mail* (July 18, 1955), box 35, folder 2, KHP, NYLPA.

89. "Just the Same as on the Screen," *West Australian*, October 31, 1955, box 35, folder 2, KHP, NYLPA.

90. Cindie Lovelace to Katharine Hepburn, May 27, 1970, box 19, folder 28, KHP, NYPLA.

91. "Hepburn Named 'Woman of the Year,'" *ATU* (January 29, 1970): 18.

EPILOGUE

1. Anita Loos, *Kiss Hollywood Good-By* (New York: Viking Press, 1974), 10.

2. Samuel Goldwyn, "Women Rule Hollywood," *New Movie Magazine* (March 1935): 18–19.

3. See Wikipedia.org entries on Joan Harrison and Virginia Van Upp, accessed May 22, 2017.

4. See IMDB.com, biography of Barbara McLean and Oliver (1996). Today, according to a study by the Center for the Study of Women in Television and Film at San Diego State, women make up 17% of all editors. See Brent Lang, "Number of Female Directors Falls Despite Diversity Debate, Says Study," *Variety* (January 12, 2017).

5. Lang, "Number of Female Directors."

6. Gay Pauley, "Career Girl Must Retain Sex Appeal," *BCE* (August 3, 1957): 11.

7. McGilligan, "Dorothy Kingsley," 117.

8. Bob Thomas, "Bette Davis Calls Directors Stars," *Troy Record* (October 10, 1970): B8.

BIBLIOGRAPHY

ARCHIVAL SOURCES

Arzner, Dorothy. Papers. Performing Arts Special Collections. University of California. Los Angeles, CA.

Bacon, Lloyd. Papers. Margaret Herrick Library. Academy of Motion Picture Arts and Sciences. Beverly Hills, CA.

Behrman, S. N. Papers. New York Public Library. New York, NY.

Bessie, Alvah. Papers. Wisconsin Center for Film and Theater Research. Madison, WI.

Bohem, Leslie. Collection. University of Southern California Cinematic Arts Library. Los Angeles, CA.

Booth, Margaret. Papers. Margaret Herrick Library. Academy of Motion Picture Arts and Sciences. Beverly Hills, CA.

Booth, Margaret. Oral history interview conducted by Rudy Behlmer. Margaret Herrick Library. Academy of Motion Picture Arts and Sciences. Beverly Hills, CA.

Brackett, Charles. Papers. Margaret Herrick Library. Academy of Motion Picture Arts and Sciences. Beverly Hills, CA.

Brown Barrett, Katharine "Kay." Papers. New York Library for the Performing Arts. New York, NY.

Bucquet, Harold. Papers. Margaret Herrick Library. Academy of Motion Picture Arts and Sciences. Beverly Hills, CA.

Caspary, Vera. Papers. Wisconsin Center for Film and Theater Research. Madison, WI.

Crawford, Cheryl. Papers. New York Library for the Performing Arts. New York, NY.

Davis, Bette. Papers. Howard Gotlieb Archival Research Center. Boston University. Boston, MA.

Deutsch, Helen. Papers. Howard Gotlieb Archival Research Center. Boston University. Boston, MA.

Ferber, Edna. Papers. Wisconsin Center for Film and Theater Research. Madison, WI.

Gaynor, Janet. Papers. Howard Gotlieb Archival Research Center. Boston University. Boston, MA.

Goldwyn, Samuel. Papers. Margaret Herrick Library. Academy of Motion Picture Arts and Sciences. Beverly Hills, CA.

Goodrich, Frances. Papers. Wisconsin Center for Film and Theater Research. Madison, WI.

Greenwood, Charlotte. Collection. University of Southern California Cinematic Arts Library. Los Angeles, CA.

Hayes, Helen. Papers. New York Library for the Performing Arts. New York, NY.

Head, Edith. Papers. Wisconsin Center for Film and Theater Research. Madison, WI.

Hellman, Lillian. Recordings. Playwright Lecture Series, New Dramatists, Inc. New York Library for the Performing Arts. New York, NY.

Hepburn, Katharine Houghton. Papers. Margaret Herrick Library. Academy of Motion Picture Arts and Sciences. Beverly Hills, CA.

Hepburn, Katharine Houghton. Papers. New York Library for the Performing Arts. New York, NY.

Hollywood Women's Press Club Records. Margaret Herrick Library. Academy of Motion Picture Arts and Sciences. Beverly Hills, CA.

Hopper, Hedda. Papers. Margaret Herrick Library. Academy of Motion Picture Arts and Sciences. Beverly Hills, CA.

HUAC Exhibits and Evidence. RG 233. National Archives. Washington, DC.

Huston, John. Papers. Margaret Herrick Library. Academy of Motion Picture Arts and Sciences. Beverly Hills, CA.

Jeakins, Dorothy. Papers. Wisconsin Center for Film and Theater Research. Madison, WI.

Jeakins, Dorothy. Oral history interview conducted by Betty Hoag. Archives of American Art. Smithsonian Institution. Washington, DC.

Lawrence, Viola. Papers. Special Collections. California State University. Fullerton, CA.

Levien, Sonya. Papers. Huntington Library. San Marino, CA.

Loos, Anita. Papers. Howard Gotlieb Archival Research Center. Boston University. Boston, MA.

Loos, Anita. Papers. New York Library for the Performing Arts. New York, NY.

Loy, Myrna. Papers. Howard Gotlieb Archival Research Center. Boston University. Boston, MA.

McCall, Mary C., Jr. Federal Bureau of Investigation Confidential File. FBI, Department of Justice. Washington DC.

McCall, Mary C., Jr. Papers. Private collection. Los Angeles, CA.

McCall, Mary C., Jr. Papers. Writers Guild Foundation Archive. Los Angeles, CA.

McLean, Barbara. Oral history interview conducted by Tom Stempel. Darryl F. Zanuck Research Project. Louis B. Mayer Library. American Film Institute Archives. Los Angeles, CA.

MGM/Paramount Script Collection. Margaret Herrick Library. Academy of Motion Picture Arts and Sciences. Beverly Hills, CA.

MGM Studio Club News. 1936–42. University of Southern California Cinematic Arts Library. Los Angeles, CA.

Minnelli, Vincente. Papers. Margaret Herrick Library. Academy of Motion Picture Arts and Sciences. Beverly Hills, CA.

Motion Picture Association of America World War II Records. Margaret Herrick Library. Academy of Motion Picture Arts and Sciences. Beverly Hills, CA.

Motion Picture Editors Guild. Archives. Los Angeles, CA.

Office of War Information Files. RG 208. National Archives. College Park, MD.

Pickman, Milton E. Papers. Performing Arts Special Collections. University of California. Los Angeles, CA.

RKO Production Files. Performing Arts Special Collections. University of California. Los Angeles, CA.

Screen Actors Guild Archives. Los Angeles, CA.

Selznick, David. O. Papers. Harry Ransom Center. University of Texas. Austin, TX.

Turner-MGM Script Collections. Margaret Herrick Library. Academy of Motion
Picture Arts and Sciences. Beverly Hills, CA.

Twentieth Century-Fox. Papers. University of Southern California Cinematic Arts
Library. Los Angeles, CA.

War Department Correspondence Relating to Motion Pictures. RG 107. National
Archives. College Park, MD.

Warner Bros. Archives. University of Southern California. Los Angeles, CA.

Writers Guild Foundation Archive. Writers Guild of America West. Los Angeles, CA.

BOOKS

Acker, Ally. *Reel Women: Pioneers of the Cinema, 1896 to the Present*. 1990;
New York: Continuum, 1993.

Alicoate, Jack, ed. *The "Film Daily" Year Book of Motion Pictures*. New York: Film Daily,
1930–54.

Allen, Jane. *I Lost My Girlish Laughter*. London: Faber & Faber, 1938.

Arnold, Rebecca. *The American Look: Fashion, Sportswear, and the Image of Women in
1930s and 1940s New York*. London: I.B. Taurus, 2009.

Balio, Tino. *Grand Design: Hollywood as a Modern Business Enterprise, 1930–1939*.
Berkeley: University of California Press, 1996.

Banks, Miranda J. *The Writers: A History of American Screeenwriters and Their Guild*.
New Brunswick, NJ: Rutgers University Press, 2015.

Banner, Lois W. *Women in Modern America: A Brief History*. New York: Harcourt Brace
Jovanovich, 1974.

Barbas, Samantha. *The First Lady of Hollywood: A Biography of Louella Parsons*.
Berkeley: University of California Press, 2005.

Basinger, Jeanine. *A Woman's View: How Hollywood Spoke to Women, 1930–1960*.
Middletown, CT: Wesleyan University Press, 1993.

Beard, Mary, ed. *America through Women's Eyes*. New York: Macmillan, 1933.

———. *On Understanding Women*. New York: Grosset & Dunlap, 1931.

———. *Women as a Force in History*. New York: Macmillan, 1946.

Beauchamp, Cari. *Without Lying Down: Frances Marion and the Powerful Women of Early
Hollywood*. Berkeley: University of California Press, 1998.

Behlmer, Rudy, ed. *Inside Warner Bros., 1935–51*. New York: Viking, 1985.

———, ed. *Memo from Darryl F. Zanuck*. New York: Grove Press, 1995.

———, ed. *Memo from David O. Selznick*. New York: Viking, 1972.

Berg, A. Scott. *Goldwyn: A Biography*. New York: Knopf, 1989.

Bergman, Ingrid, and Alan Burgess. *Ingrid Bergman: My Story*. London: Michael
Joseph, 1980.

Birchard, Robert S. *Cecil B. DeMille's Hollywood*. Lexington: University Press of
Kentucky, 2004.

Bordwell, David, Kristin Thompson, and Janet Staiger. *The Classical Hollywood Cinema*.
New York: Columbia University Press, 1985.

Britton, Andrew. *Katharine Hepburn: Star as Feminist*. 1984; New York: Columbia
University Press, 2008.

Brown, Dee. *The Gentle Tamers: Women of the Old Wild West*. Lincoln: University of
Nebraska Press, 1958.

Brownell, Kathryn Cramer. *Showbiz Politics: Hollywood in American Political Life*.
Chapel Hill: University of North Carolina Press, 2014.

Carman, Emily. *Independent Stardom: Freelance Women in the Hollywood Studio System*.
Austin: University of Texas Press, 2015.

Casper, Drew. *Postwar Hollywood*. Boston: Blackwell Publishing, 2007.

Ceplair, Larry. *A Great Lady: A Life of Sonya Levien*. Lanham: Scarecrow Press, 1996.

Ceplair, Larry and Christopher Trumbo. *Dalton Trumbo: Blacklisted Hollywood Radical*. Lexington: University Press of Kentucky, 2015.

Ceplair, Larry, and Steven Englund. *The Inquisition in Hollywood: Politics in the Film Community, 1930–60*. Urbana: University of Illinois Press, 2003.

Chafe, William. *The American Woman*. Oxford: Oxford University Press, 1982.

Chierichetti, David. *Edith Head*. New York: HarperCollins, 2003.

———. *Hollywood Costume Design*. New York: Harmony Books, 1976.

Clark, Danae. *Negotiating Hollywood: The Cultural Politics of Actors' Labor*. Minneapolis: University of Minnesota Press, 2008.

Cole, Lester. *Hollywood Red*. New York: Ramparts Press, 1981.

Coontz, Stephanie. *The Way We Never Were*. 1992; New York: Basic Books, 2000.

Cooper, Mark Garrett. *Universal Women: Filmmaking and Institutional Change in Early Hollywood*. Urbana: University of Illinois Press, 2010.

Corliss, Richard. *Talking Pictures: Screenwriters in the American Cinema*. New York: Penguin, 1974.

Cott, Nancy. *The Grounding of Modern Feminism*. New Haven: Yale University Press, 1987.

Crowther, Bosley. *The Lion's Share*. New York: E.P. Dutton, 1957.

Dahlquist, Marina, ed. *Exporting Perilous Pauline: Pearl White and the Serial Film Craze*. Urbana: University of Illinois Press, 2013.

Davis, Bette. *This 'n That: A Memoir*. London: Pan Books, 1987.

Davis, Bette, and Whitey Stine. *Mother Goddam: The Story of the Career of Bette Davis*. New York: Hawthorn Books, 1974.

DeMille, Cecil B. *The Autobiography of Cecil B. DeMille*. London: W.H. Allen, 1959.

Denton, Sally. *The Pink Lady: The Many Lives of Helen Gahagan Douglas*. London: Bloomsbury, 2012.

Des Jardins, Julie. *Women and the Historical Profession in America*. Chapel Hill: University of North Carolina Press, 2003.

Dick, Bernard. *Hellman in Hollywood*. Rutherford, NJ: Fairleigh Dickinson University Press, 1983.

Donati, William. *Ida Lupino: A Biography*. Lexington: University Press of Kentucky, 1996.

Douglas, Susan. *Where the Girls Are*. New York: Three Rivers, 1995.

Edwards, Anne. *A Remarkable Woman: A Biography of Katharine Hepburn*. New York: Morrow, 1984.

Eleventh Report of the Senate Fact-Finding Sub-committee on Un-American Activities. Sacramento: California State Legislature, 1961.

Epstein, Cynthia Fuchs. *Woman's Place: Options and Limits in the Professional Careers*. Berkeley: University of California Press, 1970.

Fagan, Myron C. *Documentation of the Red Stars in Hollywood*. Hollywood: Cinema Education Guild, 1950.

Ferber, Edna. *Cimarron*. New York: Doubleday, 1929.

Filene, Catherine, ed. *Careers for Women, New Ideas, New Methods, and New Opportunities—to Fit a New World*. Boston: Houghton Mifflin, 1934.

Forester, C. S. *The African Queen*. Boston: Little, Brown, 1935.

Francke, Lizzie. *Script Girls*. 1994; London: BFI, 2000.

Freedland, Michael. *Katharine Hepburn*. London: W. H. Allen & Co., 1984.

Frost, Jennifer. *Hedda Hopper's Hollywood: Celebrity Gossip and American Conservatism*. New York: New York University Press, 2011.

Galerstein, Carolyn L. *Working Women on the Hollywood Screen: A Filmography*. New York: Garland, 1989.

Georgi-Findlay, Brigitte. *The Frontiers of Women's Writing: Women's Narratives and the Rhetoric of Westward Expansion*. Tucson: University of Arizona Press, 1996.

Gilbert, Julie Goldsmith. *Opposite Attraction*. New York: Pantheon, 1995.

Gomery, Douglas. *The Hollywood Studio System: A History*. London: BFI, 2005.

Gregory, Mollie. *Stuntwomen: The Untold Hollywood Story*. Lexington: University Press of Kentucky, 2015.

Grisham, Therese, and Julie Grossman. *Ida Lupino: Her Art and Resilience in Times of Transition*. New Brunswick, NJ: Rutgers University Press, 2017.

Hallett, Hilary A. *Go West, Young Women! The Rise of Early Hollywood*. Berkeley: University of California Press, 2012.

Hampton, Benjamin. *A History of the American Film from Its Beginnings to 1931*. 1931; New York: Dover, 1970.

Haskell, Molly. *From Reverence to Rape: The Treatment of Women in the Movies*. New York: Holt, Rinehart, and Winston, 1973.

Hastie, Amelie. *Cupboards of Curiosity: Women, Recollection, and Film History*. Durham, NC: Duke University Press, 2007.

Head, Edith, and Paddy Calistro. *Edith Head's Hollywood*. New York: E.P. Dutton, 1983.

Hellman, Lillian. *An Unfinished Woman*. Boston: Little, Brown, 1969.

———. *Scoundrel Time*. Boston: Little, Brown, 1976.

Hepburn, Katharine. *Me*. New York: Ballantine Books, 1996.

Higham, Charles. *Bette*. New York: Macmillan, 1981.

Hill, Erin. *Never Done: A History of Women's Work in Media Production*. New Brunswick, NJ: Rutgers University Press, 2016.

Hole, Kristin Lené, Dijana Jelača, E. Ann Kaplan, and Patrice Petro, eds. *The Routledge Companion to Cinema and Gender*. London: Routledge, 2016.

Hoopes, Roy. *When the Stars Went to War: Hollywood and World War II*. New York: Random House, 1994.

Hopper, Hedda. *The Whole Truth and Nothing But*. Garden City: Doubleday, 1962.

Hutchins, Grace. *Women Who Work*. New York: International Publishers, 1934.

Huyssen, Andreas. *After the Great Divide*. Bloomington: Indiana University Press, 1986.

Johnston, Claire, ed., *The Work of Dorothy Arzner: Towards a Feminist Cinema*. London: BFI, 1975.

Jorgensen, Jay. *Edith Head*. New York: Running Press, 2010.

Jorgensen, Jay, and Donald Scoggins. *Creating the Illusion: A History of Hollywood Costume Design*. New York: Running Press, 2015.

Kaplan, E. Ann. *Women and Film: Both Sides of the Camera*. New York: Routledge, 1990.

———, ed. *Women in Film Noir*. London: BFI, 1998.

Keefe, Maryellen. *Casual Affairs: The Life and Fiction of Sally Benson*. Albany: State University of New York Press, 2014.

Kellow, Brian. *The Bennetts: An Acting Family*. Lexington: University Press of Kentucky, 2004.

Kessler-Harris, Alice. *Out to Work: A History of Wage-Earning Women in the United States*. New York: Oxford University Press, 1982.

Knight, Arthur. *The Liveliest Art*. New York: Mentor Books, 1957.

Koppes, Clayton, and Gregory Black. *Hollywood Goes to War*. New York: Free
    Press, 1987.

Leider, Emily. *Myrna Loy: The Only Good Girl in Hollywood*. Berkeley: University of
    California Press, 2012.

Lemons, J. Stanley. *The Woman Citizen: Social Feminism in the 1920s*. 1973;
    Charlottesville: University of Virginia Press, 2000.

Levy, Emanuel. *George Cukor: Master of Elegance: Hollywood's Legendary Director and
    His Stars*. New York: William Morrow, 1994.

Loos, Anita. *Kiss Hollywood Good-By*. New York: Viking, 1974.

Lucia, Cynthia. *Framing Female Lawyers*. Austin: University of Texas Press, 2002.

Lupino, Ida, with Mary Ann Anderson. *Ida Lupino: Beyond the Camera*.
    New York: BearManor Media, 2011.

Maas, Frederica. *The Shocking Miss Pilgrim: A Writer in Early Hollywood*.
    Lexington: University Press of Kentucky, 2002.

Macgowan, Kenneth. *Behind the Screen*. New York: Dell, 1967.

Mahar, Karen Ward. *Women Filmmakers in Early Hollywood*. Baltimore: Johns Hopkins
    University Press, 2008.

Marion, Frances. *How to Write and Sell Screenplays*. New York: Covici-Friede, 1937.

——. *Off with Their Heads: A Serio-Comic Tale of Hollywood*.
    New York: Macmillan, 1972.

Mason, Lucy. *To Win These Rights*. New York: Harper & Bros., 1952.

Mayne, Judith. *Directed by Dorothy Arzner*. Bloomington: Indian University
    Press, 1995.

McCall, Mary C., Jr. *The Goldfish Bowl*. Boston: Little, Brown, 1932.

McConathy, Dale, with Diana Vreeland. *Hollywood Costume*. New York: Harry
    N. Abrams, 1976.

McCreadie, Marsha. *The Women Who Write the Movies*. New York: Citadel Press, 1996.

McGilligan, Patrick, ed. *Backstory 2: Interviews with Screenwriters of the 1940s and
    1950s*. Berkeley: University of California Press, 1991.

McLean, Adrienne. *Being Rita Hayworth: Labor, Identity and Hollywood Stardom*. New
    Brunswick, NJ: Rutgers University Press, 2004.

Miller, Merle. *The Judges and the Judged*. Garden City: Doubleday, 1952.

Mitchell, Margaret. *Gone with the Wind*. New York: Macmillan, 1936.

Morley, Christopher. *Kitty Foyle*. New York: J. B. Lippincott & Co., 1939.

Mulvey, Laura. *Visual and Other Pleasures*. Bloomington: Indiana University
    Press, 1989.

Murch, Walter. *In the Blink of an Eye*. New York: Silman-James Press, 2001.

Naumburg, Nancy, ed. *We Make the Movies*. New York: Norton, 1937.

Nelmes, Jill, ed. *Women Screenwriters: An International Guide*. London:
    Palgrave, 2015.

Orgeron, Marsha. *Hollywood Ambitions*. Middletown, CT: Wesleyan University
    Press, 2008.

Parsons, Louella. *The Gay Illiterate*. Garden City: Doubleday, 1944.

Peiss, Kathy. *Cheap Amusements; Working Women and Leisure in Turn-of-the-Century
    New York*. Philadelphia: Temple University Press, 1997.

Prindle, David. *The Politics of Glamour: Ideology and Democracy in the Screen Actors
    Guild*. Madison: University of Wisconsin Press, 1988.

Rabwin, Marcella. *Yes, Mr. Selznick: Recollections of a Golden Age*.
    Pittsburgh: Dorrance, 1999.

Ramsaye, Terry. *A Million and One Nights*. New York: Simon & Schuster, 1926.

Raubicheck, Walter, and Walter Srebnick. *Scripting Hitchcock*. Urbana: University of
    Illinois Press, 2011.
Riley, Glenda. *The Female Frontier*. Lawrence: University of Kansas Press, 1988.
———. *The Life and Legacy of Annie Oakley*. Norman: University of Oklahoma
    Press, 1994.
Robson, Cheryl, and Gabrielle Kelly, eds. *The Celluloid Ceiling: Women Film Directors
    Breaking Through*. London: Supernova Books, 2014.
Rogers, Ginger. *My Story*. New York: HarperCollins, 1991.
Rollyson, Carl. *Lillian Hellman: Her Life and Legend*. New York: St. Martin's
    Press, 1988.
Roosevelt, Eleanor. *This Is My Story*. New York: Harper & Bros., 1937.
Rosen, Marjorie. *The Popcorn Venus*. New York: Coward, McCann & Geoghegan, 1973.
Rosenberg, Rosalind. *Divided Lives: American Women in the Twentieth Century*.
    New York: Hill & Wang, 1992.
Ross, Ishbel. *Ladies of the Press: The Story of Women in Journalism by an Insider*.
    New York: Harper & Bros., 1936.
Ross, Murray. *Stars and Strikes: Unionization of Hollywood*. New York: Columbia
    University Press, 1941.
Ross, Steve. *Hollywood Left and Right: How Movie Stars Shaped American Politics*.
    Oxford: Oxford University Press, 2011.
Rosten, Leo. *Hollywood: A Modern Business Enterprise*. New York: Harcourt,
    Brace, 1941.
Sanders, Marion K. *Dorothy Thompson: A Legend in Her Time*.
    Boston: Houghton-Mifflin, 1973.
Sarris, Andrew. *The American Cinema: Directors and Directions, 1929–1968*.
    New York: Da Capo, 1968.
Schatz, Thomas. *Boom and Bust: American Cinema in the 1940s*. Berkeley: University of
    California Press, 1997.
———. *The Genius of the System*. New York: Pantheon, 1988.
———. *Hollywood Genres*. New York: Random House, 1981.
Schwartz, Nancy Lynn. *The Hollywood Writers Wars*. 1982; Lincoln: iUniverse, 2001.
Selznick, Irene Mayer. *A Private View*. New York: Knopf, 1983.
Sigal, Clancy. *Black Sunset: Hollywood Sex, Lies, Glamour, Betrayal, and Raging Egos*.
    Berkeley: Soft Skull Press, 2016.
Slide, Anthony. *The Hollywood Novel: A Critical Guide to Over 1200 Works with Film-
    Related Themes or Characters*. Jefferson, NC: McFarland, 1994.
Smith, Bonnie. *The Gender of History: Men, Women, and Historical Practice*. Cambridge,
    MA: Harvard University Press, 1988.
Smyth, J. E. *Edna Ferber's Hollywood*. Austin: University of Texas Press, 2010.
———. *Reconstructing American Historical Cinema*. Lexington: University Press of
    Kentucky, 2006.
Snelson, Tim. *Phantom Ladies: Hollywood Horror on the Home Front*. New Brunswick,
    NJ: Rutgers University Press, 2014.
St. Johns, Adela Rogers. *The Honeycomb*. Garden City: Doubleday, 1969.
Stacey, Jackie. *Stargazing: Hollywood Cinema and Female Spectatorship*.
    London: Routledge, 1994.
Staggs, Sam. *All About "All About Eve."* New York: St. Martin's Press, 2000.
Staiger, Janet, ed. *The Studio System*. New Brunswick, NJ: Rutgers University
    Press, 1995.
Syrett, Netta. *Portrait of a Rebel*. New York: Dodd, Mead & Co., 1930.

Taylor, Helen. *Scarlett's Women: Gone with the Wind and Its Female Fans.* New York: Virago, 1989.

Thomas, Bob. *King Cohn.* 1967; Beverly Hills, CA: New Millennium Press, 2000.

Thomson, David. *Showman: The Life of David O. Selznick.* New York: Knopf, 1992.

Tucker, Sherrie. *Dance Floor Democracy.* Durham, NC: Duke University Press, 2014.

U.S. Congress House Committee on Un-American Activities Hearings, 1951–52. 10 volumes. Washington, DC: US Government Printing Office, 1951–1952.

Vieira, Mark. *Hurrell's Hollywood Portraits.* New York: Harry N. Abrams, 1997.

———. *Irving Thalberg: Boy Wonder to Producer Prince.* Berkeley: University of California Press, 2009.

Viertel, Salka. *The Kindness of Strangers.* New York: Holt, Rinehart, and Winston, 1969.

Wallace, Eileen V. *Earning Power: Women and Work in Los Angeles, 1880–1930.* Reno: University of Nevada Press, 2010.

Ware, Susan. *Holding Their Own: American Women in the 1930s.* Boston: Twayne, 1983.

Watts, Jill. *Mae West: An Icon in Black and White.* Oxford: Oxford University Press, 2001.

Whitfield, Eileen. *Pickford: The Woman Who Made Hollywood,* Lexington: University Press of Kentucky, 2007.

Wiley, Mason, and Damien Bona. *Inside Oscar: The Unofficial History of the Academy Awards.* New York: Ballantine Books, 1987.

INDEX

Walsh, Raoul, 164

Walters, Barbara, 86

Wanger, Walter, 43, 48, 80, 94, 102

War Activities Committee, 6, 8, 139–40, 142, 145, 240

Ward, Anna Bell, 7

Ware, Susan, 17

Warner, Harry, 26, 89, 136

Warner, Jack, 12–13, 26, 29, 31, 33, 45, 89, 131–132

Warner Bros., 12, 21, 28–31, 33–38, 45–46, 49, 51, 53, 55, 69, 78, 89, 93, 95, 97–100, 103, 111, 120, 123, 126–28, 130–31, 142, 145, 161, 178, 183, 217, 234, 236

Warren, Eda, 6, 156

Warrior's Husband, The (1932), 214

Watch on the Rhine (1943), 39, 44

Watkins, Maureen, 15

Watt, Lois, 1

Weaver, Sylvia, 181, 197

Webb, Helen, 255n42

Weber, Lois, 15–16, 96, 116

Webster, Margaret, 40

Weidler, Virginia, 195

Weisberg, Brenda, 69, 120

Welles, Orson, 7, 56, 62, 109, 158, 223, 253n96

Wellesley College, 63, 110

Wells, Laura, 83

West, Claire, 182–83

West, Claudine, 5, 15, 218

West, Mae, 5, 13, 96, 116, 217, 231

West, Nathaniel, 59

West, Vera, 3, 21, 181–84, 192–93

Westman, Nydia, 4

Wetzel, Lela, 155

Wharton, Edith, 30, 218

What If They Quit? (1944), 140

What Price Hollywood? (1932), 32, 59, 62

Whatever Happened to Baby Jane? (1962), 54

Whitbeck, Frank, 228

White, Pearl, 15

Whitney, Anita, 230

Who's That Knocking at My Door (1967), 157

Wife Wanted (1946), 95

Wiggins, Mary, 247n47

Wild Party, The (1929), 106

Wilde, Cornel, 93

Wilde, Hagar, 223

Wilkerson, William R., 48–49

Will the Real Killer Please Stand Up? (1962), 69

Willebrand, Mabel Walker, 77

Williams, Esther, 13, 81

Wills, Mary, 182

Wilson (1944), 154–55, 170, 172

Wilson, Elizabeth, 5

Wilson, Sloan, 68

Winn, Marcia, 8–9, 143

Winsten, Archer, 128–29

Wise, Robert, 159

Wizard of Oz, The (1939), 156

Woll, Matthew, 49

Woman in Red, The (1935), 127

Woman in the Window, The (1944), 84

Woman of the Year (1942), 51, 62, 199, 211, 218, 225–26, 234–35, 238

Woman Rebels, A (1936), 217–20

Women, agents, 3, 8–9, 59, 63–67; anti-communist attacks on, 12–13; 48–49, 54, 70–74, 148–50, 228–31 (*see also* Hollywood blacklist); costume designers, 21, 181–209 (*see also* Head, Edith and Jeakins, Dorothy); decline in Hollywood, 11–14, 22–23; 56–57, 116–18, 157; employment in Hollywood, 5, 10–11, 14–16, 120; employment in US, 10; equal pay in Hollywood, 33; executives, 1–7, 11 (*see also* Colby, Anita; Koverman, Ida; Van Upp, Virginia); film editors, 6, 10, 42, 155–56 (*see also* Booth, Margaret and McLean, Barbara); Great Depression and, 17, 22, 26, 61, 114, 137, 170, 217, 220, 222; heads of house, 41; Hollywood journalists, 7–8, 28, 199 (*see also* Hopper, Hedda and Parsons, Louella); migration west, 16; onscreen image of, 21, 29, 36, 128–30, 214–26 (*see also* Kitty Foyle); political leadership, 17, 46–50, 54, 76–82, 91–93, 139–40; 228; producers, 3–4, 7–8, 18, 51, 83–86, 89–118, 148, 167–70, 175, 243; screenwriters, 5, 120, 131, 133–35 (*see also* McCall, Mary C. Jr); story editors, 2, 62–72, 79; union activities, 3–6, 146–47 (*see also* McCall, Mary C. Jr.); war work, 6, 43–47, 72, 146 (*see also* Hollywood Canteen)